Information Technology and the Ethics of Globalization:
Transnational Issues and Implications

Robert A. Schultz
Woodbury University, USA

INFORMATION SCIENCE REFERENCE

Hershey · New York

Director of Editorial Content: Kristin Klinger
Senior Managing Editor: Jamie Snavely
Assistant Managing Editor: Michael Brehm
Publishing Assistant: Sean Woznicki
Typesetter: Mike Killian, Sean Woznicki
Cover Design: Lisa Tosheff
Printed at: Yurchak Printing Inc.

Published in the United States of America by
        Information Science Reference (an imprint of IGI Global)
        701 E. Chocolate Avenue
        Hershey PA 17033
        Tel: 717-533-8845
        Fax: 717-533-8661
        E-mail: cust@igi-global.com
        Web site: http://www.igi-global.com/reference

Library of Congress Cataloging-in-Publication Data

Schultz, Robert A., 1942-
  Information technology and the ethics of globalization : transnational issues and implications / by Robert A. Schultz.
     p. cm.

  Includes bibliographical references and index.
  Summary: "This book summarizes the main theories of globalized ethics and show their inadequacies in dealing with IT-enabled global ethical problem"--Provided by publisher.

  ISBN 978-1-60566-922-9 (hardcover) -- ISBN 978-1-60566-923-6 (ebook) 1.
Information technology. 2. Technology--Moral and ethical aspects. 3.
Globalization--Moral and ethical aspects. I. Title.
  HD30.2.S387 2009
  174--dc22
                        2009015724

British Cataloguing in Publication Data
A Cataloguing in Publication record for this book is available from the British Library.

Table of Contents

Section 1
IT-Enabled Globalized Ethical Problems

Section 3
A Social Contract for Globalized Institutions

Section 4
Ultimate Questions

Foreword

People who care about ethics should read this book. Particularly those in global organizations, and especially those concerned about information technology. As a university professor, I see a host of uses for the book in my business courses, and am convinced that the book would serve liberal arts faculty and students as well.

Globalization is a powerful force, but because it by definition extends across political and social boundaries, the traditional mechanisms which shape and control human behavior and decision making may prove ineffective in maintaining ethical behavior and decision making. This book deals with the problem by amply illustrating how globalized ethical challenges arise in the most transnational of activities – IT – helps actors identify what novel dimensions arise due to their global setting, and provides a framework for decision makers to allow them to clearly and consistently analyze the implications of alternatives and chose ethical paths.

Dr. Schultz aptly uses IT as a playing field, where he has been both a senior level IT practitioner as well as an academic who built a highly successful IT department in a long established business school. Rare as this combination of town and gown is, the author adds one more key pillar of wisdom which makes him unique: he earned a PhD in Philosophy under at Harvard under one of the most astute ethicists of the 20th Century, John Rawls.

Because of this background, Dr. Schultz brings to bear a wealth of experience and expertise in identifying situations which highlight the pressing need for individuals to apply an ethical framework in determining what they will do. And, after providing an insightful explanation of ethical theories, he outlines an eminently useful "social contract" frame of reference to help people think about the ethical aspects of their actions, and make informed, consistent, ethical decisions. These are tasks which are increasingly important in today's world.

It has once again become fashionable to talk about ethics, particularly at universities and in big companies. Alas, mostly it is just talk. And all too often the discussion is not really about ethics, but merely about the ugly imposition of the social values articulated by the power elite. As such, the focus – and the results – tend to be *ad hoc*, self oriented, semi- utilitarianism. (One example of this which comes to mind is one of my students' conclusions that "ethics is when the bookstore lowers its prices on textbooks.")

To the contrary, this book is not value laden. Nor is the ethical decision making framework outlined in the book. For example, even though this book focuses on IT-enabled ethical problems in globalized operations, the book is neither pro-globalization nor anti-globalization. These value sets are not at issue. Instead, globalization is viewed as another developing form of human cooperation. Rather than focus on whether globalization is good or bad overall, the author presents a highly developed, very useful framework for identifying ethical issues and determining how to act ethically. In other words, Dr.

Schultz presents ethical standards for dealing with the impacts of globalization, rather than supporting or condemning it.

It is refreshing to see instead how ethics can be viewed as a set of principles of cooperation, sharply distinguished from morality as founded on custom, religion, ethnicity, culture, power, or authority. This book does so by presenting a social contract theory inspired by the work of John Rawls as a means of determining ethical principles of cooperation.

The author proposes two global social contracts, one for ethical relations between states, and one governing the global economy. This global two-contract theory differs from other theories of globalized ethics. On the one hand, it acknowledges that a social contract is needed for the global economy which goes beyond a contract just for states. Most ethical frameworks do not go beyond this. Unlike cosmopolitan ethical theories which apply to all human beings as human beings, Dr. Schultz' two-contract approach theory allows ethical standing for cooperative groups such as countries and national economies, not to mention tribes, clans, and social cohorts.

Other distinctive features of the book include an assessment of current and new institutions with an eye towards showing how to implement global ethics while extending authority as little as possible. Like gravity, there may very well be an inverse square rule for driving behavior through authority. The farther the authority is physically from the actor, the less effective the authority is in shaping the actor's behavior. Globalized IT has proven an excellent laboratory to test this; Dr. Schultz' insight in this area is astute and sorely needed.

But wait, there's more! This book also provides a separate, non-social-contract treatment of environmental ethics as prior to human ethics, and discussions of the ultimate value of globalization for humanity. These are topics which we as citizens ought to be thinking about as we vote and go about our public lives. Let me suggest that you treat yourself to Dr. Schultz' insights, and read this book.

John E. Karayan

*Formerly Director of Taxes of a New York Stock Exchange-listed high tech multinational (which was then one of the world's largest software concerns), **John Karayan** is a tax attorney with a "Big 8" CPA firm background. Dr. Karayan remains active outside academia with service on public and private Boards, as well as testifying as an expert witness in complex business litigation. John serves on the Board of Directors of Delta Scientific Corporation. (http://www.deltascientific.com/). A family business headquartered in Southern California, Delta is the world's foremost manufacturer of anti-terrorist vehicle barricades, and was featured in Tom Peters' "Thriving on Chaos" Series on PBS, Peter Drucker's "Innovation on the West Coast" video series, and articles in newspapers, such as the Wall Street Journal, along with features on television news programs, such as the NBC Evening News. Professor Karayan has co-authored several books – notably Strategic Business Tax Planning (Wiley 2006) -- and published articles in journals ranging from The Tax Advisor to the Marquette Sports Law Review. He also has spoken before professional groups such as the World Trade Institute, the Tax Executives Institute, the California Continuing Education of the Bar, the California Society of CPAs, and the Beverly Hills Bar Association.*

Preface

Globalization—the coalescence of the economies and cultures of this planet—has definitely been enabled by Information Technology (IT). Globalization, in altering previous economic and social structures, also raises new ethical issues. But IT is much more, I think, than a mere enabler of globalization. Within globalization, IT produces new ethical problems all by itself.

Globalization has become a contested concept. In this book my aim is neither to condemn globalization nor to praise it. Globalization is a form of human social cooperation with both good and bad aspects. To try to prove that globalization is in itself good or bad would be just as nonsensical as to try to prove that human social cooperation is in itself good or bad. Human social cooperation has produced a technological lifestyle which is dramatically better for many people. It has also produced great evils such as wars and the potential collapse of the ecosystem. Globalization has also produced benefits and harms. So instead of trying to determine whether globalization is good or bad, I will determine how globalization can be implemented in a just and ethical way.

There is already a substantial literature in philosophy and political theory on globalized ethics. I will examine the major possibilities. But for the most part theories of transnational ethics proceed by allocating ethical problems to different states and therefore are not helpful in dealing with ethical problems of ethically globalized institutions, most of which would not exist were it not for IT. (Throughout this book I use 'global' and 'transnational' to mean the same thing. I believe this is standard usage.)

In Section 1, *IT-enabled Globalized Ethical Problems*, I will show how these IT-enabled global ethical problems come about. One recent example is Yahoo's difficulties with e-mail in China. Around 2002, Yahoo provided the Chinese government with information about two pro-democracy journalists who were subsequently jailed and apparently tortured. The journalists later successfully sued Yahoo. Yahoo initially claimed that it was merely complying with Chinese law. The obvious ethical issue is whether Yahoo should do this, whether the law of a country not recognizing basic human rights should be followed. The background question is whose law, if any, should be followed by a transnational IT company? At Yahoo's 2007 annual meetings, Yahoo shareholders voted overwhelmingly against a proposal for Yahoo to reject censorship. Obviously Yahoo, as a corporation, is bound by the vote of its shareholders. But ethically do the shareholders of transnational corporations have the last word? What IT has produced in the case of Yahoo and other Internet communications companies are *ethically globalized* companies, companies whose ethical problems cannot be solved by dividing them up among different nations.

Chapter 1, *IT-enabled Global Ethical Problems*, lists the various kinds of globalized ethical problems that have arisen. **Chapter 2**, *Current Ethically Globalized Institutions*, records the globalized institutions currently involved with global ethical problems. In **Chapter 3**, *IT's Contribution to Globalization*, the nature of globalization is examined in some detail. Some concepts of globalization such as Thomas

Friedman's "flattening" encapsulate contested value judgements. After separating out a more neutral concept of globalization, I examine what aspects of IT play a role in the ethics of globalization.

Then, in Section 2, *Theories of Globalized Ethics*, I summarize the main theories of globalized ethics and show their inadequacies in dealing with IT-enabled global ethical problems. **Chapter 4**, *The Basis of Ethical Principles*, provides a background in ethical theory. I make a distinction between ethics as principles of social cooperation and morality as rules depending on special beliefs. **Chapter 5**, *Domestic Theories of Justice, discusses various theories of justice, or ethics for particular societies*. I decide on John Rawls' two Principles of Justice (1999a) as the best theory of ethics for social cooperation.

Chapter 6, *Political Realism and the Society of Societies*, and **Chapter 7**, *Cosmopolitanism*, present current theories of globalized ethics. Authors of some of these theories do not sufficiently appreciate the changes IT makes to underlying social and economic structures. Others don't take social cooperation seriously enough. **Chapter 8**, *The Ethical Status of Globalized Institutions*, determines where globalized institutions need ethical principles, and of what kind. **Chapter 9**, *IT and Globalized Ethics*, does the same for IT in the service of globalization. A preliminary version of a global social contract is presented, and IT's special role in that contract is discussed.

In Section 3, *A Social Contract for Globalized Institutions*, I sketch a social contract approach to deal with these IT-enabled global ethical problems. The essence of this approach is that people in societies live under principles which they themselves could have chosen.[1] Its political and ethical attractiveness is that coercive social and governmental commands are grounded in free agreement rather than in arbitrary force. This approach derives from the work of John Rawls on domestic and international justice (Rawls 1999a, 1999b). **Chapter 10**, *Elements of a Global Contract*, lays out all the elements of the Global Contract. Actually two social contracts are required, the International Social Contract and the Global Economy Social Contract. The International Social Contract is a revision of Rawls' version of international ethics. Two distinctive features of the Global Economy Social Contract are that it applies only to participants in the global economy and that corporations cannot be parties to the contract. **Chapter 11**, *Globalized Ethics and Current Institutions*, explores the extent to which current institutions are in compliance with the global social contracts. **Chapter 12**, *New Globalized Institutions*, discusses whether additional institutions would be required to implement the principles of the global social contracts. An important consideration is whether cooperation between existing states or other institutions would be sufficient. Simply adding new institutions for the sake of adding them raises difficult questions about authority and oversight, so cooperative solutions between existing institutions are in general preferable. **Chapter 13**, *Ethical Implications for IT*, explores the implications of the global social contracts for IT.

Then, in the Section 4, *Ultimate Questions*, I will consider issues beyond the reach of justice and social contracts, including issues of environmental ethics. These issues need to have priority even over the requirements of fair and just social contracts. **Chapter 14**, *IT-enabled Globalization and the Environment*, deals with globalized environmental issues and IT's role in those issues. **Chapter 15**, *The Value of IT-enabled Globalization*, deals with the value of cultural and economic globalization. Modern technology's special value status is discussed, as well as the point of view of *being* on the value of IT and globalization.

This book reflects my practical experience with IT management, both for a Forbes 500 company and as Director of Academic Computing for Woodbury University. My academic qualifications include a Ph.D. dissertation in ethics done with John Rawls and teaching many graduate and undergraduate ethics courses. My previous book for IGI-Global Press, *Contemporary Issues in Ethics and Information Technology* (2006), discussed professional and individual ethical issues connected with IT. Globalization was discussed briefly in connection with offshoring. I believe a more complete discussion is now called for.

The primary intended audience for this book is IT professionals and IT users with ethical concerns. It is not intended as a contribution to professional philosophy.[2] This is very much a book of *applied* ethics. But I have tried my best to be faithful to the spirit of Rawls' work on social contracts. As I worked on the various issues discussed in the book, I experienced once again the power of the idea of a social contract. Rawls' work has the "unique distinction among contemporary political philosophers of being frequently cited by the courts of law in the United States and referred to by practicing politicians in the United States and United Kingdom" (Wikipedia 2008). President Bill Clinton stated that Rawls's thought "helped a whole generation of learned Americans revive their faith in democracy itself" (Clinton 1999).

REFERENCES

Clinton, B. (1999). *Remarks by the President at presentation of the National Medal of the Arts and the National Humanities Medal*. Retrieved September 15, 2008, from http://clinton4.nara.gov/WH/New/html/19990929.html

Rawls, J. (1999a). *A theory of justice*. Cambridge, MA: Harvard University Press.

Rawls, J. (1999b). *The law of peoples*. Cambridge, MA: Harvard University Press.

Schultz, R. (2006). *Contemporary issues in ethics and information technology*. Hershey, PA: IRM Press.

Wikipedia. (2008). *John Rawls*. Retrieved on July 20, 2008, from http://en.wikipedia.org/wiki/John_Rawls

ENDNOTES

[1]   Classic social contract theory was developed by the 17th and 18th century philosophers Hobbes, Locke, and Rousseau. These theories were the basis for American and French democracies.

[2]   It seems to me that if social contract theory can't be understood without the substantial added complexity of professional philosophy, then it is probably not workable as a practical basis for ethics--or for society.

Acknowledgment

I would like to thank Major Johnson, Douglas Cremer, and the IGI-Global reviewers for helpful suggestions. I would also like to thank David Rosen of Woodbury University for a grant to present the ideas of this book at an InSite conference in Bulgaria in 2008. The Rinker Law Library of Chapman University and the Woodbury University Library were helpful in obtaining materials. Christine Bufton of IGI-Global was a very helpful and sympathetic editor.

For their encouragement, I would like to thank John Dittmeier and my daughters Katie and Rebecca. David Rosen, John Karayan, and other former colleagues at Woodbury University also cheered me on. Finally, my cat Zuni helped in many ways I am sure he did not understand.

Robert Schultz

Section 1
IT–Enabled Globalized Ethical Problems

Chapter 1
IT–Enabled Global Ethical Problems

Problems of IT-enabled globalization are a new kind of ethical problem and require new ethical principles for their solution. I will first discuss two examples to demonstrate this: these examples are the World Bank and its IT development, and Yahoo in China. These institutions are what I will call *ethically globalized institutions,* institutions which raise ethical problems that cannot be handled as problems belonging to existing nation-states. Then I will discuss some other recognized ethical problems of IT-enabled globalization which, at first sight, involve only older ethical principles. It will turn out that these problems also have globalized aspects.

In Section 1, this section, I will be using intuitive ethical principles in evaluating the cases. These evaluations are provisional and the reader should feel free to have other opinions. In Sections 2 and 3, I will develop and defend an ethical theory which will provide a firmer foundation for my evaluations.

IT DEVELOPMENT AT THE WORLD BANK

The Harvard Business School published in 2003 a case study of IT development at the World Bank. (McFarlan 2003) The IT staff was notably successful in improving the functioning of the World Bank,

DOI: 10.4018/978-1-60566-922-9.ch001

enabling it to work better toward its stated goals. But the World Bank's stated high ideals of improving life in developing countries are, according to economist Joseph Stiglitz, not realized in practice. Stiglitz, a Nobel Prize winner and himself a former Senior Vice President of the Bank, finds that the World Bank actually often makes conditions worse in developing countries. (Stiglitz 2003, 2007)

The mission of the World Bank is to fight poverty around the world by providing resources, sharing knowledge and enabling public/private partnerships. This is to be accomplished by attracting and maintaining a committed staff with exceptional skills. The World Bank is financed by investors in 184 member countries, primarily through bond purchases. In 2003, the Bank adopted a strategy of global decentralization and facilitating knowledge transfer to developing countries. In the face of numerous challenges, their IT department succeeded in enabling these goals.[1] (McFarlan 2003)

However, decentralized administration and knowledge transfer may not, in the context of World Bank administration, succeed in improving the lot of those in developing countries. The problem, according to responsible commentators such as Joseph Stiglitz, is that the World Bank (together with the International Monetary Fund) attaches conditions to its loans and grants which reflect more the ethics of international banking than that of alleviating poverty. Typically, keeping to agreements to repay loans and privatization of government services are required. During the 2002 Argentina default, enormous increases in debt service on its loans triggered by events in the U.S. and East Asia, together with loss of revenues caused by privatized services moving out of the country, were simply made worse by IMF and World Bank policies. (Stiglitz 2007, 220-225). Other problems include loans going to entrenched oligarchies rather than development projects. In general about 50% of World Bank projects fail. (Center for Economic Justice 2004)

There are several layers of ethical considerations to be untangled here. If one accepts Stiglitz's account of the World Bank's failings, then the IT staff at the World Bank has enabled a diminished future for many in developing countries. His views are shared by many and as of 2008 there is a boycott campaign against buying bonds issued by the World Bank. Participants include municipalities, the college pension organization TIAA/CREF, as well as a number of labor unions. (Support for the boycott is for financial risk reasons as well as socially conscious reasons). (Evans 2003)

The ethical situation has parallels to IT development for ethically flawed organizations, for example tobacco manufacturers, or, less controversially, distributors of child pornography. If, for example, an IT professional were to produce a first rate website and back office system for an outfit distributing child pornography, there would not be much question about the ethical status of his activity. The activity of the organization is highly unethical, so it is not ethical to aid and abet its implementation. Tobacco seems more of an intermediate case. Certainly tobacco manufacturers are operating legally, so ethically it is up to the IT professional whether he wants to work for this sort of company. But the difference in the case of the World Bank is that it is not immediately clear what ethical standards are appropriate for a globalized organization. Ought the IT professionals who did such a good job for the World Bank consider the Bank's negative impact on developing countries? Or do ethical standards of international banking take precedence? What ethical conclusion should they draw?

When is "I only work here. I'm only following orders" an acceptable ethical defense? Clearly it matters how directly implicated people are in ethically questionable activities. The IT professional enabling child pornography distribution clearly cannot say "I only work here" to establish that he is acting ethically. We expect him to recognize that the activity he is enabling is both illegal and unethical. However, the IT professional enabling the sale of tobacco can say "I only work here." Producing and developing tobacco products is legal. It is another question whether distributing a product which tends to kill people in large numbers should be legal. But so long as it is legal, it is a matter of personal ethical preference whether or not to aid and abet the production and distribution of tobacco. It would be ethically *better* not to aid and abet the tobacco industry but it is not ethically required.

However, why wasn't Adolf Eichmann, who was in charge of administering the Holocaust, able to use "I only work here" as a defense? He tried, unsuccessfully. (Arendt 1965) And as in the tobacco example, he was following German laws implementing the "final solution".[2] Yet a street sweeper in Nazi Germany, although he contributed to keeping Germany running and thus helped to enable the Holocaust, could legitimately say "I only work here." What's the difference? If it is ethical to aid a tobacco company in its operations, it can only be because we regard the legality of the tobacco company as at least ethically neutral. We do not regard laws mandating genocide as ethically neutral.

So is the situation with the IT staff at the World Bank more like the situation at the child Pornography website or at the tobacco company? Because of globalization, there is not an immediate answer. The World Bank is a globalized institution and so its legality is not determined by the laws of any one state. Further, the ethical status of its operations is not determined by the ethical standards of any one nation. And, as we shall see in Section II, there are several different choices for transnational ethical standards. My personal intuition would be that the World Bank case is ethically the same as the tobacco company case, but to support this intuition requires a choice of specific transnational ethical standards.

YAHOO IN CHINA

Around 2002, Yahoo provided the Chinese government with information about two pro-democracy journalists who were subsequently jailed and apparently tortured. The journalists successfully sued Yahoo. Yahoo initially claimed that it was merely complying with Chinese law. (Elias 2007) The obvious ethical issue is whether Yahoo should do this, whether the law of a country not recognizing basic human rights should be followed. The background question is whose law, if any, should be followed by a transnational company? Again, the fact that this is an IT company makes the question a lot harder to answer. With outsourced manufacturing, the choice would be the country where operations take place. With Yahoo, it is not so clear, although Yahoo itself seemingly followed some such principle by selling its Chinese e-mail operation to a Chinese company.

At Yahoo's 2007 annual meetings, Yahoo shareholders voted overwhelmingly against a proposal for Yahoo to reject censorship. (BBC News 2007) Obviously Yahoo, as a corporation, is bound by the vote of its shareholders. But ethically do the shareholders of transnational corporations have the last word? What IT has produced in the case of Yahoo and other Internet communications companies are *ethically globalized* companies, companies whose ethical problems cannot be solved by parceling them out among different nations.

Similarly, the World Bank is an *ethically globalized* institution, at least in its objectives. Its objectives cannot be understood when parceled out amongst different nations. In fact, it remains ethically globalized even if, as its critics charge, it does not live up to its stated objectives of improving the lives of those in developing countries. For critics claim instead that the World Bank is serving the interests of transnational corporations!

OFFSHORING

Perhaps the most controversial and much-discussed transnational ethical issue is *offshoring*, the practice of exporting jobs to other countries to exploit lower wages. IT is required for many types of offshoring to be possible. In Chapter 3, **IT's Contribution to Globalization,** we will consider what responsibility IT has for its contribution to globalization in general and offshoring in particular. In this chapter, we are examining the ethical status of offshoring in general.

In some circumstances, there seems to be no special ethical issue connected with offshoring. If, for example, the currency exchange rate makes work done in the U.S. cheaper than work done in France, but otherwise the standards of living of the workers in the two countries are comparable, offshoring to the US raises no ethical issue. It seems instead to be a form of arbitrage on labor prices. "Arbitrage" is a benign communication function in a market economy, helping to even out commodity prices consistently throughout markets.

Although offshoring has some of the features of arbitrage, it differs in an important respect. In offshoring, the "commodity" subject to arbitrage is labor. In a true arbitrage situation, the commodity's location does not change the nature of the commodity. This is why, for example, price differences in gold subject to arbitrage are simply fluctuations due to market functioning. But it makes a big difference where labor is located. The whole point of offshoring jobs is precisely that we don't want to move laborers from India or China to the United States, because then we would have to pay them prevailing U. S. wages. For offshoring to work, we must take advantage of a social context with prevailing lower wages.[3] Offshoring is in fact a new ethical problem brought about by the ability of information technology to make information available at any location. By the use of IT we can take advantage of social contexts with prevailing lower wages when the relevant features of the job can be performed great distances away.

I will consider three potentially ethically relevant aspects of offshoring: The loss of higher-wage jobs in developed countries; the use of child and sweatshop labor in low-wage countries; and substandard customer and technical service in those countries.

MOVING HIGHER-WAGE JOBS TO LOWER-WAGE COUNTRIES

All the normal ethical considerations for outsourcing continue to apply when the outsourcee is a continent away. These include due diligence on the part of IT professionals and managers to ensure that outsourcing will provide net benefits for the organization and its stakeholders. The primary benefit for offshoring should be to save personnel costs with at least equal quality of work. A major concern both with "regular" outsourcing and offshoring is the separability of offshored work. If constant feedback between the companies is needed, neither offshoring nor outsourcing is a good option. It is also not appropriate to outsource strategic applications, the long-term reliability and quality of the outsourcer is still important, and oversight needs to remain with the outsourcing company. (Applegate et al., 2002, 572-578) When these considerations are not taken into account, there are problems. Gartner Group estimates that fully half of offshore projects fail to deliver anticipated savings. (Procurement Insights 2008)

For offshoring, English language skills and knowledge of cultural and legal practices are also important. Also, unless responses are highly structured, offshoring service calls can cost companies customers. (Ante 2004, 36) (We will consider later whether substandard offshored customer and technical service raises other ethical problems.) Also maintaining U.S. levels of security on development projects can be difficult. Even with these difficulties, some companies continue to offshore because of the savings. But IT professional ethics requires one to be aware of the risks--both technical and business--and to manage them appropriately.

Over and above IT professional ethical considerations, the justice of the practice of offshoring is also an issue. As we just saw in the Yahoo! case, principles of justice applying within societies do not immediately apply transnationally. As we will see in Section II, **Theories of Globalized Ethics,** principles of global justice are not yet a settled matter, even when there is agreement on principles of justice within societies. Within a society, these principles apply to economic and political arrangements for members sharing cooperative benefits and cooperative burdens.

In international labor offshoring, economic benefits and burdens are experienced by different societies with different economic and political arrangements. Although it is claimed that offshoring will ultimately make everyone better off, a lot more discussion of how this will happen is necessary. John Rawls, in his discussion of transnational justice, claims that people from different societies will not choose to trade off economic benefits and burdens between societies. Rawls says:

... no people organized by its government is prepared to count, as a first principle, the benefits for another people as outweighing the hardships imposed on itself. (Rawls 1999b, 40. Italics in original.)

In other words, although we can have agreements between societies (and parties within those societies) which redistribute benefits and burdens, we must first be assured that the internal arrangements within those societies are just. It doesn't count toward the justice of institutions in the U.S. to point to our work in Kosovo. And conversely, it doesn't ameliorate injustice in Kosovo to point to our contribution to improving the lot of the least advantaged in the U. S. So the justice of transnational redistribution of benefits and burdens is necessarily a *secondary* matter, to be considered against a background of justly functioning institutions on the home front.

Rawls' theory and a popular rival theory, *utilitarianism,* will be examined at much greater length in Section II, **Theories of Globalized Ethics**. There is a major difference in how the two theories treat offshoring. A utilitarian approach to relations between societies would hold that so long as the net average value goes up, there is no further issue of justice, regardless of how the justice of the two societies is affected. Rawls' social contract alternative to utilitarianism reflects care about what happens to the individual.[4] (Rawls 1999a, secs. 27 and 28) And redistribution of benefits and burdens between societies can easily wreak havoc with the internal justice of those societies.

This is especially true when utilitarian principles govern relations between societies. Under utilitarian principles a loss on one society can be outweighed by a gain in another. So the losing society can end up, on its own terms, much worse off. A possible example is corn production in the U. S. and Mexico after NAFTA. NAFTA is regarded as overall producing a net gain for the two countries. Subsidized U.S. corn drove approximately 100,000 small Mexican corn producers out of business. Since we are separate societies, such out-of-work Mexicans who come to the U.S. to raise corn now shipped to Mexico, often come as illegal aliens. (Bensinger 2003)

It seems clear that offshoring cannot be ethically justified only by showing that people in the less-well-off society are better off because of it. For the practice to be just, it must also be shown that members of the society losing positions are not being treated unjustly. This point has been ignored by those trying to justify outsourcing. Thomas Donahue, President and CEO of the U.S. Chamber of Commerce, claims that offshoring boosts our economy and companies create new jobs with the money they save.

(Konrad 2004) This defense, if correct, would address the justice of offshoring by showing that those losing their jobs aren't harmed. But companies saving money from outsourcing are free to use the savings for whatever legal and ethical purposes they want--extra dividends for their stockholders, extra health benefits for their remaining employees, higher compensation for their top executives, grants to hospitals or educational institutions. There is no direct requirement for them to create new jobs. Indeed Marc Andreesen, the Netscape founder, although sympathetic to offshoring, remarks that believing new jobs will be created requires a "leap of faith." (Baker and Kripalani 2004) And, as Katharine Yung points out, new replacement jobs tend to be lower-wage service jobs. (Yung 2004). Adam Geller notes that a majority--53%--of new jobs are in restaurants or temp services or somewhat below-average-wage areas. Average pay is about 12% less than older jobs with 14% less benefits. (Geller 2004)

But these kinds of concerns are dismissed as "whining" by Thomas Donahue of the U.S. Chamber of Commerce. (Konrad 2004) For him, as long as companies save money and the economy is uplifted, the practice is justified. He is joined by a number of commentators who advocate offshoring as another example of the economic benefits of free trade and open markets. Examples include former Secretary of State Colin Powell (Weisman 2004), Azim Premji, the CEO of Wipro, a leading Indian offshore service provider (Rai 2004), and many IT startup venture investors including Accel. (Amte and Hof 2004)

The economist Paul Craig Roberts, writing in *BusinessWeek,* begins to articulate the difficulty: There is a difference between free trade of commodities and what he calls "labor arbitrage." Proponents of offshoring who think that the U.S. will benefit are assuming that labor will behave in the same way as commodities. (Roberts 2004) Certainly this is true of Colin Powell, who in speaking to the Indians urged them to open certain commodity markets as a quid pro quo for our allowing offshoring. (Weisman 2004) But Roberts points out that the economic doctrine of comparative advantage does not apply to labor, capital, and production technology.[5] In fact we don't have any advantage, comparative or otherwise, over countries such and India and China, and there no reason to expect a balance of trade to materialize. The offshore countries ultimately get to keep everything. The final position outsourced could be the CEO.

Although this is speculative, there is some evidence that the decline of England as a major economic power from the 19th to the 20th century was due to the English practice of offshoring increasingly complex jobs to the U.S. [6] More complex jobs represent more than labor that can be reproduced at any location; they are also a repository of skills available for innovation and new ventures. When this repository diminishes, so does the capacity for economic growth. So from the point of view of the self-interest of a society, it should be a matter of concern that highly skilled technology jobs are being moved to other countries.

Besides these self-interested considerations, there are considerations of justice. From the point of view of justice, employees are participants in a society and not just commodities. The ethical problem with offshoring is that significant economic redistribution affecting the life prospects of citizen of multiple countries is being treated as if we were already part of a global society governed by shared principles of justice. This is simply not the case now.

Transnational institutions, policies, and principles are needed to supplement arrangements within or between nations or societies. Most commentators on globalization acknowledge that current global institutions have large imperfections. Multinational corporations regularly evade one country's regulations by transferring operations to another country. This is more than a legal issue—the social benefits of a market economy require effective prevention of monopoly power, and antitrust concerns are one set of regulations being evaded. (Schultz 2006, chapter 5)

Indeed, unless and until all the world's economies are managed as a single economy, we can't directly trade off benefits and burdens between different societies. In current circumstances, the social cost to the United States of IT personnel losing skilled jobs needs to compensated for in some way. Some have suggested that corporations provide job retraining to those losing jobs.[7] The savings from successful offshoring are so substantial--on the order of 50%--that giving departing workers one-time retraining costs would not materially alter the economics of the situation.

Not only that, because the US needs to buy back goods produced in the offshored countries, there is a loss to the US economy not reflected in increased corporate profits. The loss is reflected in increased debt. In the economic meltdown of late 2008, the illusory nature of gains to the US economy became evident. *BusinessWeek* Chief Economist Michael Mandel notes that:

U.S. companies [will] *have to pay more attention to sustaining productivity growth and innovation at home rather than resorting to outsourcing as their main source of cost savings. That would boost wages and incomes for U. S. workers and reduce the need for . . . huge debts* [for the US] *to pay for foreign-made goods.* (Mandel 2008)

Because of the negative economic impact of offshoring on the domestic economy, an excess profits tax on corporate profits due to offshoring could be in order to internalize what is now an externality for corporations. (Reubens 2008)

Such an excess profits tax is one example of the background institutions and policies needed to make offshoring a just practice, especially to regulate multinationals. Offshoring may be a just practice when institutions and policies are able to regulate the sharing of benefits and burdens within the global economy. In those circumstances raising the well-being of a programmer in India may be just even though the well-being of an American is consequently reduced to the extent that we are all part of one economic system sharing benefits and burdens. However, it must also be shown that members of the society losing positions are not being treated unjustly.

Competitive pressures also need to be considered and do make a difference in the justice of the situation. Managers who are uneasy about the practice of offshoring may still feel that competition makes it necessary for them to offshore. In a competitive environment, one company may not be able to afford to behave ethically or even seriously consider behaving ethically when such behavior would produce a serious competitive disadvantage. This justification is mentioned frequently in discussions of offshoring. I may even be failing to do my (ethical and professional) duty by my company and its stockholders or stakeholders.

To some extent, this is a general problem about the ethical status of corporations, which will be more fully discussed in Chapter 8, **The Ethical Status of Globalized Institutions.** Corporations are legal constructs rather than ethical individuals, with the directive (in for-profit corporations) to maximize shareholder value. And the people running corporations have a managerial duty to maximize profits. Michael Lerner, a corporate critic, notes that "Even the corporate executives with the highest level of spiritual sensitivity . . . have no choice but to accept corporate profits as the absolute bottom line." (Lerner 2000, 311) The corporation cannot become a better *person* because it is not an ethical person at all. So what is an individual to do, who has on the one hand ethical beliefs based on his role as a citizen in a just society, and on the other hand conflicting directives based on his role as a manager or IT professional in a corporation?

One relevant ethical consideration here is that, whatever you ultimately do, the higher level principle has to be acknowledged in what you do. (Schultz 2006, 38-41) Even if the corporation is not an ethical individual, you as a manager are. You embody *both* points of view: A citizen concerned with justice and a responsible corporate manager. So you may be in the unfortunate position of believing that offshoring is unjust as currently practiced and at the same time know that your corporation would be at a severe competitive disadvantage if it did not send jobs offshore. The critical point here is that even if reasons of interest make it difficult or impossible for you to do what you believe is ethical, it is still necessary in what you do to acknowledge your own ethical principles. If the fact that other people are not behaving well were a sufficient reason for you not to behave well, the situation could never improve. It may be foolhardy and completely unproductive to do the right thing in circumstances where ethical principles do not hold sway. But if so, such action is not an ethical requirement.

LABOR STANDARDS/CHILD LABOR

Offshoring also raises ethical concerns when the ethical standards of the offshored country concerning labor differ in significant ways from those of developed countries. It is a somewhat frequent embarrassment for multinational corporations when it is revealed that their products have been produced--usually in developing countries--by workers working in inhumane conditions or by child labor. Historically working conditions in industrialized countries in the earlier days of the industrial revolution were very harsh, and it is only relatively recently that labor exploitation and child labor have become unacceptable in developed countries. Some authors such as conservative Nobel economist Milton Friedman claim that child labor actually decreased during the industrial revolution. He argues that before the industrial revolution almost all children were working in agriculture, either on their family's farm or elsewhere. (Friedman 1999)

Other commentators such as E.P. Thompson (1968) have pointed out that there is a difference between children doing agricultural or other work with their families and in factories as part of the labor market. The International Labor Organization (ILO Convention 138) distinguishes between child work and child labor. *Child work,* children's participation in economic activity that does not negatively affect their health and development or interfere with education, is permitted from the age of 12 years. In contrast, *Child labor* is children working in contravention of the above standards. This means all children below 12 years of age working in any economic activities, those aged 12 to 14 years engaged in harmful work, and all children enslaved, forcibly recruited, prostituted, trafficked, forced into illegal activities and exposed to hazardous work. (UNICEF 2008)

As it turns out, Friedman's ideology that unhampered free markets result in better outcomes for all social problems[8] figures prominently in the policies of many ethically globalized institutions. We will return to this topic in Chapter 2, **Ethically globalized Institutions**. We can use the ILO's definition of child labor and consider the nature of ethical issues here. It is clearly part of the profitability of offshoring to use labor which is extracted from workers under conditions we would find substandard.

But revelations that child labor is being used to produce Ikea furniture or Nike shoes are very damaging to the reputations of those organizations and can potentially affect sales. Many companies have taken steps to insure that child labor or seriously exploited labor is not used in the offshore production of their products. One constructive response by these corporations is to set standards for their suppliers. In November 2005 Apple responded to allegations of inhumane working conditions by its Chinese suppliers of iPods by setting standards. The standards ban child labor and set a maximum of 60-hour work weeks, including overtime. The provisions also require suppliers to comply with applicable laws on minimum wages and to keep worker dormitories clean and safe. Apple's code of conduct for its suppliers was modeled after the Electronic Industry Code of Conduct and other labor standards. (Associated Press 2006) The Electronic Industry Code of Conduct was developed to provide standards for working conditions and environmental responsibility throughout the supply chain for electronic equipment, which involves many developing countries. (EICC 2007)

Three related ethical points need to be kept in mind: First, although concern for reputation is an important ethical motivation, it only goes so far. For a corporation maximizing profits, the ideal would be only to appear to deal with labor inequities and yet get the benefit of exploitative lower labor costs. This would not be ethical.[9] Second, the standards being appealed to are those of the developed countries. To apply them, further justification is needed besides just saying that we are in a position to require them. Obviously, there is an ethical case for developed countries' standards for child labor and non-exploitative work. But this case needs to be made in the context of a transnational theory of justice.

It has also been pointed out that strict enforcement of child labor standards in factories in impoverished countries can result in children being forced into even more exploitative pursuits such as prostitution. (Bhagwati 2007, 71) In any case, if there is no internal motivation within the developing country for enforcing labor standards, enforcement will be haphazard. IKEA, faced with allegations of substandard labor practices in some of its suppliers, went to great lengths to ensure decent labor standards, but with imperfect results. (Bartlett et al. 2006)

Some conservative defenders of globalization deny that there is any problem here, ethical or otherwise. Jagdish Bhagwati argues that workers prefer working in harsh conditions because it is better than their alternatives, and that labor standards cannot be enforced transnationally. "It will produce chaos," he says. (2007, 178) Even if these observations are true, they concern the practicality of the enforcement of ethical principles. They do not provide reasons for or against ethical principles concerning labor standards. It may very well be true for a variety of reasons that sweatshop workers have no better alternative. But do the employing companies really require conditions that harsh in order to survive and prosper? And, ethically, should they? It needs to be remembered that decent working conditions came about in the developed countries only after great strife with corporations--which survived quite well. These issues will be revisited in more detail in Chapter 8, **The Ethical Status of Globalized Institutions.**

INTELLECTUAL PROPERTY

Intellectual property becomes an ethically globalized issue primarily through IT. Content is now readily available in electronic form across national boundaries. Different nations or nation-groups have different regulations for a creator's property rights in his or her written (or otherwise produced) creations. Asian and eastern European countries have a reputation for "pirating" software. Thus exercising intellectual property rights is in some ways similar to Yahoo's globalized ethical problem. There are different standards for such rights in different nations, and how are they to be harmonized? There is a common standard proposed by the World Trade Organization (WTO), but it is not clear that it is the ethical one. The WTO has introduced the Trade-Related Intellectual Property Rights (TRIPS) agreement to broaden the scope of protection of Intellectual Property Rights. (Chang 2008) This agreement is transnational and applies to all members of the WTO, currently 150 nations. This is a substantial percentage of the 192 total current nations.

The ethical question comes about because to hold developing countries to our standards may make these countries much worse off than they need be. This is perhaps clearest in the area of patents on drugs. When African governments imported copies of HIV/AIDs drugs at cost savings of 95% off drug companies patented originals, 41 drug companies sued South Africa for violating the TRIPS agreement. Many African countries have the most serious HIV/AIDs epidemics and the prices for the originals were from 3 to 40 times the average annual income of citizens of these countries. The ensuing public uproar resulted in the drug companies' withdrawing their suit. (Chang 2008, 123-125)

It may come as a surprise to readers used to the "piracy" rhetoric of entertainment and drug corporations that historically copyright and patent are not just property rights. All societies balance the right to exclusive use of the creation against the public benefit of the creation being freely available for others to build upon. The original stated purpose of copyright is to give the artist or creator of intellectual property the exclusive right to reproduce it, but not just for the artist or creator to be able to reap suitable rewards for his creation. Ultimately the existence of this right is to stimulate creativity. U.S. Supreme Court Justice Sandra Day O'Connor writes:

The primary objective of copyright is not to reward the labor of authors, but 'To promote the Progress of Science and useful Arts.' To this end, copyright assures authors the right to their original expression, but encourages others to build freely upon the ideas and information conveyed by a work. (Lewis 2001, 1)

Drug companies (through the International Federation of Pharmaceutical Manufacturers Association) argue that 'without [intellectual property rights] the private sector will not invest the hundreds of millions of dollars needed to develop new vaccines for AIDS and other … diseases.' (Bale 2005) However, in 2000, a typical year, only 43% of US drug research funding came from the pharmaceutical industry. The remainder came from the government, private foundations, and universities. (Chang 2008, 125)

In the 19th century, the British free-market magazine *The Economist* argued forcefully against patents on the grounds that the social costs would be greater than the benefits. It was claimed that first-mover advantage for innovators would be enough of a compensation. The US itself refused to protect foreigner's copyrights from 1790 to 1891. Copyrights on materials printed outside the US were not recognized until 1988. (Chang 2008, 127, 134)

The original intent of copyright has clearly been attenuated (and apparently distorted) in recent years as corporations come to hold copyrights and to use their influence in congress to extend the copyright period indefinitely. The Digital Millennium Copyright Act of 1998 criminalizes for the first time "unauthorized access" to works that are published and sold. The 2004 Supreme Court case *Eldred vs. Ashcroft* upheld legislation by the late Sonny Bono extending copyrights for an additional 20 years.[10] The original copyright period of 14 years is now 70 years for individuals and 95 years from publication and 120 years from creation for corporations! (Lewis 2001) Since the greatest benefit from the extended copyright is enhanced corporate profits, any connection to stimulating creativity is indirect at best. The ethical question in the case of digital copying is how far the rule not to copy extends, and how to balance the property rights of the copyright owners with the public's right to free exchange of ideas as the basis for social progress. The globalized ethical question is how to extend these considerations to transnational contexts, taking into account that the development of poor countries can be seriously hampered by license fees reasonable for the US but prohibitive for them.

The Supreme Court Betamax decision of 1984 held that noncommercial home use recording of material broadcast over the public airwaves was a fair use of copyrighted works and did not constitute copyright infringement.[11] Further, makers of VCRs could not be held liable as contributory infringers even if the home use of a VCR was considered an infringing use. Fast forward 20 years and we find music and movie companies hard at work demonizing, prosecuting, and persecuting individuals for making copies for their own use.[12] In the year before August 2004, the recording industry sued just under 4,000 individuals for downloading copyrighted music. The Motion Picture Association of America announced in November 2004 that it would begin employing the same tactics, suing downloaders for amounts of $30,000 to $150,000. The MPAA apparently draws no distinction between downloading for personal use and downloading for resale (Hernandez 2004).eHH

A California district court in 2005 held that the fileswapping service Grokster was not liable if its software is used to make illegal copies. Although this parallels the 1984 Supreme Court Betamax decision, the US Supreme Court[13] held in 2005 that Grokster was liable. (www.techlawjournal.com 2005) A number of senators with corporate ties introduced legislation to make it a crime to "induce" people to violate copyright. The proposed Inducing Infringement of Copyright Act has the backing of most of the recording and music industry, as well as Microsoft. Opponents include Intel, Sun Microsystems, and Verizon Communications. These opponents are concerned that the act may stunt technological development (Woellert 2004).

Recall Justice O'Connor's statement about the purpose of copyright, which was "To promote the Progress of Science and useful Arts and to encourage others to build freely upon the ideas and information conveyed by a work." Clearly digital copying helps greatly in disseminating intellectual property and in this respect furthers intellectual progress. Further, noncommercial possession of digital copies by individuals seems to be an important part of their right to personal property. The conflict between the interests of corporations and individuals just discussed will receive further ethical discussion in a transnational context in Section 2, **Theories of Globalized Ethics**, and Section 3, **A Social Contract For Globalized Institutions**.

SERVICE LEVELS: AN ETHICAL PROBLEM?

We noted earlier that English language skills and knowledge of cultural and legal practices are also important, especially for offshored technical and customer service calls. As of 2004, poor technical and customer service because of offshoring was costing companies customers. (Ante 2004, 36) Since then, offshored service calls have become so ubiquitous that it is difficult if not impossible to switch to a company whose service calls are not offshored.

Common advice about offshoring notes that only highly structured service calls can safely be outsourced. It is true that current outsourced calls are highly structured. The difficulty is that problems falling outside the structure can't be handled. Since I can handle the structured problems myself, that leaves close to 100% of my problems unresolved by calls to technical service or customer service. I vowed never to do business with Amazon because of a delivery foul up, and so informed the (apparently Indian) customer service rep on the line. It was pretty clear that my message would never get forwarded.

Normally it would be a function of market competition to weed out inferior customer and technical service. But it seems that nearly all hardware and software manufacturers, nearly all ISPs, and most major web commerce companies, have offshored customer and/or technical support. So there is no one to switch to. I have not seen any data on this phenomenon, so to that extent my discussion of this issue is hypothetical: *If* it were the case that competition is currently helpless to weed out substandard customer and technical service, is there an ethical issue here, and if so, what?

I believe the ethical issue is the same as when there is no competitive pressure to fix a defect in a product, while at the same time there is no compensation such as a reduced price for the product. In the case of offshoring service calls, the motive for offshoring is to save money. So the case is essentially the same as that of a manufacturer who substitutes inferior materials and charges the same price. The ethical failing on the part of companies' offshoring customer or technical service is misrepresentation. It would be fraud if there were explicit standards for technical or customer service, but with informal standards there is no legal case.[14]

So in this case there is a standard ethical problem, namely supplying shoddy goods or services. The transnational aspect comes about because language and cultural differences are overlooked or ignored in providing the service. In this case as well as in manufacturing (although for a different reason), labor is not a commodity. For companies to overlook this is to fob off inferior services on their customers.

Of course, in other cases, notably software development, offshore services can be superior to those in the offshoring country. But even there cultural factors are important. Professor S. Krishna of Indian Institute of Management Bangalore reported[15] that an English firm, impressed with the IT productivity of its Bangalore firm, moved its entire English staff and operations to Bangalore. The resulting crash in productivity occurred because of the unwitting clash between English business customs and Indian business customs. For example, Indian employees were unwilling to disagree publicly with a superior's opinion, and unwilling to engage in public drinking to celebrate accomplishments.

CONCLUSION

Obviously all these cases require us to appeal to some sort of transnational code of ethics. In Section II, we will examine the possibilities. But before that, we need to understand what currently exists in the way of transnational institutions and what principles they are governed by. This is the topic of the next chapter. The final chapter in this first section will examine globalization itself more closely, as well as the contribution of IT to globalization.

REFERENCES

Ante, S. E. (2004, January 12). Shifting work offshore? Outsourcer beware. *BusinessWeek*.

Ante, S. E. & Hof, R. (2004, May 17). Look who's going offshore. *BusinessWeek*.

Applegate, L. M., Austin, R. D., & McFarlan, F. W. (2003). *Corporate Information Systems: Text and Cases*. New York: McGraw-Hill Irwin.

Arendt, H. (1965). *Eichmann in Jerusalem*. New York: Viking Press.

Associated Press. (2006). *Apple launches China labor probe*. Retrieved February 11, 2008, from http://www.wired.com/science/discoveries/news/2006/06/71176

Baker, S. & Kripalani, M. (January 20, 2004). Will outsourcing hurt America's supremacy? *Business-Week*.

Bale, H. E. (2005). *Access to essential drugs in poor countries.* Retrieved March 11, 2008, from http://www.ifpma.org/News/SpeechDetail.aspx?nID=4

Bartlett, C. A., Dessain, V., & Sjöman, A. (2006). *Ikea's global sourcing challenge* (Harvard Business School Case #9-906-414).

Bensinger, K. (2003, September 9). Mexican corn comes a cropper. *Washington Times.*

Bhagwati, J. (2007). *In defense of globalization.* Oxford, UK: Oxford University Press.

Center for Economic Justice. (2004). Investing in World Bank bonds: What are the risks? Retrieved December 3, 2007, from info@econjustice.net

EICC. (2007). *Electronic Industry Code of Conduct.* Retrieved February 11, 2008, from http://www.eicc.info

Elias, P. (2007). *Yahoo, jailed journalists, settle lawsuit.* Retrieved November 13, 2007, from http://news.yahoo.com.

Evans, M. D. (2003) *Bankbusters: the boycott of World Bank bonds is spreading.* Retrieved March 24, 2009 from http://www.thefreelibrary.com/Bankbusters:+the+boycott+of+World+Bank+bonds+is+spreading,+writes...-a0100462820

Friedman, M. (1999). *Take it to the limits: Milton Friedman on libertarianism.* Interview filmed on February 10, 1999. Retrieved February 11, 2008 from http://www.hoover.org/multimedia/uk/3411401.html

Geller, A. (2004, August 1). How good are the new jobs? *San Fernando Valley Daily News.*

Goodman, D. (2008, March 12). War against Web tops music biz "screw-ups" list. *Reuters.* Retrieved March 14, 2008 from news.yahoo.com

Herbst, M. (2008, February 11). Are H1-B workers getting bilked? *BusinessWeek.*

Hernandez, G. (2004, November 5). Taking aim at film thieves. *San Fernando Valley Daily News.*

Hopkins, M. (2003). *The planetary bargain.* London: Earthscan Publications.

Kant, I. (1970). Perpetual peace. In H. Reiss (Ed.), *Kant's political writings.* Cambridge, UK: Cambridge University Press.

Kohlberg, L. (1976). Moral stages and moralization. In T. Lickona (Ed.), *Moral development and behavior.* New York: Holt, Rinehart & Winston.

Konrad, R. (2004, July 1). U.S. Chamber President promotes outsourcing. *San Fernando Valley Daily News.*

Lerner, M. (2000). *Spirit matters.* Charlottesville, VA: Hampton Roads Publishing Co.

Lewis, M. B. (2001). *Music length protection.* Retrieved June 30, 2004 from http://www.serve.com/marbeth/music_length_protection.html

Locke, J. (2004). *The second treatise of government.* Retrieved July 13, 2004 from http://www.constitution.org/jl/2ndtreat.htm

MacDonald, G. J. (2006, February 14). Congress's dilemma: When Yahoo in China's not Yahoo. *The Christian Science Monitor*.

McFarlan, W., & DeLacey, B. (2003). *Enabling business strategy with IT at the World Bank* (Harvard Business School Case No. 304-055).

Mulligan, A. C., Hay, R., & Brewer, T. (2000). *David Ricardo and comparative advantage*. Retrieved July 21, 2004 from http://iang.org/free_banking/david.html

News, B. B. C. (2007, June 12). *Yahoo's China policy rejected*. Retrieved December 2, 2007, from http://news.bbc.co.uk

Plato. (2009). *Republic*. Retrieved May 10, 2004, from http://classics.mit.edu/Plato/republic.html

Procurement Insights. (2008, July 10). What would you prefer for cost cutting, offshoring or process improvement? *Procurement Insights*. Retrieved March 30, 2009, from http://procureinsights.wordpress.com/2008/07/10/what-would-you-prefer-for-cost-cutting-offshoring-or-process-improvement-a-pi-qa/

Rai, S. (2004, March 21). An outsourcing giant fights back. *The New York Times*.

Rawls, J. (1999a). *A Theory of Justice* (rev. ed.) Cambridge, MA: Harvard University Press.

Rawls, J. (1999b). *The Law of Peoples*. Cambridge, MA: Harvard University Press.

Reich, R. (2007, September 10). It's not business' business. *Business Week*.

Roberts, P. C. (2004, March 22). The harsh truth about outsourcing. *BusinessWeek*.

Rousseau, J. (2004). *The social contract*. Retrieved July 13, 2004 from http://www.constitution.org/jjr/socon_01.htm

Schultz, R. (2006). *Contemporary issues in ethics and information technology*. Hershey, PA: IRM Press.

Singer, P. (2004). *One world* (2nd ed.) New Haven, CT: Yale University Press.

Stiglitz, J. (2003). *Globalization and its discontents*. New York: W. W. Norton.

Stiglitz, J. (2007). *Making globalization work*. New York: W. W. Norton.

Supreme Court Rules in MGM v. Grokster. (2005). Retrieved March 24, 2009 from http://www.techlaw-journal.com/topstories/2005/20050627a.asp

Thompson, E. P. (1968). *The making of the English working class*. London: Victor Gollancz Ltd.

UNICEF. (2008). *Child protection from violence, exploitation and abuse*. Retrieved February 11, 2008, from http://www.unicef.org/protection/index_childlabour.html

Weisman, S. R. (2004, January 21). Powell defends outsourcing. *The New York Times*.

White, T. (2007). *Data, dollars, and the unintentional subversion of human rights in the IT industry*. Waltham, MA: Center for Business Ethics.

Wikipedia (2007a). *Global Justice*. Retrieved December 2, 2007 from http://en.wikipedia.org

Wikipedia (2007b). *Sovereignty*. Retrieved February 20, 2007 from http://en.wikipedia.org

Woellert, L. (2004, July 19). Piracy wars: Hollywood turns its guns on tech. *BusinessWeek.*

Yung, K. (2004, August 2). Can't we work this out? *Dallas Morning News.*

ENDNOTES

[1]   The global reach of this project extended far beyond the usual suspects, including such places as Ouagadougou, Burkina Faso.

[2]   My thanks to a reviewer for the 2008 InSite conference for pointing this out.

[3]   Although foreign recipients who receive H1-B visas and work in the U.S. receive substantially less than U.S. workers, this practice is considered abuse. (Herbst 2008)

[4]   Rawls' own account of transnational justice has flaws. I will ultimately present a different social contract approach to transnational justice in Section 3, **A Social Contract for Globalized Institutions.**

[5]   The economist David Ricardo developed the economic theory of competitive advantage in the early 19th century. See Mulligan, Hay, Brewer 2000.

[6]   Personal communication from Bradley Zucker.

[7]   See www.brookings.edu/comm/policybriefs/pb132.htm.

[8]   Critics call Friedman's doctrine "market fundamentalism."

[9]   Plato deals with appearing to be ethical in his *Republic* (360 BCE), 357A-367E. See also Chapter 4, **The Basis of Ethical Principles**, p. 45.

[10]   I am indebted to Eric Eldred, the plaintiff in this case, for helpful comments both on the case and its context.

[11]   U.S. Supreme Court SONY CORP. v. UNIVERSAL CITY STUDIOS, INC., 464 U.S. 417 (1984) (FindLaw Legal News http://news.findlaw.com)

[12]   Goodman 2008 reports that the music industry's decision to go after noncommercial copiers is considered its worst mistake, and probably responsible for its tailspin in profits since closing down Napster. Blender magazine suggests that the industry should have instead figured out how to make money from downloading.

[13]   The Court's taking the 2000 election decision out of the hands of the voters casts doubts on its intelligence and respect for law and the Constitution.

[14]   Dell is reputed in 2004 to have responded to complaints about its Indian technical service to have instituted training for its Indian service employees to improve their American English accents.

[15]   Lecture given to the BIT group at UCLA, Los Angeles, October 2007.

Chapter 2
Current Ethically Globalized Institutions

As I noted in the previous chapter, the world is currently not organized into a single economy sharing benefits and burdens. But at the same time, institutions have developed which transcend national boundaries. We are looking for ethically globalized institutions, those which raise ethical problems which cannot be divided into pieces belonging to different nations. I will begin with a list of international organizations. International organizations are those which have an official presence in more than one nation. Among these, we will separate out those which are ethically globalized institutions and therefore the concern of this book. Here is a list of the different types of international organizations which may or may not be currently operating as ethically globalized institutions:

- The United Nations and its agencies; the World Court
- World financial and economic institutions such as the World Bank, the International Monetary Fund (IMF), and the World Trade Organization (WTO). These institutions have ties to existing powerful states.
- Superpowers
- Multinational Corporations (MNCs)

DOI: 10.4018/978-1-60566-922-9.ch002

- Non-Governmental Organizations (NGOs) without ties to existing states
- Websites with international presence

Before we examine these organizations, a general problem with transnational institutions should be acknowledged. The 18th century philosophers Kant and Hume noted that a world state was undesirable if not impossible. Kant's reason was that it was contradictory for a sovereign entity (a state) to have another sovereign entity (the world state) with sovereignty over it. (Kant 1795, 102) In practice, we can see how this works out in the "states" of the so-called United States. The states invoke what are called 'states rights' to claim sovereignty over matters sometimes also claimed by the Federal government. The tenth amendment to the US Constitution states:

The powers not delegated to the United States by the Constitution, nor prohibited by it to the States, are reserved to the States respectively, or to the people. (The US Constitution 1997)

The interpretation of this amendment and related parts of the United States Constitution has a long and complex history. Kant himself argues that a *federation* of independent states is necessary to prevent war. Arrangements for sovereignty distributed piecemeal between a sovereign over states (the U.S. Federal Government) and lesser sovereigns (the various states) are possible.[1] These arrangements are clearly tricky and difficult to define once and for all, but the example of the United States (and other nations with similar federal arrangements) shows that it can be done.

THE UNITED NATIONS (UN)

Is the United Nations an ethically globalized institution, or is it only an international organization? Recall that an ethically globalized institution is defined as one whose ethical problems cannot be solved by dividing them up between different nations or societies. Transnational ethical problems for ethically globalized institutions tend to arise in connection with issues of sovereignty or ultimate control. Indeed, discussions of reform of the UN revolve around precisely these issues, as we will see.

The stated aims of the UN are to facilitate cooperation in international law and security, and promote economic development, social progress and human rights. Founded in 1945 just after World War II, it was hoped that the UN would settle conflicts between states and thereby avoid war. Its main branches with transnational responsibility are the Security Council, which passes resolutions for peace and security; and the International Court of Justice, which adjudicates disputes between states; the separate International Criminal Court tries individuals for crimes against humanity and the like.[2]

The ethical status of the UN is determined by the nature of its powers with respect to the sovereignty of its member nations, now virtually all independent states on the planet. The UN, primarily through the Security Council, has in many cases asserted its power over sovereign nations, but in a number of cases (often involving the so-called 'superpowers') it has been unable to prevent wars. The typical UN force authorized by the Security Council is a peacekeeping force, either unarmed or armed only for self-defense. The force is present only at the request of both warring parties and is usually authorized by the Security Council. Such forces have been used numerous times in conflicts between Israel and its Arab neighbors, in the former Belgian Congo, between Greece and Turkey on Cyprus, and between India and

Pakistan over Kashmir. These UN operations have succeeded in reducing the level of violence, though the underlying conflicts tend to remain. (Frängsmyr 1989)

This peacekeeping use of transnational force clearly threatens no nation's sovereignty--the nations impacted have to agree to have the force present. Also, the peacekeeping force itself is not designed for aggressive use. However, in the 1950s the UN actually approved the use of military force in the Korean War. Korea had been partitioned into North Korea under Russian influence and South Korea under American influence. The North invaded the South, and the UN Security Council approved the use of force to meet the challenge. The military that was fielded was called a UN force, even though about 90% of the personnel and expenditure was American. Russia did not veto the authorizing Security Council resolution because it was at that time boycotting the UN for seating Nationalist China rather than Communist China. (Wikipedia 2009)

Using aggressive military force to deal with transgressions against peace and national sovereignty has not been, except in the case of Korea, UN policy. American use of military force in Vietnam and Iraq did not have UN approval, and indeed was contrary to the very purposes of the UN. The more limited military incursion in Kosovo/Serbia was done under the auspices of NATO, an American-led military alliance with mainly European members. Other uses of military force in Somalia, Panama, and Grenada were unilaterally American, and transnational only because superpowers are transnational. Russia, the other superpower during this same period, was putting down uprisings in Hungary and Czechoslovakia and waging aggressive war in Afghanistan.

We can see that the UN has very limited powers in dealing with aggression by superpowers and thus there are no ethically globalized issues involving the UN having to do with the security of nations. Those ethical issues remain lodged in the nation states which continue to wage war. In fact, whether the UN has any real transnational powers has been questioned in proposals for reform. Some proposals are for the UN to play a greater or more effective role in world affairs; others are to reduce its role to humanitarian work only. The nations that have veto power in the Security Council were fixed at its founding in 1945 and there are proposals to alter its membership. This has not happened. UN Secretary-General Kofi Annan also called for making UN governance more democratic and imposing an international tariff on arms manufacturers worldwide. These proposals were not adopted. (Wikipedia 2008b)

An international tariff imposed by the UN, as well as some power to penalize nations which go to war (currently mostly the US), would indeed make the UN an ethically globalized institution. But so long as it has to depend on the agreement of the most powerful states even to prevent war, any ethical problems involving its member states have to be resolved within those states.

Despite its lack of power, the UN has played a significant role in formulating and promulgating trans-national standards, especially for human rights (the Universal Declaration of Human Rights in 1948) and also for transnational business (the Global Compact in 2000). When the UDHR was initially adopted, the Soviet bloc nations, South Africa, and Saudi Arabia abstained. In 2000, 57 Islamic nations moved their allegiance to the Cairo Declaration of Human Rights which gives priority to Islamic religious law. (Cairo Declaration 1990) The Global Compact is a voluntary set of standards for transnational corporations, and I will discuss its effectiveness in Chapter 11, **Globalized Ethics and Current Institutions.**

An international judicial body, the International Court of Justice (ICJ), adjudicates disputes between states; the separate International Criminal Court (ICC) tries individuals for crimes against humanity and the like. The ICJ tries cases between states, and states must accept its jurisdiction, either overall or on a case-by-case basis. The ICC also requires acceptance of its jurisdiction, but a number of states refused to accept its jurisdiction at its founding in 2002. These included pre-war Iraq, Israel, China, and the

United States.[3] (Scharf 1998) So the remarks about the UN on national security apply here as well: So long as these courts require the consent of states to have jurisdiction, they are not ethically globalized institutions.

Both the UN and the International Courts are probably best understood ethically as nongovernmental organizations (NGOs), operating transnationally but without any power or sovereignty over the various nations they are operating within. The ethical status of NGOs will be discussed further below.

WORLD FINANCIAL AND ECONOMIC INSTITUTIONS

World financial and economic institutions such as the World Bank, International Trade Organization (ITO), and the International Monetary Fund (IMF), have ties to existing powerful states, but also have the ability to act without the consent of any states. Like the UN, the World Bank and the IMF were founded after World War II, mainly to aid in rebuilding Europe and in preventing another Great Depression. (Stiglitz 2003, 11-12) Their aims have changed and expanded, to provide support to developing countries. The World Trade Organization was founded in 1995 as a successor to the General Agreement on Tariffs and Trade (GATT). GATT began in 1947 as a multinational agreement to reduce trade restrictions and to adjudicate trade disputes between signatories to the agreement. The aims of the WTO have likewise changed and expanded. Under GATT, members could choose which of a bundle of trade-related agreements they would comply with. Under the WTO, members must sign up with all agreements. Some commentators believe that the changes are very much to the detriment of developing countries. (Chang 2008, 74-77)

It will help in placing these world institutions to compare the World Bank with a branch of the UN, the Economic and Social Council, ostensibly with similar aims. The Economic and Social Council has a rotating membership and engages in information gathering, advising member nations, and making recommendations. It also coordinates overlapping functions of other UN agencies. Since 1998, it also meets with important ministers of the IMF and World Bank, again primarily for coordination. Obviously, unlike the IMF and World Bank, it has no power over these institutions nor over its member nations, but is in a position to provide input to these organizations.

The power of the IMF and World Bank resides in their being able to grant or withhold loans to developing countries. The IMF's approval of a country's economic policy is often a condition for the World Bank, the European Union, or other lenders to provide funds. Conditions on loans to developing countries include liberalizing financial markets to allow more foreign investment, having an independent central bank which keeps inflation down, and trade liberalization.

As noted in Chapter 1, some commentators have felt that these world financial and development institutions have been a failure, making conditions in developing countries worse. Joseph Stiglitz finds their failure to have two main causes: (1) adherence to an incorrect economic theory called "market fundamentalism" by its critics; and (2) placing the interests of international finance above the interests of developing countries. (Stiglitz 2003) In order to determine whether these failures are ethically relevant, we need to determine to what extent these institutions have power over sovereign nations. So we need to examine the governance of these institutions and their relationship to developed and developing nations.

There are twenty-four seats on the governing boards of the IMF and World Bank. Each seat represents several countries, but votes are allocated on the basis of economic power. All three institutions are said to be public, but it is not entirely clear what this means. The World Bank is a bundle of institutions, the most important being: The International Bank for Reconstruction and Development (IBRD), organized as a cooperative of its 185 member countries; and the International Development Association (IDA) whose aim is to give interest-free loans to the 80 poorest countries. The same staff and "rigorous standards" are used by both organizations. The five largest shareholders, France, Germany, Japan, the United Kingdom and the United States appoint an executive director, while other member countries are represented by 19 executive directors. (The World Bank 2008). Thus the World Bank is truly transnational, and in practice has the ability to override the sovereignty of developing nations. However, the developed nations just mentioned have much greater say in the operations of the Bank than developing nations, about nine times as much.

Membership in the IMF is a condition for membership in the World Bank, and in fact all members of the IMF are also members of the World Bank. Also, with the exception of North Korea, Cuba, Andorra, Monaco, Liechtenstein, Tuvalu, and Nauru, all UN member countries are also members of the IMF. Also, with the exception of North Korea and Cuba, the remaining non-members are among the world's smallest countries. North Korea and Cuba are presumably nonmembers because of the disapproval of the larger members, notably the United States. The concurrent IMF support of other military dictatorships has given rise to an anti-globalization movement targeting the IMF. The IMF's defense is that it has no power to enforce democratization.

The IMF's governing structure has similarities to the World Bank. The board of directors consists of a member from each nation, normally the finance minister or central bank governor. There is an executive board of the same five member nations, but each member has voting strength proportional to its economic power expressed as quotas in units of SDRs[4] The IMF itself determines these quotas. It is also in the process of revising the quota system to give developing countries a bigger voice. (International Monetary Fund 2008) Again, its power over developing countries lies in the fact that it must approve the financial operations of a developing country before that country can get a loan from the World Bank.

So are the World Bank and the IMF ethically globalized institutions? Unlike the UN, they have *de facto* enforcement power over the financial structure of countries which need capital. However, the much greater say of developed countries over the policies of these organizations is built into their organizational structure. So the question is whether the interests of the major powers and (transnational) corporations get more weight than they should. It should be noted that the *official* aim of the World Bank is an ethical one. The World Bank's stated mission is to fight poverty around the world. The IMF's stated aims are somewhat more indirectly ethical: To foster global monetary cooperation, financial stability, facilitate international trade, promote high employment and sustainable economic growth, and reduce poverty. Although many of these aims tend to promote the well-being of the peoples of various countries, even the worst off, some of them may conflict with ethical aims. Indeed there is a dispute among economists whether the actual decisions of these organizations promote their own stated aims. This dispute is in part a dispute about economic theories and their results, and it will need to be examined in the course of examining the ethical status of these organizations.

The third organization, the World Trade Organization, has 150 member nations, and decisions (trade agreements) are reached by consensus. As previously mentioned, members must agree to all or none at their biennial meeting. The WTO has probably drawn the most visible criticism of the three organizations, including massive demonstrations at biennial meetings in Seattle and Genoa. It also has the most ethically neutral mission, which is to supervise and liberalize free trade. Whether or not free trade is always or even mostly ethically desirable is an issue argued by economists. (Stiglitz 2003, Chang 2008)

The WTO's power stems from its ability to impose significant trade sanctions for noncompliance. Other WTO members, nearly all countries, must cooperate in enforcing sanctions or be subject to sanctions themselves

Critical claims of the WTO include: WTO rules are written by and for corporations with inside access to the negotiations. Citizen input by consumer, environmental, human rights and labor organizations is consistently ignored. The WTO has ruled that it is illegal for a government to ban a product based on the way it is produced, such as with child labor. It has also ruled that governments cannot take into account "non commercial values" such as human rights, or the behavior of companies that do business with vicious dictatorships such as Burma when making purchasing decisions. The WTO requires privatizing public assets and services to profit-making corporations, raising costs for those least able to pay. The WTO dismantles environmental protections. The WTO's 'Trade Related Intellectual Property' rights (TRIPs) protect pharmaceutical companies' right to profit and increase the death toll from HIV/AIDS. WTO's Agreement on Agriculture--that market forces should control agricultural policies—again puts profits above reducing hunger. The WTO hurts poor, small countries in favor of rich powerful nations by prohibiting conflicting local laws. Even entire sections of California and US laws have had to be rewritten. (Global Exchange 2007)

The WTO clearly qualifies as an ethically globalized institution. It is officially transnational in its governance and its decisions impact the well-being of people in many different nations. Since it can even force nations to revise laws and its directives have their own legal force, its actions raise ethical issues that cannot be divided up between nations. Critics feel that the WTO reflects the interests of (multinational) corporations and the most powerful nations and thus needs to be replaced by a more democratic institution also reflecting concerns of ethics and justice. These are precisely the areas globalized ethics needs to address, and we will address them in Section 2, **Theories of Globalized Ethics,** and Section 3, **A Social Contract For Globalized Institutions.**

Another international organization, the Organisation for Economic Cooperation and Development (OECD) has thirty high-income and a few middle-income countries as members. Members must accept the principles of representative democracy and free-market economy. It is more of a forum for economic, social, and environmental issues. But its directives can, if adopted by all its member nations, have a great deal of force, if not full legal status. It deals with issues such as corporate tax evasion, corruption, educational assessment, and environmental issues. Its 1997 MAI (Multilateral Agreement on Investment) was scuttled by a campaign by NGOs. This agreement would have greatly restricted the powers of sovereign states to regulate investment or any enterprise within their borders. The OECD's ability to put forth an agreement radically altering state sovereignty makes it an ethically globalized institution. (OECD 2008)

SUPERPOWERS

These are nations with the ability to dominate the politics and economies of other nations. The former Soviet Union qualified, with satellite states in Eastern Europe and Cuba in America. The United States qualifies because of its propensity to destabilize democratically elected governments with political ideologies it dislikes, such as in Guatemala, Iran, and Chile. The United States claims that it is not an 'imperial power' because it does not install its own government officials (that is, US citizens) in countries that it dominates. However, it supports regimes that it feels are favorable to its policies with financial and military aid. The ethical status of these regimes is usually not a consideration for the US. The ideological status of the regimes usually is. So military dictatorships which have overthrown democratically elected governments are supported, as in Chile, Guatemala, and Iran. In these cases, the democratically elected governments were socialist. Repressive military dictatorships such as Chile and Burma have gotten US support, while repressive military dictatorships such as Cuba and North Korea have strict economic sanctions from the US. Although Cuba and North Korea have communist governments, Iran and (pre-war) Iraq, also subject to sanctions, did not. The official US explanation is that these countries are especially repressive.

During the G. W. Bush administration, US international policy was determined by a group referred to as the "neocons" or neo-conservatives. Members include former World Bank head Paul Wolfowitz, Richard Perle, Eliot Abrams, Robert Kagan, and William Kristol. All are key players in designing the strategy of preemptive war. Others included: Michael Ledeen of the American Enterprise Institute; former CIA Director James Woolsey; Bill Bennett; former Vice President Dick Cheney; and former Secretary of Defense Donald Rumsfeld.

In the late 1990s, a number of these people, including virtually all members of the George W. Bush administration, signed a statement called "Rebuilding America's Defenses" to the effect that since the Soviet Union had collapsed, America, the remaining superpower should seize the opportunity to dominate the world by increased military might. The statement suggested beginning this domination with regime change in Iraq. It also noted that a "new Pearl Harbor" event would be required to obtain the support of the American people for this regime. (Project for the New American Century 2000)

Although the neocons made it explicit, since World War II the United States has always maintained by far the largest military force in the world, and spends a percentage of its GNP on military expenditures dramatically greater than any other nation. Former President Eisenhower warned of the self-perpetuating nature of this state of affairs through what he called "the military-industrial complex." (American Rhetoric 1961) Military incursions into other countries to preserve US interests are numerous: Panama, Grenada, Vietnam, Afghanistan, Iraq. Even before World War II, the US Military sent force into other countries. Visitors to Mexico City can see the substantial monument to the boy heroes (Monumento de los Niños Heroes) who threw themselves to their deaths over a parapet at Chapultepec Castle rather than surrender to the US Marines--in 1847. Presumably the Marines were there to restore order, and presumably those who erected the monument had another view.

The neocon's late 90s statement disturbingly suggests that the 9/11 event may have been strategically staged or deliberately allowed to happen.[5] Various features of the event make staging unlikely, but unfortunately the possibility that the event was deliberately allowed to happen cannot be dismissed because the Bush administration has revealed over and over again that truth is not one of its values--rather power is. Possibly the best argument that the 9/11 event was not staged is that staging that event would have required a level of competence impossible for the Bush administration.[6]

Some commentators assert that the entire system of transnational institutions is just a front for US transnational corporate interests. John Perkins, in his *Confessions of an Economic Hit Man* (2006) and other books, maintains that what he calls "the corporatocracy" has as its aims the economic and political subjugation of developing nations by forcing on them loans they will never be able to repay. These loans are typically for the purpose of developing infrastructure which will theoretically aid in economic development. The infrastructure is developed by such American multinationals as Halliburton and Bechtel, with the result that much of the loan money rapidly leaves the country. Perkins does not discuss whether the infrastructure development actually led to economic development, but he is able to testify that his own estimates of benefits of economic development were required to be grossly exaggerated.

The ethical question which needs to be answered is whether the US has a right to behave as an imperial power enforced by a strong military. At least one theory of globalized ethics, political realism (to be discussed in Chapter 6) says that there is no ethical question here at all. Other theories would strongly disagree. In any case, if there is no further justification for US hegemony than the fact that it has the power (both economic and military) to maintain its domination, then attempts to justify US actions ethically become pure rhetoric, essentially exercises in public relations.

The question whether the US (or other superpowers) are ethically globalized institutions thus depends on what transnational ethical theory one holds. At present, the question may be moot if there is no countervailing power, either another nation or some transnational power such as the World Court, that can call the US to account for its actions. But should the actions of the US turn out to be unethical by some reasonable standard, it still matters ethically to make this known and to consider steps by which the US (or other superpower) might become subject to these ethical considerations and any possible penalties or sanctions.

Other nations (usually major powers themselves) do supply aid and military support to other countries and sometimes invade other countries with military force. Sometimes regime change is the result. So such countries are acting transnationally. The ethical considerations that would apply, would be the appropriate ethical standards between states. The interaction between states here is of the same kind that has always existed between states. There seem to be no additional transnational aspects, as there might be for superpowers who define themselves as transnational actors.

MULTINATIONAL CORPORATIONS (MNCS)

The well-being of a significant portion of world citizens is tied up with the operations of multinationals, since multinational corporations account for over 60% of world economic output. (Ionescu & Oprea 2007) Since corporations are legally individuals but not ethically individuals, there are unresolved ethical issues with both multinational corporations and corporations within nations. We return in Chapter 8, **The Ethical Status of Globalized Institutions** and in Chapter 11, **Globalized Ethics and Current Institutions,** to ethical issues affecting corporations regardless of their national or multinational status.

Multinational corporations are almost by definition ethically globalized institutions. As business entities in a market economy, they automatically encounter two ethical issues: (1) Paying support for the political and social infrastructure that makes it possible to do business. These are called *taxes.* (2) Colluding with competitors to fix prices. This is called *anticompetitive behavior* and can also take the form of creating and maintaining a monopoly or oligopoly. Such behavior prevents a market economy from delivering its benefits to society. Unethical behavior in these areas is now handled *within* states. But multinational corporations can and do use their presence in multiple states to get around any sanctions for such behavior.

The goal of a corporation is to maximize profits, so by saying that corporate behavior is unethical I do not mean to imply that we can expect it to desist, or pay attention to anyone's saying "You naughty, naughty corporation." How to deal ethically with corporations is the subject of Chapter 8. The subject of this chapter is ethically globalized issues in different types of organizations. The organizations we are now dealing with are multinational corporations.

Corporations can avoid dealing with their fair share of infrastructure support by shifting their tax burden to a country with lesser or no corporate taxes. Accenture, Fruit of the Loom and Stanley are among corporations moving to Bermuda, which has no corporate tax. (Welch 2008) Attempts are being made to legislate away this form of tax avoidance, but corporations naturally defend it. One penalty would be the inability of a corporation incorporated in a tax haven to receive contracts in the nation not receiving taxes. If possible, this seems an appropriate remedy for a corporation failing to pay its fair share of infrastructure support. So at least in theory this sort of tax avoidance is manageable through current national legal structures and does not require transnational authority. There may be practical difficulties, but the ethical solution seems to be deny the corporation access to whatever part of the national infrastructure it is failing to support.

The ethical solution is not so easy with another form of tax avoidance, through internal transfer pricing between different branches of a multinational corporation. The idea is for subsidiaries to overcharge or undercharge each other so that the highest profits end up in subsidiaries in countries with the lowest corporate tax rates. Examples are bulldozers in Bolivia at $528 (increasing Bolivian profits) and German hacksaw blades at $5,485 each (decreasing German profits). (Chang 2008, 89-90) It is hard to see how to prohibit such transfer pricing without something like transnational accounting standards and the institutions to enforce them.

Similarly, although different nations with market economies have institutions and laws to deal with anticompetitive behavior, powerful multinationals can ignore them. When South Korea tried to impose anticompetitive conditions on Microsoft, Microsoft merely threatened to withdraw completely from South Korea. (Stiglitz 2007, 58) In any case, the bad effects of monopolistic and oligarchic behavior occur within individual economies and yet any action in the economy of one state will have little or no effect on this behavior in others. It should be mentioned here that monopolistic behavior is not only inefficient economically; it is a gross violation of the principles of justice underlying a market economy. It makes everyone worse off except possibly the monopolist.[7] So the solution here has to be some sort of transnational institution or policy able to prevent or eliminate monopolistic behavior. Joseph Stiglitz, in his *Making Globalization Work (*2007), maintains that such an institution is necessary. There will be more discussion of this issue in Section 3, **A Social Contract For Globalized Institutions**.

Multinational corporations also have impact on the well-being of countries with respect to each other. As we saw in the case of the offshoring of jobs, the well-being of those gaining jobs in one country is improved at the expense of those losing them in another. Policies within those countries can ameliorate the situation, but it should not be taken for granted that multinationals have carte blanche over the economies of nation states. Therefore, world financial and economic institutions would be necessary to provide oversight on multinationals and to insure that their actions are compatible with principles of justice. Institutions such as the World Bank, International Trade Organization (ITO), and the International Monetary Fund (IMF) are the exact type of institutions required. But as presently constituted, they tend to promote the interests of the developed countries and powerful multinationals at the expense of the less developed countries. Again, in Section III, we will examine the ethical possibilities for changing this situation.

NON-GOVERNMENTAL ORGANIZATIONS (NGOS)

Wikipedia defines a non-governmental organization (NGO) as:

a legally constituted organization created by private persons or organizations with no participation or representation of any government. In the cases in which NGOs are funded totally or partially by govern-

ments, the NGO maintains its non-governmental status insofar as it excludes government representatives from membership in the organization. (Wikipedia 2008a)

One problem with the definition is that "legal constitution" at this point has to be according to the legal system of some state. So there has to be some participation in some government. However, the exclusion of government representatives does limit government influence. There are about 40,000 NGOs operating transnationally, and much larger numbers operating within nations--Russia alone has 40,000.[8] (Wikipedia 2008a) NGOs tend to be humanitarian or social activist organizations performing functions that governments or government-sponsored organizations cannot. The United Nations specifically recognizes a place for organizations which are neither governments nor member states. They have a consultative role within the UN. Their power is of the same kind as any activist group-- networking, lobbying, conferences, use of the mass media, involvement in elections, and protests. The difference is that they act on transnational issues. (Global Policy Forum 2006) So NGOs can and do deal directly with ethically globalized issues. Examples include human rights, the environment, social programs, and women's rights.

A group of NGOs calling themselves "civil society" engaged in "civil regulation" have mounted successful campaigns against transnational corporate injustice by such corporations as Shell, McDonald's, Nike, Levi Strauss, Citibank, Nike, Reebok, and others.[9] These NGOs apparently make up for part of the ethical deficit of corporations and world financial and economic institutions such as the World Bank. We will consider the ethical status of these NGO activities in Chapter 8, **The Ethical Status of Globalized Institutions,** and in Chapter 11, **Globalized Ethics and Current Institutions.** The extent of bias against NGO activity is demonstrated by a breathtakingly irrelevant remark by economist Lawrence Summers. He was "deeply troubled" by the World Bank's paying attention to NGOs in design projects for democratic countries, (Fidler 2001, 46) presumably because the NGOs aren't democratically elected. But no one, not even the World Bank, has ever claimed that the World Bank respects the wishes of democratic countries. Or that the World Bank itself is democratically elected. So, one should be just as "deeply troubled" by the World Bank itself.

NGOs may be subject to undemocratic repression in states which do not acknowledge human rights. Russia in 2006 passed a law providing restrictions on NGOs which violate "morals" or national security. The US and other European nations protested this Russian action. (Voice of America 2006) This human rights issue about NGOs may itself be an ethically globalized issue. Also, although these organizations *deal with* transnational ethical issues and thus should be consulted, they do not have the power to *enforce* their judgements. Local and international NGOs sometimes act irresponsibly. Providing accountability is an unresolved challenge for NGOs and an important issue for globalized ethics and the structure of global democracy.

Jagdish Bhagwati maintains that standards of transparency and regulation which apply to governments, corporations, and transnational organizations should also apply to multinational NGOs. (2007, 43) His point is certainly well-taken, and such standards need to be in place and enforced.[10] Within nations, such standards have brought down companies committing egregious fraud such as Enron. And NGOs such as the Red Cross have been caught out reassigning funds collected for 9/11 to its general fund.[11] But who formulates such standards for transnational organizations, adopts them, and enforces them? One complaint against the IMF is egregious lack of transparency, in one case refusing to provide information on a policy not only to affected developing countries but to the US Congress! (Stiglitz 2003,

51-52) There is currently no institution the IMF is answerable to. This topic will be revisited in Chapter 11, **Globalized Ethics and Current Institutions.**

Religions also fit the definition of NGO. Some, such as Roman Catholicism and Islam, have global presence and are often able to insure that governments follow their principles. Even less organizationally coherent groups such as US Christian fundamentalists actively campaign for laws and even constitutional amendments which have a basis only in religious belief. Opposition to same sex marriage is a case in point. Such activity clearly violates principles of justice. In line with these principles, the constitutions of many states prohibit making religious belief the basis of public policy. So, insofar as a religion is an ethically globalized institution, it should not have any direct say on public policy, although the same freedom of religious belief should allow anyone to have whatever religious beliefs he or she wants.

Fundamentalists sometimes argue that their freedom of belief is violated unless they are permitted to discriminate against, say, homosexuals. In a just society, the answer is that one does not have the freedom to deny others their freedom unless greater freedom for all is achieved that way. That is clearly not what is going on here. Thus in a just society, toleration is extended to religious beliefs, however outlandish, only on condition that those so tolerated are willing to tolerate others.[12]

WEBSITES WITH INTERNATIONAL PRESENCE

Because of the nature of the Internet, all websites have international presence, in the sense that they are visible in all areas where they are not blocked. But many websites have only local relevance. A list of restaurants in Beverly Hills, CA, USA, is almost entirely of interest only to those who are interested in that area. They may be trying to find a restaurant, or just in seeing what's around on Rodeo Drive. We can contrast these local websites with websites intended, not only to have an international audience, but to function transnationally.

Ethical issues are raised in two types of cases: First, some websites are located in other countries in order to circumvent the laws of countries where the website will be viewed. For a period of time, music websites offering free downloads functioned in countries where their activity was not forbidden. The Napster and Grokster free services were effectively terminated by court decisions in the US. Grokster's server was located outside the US in the West Indies. Second, other websites are banned for political or ideological reasons from their country of origin and must relocate to continue to be available. The Great Firewall of China, under construction, blocks content which might be threatening to the Chinese government, including sites such as Wikipedia and BBC News, and topics such as freedom of speech and democracy. (Elgin 2006) In countries which respect human rights such as the US and most developed countries, requests to shut down sites are rarely honored, except for obscenity and commercial reasons.

The globalized ethical issue raised by these two kinds of cases is clear: To what extent do the laws and customs of a particular company apply to websites which are operating transnationally? The fact that the music downloading website Grokster was operating from a server in the Caribbean did not shield it from the US court decision that shut it down. I am sure Chinese officials regard attempts to circumvent the "Great Firewall of China" from outside with the same amount of tolerance.

In early 2008, the whistleblowing website Wikileaks, with its server in San Mateo, CA, was ordered shut down because the Zurich bank Julius Baer Bank and Trust claimed that the site had posted stolen and confidential material. Interestingly enough, the exact location of the organization is unclear. It has spokespersons in Paris and posts material from Chinese dissidents. Wikileaks argued unsuccessfully initially in US court that US courts did not have jurisdiction. (Elias 2008) The argument later prevailed that shutting down an entire website constituted illegal "prior restraint" in US Law, and that even removing the documents was unconstitutional. (Kravets, 2008)

Most developed countries have strong free speech protection, and thus from an ethical point of view including justice, legal findings in these countries are ethically more desirable. But from a procedural point of view, locating an action in the country likely to be most favorable to a just decision, may not be most defensible principle. There is definitely an ethically globalized issue here, without an institution or policy to handle it. The International Court of Justice (ICJ) adjudicates disputes between states; and the separate International Criminal Court (ICC) tries individuals for crimes against humanity. But neither court is designed to handle essentially routine legal disputes which are difficult or impossible to locate in any national jurisdiction. A framework for these issues will be addressed in Section 3, **A Social Contract For Globalized Institutions.**

CONCLUSION

So the existing ethically globalized institutions we have discovered are: The World Bank, World Trade Organization (WTO), the International Monetary Fund (IMF), the OECD, and multinational corporations. Other organizations, although they *deal with* transnational issues, they do not *take action* in a global way. These would include the United Nations (UN) and World Court, and the transnational non-governmental organizations (NGOs). Then there are superpowers (currently the US) which, although one nation-state, have power over other states. A superpower of this kind is not an ethically globalized institution because the rules of the one state take priority over the rules of all the other states, so the rules aren't globalized. The related ethical question is the ethical status of this situation.

In the course of examining these existing institutions, we have also discovered the need either for reform of some current institutions, or for new globalized institutions. For the UN and World Court to function as ethically globalized institutions, they need more power, the UN actually to take action against states making war, and the two International Courts having universal jurisdiction. The world financial and economic institutions need a more impartial and democratic governance. The NGOs need some structure of accountability. Multinationals need some form of ethical accountability and possibly a global tax system and also (assuming that a market economy is part of a just global order) transnational regulation of competition. Finally, because of organizations whose main presence is on the web, there should be some transnational organization or policy to adjudicate disputes between such organizations and other organizations.

There are several possibilities for ethical principles for existing and possible globalized institutions, and we need to settle on one possibility before we can justify specific ethical principles. In Section II, **Theories of Globalized Ethics,** I examine these possibilities. Before that, however, the scope of globalization needs a closer look, as well as the place of IT within globalization. These are the topics of the next chapter.

REFERENCES

American Rhetoric. (1961). *Eisenhower's farewell address*. Retrieved February 29, 2008, from http://www.americanrhetoric.com

Chang, H. (2008). *Bad Samaritans*. New York: Bloomsbury Press.

Elgin, B., & Einhorn, B. (2006, January 12). The great firewall of China. *BusinessWeek*

Elias, P. (2008, February 19). Web site 'Wikileaks' shuttered over post. *Associated Press*. Retrieved February 20, 2008, from http://news.yahoo.com

Exchange, G. (2007). *Top reasons to oppose the WTO*. Retrieved February 28, 2008, from http://www.globalexchange.org

Fidler, S. (2001, September/October). Who's minding the bank? *Foreign Policy*, 126.

Frängsmyr, T. (Ed.). (1989). *The Nobel Prizes 1988*. Stockholm: Nobel Foundation.

Global Policy Forum. (2006). *NGOs*. Retrieved March 8, 2008 from http://www.globalpolicy.org/ngos

International Monetary Fund. (2008). *What the IMF does*. Retrieved February 27, 2008 from http://www.imf.org

Ionescu, R., & Oprea, R. (2007). *Multinational corporations and the global economy*. Retrieved March 24, 2009, from http://www.idec.gr/iier/new/3rd Panhellenic Conference/Ionescu-Oprea-Multinational Corporations And The Global Economy.pdf

Kant, I. (1970). Perpetual peace. In H. Reiss (Ed.), *Kant's political writings*. Cambridge, UK: Cambridge University Press.

Kravets, D. (2008, February 29). *Judge backtracks: WikiLeaks resumes U.S. operations*. Retrieved March 11, 2008 from http://blog.wired.com

Lodge, G., & Wilson, C. (2006). *A corporate solution to global poverty*. Princeton, NJ: Princeton University Press.

OECD. (2008). For a better world economy. *Organisation for Economic Cooperation and Development*. Retrieved September 19, 2008 from http://www.oecd.org

Perkins, J. (2006). *Confessions of an economic hit man*. London: Penguin Group.

Project for the New American Century. (2000). *Rebuilding America's defenses*. Retrieved March 9, 2008, from http://www.newamericancentury.org

Scharf, M. P. (1998). *Results of the Rome Conference for an International Criminal Court*. The American Society of International Law. Retrieved February 21, 2008.

Southparkstudios.com. (2006, October 11). Mystery of the Urinal Deuce. *South Park* (Episode 1009). Retrieved March 27, 2009 from http://www.southparkstudios.com/episodes/103775

Stiglitz, J. (2003). *Globalization and its discontents*. New York: W. W. Norton.

Stiglitz, J. (2007). *Making globalization work*. New York: W. W. Norton.

TheCairo Declaration on Human Rights in Islam. (1990). Retrieved March 24, 2009 from http://www.religlaw.org/interdocs/docs/cairohrislam1990.htm

The World Bank. (2008). *FAQs*. Retrieved February 27, 2008 from http://web.theworldbank.org

US Constitution. (1997). Retrieved December 7, 2008 from http://www.usconstitution.net/const.html

Voice of America. (2006, January 27). *U.S. on Russian N-G-O law*. Retrieved March 8, 2008 from http://www.voanews.com/uspolicy/archive/2006-01/2006-01-27-voa2.cfm

Welch, W. M. (2008, March 8). Offshore tax shelters under fire. *USA TODAY*. Retrieved March 8, 2008 from http://www.usatoday.com

Wikipedia. (2008a). *Non-governmental organization*. Retrieved March 7, 2008 from http://en.wikipedia.org

Wikipedia. (2008b). *The United Nations*. Retrieved September 13, 2008 from http://en.wikipedia.org/wiki/United_Nations

Wikipedia. (2009). *The Korean War*. Retrieved March 24, 2009, from http://en.wikipedia.org/wiki/Korean_War#Invasion_of_South_Korea

ENDNOTES

[1] Sovereignty is usually defined as "the exclusive right to complete control over an area of governance, people, or oneself." (Wikipedia 2007). However, the possibility of the distributed sovereignty of a federal system such as the U.S. is also acknowledged, although strictly speaking this is contradictory.

[2] The other branches of the UN are: The General Assembly; The Secretariat (provides background information needed by the UN); the World Health Organization (WHO) and United Nations Children's Fund (UNICEF). The Economic and Social Council, which promotes international economic and social cooperation and development, is clearly a transnational organization; I will discuss it in connection with the other transnational economic organizations, the IMF, World Bank, and WTO.

[3] A complete list is Iraq, Israel, Libya, the People's Republic of China, Qatar, the United States, and Yemen. Israel and the United States have severed all connection with the court.

[4] Special Drawing Rights. The value is a function of a basket of currencies. See International Monetary Fund 2008.

[5] There are believable claims that fairly explicit advance intelligence warnings of 9/11 were simply ignored by the Bush administration.

[6] My thanks to Neil Anapol for this point. For a very funny (if scatological) riff based on this observation, see southparkstudios.com (2006) episode 1009. Thanks to John Karayan for calling my attention to the episode.

7   I can't resist a footnote while writing in Microsoft Word, a program with myriad defects in the use of formatting that Microsoft has zero incentive to correct.

8   In India, with over 1,000,000 NGOs, "NGO" seems roughly equivalent to what would be a non-profit in the US.

9   Lodge and Wilson (2006, Chapter 3) call these campaigns "attacks," thereby revealing their pro-corporate bias.

10 The economic collapse of late 2008 demonstrates that standards of transparency and regulation for corporations--especially financial institution--were considerably below what they should have been.

11 I have seen cases in which presidents of nonprofits have casually reassigned grant money to different uses, apparently feeling that free money can be freely spent. Legally, however, this practice is criminal fraud.

12 See Rawls 1999a, sec. 53, "Tolerating the Intolerant."

Chapter 3
IT's Contribution to Globalization

In this chapter we will consider this question: To what extent is IT responsible for globalization? But before we can address this question, we need more clarity on what globalization is. Some authors, for example, Thomas Friedman, view globalization very broadly. Friedman uses an invented term, *flattening,* to include a wide range of phenomena both social as well as economic.[1] (Friedman 2005) Friedman's flattening is always a good thing. The danger in this approach is that there cannot be bad cases of flattening; good and bad aspects of globalization can seem to be completely linked when in fact they are not. For example, I believe that Friedman may tend to view negative features of offshoring to be compensated for just by offshoring's contribution to "flattening."

GLOBALIZATION AND 'FLATTENING'

It is worth some effort to unpack what Friedman means by flattening, because that will enable us to gain some insight into what does and does not belong to globalization. For Friedman, flattening can occur within one nation or economy. IT and improvements in communication are very largely its causes, and its effects are largely economic. Some hallmarks of flattening are greater equality in access to information,

DOI: 10.4018/978-1-60566-922-9.ch003

greater speed of access to information, greater collaboration, shared standards, dissolving boundaries (both national and company), and greater productivity brought about by these hallmarks. (Friedman 2005)

New business models are valuable for Friedman not just because of their increased efficiency or productivity, but because they contribute to "flattening." For example, Wal-Mart's supply chain efficiency and UPS's supply chain management produce their beneficial results by breaking down barriers between separate companies and intermingling their business processes.

About halfway through the book, Friedman quotes (apparently approvingly) Harvard political theorist Michael Sandel's short definition of Friedman's term "flattening":

What you [Friedman] *are arguing is that developments in* [IT] *are enabling companies to squeeze out all the inefficiencies and friction from their markets and business operations.* That is what your notion of 'flattening' really means. (Friedman 2005, 203-4; my emphasis)

In other words, "flattening" is untrammeled free market capitalism enable d by IT. Friedman follows Sandel's discussion with a long quote from *The Communist Manifesto* of Marx and Engels which, in 1848, presciently describes globalization or "flattening" as an inevitable stage in the development of capitalism. (Marx and Engels 1848, section 1) Of course, Marx and Engels see this state of no boundaries and cosmopolitanism as the precursor to the inevitable death of capitalism. Friedman, on the other hand, sees that other values than market efficiency need to be taken into account, such as "social cohesion, religious faith, and national pride." We also need to determine what to keep in the way of worker protections and democratic traditions. Friedman calls this process 'sorting out.' (Friedman 2005, 204-205)

Two points are worth noting about this discussion so far: First, both Friedman and Marx regard globalization as inevitable, but have opposing views about its value. Second, on Friedman's account, IT plays an enormous role in globalization. It turns out that Friedman believes what I have called the Technology Principle:

Technological progress is inevitable, unstoppable, and mostly beneficial. The results of technology come about through its unimpeded progress. Hence, technological development must have priority over other considerations. (Schultz 2006, Ch. 11, 165)

Friedman actually believes that technology is *entirely* beneficial. Friedman says in italics, "*I am a technological determinist!* (2005, 374) People can *misuse* technology, but technology itself does nothing but provide opportunities on which we must capitalize or go under.

This raises a large topic which we will discuss later more thoroughly in Chapter 15, **The Value of IT-enabled Globalization.** But the view of technology as a neutral enabler, providing only positive opportunities, is very naïve at this point in history. Friedman recognizes threats to the ecosystem as important. But he does not recognize technology's role in this threat. Global warming and ozone depletion are only two of the threats technology is totally or largely responsible for. The critical feature of modern technology is its willingness to treat anything as a resource to be reordered in the furtherance of human aims, including its own. It builds a new and incompatible order on top of what was there. The point of view of modern technology regards everything as a potential resource, as "standing reserve" to be used or reused later in other processes of the same kind.[2] A forest has status only as a timber resource. Land itself is only a resource for the building industry. Even human beings themselves, from this point of view, become "human resources." (Heidegger 1955, 14-17) Friedman's world is a technologized world, the pattern of production and consumption enabled by technology. His flattened world contains resources, with human beings having roles only as producers and consumers.

Turning now to ethics in Friedman's flat world: Friedman calls the process of determining appropriate ethical constraints on globalization, 'sorting out.' The constraints he comes up with are:

- The well-being of everyone involved in globalization has to be considered (low-paid Indian workers as well as Americans losing jobs, possibly equally).
- The relation between (multinational) corporations and the countries (communities) they are headquartered has become "unclear."
- The 19th-century conflict of interest between labor and capital has become a conflict between customer and worker, with the company in the middle. For example, to what extent should a company reduce worker health care benefits to make greater profits (possibly reducing prices to customers in the process)?
- Intellectual property rights need a "system of global governance that keeps up with all the new legal and illegal forms of collaboration." (Friedman 2005, 218)

(Friedman seems to be assuming that current definitions of what is legal and what is not will somehow apply globally, although they are different in different countries.)

Friedman's conclusion is that whether departures from corporate efficiency are worth preserving will be determined by those who understand "the real nature and texture of the global playing field [i.e., flattening] and how different it is from the one that existed in the Cold War era and before." (Friedman 2005, 222) There is no mention of the fact that the ethically globalized problems are new and clearly require new ethical principles. As we have defined them, they are problems that cannot be divided up between existing countries and solved using the ethical and legal systems of those countries. Although Friedman has done a very good job in describing the various facets of globalization and how they operate, without some attention to the new ethical issues and value issues raised by globalization, we will likely give answers to questions of ethics, justice, and value based on our old principles. And thus we will be likely to get them wrong.

Indeed, there is a disconnect in Friedman's book. Although "flattening" is definitely about dissolving national boundaries, the second section of the book, "America and the Flat World" is about what the US must do to "win" in a "flattened" world. Exactly what this is supposed to mean in a globalized world is not clear. Thinking of the US economy as a standalone entity among others is "unflattened" thinking. But we may want to continue thinking this way, even in a globalized world. Although each nation cannot think of its interests as independent of those of others, we are still organized as national economies, as Friedman unwittingly admits.

Americans are very fond of thinking of everything as a sports competition. The part of globalization Friedman is ignoring when he thinks in terms of America's winning or losing is the infrastructure that makes the game possible and also fair. Who, in a global economy, are the impartial referees? Who provides the equipment and constructs the playing field? Without attention to such infrastructure elements and their ethical provenance, all we get is pep talk. Later on in Chapter 11, **Globalized Ethics and Current Institutions,** we will consider the nature of the ethical constraints on nations in a world of globalized institutions.

The problem of infrastructure also impacts Friedman's discussion of what developing countries need to do to get out of poverty and join the globalized economy. His prescription is the standard one of the

World Bank, IMF and WTO: No trade barriers, open the economy to foreign investment, and privatize state-supported institutions. (Friedman 2005, 314) However, other commentators such as economists Joseph Stiglitz (2003, 2007) and Ha-Joon Chang (2008), as well as social commentators such as Naomi Klein (2007), point to limitations in the functioning of free trade and free markets in improving the lot of less developed countries.

Any reasonable ethical theory would approve of reducing poverty in developing countries. Although there are important differences between theories of globalized ethics, they would all agree on this. However, there is serious disagreement between economists on which policies to adopt to obtain this result. There are actually disagreements on two levels: One is the actual results of macroeconomic policies in bettering the lot of those in developing countries. The second is whether a given policy caused the results of making those in developing countries better off or worse off.

Thus Stiglitz points out that the standard World-Bank-IMF-WTO policy of no trade barriers, opening the economy to foreign investment, and privatizing state-supported institutions was not the route taken by successful developing countries such as China, Indonesia, Malaysia, and South Korea. Whereas, the standard policy was the route taken by Russia to economic and social disaster. (Stiglitz 2007, Ch. 2) Stiglitz believed the problem was that background institutions were not in place for free markets to function effectively or justly. Believers in the standard policy of openness and free trade tend to counterargue that free market policy was not applied thoroughly enough.[3]

It seems as though economists should agree on the results—China and South Korea, for example, have sustained high growth rates and poverty reduction and Russia a huge increase in poverty and a drop of four years in life expectancy. Yet this is not always the case. For example, Jagdish Bhagwati argues in his *In Defense of Globalization* that the supposed failures of free trade and free markets are actually due to other causes, usually bad governmental policies. "….appropriate policies will always enable us to profit from growth [ie globalization] and to moderate (or even prevent) unpleasant outcomes for the poor." (Bhagwati 2007, 56)

So what are we going to do with these disagreements when we come to judge globalized situations ethically? I think we will have to state ethical conclusions conditional on the truth or falsity of claims about the results of economic policy. In other words, we can say *if* free trade produces better results for the poor in an underdeveloped country, *then* that is the ethical policy to follow (for example). Unfortunately economics has an ideological or political aspect, so it may not be possible to have the firm basis we would like for our ethical conclusions.

It needs to be pointed out here that a market economy and free trade are not automatically the ethical or just choice for a society. They are very likely to be the just or ethical choice because, under moderately favorable circumstances, they make everyone better off economically. They are efficient.[4] But this result depends on a number of other factors, including everyone involved in the market being part of the same economy or society. It also requires that there be background institutions in place, such as a body to enforce antitrust violations. The free market produces its results through the "invisible hand" of competition. Monopolies and oligopolies need to be dismantled because they drastically reduce or eliminate competition. Thus they can easily produce results which make everyone but themselves worse off than might have been. A robust legal system is also necessary to deal with ethical infractions.[5]

When it comes to developing countries, Friedman advances "the irrefutable fact that more open and competitive markets are the only sustainable vehicle for growing a nation out of poverty, because they are the only guarantee that new ideas, technologies, and best practices are easily flowing into your country" (Friedman 2005, 314-315) and your institutions are turning them into jobs and products. The experience of Russia, of Argentina in the late 90s, and Africa refute this supposed irrefutable fact. Open and competitive markets in the case of Russia produced an enormous decline in output and an enormous increase in poverty—from 2% in 1989 to 24% in 1998. Basically, nationalized institutions were sold off to oligarchs at very low valuations. Then these people stripped and sold the assets and shipped the money offshore using the liberalized finance markets. Natural resources were also privatized before the state was able to collect taxes on them. As Joseph Stiglitz puts it, "Russia's ... ersatz capitalism did not provide the incentives for wealth creation and economic growth but rather for asset stripping." (Stiglitz 2003, 162) Stiglitz puts the blame on the absence of an institutional infrastructure to allow markets to function as they should—to make everyone better off. In Russia private ownership simply meant you could sell the assets—much easier than putting all that effort into running an enterprise.

Friedman quotes with approval the reforms advocated by the World Bank's International Finance Corporation: Don't "overregulate"; enhance property rights; reduce court involvement in business matters. The IFC also advocates using the Internet for regulation fulfillment, providing expanded education opportunities, and investing in infrastructure. Education and infrastructure are obvious winners.

The Internet suggestion is peculiar, given that many developing countries have poor Internet availability. There was only one Internet user for every 750 people in Africa as compared to the world average of one user for every 30 people and one user per 2-3 people in North America and Europe. A major constraint is average African internet service provider prices of US$ 50 per month, which is close to an average monthly salary. (ITU 2000) In 2007, 3.7% of Africans had internet access. In Latin America, it was about 20%, the world average. By contrast, the US had 71%. (Internet World Stats 2007)

But the first three "reforms"—don't "overregulate", enhance property rights, reduce court involvement in business matters—read like campaign items from a US Republican businessman candidate operating in an environment with an institutional cushion to prevent business from riding roughshod over the well-being of everyone else. Very one-sided, and predictably guaranteed to entrench or create a wealthy oligarchy at the expense of the rest of the population.[6]

Friedman's flattening seems to encapsulate three biases: Two seem to be leftovers from the dot-com days, and a third is from neoconservative economics. The leftovers are these: First, technology is always good, and the opportunities it presents must be seized and developed as soon as possible. We saw how well this principle worked in the dot-com days. Just because the technology was new did not mean it had a useful or practical application, or would in the foreseeable future. Second, first-mover advantage, which justified nearly every departure from sound business practice in the dot-com era. Third, the neoconservative bias in favor of free trade and privatization has serious critics. In any case, these assumptions can hardly be the starting point for a definition of globalization.

Before we attempt a definition, two other components of globalization need to be examined. These are transportation costs and enhanced information availability.

GLOBALIZATION AND TRANSPORTATION COSTS

Friedman's view of globalization compressed into a nutshell is that globalization is advances in IT enabling more efficient business practices. There is no question that this is a huge part of globalization. Yet there are at least two other components to globalization that are important. One is that the globalization of manufacturing and agriculture requires the economic feasibility of transporting products long distances. This aspect of globalization is independent of IT's enabling information to be available globally at low cost.

Second, IT's properties of speed and availability of information at any location have enabled not only more efficient business processes but also greatly enhanced the availability of information in other ways. Friedman is sensitive to some of these. For example Wikipedia, the user-generated online encyclopedia, has come close to its founder Jimmy Wales' goal of giving "every single person on the planet... free access to the sum of human knowledge." (Miller 2004) Also, the Internet search engines such as Google enable users to locate virtually any information quickly, easily, and with great relevance. We will return to the role of enhanced information in globalization after discussing transportation costs.

If globalization were confined solely to advances in speedy availability of information, it would still be a huge force. Any part of any enterprise that can be digitally transmitted has the potential to be part of a globalized enterprise. Large parts of the IT business involving software such as programming can be conducted globally. Likewise, service provided essentially over the telephone such as customer service can now be conducted globally. But many parts of businesses which involve physical products often require shipping. It is certainly possible for globalized business to produce products in the same international locale they are sold in to minimize shipping costs, but this is a much more limited form of globalization than is now practiced.

A dramatic improvement in transportation took place beginning in the last half of the 18th century with railroads and continuing in the 20th century with cars, trucks, planes, and ships running on internal combustion engines. Before these improvements, only high value items such as gold or slaves or unique items such as art objects were regularly imported over long distances. Now relatively low-value items such as cheap toys are regularly imported over half the globe from China to the US. Fresh fish is regularly imported from Vietnam to the US.

One question to be raised about this aspect of globalization is whether the social cost of transportation is accurately reflected in a company's economics. Are there what the economists call "externalities" which make the social cost of transporting goods greater than what companies utilizing transportation pay? Transportation speedy enough to serve the purposes of globalization requires transport using internal combustion engines running on fossil fuel. The resulting air pollution and carbon emissions are externalities which do not add to the company's cost. The transport of fossil fuel by tanker produces another externality in the form of massive environmental damage when there are tanker accidents such as the Exxon Valdez. (Such accidents seem to occur with regular frequency.) Trucks and air transport require massive social expenditures for such infrastructure as roads, airports, and air traffic control systems.

If we took such externalities into account, would it actually be economic to import cheap plastic toys from China? It would be very hard to say because it is currently not easy to estimate the cost of excess carbon emissions. That would require predicting the relatively long-term effects of global warming. Given that we do need to reduce carbon emissions, some sort of mechanism is necessary to give a shipment of AIDS drugs priority over a shipment of plastic toys.

A dramatic improvement in shipping methods since World War II has contributed to product globalization, and that is containerized shipping. Michael McLean, the shipping magnate who invented containers, found that in 1956 loading loose cargo cost $5.83 per ton. That same year, his first container ship cost less than 16 cents a ton to load. (Krueger 2006) Fifty years ago, businesses and regulators treated distribution not as a single process but as a series of distinct modes: ships, trucks and trains. Every time the transportation mode changed, somebody had to transfer every item physically. Half the cost of shipping was transferring the cargo between ship and truck or train. Transfers and delays made shipping slow and schedules uncertain. The simple idea of containerization was to move trailer-size loads of goods seamlessly among trucks, trains and ships. But many additional innovations were needed: Dockside cranes, standard container sizes, strengthened wharves, connections to rail lines and highways, storage places for containers and new deals with unions. The result was that "[j]ust as the computer revolutionized the flow of information, the shipping container revolutionized the flow of goods," (Thoma 2006) and made complex globalized supply chains possible.

The previous discussion assumes that managers considering outsourcing and offshoring are rational economically and consider all the relevant economic costs—excluding difficult-to-quantify considerations such as long-term environmental damage. However, as Ralph Bernstein points out, even relatively sophisticated managers miss important considerations. (Bernstein 2008) Bernstein discusses the analysis of Michael Marks, an equity fund manager, of outsourcing costs. This manager has found that companies he advised considered labor hours and labor costs only: "That was it! No analysis of overhead costs, transportation costs, labor efficiencies, power costs, average hours worked, overtime policies." He then offered his own analysis including labor costs, factory general and administrative expenses, manufacturing overhead, freight in (meaning the cost of transporting materials from suppliers), scrap, cost of materials, and real estate costs. He concluded that the full factory level costs for a product with material cost of $100 are $127.20 in California, $113.40 in Eastern Europe, $110 in Mexico and $98.90 in China, but also comments:

.... these costs are at the factory location, and don't take into account the cost of freight to the customer's location. That cost can be substantial, and has been increasing quickly with the increase in the cost of oil. So transporting Chinese-made goods to the U.S. costs more, and for some products, makes moving manufacturing back to the U.S. or at least to Mexico more reasonable. (Marks 2008)

Bernstein notes that obviously cost of freight to the customer's location should have been factored in. Also relevant are "issues of time to market, ability to respond quickly to market changes, quality and all those other pesky problems that can arise when you move your manufacturing several thousand miles away... Transportation across thousands of miles is a big waste" (Bernstein 2008)

The ethical consideration here is due diligence. It is a professional duty of a manager to take into account the features relevant to a decision, especially an outsourcing or offshoring decision. Failure to take into account costs directly related to the distance of the offshored process is a failure of due diligence. If Bernstein is correct, this failure may be more common than one would like to believe. Bernstein's observations may have been taken to heart in the recent practice of "nearshoring" rather than "offshoring." (Sourcingmag.com 2005)

ENHANCED INFORMATION IN GLOBALIZATION

Besides enabling new business structures, IT has contributed to globalization through making all sorts of information much more available. As I noted, Wikipedia, the user-generated online encyclopedia, has come close to its founder Jimmy Wales' goal of giving "every single person . . . free access to the sum of human knowledge." (Miller 2004) And Internet search engines such as Google enable users to locate virtually any information quickly, easily, and with great relevance.

The name 'Wikipedia' is a combination of 'Wiki' and 'encyclopedia.' A wiki is a collection of web pages which can be changed by anyone who accesses it.[7] So Wikipedia is a user-generated and maintained encyclopedia. There are standards and it is possible for users to challenge content. Two differences of

Wikipedia from traditional encyclopedias are its range and its currency. It is almost impossible to find an uncovered topic. Wikipedia is light years more current than traditional encyclopedias, which, after all, use a central authority to decide on topics, decide and approach authors to write on them, and then collect, edit, and publish the various entries. For example, even though the Encyclopedia Britannica has a policy of continuous revision, so that roughly 40% of its articles will be revised in a three-year cycle, this still means that the latest print version will still be at least two years old, and probably much more than that. Also, the centralized hierarchical structure of Britannica and traditional encyclopedias does not exempt them from problems of inaccuracy and bias. After years of resistance, academics now allow students to cite material from Wikipedia.

Although e-commerce was over-hyped during the dot com years, it has still grown explosively since then. (US) online retail sales have been increasing at annual rates from 19% to 24%, with no sign of slowdown. (*Double Digit Growth for E-Commerce,* 2008) Virtually any item one could imagine is available online, either through the manufacturer, distributor, or another consumer. EBay and Craigslist are successful sites that offer more than any garage sale ever could have dreamed. From the point of view of globalization, the location of a sales site does not matter much. Shipping costs may be greater if the product you are purchasing is in India, and there may be greater difficulties if the company is not operating through a distributor in your own country and something goes wrong. But e-commerce is globalized commerce.

There are some legal issues (which can also be ethical issues) about the actual location of the company. For example, the issue of when sales tax should be charged. The ethical basis for many taxes is that an entity is taxed because it uses the social infrastructure provided by the government and the government is ethically entitled to compensation to maintain that structure. The current rule is that if a company has a physical presence in a state, it must collect and pay sales tax from that state. But Internet business transactions simply do not take place at a few specific physical locations. Mail-order (and phone-order) sales transactions still take place at particular physical locations. The selling organization has its operations at one place, and the customer is at another. But with IT, the various parts of a sales transaction can easily be scattered across many states or many countries. Where is the sales transaction when the product information is planned in San Francisco and accessed from a server in New Jersey and the order information is taken from a customer in Iowa and processed by someone in Ireland and shipping is coordinated in Seattle for shipment from a warehouse in Colorado and payments are processed in the Bahamas and questions about the transaction handled in Bangalore?

The ethical consideration underlying the location of the collection of sales tax is helping to support the infrastructure of the location where you do business. So it seems very wrongheaded to attempt to extend traditional sales tax collection to e-businesses, as a number of states are trying to do. California's "use tax" on items acquired through the internet seems particularly unjust, since the amount is the same as sales tax. There would be some justice in having a separate national (or even international) tax to help support the IT infrastructure.[8] But there is no requirement in a market economy to make life safe for bricks-and-mortar companies. Within a market economy, competition should decide. There is no ethical requirement, and indeed it would be misuse of government power, to use government redistributive power to make traditional businesses competitive. It would be just as inappropriate for the government to prevent airlines from charging less for e-tickets even though travel agents are put out of work. A certain amount of economic dislocation is part of the workings of a free market, and a market economy is an important part of a just social system.

Sales tax is one of a number of issues which arise because of the fact that companies may no longer be located in any one state, nor indeed in any one country. The ethical issues in this area will be discussed further in Chapter 9, **IT and Globalized Ethics,** and Chapter 13, **Ethical Implications For IT.**

The consumer-to-consumer site Craigslist also functions as a social site, along with many others such as Match.com. Meeting people through the internet is moderately common, and has its benefits and drawbacks. One benefit is the availability of a larger pool of prospective people. This can be especially important for those in smaller towns. One drawback is that the actual person may be different from what they present themselves as on the Internet. Sometimes the actual person may be thoroughly bad and may be using the Internet to exploit people. Sometimes the actual person may be a total fiction set up to entrap an unsuspecting pedophile.[9]

The effects on culture of Internet-mediated relationships will probably take some time to shake out. When Internet-mediated relationships actually *replace* face-to-face relationships, there may be a problem. People do become addicted to sexually charged chatrooms and Internet pornography. But if the description of "addicted" is correct, then this is not an ethical problem but rather a personal problem, a psychological illness, for which some form of treatment is necessary. In any case, there are no obvious special transnational aspects to social uses of the Internet.

CHARACTERIZING GLOBALIZATION

Globalization has the following aspects: Economy, politics, culture, and law. Friedman's "flattening" is primarily an economic phenomenon, with consequences in the other areas. For example, economic globalization forces changes in culture, and cultural globalization forces changes in politics and law. Farmers in Mexico who cannot compete with US agribusinesses are forced to become manufacturing laborers or illegal immigrants to the US. Cultural globalization has made child labor and battering of women less acceptable. Because of this interdependence of aspects of globalization, they cannot be considered completely separately. Friedman's "flattening" expresses this insight to some extent, but gives globalization as flattening a positive value without any real examination of its pros and cons.

In this book, there are two focal points which determine how we will consider globalization: One is Information Technology and the other is ethical issues which emerge only at a transnational level. Keeping these in mind, we can characterize **globalized properties** as properties of institutions (whether economic, cultural, political, or legal) which emerge only at the transnational level, and which are enabled either by advances in information technology or in transportation technology. **Globalization** is the accumulation of institutions with globalized properties.

I initially characterized globalization as "the coalescence of the economies and cultures of this planet." The fuller characterization just given makes clear that the reason for the coalescence is technological advances, both in information technology and transportation technology. It is not as though people all over the world suddenly decided to globalize for no special reason. My characterization of globalization also makes it a recent phenomenon. Without IT, for example, it would just not have been possible to manage pieces of the same business in a single transnational supply chain. The IT applications which made such supply chains possible did not begin to emerge until the 1970s and 1980s, and were dramatically enhanced by the arrival of the Internet for business use in 1994. Also, as we saw, transportation technology improvements in the late 1950s and early 1960s made it more feasible to do manufacturing on the other side of the world.

Ultimate questions are difficult but nevertheless need to be addressed. There is probably no question that economic globalization has improved productivity overall. The value of cultural globalization is not so clear cut. It is probably good that democratic and human rights ideals are promulgated throughout the world. But it is not so clear that the proliferation of the shallow consumer culture prevalent in the US is an unalloyed good. The ultimate question of the value of the changes we are calling globalization will be discussed at some length in Chapter 15, **The Value of IT-Enabled Globalization.**

PLACING IT WITHIN GLOBALIZATION

As I have characterized globalization, IT is a major enabler. IT also participates in globalization in a major way. Hardware manufacturers typically use global supply chains and market around the globe. For example, a typical Dell Inspiron notebook will have been codesigned in Austin, TX, and Taiwan. It will be assembled in Malaysia with parts from the Philippines, Japan, Korea, Costa Rica, Mexico, Taiwan, Israel, or China. (Friedman 2005, 415-417) Software developers also typically develop globally and market around the globe. The ethically globalized issues raised by their activities are basically the same as for any multinational corporations. Those issues will be discussed in Chapter 8, **The Ethical Status of Globalized Institutions,** and Chapter 9, **IT and Globalized Ethics.**

As an enabler, the position of IT with respect to globalization is very much like the position of the IT staff of the World Bank we discussed in Chapter 1. The stated aims of globalization are often praiseworthy, even laudable. But when globalization produces results which are bad for people, who shall we say is responsible? Can those building information systems say, "It's not up to me that they were used badly?"

We need to consider exactly how much of an enabler of globalization IT is. I think there is no question that globalization as we now experience it could not have taken place without IT. This is especially true of economic globalization. But was globalization, especially economic globalization, inevitable once IT and the Internet came along? Thomas Friedman seems to believe something close to this—he calls himself a "technological determinist" (Friedman 2005, 374)—but the question is, is it so? If it is so, then IT is 'off the hook' ethically, so to speak. IT is simply an enabler in a process beyond its control or anyone's control.

As I mentioned at the beginning of this chapter, technological determinism is, at this point in history, a very naïve view as well as a dangerous one. There are really two distinct views possible within technological determinism. One view is that the development of technology, the appearance of technological advances, is determined. I will call this view *advance determinism.* The second view is that, once a technological advance appears, its widest useful application is inevitable. I will call this view *application determinism.* Application determinism is the dangerous view. Friedman is an application determinist. There is no evidence one way or the other that he is an advance determinist.

The danger in application determinism comes from the accompanying claim that technology (including information technology) is always an improvement (which I earlier called the Technology Principle[10]). The claim that technology is always an improvement ignores the fact that technology is a new order imposed on an older order and can easily have deleterious side effects which cannot be prevented by due diligence in development. The development of chlorofluorocarbons (CFCs) is a counterexample. CFCs were inert at surface levels but highly destructive of the ozone layer necessary for life on the planet.[11] So application determinism is false as the view that new technology is necessarily an improvement.

Advance determinism is not a particularly dangerous view, but it is also clearly false. Most technological advances were not predictable and appeared only as a result of chance factors. In this respect, technological advance is similar to the evolution of organic life forms. Important technological developments have arisen in very unlikely ways, and certainly not as the result of predefined rigid research programs. This is especially true of IT, and, within IT, of the Internet and World Wide Web. The Internet itself was originally a US Defense Department project, and such vital characteristics as no central computer were required to make the system impervious to nuclear attack. The World Wide Web was developed by Swiss physicist Tim Berners-Lee as a method of exchanging scientific information including both text and graphics. The web browser—essential to widespread use of the Internet—was developed by graduate students at the University of Illinois. (Kristula 2001) A useful peer-to-peer filesharing application (Napster) was developed by an undergraduate at Boston University. (Wikipedia 2008b) So the Internet technology necessary for globalization was no more inevitable than was the rise of mammals after the age of dinosaurs.

The Napster example also shows the falsity of application determinism. Music companies used the courts to shut down a free music-sharing service in 2001. Several years later, some commentators believe the poor showing of the music industry stemmed from their failure to find a way to make money from peer-to-peer technology rather than shutting it down.

However, the Napster example still supports a version of application determinism. For Friedman, the force which drives application determinism is competition within a free-market economy. He notes "if you can do it [apply the technology], you must …, otherwise your competitors will." (2005, 374) In the case of the music industry, they didn't, and merely worked through the courts to extend their (monopoly) property rights. Thus people can fail to exploit technologies, but ultimately the market will destroy them. This brand of application determinism is probably correct. But obviously it depends on the market functioning as a free market, without monopolistic or oligarchic impediments. Free-market application determinism is thus more-or-less the claim that a properly functioning market economy will deliver good economic results. This is not a dangerous claim and is correct.

Therefore we are left with an ethical question: Who is responsible for technology's being used properly and beneficially? This question becomes much harder when IT applications are used across the globe. Some sort of transnational code of ethics is clearly necessary. In the next Section, Section 2, **Theories of Globalized Ethics,** we will examine the various possibilities. But we will see that many theories of transnational ethics proceed by considering ethical problems as occurring within and between states and therefore are not helpful in dealing with ethical problems of ethically globalized institutions.

We have seen that these institutions could probably not exist were it not for IT. Yet it cannot be correct to hold IT responsible for *every* bad consequence of every IT application. For one thing, not all consequences are predictable, even with the best due diligence. For another, no institution is ethically responsible for all consequences of an action. The Chapter 1 example of IT responsibility for what the World Bank does is a similar sort of case. There we used intuitive ethical judgements to render a tentative decision. But it is hard, using intuitive judgements, to have much confidence that those judgements are correct, and hard to be clear on when they can be extended to other cases and when not. To accomplish this, we need ethical principles based on a comprehensive ethical theory. To examine the alternatives and produce such a theory will be the aim of Section 2, **Theories of Globalized Ethics,** and Section 3, **A Social Contract for Globalized Institutions.**

REFERENCES

Bernstein, R. (2008, January 21). *Failing to grasp the true costs of outsourcing.* Retrieved March 28, 2008 from http://lean.insider.com

Bhagwati, J. (2007). *In defense of globalization.* Oxford, UK: Oxford University Press.

Chang, H. (2008). *Bad Samaritans.* New York: Bloomsbury Press.

Double Digit Growth for E-Commerce. (2008). Retrieved April 2, 2008 from http://onlinebusiness.about.com.

Friedman, T. (2005). *The world is flat.* New York: Farrar, Straus and Giroux.

Heidegger, M. (1955). The question concerning technology. In *The question concerning technology and other essays.* New York: Harper & Row.

Internet World Stats. (2007). Retrieved March 21, 2008 from http://www.internetworldstats.com

ITU. (2000, June 5-9). *Conclusions: The African Internet & Telecom Summit,* Banjul, Gambia. Retrieved March 21, 2008, from www.itu.int/africainternet2000/conclusions.html

Klein, N. (2007). *The shock doctrine: The rise of disaster capitalism.* New York: Henry Holt and Company.

Kristula, D. (2001). *The history of the Internet.* Retrieved April 3, 2008, from http://www.davesite.com/webstation/net-history.shtml

Krueger, A. O. (2006, May 11). *Globalization and international locational competition.* Lecture given at the IMF at the Kiel Institute.

Marks, M. (2008). Some truth about costs. *Forbes.* Retrieved March 28, 2008 from http://www.forbes.com/home/opinions/2008/01/03/marks-mfg-costs-oped-cx_mem_0104marks.html

Marx, K., & Engels, F. (1848). *The manifesto of the Communist party.* Retrieved March 17, 2008 from http://www.marxists.org/archive/marx/works/1848/communist-manifesto/

Miller, R. (2004, July 28). Wikipedia founder Jimmy Wales responds. *Slashdot.* Retrieved October 31, 2008 from http://interviews.slashdot.org/article.pl?sid=04/07/28/1351230.

Sourcingmag.com. (2005). *Nearshoring.* Retrieved December 7, 2008, from http://www.sourcingmag.com/dictionary/Nearshoring-115.htm

Stiglitz, J. (2003). *Globalization and its discontents.* New York: W. W. Norton.

Stiglitz, J. (2007). *Making globalization work.* New York: W. W. Norton.

Thoma, M. (2006, March 23). *Transportation costs and globalization.* Message posted in Economics, International Trade, Technology. Retrieved January 6, 2008, from http://economistsview.typepad.com

Wachowski, L., & Wachowski, A. (Producers/Directors). (1999). *The matrix* [Motion picture]. United States: Warner Bros.

Wikipedia. (2008a). *Wiki*. Retrieved April 1, 2008 from http://en.wikipedia.org/wiki/Wiki

Wikipedia. (2008b). *Napster*. Retrieved on April 3, 2008 from http://en.wikipedia.org/wiki/Napster

ENDNOTES

[1] The title of Friedman's best-selling book *The World is Flat,* includes the invented term.

[2] The most chilling image of the film *The Matrix* (Wachowski, 1999) is of banks of human beings become pure standing reserve.

[3] This type of view is usually espoused by followers of the Chicago economist Milton Friedman (also a Nobel-Prize winner), who hold that unconstrained markets always produce the best results. The view is sometimes called "free market fundamentalism." The financial crisis of late 2008 is almost certainly a counterexample.

[4] Economists call this property "Pareto optimality."

[5] It is disturbing that anti-monopoly (antitrust) enforcement in the US seems to have broken down. For whatever reason, the interests of large corporations such as Microsoft have taken precedence in the courts over the interests of a free market society in not tolerating monopolies. See Schultz 2006, Ch 5, for a summary.

[6] Increasing inequality seems to be the goal of US policy until 2009.

[7] 'Wiki' is the Hawaiian word for 'fast,' and the Wiki software was intended to be "the simplest online database that could possibly work." (Wikipedia 2008a, "Wiki")

[8] Possibly an EU-style value added tax would be more appropriate as well as easier to administer for this purpose.

[9] An MSNBC show does this extensively. Although I believe sexually exploiting children is very wrong, I also believe entrapment is also very wrong. The show has produced a number of broken lives and at least one suicide. At very least, the producers of the show should be held liable as accessories. Who knows whether the people they catch would have gone after kids without the Internet posting? Also, any one who thinks that teenagers are sexually innocent has not been in an American high school or junior high for any time in the past century.

[10] See "Globalization and Flattening" at the beginning of the chapter.

[11] This issue will be discussed further in Chapter 14, **IT-enabled globalization and the environment.** See also Schultz 2006, Chapters 12 and 13.

Section 2
Theories of Globalized Ethics

Chapter 4
The Basis of Ethical Principles

My aim in Section 1 was to locate and describe areas of ethical concern in IT-enabled globalization. Yet in doing so, I was not ethically neutral in my judgements. The reader, especially the reader who disagreed with some of those judgements, may wonder how they are justified. In this section, Section 2, I will address precisely that question. I will begin by showing that ethical judgments can be justified. Then I will state a theory of ethical development which I think allows great insight into conflicts of ethical principles. Next I will describe a method for justifying ethical principles called *reflective equilibrium*. Finally, the rest of Section 2 will examine ethical theories relevant to ethical problems of globalization.

RELATIVISM

Ethical relativism is the view that all ethical views are equally good. The relativist answer to the question *who's to say what's right and wrong?* is "anyone and everyone." For the relativist, there are no better or worse answers to ethical questions, there are merely different answers. Contrary to relativism, I think it is worthwhile to attempt to find the best answer we can to ethical questions. The obvious fact that there is disagreement about ethical questions does not show that it is pointless to try to determine the best

DOI: 10.4018/978-1-60566-922-9.ch004

answer to ethical questions. Disagreement about scientific issues--sometimes long and unsettled--does not show it's pointless to try to resolve scientific disagreements. Disagreement about scientific issues can also be severe and can also last a long time. In the case of ethical issues, however, there is evidence of progress. Practices such as slavery and racial discrimination were condoned in the United States less than 200 years ago. These practices are now regarded as ethically outrageous.[1] So consensus can develop over time on the answers to ethical questions.

There is a very short way of dealing with a relativist. He or she believes that the last word in ethical judgements is each of our beliefs. So *my* belief is that there are ethical judgements that are better justified. The relativist can have nothing to say about this belief, since according to him or her, my belief is the last word. This objection is more of a debater's (or philosopher's) point, so I don't think it gets to the real issue, which is whether there is or is not a basis for the justification of ethical principles. I now turn to this question.

THE RATIONAL BASIS OF ETHICS

Ethical problems first arise because there are conflicts between different interests which cannot be resolved on the level of interests alone. Higher level principles need to be applied. The role of ethical principles of higher level is to resolve conflicts between lower-level principles which cannot be resolved on the same level as the conflicting principles. Perhaps I do best if I sell you accounting software, take the money and run and forget about support. Yet it is definitely in your interest to have support for the software. So we reach an agreement to limit our interests in a way that is fair to both of us. I agree to provide support (probably for an agreed-on fee), and you agree to pay for the support.[2]

There might actually be no need for ethics if everyone could get everything they wanted with no conflict with other people. But we live in a world (and in societies) in which this is not true. There are conflicts of interest. These need to be resolved in a fair way. It is also to everyone's advantage to have procedures for handling recurring conflicts which people accept. This gives rise to principles involving negotiated agreements and keeping them. Enough people see that reasons for keeping cooperative agreements have to be given higher priority than reasons of individual interest for cooperative benefits to be produced. Actually it is incorrect even to think that human beings have any alternative but to live in society. Human beings have evolved as social animals, and this means it is almost impossible for them to survive outside of a society. But there are still questions about the constitution of societies. Individuals can sometimes join a different society or consider alternative arrangements of social rules for their own society. But, just as all individuals can't get everything they want, so no set of social rules satisfies everyone's interests perfectly. The question is how to handle cases in which generally beneficial social rules are worse than they could be for some members of a society.

There are two conflicting considerations in these cases: First, the fact that there is a grievance against the social rules isn't enough by itself to release people from the obligation to obey the rules. The individual can't *directly* opt out of social rules.[3] And, second, ultimately a just society is for the individual, so ultimately the individuals in the society have the right (and sometimes the obligation) to decide that some rules are no longer to be followed. John Locke, the strongest influence on the founding fathers of the United States, put this point very strongly: "Who shall be judge whether [government] act contrary to their trust?...The people shall be judge." (Locke 1690, Chapter XIX)

Table 1. Prisoners' Dilemma Payoff Matrix

	Prisoner A confesses	Prisoner A does not confess
Prisoner B confesses	(2,2)	(4,1)
Prisoner B does not confess	(1,4)	(3,3)

Once again, if this conflict is going to be resolved in an ethical way, there must be higher-level principles to appeal to. In the case of a constitutional democracy, higher level appeals can be to the electorate, through changing legislators or through initiatives. Or appeals can be made to the constitution through the court system. But it certainly has been experienced in constitutional democracies and in the United States, that the constitution itself has been flawed and requires revision, or that the electorate itself is unresponsive. The prime example was slavery and the ensuing treatment of African-Americans. The principles appealed to in cases where the regular institutional paths have failed to address the issue are the principles of justice behind the constitution.

In cases of civil disobedience, perhaps most clearly in the United States as practiced by Martin Luther King, Jr., the law is broken not on the grounds that the lawbreakers now have the right to break any law or even particular laws, but rather to address the sense of justice, the commitment of the people to the principles underlying the laws. (King 1963) It should be noted again, that although majority rule is a good choice of procedure to make a group decision, it by no means guarantees a reasonable or fair decision and there is no reason to change one's beliefs just because of what the majority thinks.[4] There are actually built-in guarantees that systems of social rules won't work perfectly.

Also, if it is decided that the constitution needs to be revised, the appeal has to be to principles above and beyond the constitution, so once again we need to appeal to principles deciding what institutions and social arrangements are truly just and which are not. I will discuss principles of justice in the next Chapter, Chapter 5, **Domestic Theories of Justice.**

THE RATIONALITY OF COOPERATIVE PRINCIPLES

It is important to see the nature of the conflict between interests and higher-level ethical principles. It can always look as though one can do better by not being ethical, and thus that ethics demands a departure from rationality. The situation is discussed in Game Theory, the theory of rational choices. The name of the type of choice situation is the Prisoner's Dilemma. The classic story which gives it that name is this: A prosecutor is sure that two prisoners are guilty, but does not have enough evidence to convict them. He offers each of them (separately) a deal: If neither confesses, they will receive long sentences. If both confess, they will receive light sentences. If one prisoner confesses, he will be released, but the non-confessing prisoner will receive a maximum sentence. (Luce & Raiffa 1957, 94-97) The situation can be represented as a *payoff matrix*, shown in Table 1.

The pairs of numbers give Prisoner A's and then Prisoner B's ranking of the outcome. Thus, if prisoner A confesses and prisoner B does not, prisoner A gets his first choice outcome (most lenient sentence) and prisoner B gets his worst choice outcome (maximum sentence).

Table 2. Cooperative Benefits Payoff Matrix

	Person A obeys principle	Person A disobeys (acts selfishly)
Person B obeys principle	(2,2)	(4,1)
Person B disobeys (acts selfishly)	(1,4)	(3,3)

The payoff matrix applies unchanged to most situations in which there is a higher-level ethical principle providing cooperative benefits, and the choice is to observe that principle or not to observe and act on self-interest instead[5] (see Table 2).

What the payoff matrix reflects is that one can always do better from a selfish or self-interested point of view if everyone else obeys the (cooperative ethical) principle but you do not. For example, obeying traffic signals. If I obey, I may have to wait extra time. But if I am thinking in a purely self-interested (selfish) manner, I may go through the red light when it looks safe to me. I am attempting to avoid whatever disadvantage or burden there is for obeying and at the same time get the cooperative benefit. Of course, the rub is that if everyone acts this way, the cooperative principle with its cooperative benefits is no longer available--we are at alternative (3,3), which means everyone is *collectively* worse off than if everyone obeyed (2,2). Therefore, the only way we can have ethical principles is if we treat principles which are cooperatively rational (produce 2,2 as opposed to 3,3) as of higher priority than considerations of self-interest. (Schultz 1971, 211-217) A more extreme but maybe more compelling example is that we agree not to use deadly force against each other and relegate the use of deadly force to a sovereign. The philosopher Hobbes thought this agreement was the essential social contract which removes us from a state of nature, described by Hobbes as a "war of all against all," guaranteeing that our lives will be "solitary, poore, nasty, brutish and short." (Hobbes 1651, Ch. XIII)

People taking advantage of cooperative schemes are called "free riders." Although enforceable penalties help with free riders and may sometimes be necessary, they reduce cooperative benefits. And in general people expect to obey ethical principles even though there may be no obvious or immediate penalties.

The reasoning involved in giving principles yielding cooperative benefit higher priority than self-interest can be applied at higher levels: Whenever principles conflict for a type of action, there is the possibility of higher-level principles resolving the conflict in a way that adds value. Thus there is the possibility of higher-level principles for the behavior of nations which add value if they are treated as higher level. A principle not to settle disputes with other nations by making war would be an example. Without such principles, we are left with wars which are rarely in any society's interest.

The rational basis for ethics is thus the principle of higher level principles. It states that other things being equal, it is rational to follow a higher-level principle when that principle needs to be treated that way in order to resolve conflicts between lower-level principles. (Schultz 1971, 216-217) "Other things being equal" includes the reasonableness of other principles already being followed, and the likelihood of the principle being publicly adopted. The task of ethics, so conceived, is to discover, formulate, and promulgate such a system of principles. It is a task we human beings began at least 2500 years ago, and we have made some progress. As we rapidly expand the scope of our powers of action through technology and information technology, one can hope that our progress in our ability to understand how to use these powers in the highest and best ways will keep pace.[6]

ETHICAL DEVELOPMENT

My view of ethics as higher-level principles settling conflicts of interest can provide a basis for saying what is right and wrong. Ethical principles themselves can conflict, and it requires higher-level principles to settle those conflicts. Some principles are clearly higher level than others. The social psychologist Lawrence Kohlberg, a pioneer in this area, developed a theory of different levels of ethical principles. Kohlberg believed that ethical reasoning develops in stages in human beings. (Kohlberg 1976) People move to a different stage--and higher level of principle--precisely because they encounter unresolvable conflicts of principles at lower levels.[7]

His stages are:

Stage One: Punishment and obedience
Stage Two: Interests of only oneself
Stage Three: Conformity for social approval
Stage Four: Law and order
Stage Five: Social contract based on utility
Stage Six: Universal principles.

Kohlberg thinks of children as moving through these stages. A person's development can stop at various stages. Children begin by obeying those in authority, usually parents, and are motivated to do so by the threat of punishment. Eventually, the child realizes that his own needs are not always satisfied by obedience. So his motivation changes: He obeys when it satisfies his own needs, and may not obey when his needs come into conflict with parental demands. He is at Stage Two, and is characterized by Kohlberg as being an "instrumental relativist." Those who never get beyond Stage Two, acting only on what they perceive satisfies their needs only, often spend large periods of time incarcerated. The major impetus for advancing to the next stage is conflicts which cannot be resolved at the stage below. Thus the Stage Two instrumental relativist must recognize social norms that come before self interest in order to do at all well in the social context in which his needs have to be met. The relativist is at Stage Two and thus, as I claimed earlier, cannot acknowledge that there is a binding basis for principles of social cooperation. A little reflection will make clear that human society as we now know it, or even primitive human society, could not exist without principles of social cooperation overriding self-interest. Any sort of commerce would be unthinkable. And a little reflection will make clear that human beings cannot survive without society. Therefore relativism is not possible as an ethical theory.

Individuals at the next Stage Three (Conformity) are motivated primarily by considerations of 'looking good' in the eyes of others.[8] And a person may find it impossible to be all things to all people. A common teenage conflict is between peer approval and the approval of older authorities such as parents. And… "who's to say who's right?" Obviously neither. We need to move beyond social approval as the basis for ethical judgements.[9] Instead, we look to the social order, to laws and duties prescribed by society. This is Stage Four (Law and Order); now we obey to preserve social harmony.

Because of the nature of corporations, it may be that they are capable of at most Stage Three morality. The key to identifying someone at Stage Three is that the *appearance* of doing the right thing is more important than actually doing the right thing. The goal of a corporation is to maximize profit. So, if through public relations and advertising, a corporation gains the reputation (or image) of being honest and caring, it will be the reputation that enhances the bottom line, and not the unrecognized sacrifice to do the right thing.[10]

As we consider the different stages, we can recognize people who simply stop at a given stage. Those who stop at Stage Three (Conformity) tend to be shallow people, and unless protected by others, will probably never have really fulfilling lives. Those who stop at Stage Four (Law and Order) are often quite functional. Stage Four is not the end of the line because laws and duties prescribed by society can conflict, either within a society, or across different societies or social groups, or with other values. The question is then, where do these laws and duties get their authority? The Stage Four answer is, "They just are what they are, period." Digital entertainment companies encourage a Stage Four attitude toward noncommercial copying, without noting that they themselves were responsible for criminalizing this activity for the first time in the late 1990s. Stage Four responses also occur with some frequency in letters to the editor which point out that illegal immigration or medical marijuana are illegal and regard this observation as the final word in the discussion.

The Stage Five (Social Contract) answer goes beyond this. Kohlberg's Stage Five, which he thinks is embodied in the U.S. Constitution and its government, derives the authority of the law and social duties from the consent of the governed. There is a social contract and laws and duties can be changed to maximize social utility, "the greatest good for the greatest number." In certain circumstances, it can even be justified to break a law to demonstrate a higher principle. This is what Martin Luther King called *civil disobedience.* (King 1963)

Stage Five (Social Contract) is not itself without conflict. Doing the greatest good for the greatest number may not actually produce the best result. For example, enslaving 10% of the population may produce greater overall economic benefits but could no longer be accepted as a just social organization. If we generalize on Stage Five, we arrive at the more abstract social contract of Stage Six. At Stage Six (Universal Principles), principles are chosen that best express ourselves as free and equal rational beings living together in a society, as in the U.S. Declaration of Independence and Constitution. Differences between Stage Five and Stage Six are discussed at length in Chapter 5, **Domestic Theories of Justice.**

The principles arrived at in the various stages are discussed in traditional ethical theory. A major advantage of Kohlberg's staged approach is that it makes clear the reasons for the priority of some principles over others, and thus a basis for answering the question, who's to say what's right and wrong? The answer is: "The person with the most overall view using the highest level principles." And a principle is not higher level because someone says it is, but because in fact it can settle conflicts unresolvable by lower-level principles.

REFLECTIVE EQUILIBRIUM

The determination of the Kohlberg stages of ethical principles may make it clear when one principle is better justified than another. But it is not unusual to find that there are conflicting principles in the same stage or conflicting opinions about the stage of ethical principles. There is a more general method for justifying ethical principles which will be used in this book. The method is called *reflective equilibrium*[11]. (Rawls 1999c) We each have particular ethical judgements and we each have ethical principles at various levels of generality. Reflective equilibrium calls for striking a balance between our particular judgements and our more general principles.

Here is an example from my own life. At a dinner party with my parents and a liberal Hollywood screenwriter couple, my (late) mother announced that she thought interracial marriages and families were immoral. I was able to inform her that her grandchildren were one-sixteenth black, the result of my ex-wife's old Southern family running out of male heirs and promoting a 'mixed' heir to full status so that the family line could be carried on. Reflective equilibrium would call for her either to renounce her grandchildren or to renounce her repellent racist principle. She renounced the principle.

I believe we employ this procedure all the time in daily life. We adopt general principles but are willing to abandon or amend them when shown consequences that we are not willing to accept. And we also will abandon or amend particular judgements if we feel more strongly about a principle that may conflict with them. The goal of reflective equilibrium is a consistent and coherent set of ethical beliefs and principles.

Another example may be in the area of international labor standards. We may subscribe to the UNICEF principle that no children below 12 years of age should work in any economic activities, those aged 12 to 14 years should not do harmful work, and no children should be enslaved, forcibly recruited, prostituted, trafficked, forced into illegal activities or exposed to hazardous work. But it may also be true that conditions are so harsh that a family in poverty can survive only by violating this principle.[12] In such a case, we may want to make an exception to the principle. But reflective equilibrium should also make it an ethical requirement to do something to help change such appalling circumstances.

The method of reflective equilibrium may be an especially good one for use with new ethical problems. For new ethical problems, it may be more necessary to go back and forth between particular ethical judgements and more general principles until we reach a balance. In addition to any usual levels of generality, we will also be dealing with the three different levels of individual, societal, and transnational ethics. There are possible ethical conflicts between each of these levels which cannot automatically be resolved. To enable cooperative benefits, usually the ethical rules of society override individual ethics, but certainly not always. When a given society's rules do not respect human rights, individual ethics should have precedence. In some cases, notably with Martin Luther King or the abolition of slavery, society's principles themselves change.

When it comes to transnational ethics, things are much more up for grabs. Powerful nations sometimes attempt to impose their own ethical standards on developing nations. One example would be the TRIPS (Trade-Related Intellectual Property Rights) Agreement of the WTO. This agreement forces WTO members to adopt the patent and intellectual property policies of the developed countries, but it will definitely hinder the developing countries in improving their conditions. (Chang 2006, Stiglitz 2007) At this point in time, there are no settled transnational principles to appeal to, although there is broad agreement on general principles such as that the more developed countries have a duty to help the less developed countries.

One of the main aims of this book is to develop a set of transnational principles which is in reflective equilibrium with our best judgement about principles for given societies. In order to do this, I will start with individual ethics, then proceed through ethics for societies (i.e. principles of justice for societies), and then to the various possibilities for transnational ethical principles.

ETHICAL PRINCIPLES FOR INDIVIDUALS

In this book I am going to deal with *ethics* rather than morality. I am going beyond the root meaning of ethics which derives from the Greek εθικη (*ethike*), which means "character." *Morality* derives from the Latin *mores* which means "custom." I believe the useful content of the ethical is principles which express our human nature as social beings and allow us cooperative benefits. Obviously making and keeping agreements are a major part of ethics so conceived. And prisoner's dilemma type arguments show why it is that ethics must override individual self-interest. But ethical principles allowing us cooperative benefits involve more than keeping agreements. The principle of benevolence[13]--to give aid to others in need--holds without any agreement. Prisoner's dilemma arguments also apply to such Golden Rule[14] cases. We simply assume that human beings recognize each other as fellow human beings and give aid because in so doing they expect that they will receive aid when they are in trouble.

By contrast, morality as mores has a large arbitrary element often based on nonrational religious[15] or cultural peculiarities. The principle that one ought to kill one's daughter if she marries an infidel can hardly be based on anticipated cooperative benefits. It is a stringent membership rule for a religious sect. Failure to appreciate the distinction between ethical principles that insure cooperative benefits and moral principles that reflect mainly arbitrary religious or cultural beliefs may be responsible for the attractiveness of relativism. Indeed, virtually all principles having to do with human sexual behavior not based on considerations of actual harm to the participants are arbitrary moral principles rather than ethical principles.[16]

So how do we tell which principles of right and wrong action best produce cooperative benefits? Considerations of value are also important to ethics. A very plausible theory of right action is that the right thing to do is what produces the greatest good for the greatest number. This theory is called *utilitarianism*. (Mill 1863) [17]

Besides utilitarianism, there are two other theories of right action: Intuitionist and universal principle. Intuitionism is actually a non-theory. It says that there is no good explanation of right and wrong, but we nevertheless have strong intuitive feelings about what is right and wrong. For the intuitionist, these feelings need no justification. The Ten Commandments, taken on their own, are an intuitionist theory. Two major difficulties with intuitionism are, first, that it is very unsatisfying just to be told that certain actions are right or wrong with no further justification. Second, when different principles of right action conflict, we have no way of deciding priorities. If we are told: Honor thy father and mother. And also told: Do not steal. Then what do we do if our father orders us to steal? In an episode of the TV show *The Simpsons* dealing with the Ten Commandments, Homer (the father) has stolen cable TV access. His daughter Lisa's spiritual advisor reminds her that to turn her father in would violate the commandment to honor thy father and mother. (Pepoon 1991, episode 7F13) The answer may be obvious to us that the command 'Do not steal' has precedence. But if so, we are using something in addition to an intuitive list of wrong actions to decide.

Utilitarianism is the most popular of end-based theories of right action. End-based theories simplify things by reducing considerations of right action to considerations of pursuing some end, usually goodness. Utilitarianism can be stated:

Act so as to Produce the Greatest Amount of Good for the Greatest Number

Utilitarianism has much plausibility. For how could it possibly be wrong to do the action that produces the greatest good? How could it possibly be right to do an action which produces less good when you could have done better?

Although a plausible idea, utilitarianism suffers from two major difficulties. One is that if we consider actions in isolation from one another, it is easy for a utilitarian to break promises or fail to fulfill contracts when more good would be produced in that case. Breaking copy protection to give software to a needy organization doing good for homeless people seems acceptable on utilitarian grounds. The trouble is that then institutions which allow cooperative benefits, to live and work together, would disintegrate. If in individual cases breaking copy protection may produce more good, we cannot realize the overall good of not allowing copying and thus providing an environment for software development. Thus important goods are not available unless we consider ourselves bound to follow certain non-utilitarian rules.

But utilitarianism can achieve these goods if it is considered as a theory of just institutions rather than individual acts. Then one is still bound by social rules governing the institutions of keeping agreements and fulfilling contracts even though more good might be done in the individual case by breaking the social rule. One does actions not because the individual actions produce the greatest amount of good, but because the right action is to follow social rules which produce the greatest amount of good. This theory is called *rule utilitarianism.*

But how do we tell which rules these are? The second major difficulty is that summing goodness over individuals in any precise way has been proved to be impossible. So the notion of the greatest good for the greatest number can only serve as a metaphor. It simply can't be made precise. (Arrow 1951)[18]

Nevertheless, there is something very intuitive about trying to adopt policies and principles which would produce the greatest amount of good. As mentioned in the discussion of the offshoring of jobs in Chapter 1, **IT-Enabled Global Ethical Problems,** the practice of offshoring jobs is often justified in a utilitarian way. It is noted that the net average value goes up. For a utilitarian, there is no further issue of justice, regardless of how the members of the two societies are affected. We will return to utilitarianism in the next chapter, Chapter 5, **Domestic Theories of Justice**, and in Chapter 7, **Cosmopolitanism.**

The major alternative to a utilitarian theory of right action is a universal principle theory. Universal principle theories insist that rightness is independent of goodness. Perhaps the most developed universal principle theory is due to the philosopher Immanuel Kant (1785), founded on his *Categorical Imperative*:

Act on Principles that Could be Willed to be Universal Law

For example, making an agreement you have no intention of keeping could not be willed to be universal law because then no one would make agreements. The biblical Golden Rule, do unto others as you would have them do unto you, is a similar but less formal version of The Categorical Imperative.

A number of superficial criticisms of Kant's Categorical Imperative are mainly about technicalities in its wording and application. It is important in Kant's theory that what is judged for rightness or wrongness is your action together with its motive. The test of rightness is whether your action *as done from that motive* could be made a universal principle of action. (Nell 1975, 34-42) So the Categorical Imperative, correctly understood, does not allow "tailoring" the action to the circumstances. For example "I will fail to keep agreements only to people without the resources to sue" when your agreement is with people without the resources to sue, is not a legitimate application of The Categorical Imperative. (Insurance companies would therefore sometimes be in violation of The Categorical Imperative.)

The Categorical Imperative would handle the case of breaking copy protection to give software to a needy organization doing good for homeless people by a careful (self-) examination of motives. Is my principle to do good in a particular case regardless of the social rules? Everyone's acting on that principle will result in there being no rules and thus no software and thus no opportunity to break copy protection. This cannot be a right action with that motive. But if my principle is to break the social rule only in cases where great harm would otherwise occur, this could be a right action. For example, breaking an encryption to obtain medical information needed immediately to save someone's life would clearly be the right thing to do. The tricky thing is to estimate the relative consequences. It is important to consider actual social rules, and there is clearly a presumption that they are not to be broken lightly.

Frequently the consideration of *publicity* can provide guidance in using the Categorical Imperative. Publicity requires that everyone concerned be aware of the principle you are using. This immediately rules out exceptions to principles that can't be publicized because those not granted the exception would know they had been unjustly treated. For example, a student does not satisfy a requirement for graduation but is granted a diploma on the condition that he is not to tell anyone that the exemption was made. The Categorical Imperative is clearly not satisfied.

Kant has little guidance for what to do when right actions conflict, except to say that the stronger ground of obligation has precedence. (Kant 1797b) But he doesn't give directions on how to determine this. So in this respect, Kant's theory of right action is incomplete and needs the addition of a theory of just social rules, especially how they fit together into a system without conflicts. Kant has such a theory, in his *Metaphysical Elements of Justice*. (Kant 1797a) But rather than discuss Kant's theory of justice, I will discuss a modern update by the 20th century philosopher John Rawls. (Rawls 1999a)

Richard Dawkins, in his *The God Delusion,* mentions both utilitarianism and universal principles (Kant's Categorical Imperative) as plausible non-religious ethical theories. Dawkins believes that universal principle theory is too limited to serve as a basis for ethics and that utilitarianism is preferable. (Dawkins 2008, 264-267)

Both rule utilitarianism and the Categorical Imperative offer similar and often identical answers to questions of right and wrong. But there are cases in which they differ. If there are grounds for deciding between them, it lies in the nature of the contribution each makes to a theory of justice, of what systems of social rules deserve our obedience. The question of justice is the question of the ethics of a society. This is the topic of the next chapter, Chapter 5, **Domestic Theories of Justice**

OTHER INDIVIDUAL ETHICAL ISSUES

Some other issues about ethics for individuals are worth mentioning. Some think that the attempt to reduce ethics to rational calculation is misguided. The 18th century philosopher David Hume, for example, thought that ethics would not be possible without feelings of sympathy of one human being for another. (Hume 1739 and 17511751) Without these feelings, it would not be possible for us to include others within the sphere of our own interests.[19] The claim is that formal ethical theories, especially Kant's, ignore the importance of moral feeling. We are inclined to help other people not because we see that the principles of our action could be willed to be universal law, but because we feel for other people's predicaments and are moved to help them. (Baier 1992, 56-8)

Kant does derive the duty of mutual aid from the Categorical Imperative: A principle of not helping others when they are in need could not be universal law because one would want such aid oneself when one was in need. (Kant 1797b, 451-3) Although this seems cold and unfeeling, Kant also discusses the role of feeling. Although moral feelings such as sympathy are important and need to be cultivated, they can't be the ground for the rightness of the action. Otherwise one could avoid helping other people on the ground that one simply didn't feel like it. One is probably a better person (good character again) if one has a robust set of moral feelings which help one make the correct ethical decisions and help one carry through one's ethical decisions. But such feelings are not the basis of rightness or goodness or justice. The feelings follow from rightness, goodness, and justice as determined by rational ethical principles.

DUTIES, OBLIGATIONS, RIGHTS

Besides right and wrong actions, several other terms are often used in ethical discussions. They are: Duties, obligations, and rights. All three can be defined starting with right and wrong action. *Duties* and *obligations* are actions it would be <u>wrong</u> not to do. *Duties* come about just from the nature of the situation one is in, for example, being a parent. Whereas *obligations* come about because of something one has done to obligate oneself, for example sign a contract or accept a benefit. A person has a *right* to do something or have something when it would be *wrong* to prevent him from doing the action or having the object.

Duties and obligations have different characteristics. Normally obligations require one to do a specific action or set of actions. For example, if I have an obligation to correct the faults in my installation of your network, that is the action I am ethically required to do. But if I have a duty as an I.T. professional to help underfunded educational facilities, it is to a large extent my choice which educational facilities I help--I obvious am not ethically required to help *all* educational facilities. I cannot be required to help them all because the cost to myself would be too great.[20] This is very often the limiting condition on duties--the actions mentioned in a duty are required only if the cost to oneself is not too great.[21] (Kant 1797b, 392)

It is not uncommon for people to think that, because they have a right to do something, that that is the end of the story, ethically speaking. But a right is based on reasons for not interfering with a person's doing an action. So the right may have to be weighed against reasons for not interfering with other people's doing conflicting actions. I may have a right to buy a competing software company, but that right may be outweighed by society's right to prevent monopolies. Because rights can easily conflict, they should always be regarded as derived from principles of right and wrong action. It is clearer to work in terms right and wrong action than rights. For example, if society has a right to prevent monopolies, the corresponding ethical principle is that it is wrong to create monopolies and that one's rights to acquire property can be superseded.

VALUE AND GOODNESS

To understand value or goodness, we should look at interests considered from a point of view. A good or valuable object is one that, to a greater degree than average, answers to the interests one has in the object from a certain point of view.[22] Thus a good disk drive is one that answers to the interests of a computer user in safely storing information. Very often the objects that we deal with are actually defined in terms of functions, and then the value of that object simply consists in its performing that function to a greater degree than average. That is, good antivirus software must prevent and destroy viruses; good keyboard cleaner must clean keyboards well, and so on.

Very often we simply assume that the point of view from which value is to be evaluated is our own, or that of our group. Most disagreements about value are in fact disagreements about the appropriate point of view to use for evaluation. But within a point of view, there is nothing subjective about value. Whether something is valuable from a point of view is a matter of fact.

One especially important set of values are *enabling* values, for example health, education, wealth. We must have these things to a certain level if we are going to be able to pursue any interests at all.[23] They need not lead to the fulfillment of some particular ends or realization of some particular function. These enabling values are especially important in considering the justice of social arrangements because if people are unable to have them, their ability to live satisfactory lives is greatly reduced. They thus provide a basic measure for when people are better and worse off. In Rawls' social contract theory of justice discussed in the next chapter, enabling values play a critical role.

REFERENCES

Aristotle. (n.d.). *Nicomachean ethics*. Retrieved March 10, 2004 from http://classics.mit.edu/Aristotle/nicomachean.html

Arrow, K. (1951). *Social choice and individual values*. New York: John Wiley & Sons.

Baier, A. (1992). *Moral prejudices*. Cambridge, MA: Harvard University Press.

Binmore, K. (1994). *Playing fair: Game theory and the social contract*. Cambridge, MA: The MIT Press.

Dawkins, R. (2008). *The selfish gene*. New York: Houghton Mifflin.

Gauthier, D. (1967). Morality and advantage. *The Philosophical Review*, *27*, 460–475. doi:10.2307/2183283

Gauthier, D. (1986). *Morals by agreement*. Oxford, UK: Clarendon Press.

Hobbes, T. (1999). *Leviathan*. Retrieved May 20, 2004 from http://darkwing.uoregon.edu/~rbear/hobbes/leviathan.html

Hume, D. (1739). *A treatise of human nature*. London: John Noon.

Hume, D. (1751). *An enquiry concerning the principles of morals*. Retrieved August 7, 2005 from http://www.gutenberg.org/etext/4320

Kant, I. (1785). *Groundwork of the metaphysics of morals*. Retrieved May 10, 2004 from http://www.swan.ac.uk/poli/texts/kant/kantcon.htm

Kant, I. (1797a). *Metaphysical elements of justice. Metaphysics of morals, part I*. Koenigsberg: Friedrich Nicolovius.

Kant, I. (1797b). *The doctrine of virtue. Metaphysics of morals, part II*. Koenigsberg: Friedrich Nicolovius

King, M. L. (1963). Letter from Birmingham city jail. *Liberation (New York, N.Y.)*, 10–16.

Locke, J. (2004). *The second treatise on government.* Retrieved May 10, 2004 from http://www.constitution.org/jl/2ndtreat.htm

Luce, D., & Raiffa, H. (1967). *Games and decisions.* New York: John Wiley & Sons.

Mill, J. S. (1863.). *Utilitarianism.* Retrieved on May 10, 2004 from http://etext.library.adelaide.edu.au/m/mill/john_stuart/m645u/

Nell (O'Neill). O. (1975). *Acting on principle.* New York: Columbia University Press.

Pepoon, S. (1991). Homer vs. Lisa and the 8th Commandment [*The Simpsons*]. Episode 7F13.

Rawls, J. (1999a). *A theory of justice* (rev. ed.). Cambridge, MA: Harvard University Press.

Rawls, J. (1999c). Outline of a decision procedure for ethics. In S. Freeman (Ed.), *Collected papers.* Cambridge, MA: Harvard University Press.

Schultz, R. (1971). *Reasons to be moral.* Ph.D. Dissertation, Harvard University, Cambridge, MA

ENDNOTES

[1]   Current attempts to prohibit same-sex marriage by constitutional amendment may end up the same way. Certainly very few would now approve of the early 20th-century attempts to pass a constitutional amendment to prohibit interracial marriage.

[2]   I know of a technologically naïve company some years ago who purchased accounting software from someone who disappeared. They discovered too late that the software was not subtracting payables from net profit. They declared bankruptcy when they were a few million dollars in the hole with no way of recouping their losses.

[3]   Although in extreme circumstances they can ignore social rules-for example, if the society is killing its own members, most obligations to follow the rules are void.

[4]   See Arrow 1951 and Sen 1961. The problem is that majority rule violates some minimal conditions on fair and reasonable group decisions. An even worse problem is that all procedures for group decisions violate the same minimal conditions. This result is called the Arrow Possibility Theorem. See also note 18 on Kenneth Arrow, this chapter.

[5]   The application of the matrix to ethical principles is due to David Gauthier 1967, "Morality and Advantage"

[6]   Recent authors using game theory and the prisoner's dilemma as foundations for ethics include Ken Binmore (1994) and David Gauthier (1986).

[7]   Social psychologist Carol Gillligan claims that Kohlberg's stages apply primarily to men. Since she also at one point claimed that women were much more likely to take a "correct" moral perspective, it is difficult to know how much weight to give to her claims. See Gilligan 1982.

[8]   As we will see, corporations tend to be at Stage Three.

[9]   Character-based Greek ethics, and the ethics of reputation, are at this stage. We don't necessarily leave such earlier stages behind; rather, we add higher-level considerations.

[10] This issue is discussed at length in Chapter 8, **The Ethical Status of Globalized Institutions.** I know of an auto insurance corporation which advertises its helpful agents but which in fact normally

has to be sued by its clients in order to get payment for a claim.

[11]   A good brief account of reflective equilibrium is Daniels 2003.

[12]   Conservative apologists for child labor bring up this general possibility as a blanket justification. Rather, it needs to be demonstrated that it actually holds in given circumstances.

[13]   'Beneficence' is the more precise term, because it means 'doing good.' Although 'benevolence' means only 'willing good,' in common usage it means also 'doing good.' To use 'beneficence' would send most readers running to their dictionaries for no good reason.

[14]   The Golden Rule is to do unto others as you would have them do unto you.

[15]   Most religions say their special beliefs require faith. However, since there are a number of seriously conflicting faiths, the chances that any are correct is very small.

[16]   In developing his theory of justice, John Rawls distinguishes principles of justice regulating cooperative behavior and comprehensive doctrines which are not allowed to affect the social contract. His distinction is similar to my distinction between ethics and morals.

[17]   Earlier versions were developed by David Hume and Jeremy Bentham.

[18]   Kenneth Arrow won the Nobel Prize in 1972 by proving in his "general possibility theorem" that a consistent and very minimally just amalgamation of individual preferences is impossible. Such an amalgamation is called a "social choice." Utililitarianism as a usable theory would need to make such impossible social choices. Arrow's proof uses fairly abstract mathematics (theory of partial orderings) and is not accessible to non-mathematicians. For a brief (but still technical) account, see encyclopedia.thefreedictionary.com/Arrow's+**theorem**.

[19]   Other philosophers, notably the Logical Positivists centered in Vienna until Nazism forced their dispersal, thought that this emotive content was all that there was to ethics. In effect, all ethical judgements are similar to cheers or boos: Murder, boo! Or Unselfishness, yea! This view would make it nonsensical to debate ethical issues, as people have done for several thousand years at least. So there would need to be a very good reason for holding this radical view. And there really isn't. The Logical Positivists generalized on a narrow view of science, which they took to be a standard of meaningfulness. For them, since ethical judgements didn't meet these narrow standards (direct verification by experience), they had to be explained some other way. However, theoretical scientific statements are rarely directly verifiable by experience. Also, the positivist standard of meaningfulness isn't verified by experience either. So on their own terms, the positivists were really saying, Direct verification by experience, yea!

[20]   These distinctions follow those drawn by Rawls. See Rawls 1999a, sections 18 and 19.

[21]   The cost would be too great if doing the action would interfere with your ability to fulfill your duties and obligations. That includes keeping up one's own well-being. For example, working for charitable organizations to such an extent that one's health is damaged would be too great a cost.

[22]   Similar versions of this definition of value appear in Aristotle 350 BCE, Ziff 1960, and Rawls 1999a.

[23]   Rawls (1999a) calls these *primary goods.*

Chapter 5
Domestic Theories of Justice

In this chapter I will deal primarily with principles of justice for a particular society, a society whose members share benefits and burdens and regard themselves as cooperating members of that society. This type of justice is called *domestic* justice, to contrast it with *transnational* or *global* justice. Usually it is people in a given nation who constitute a society and regard themselves as belonging to a single economic and political unit. As I mentioned in the discussion of globalized institutions in Chapter 2, federal arrangements such as the US and the EU are possible with subsidiary units with partial autonomy, both economic and political.

Although such divided autonomy can raise problems of justice, they are minor compared to the problems raised by ethically globalized institutions. As a comparison, at the domestic (federal) level, consider the (so-called) Clean Air Act of 2007. This act prohibits states from setting their own fuel efficiency standards. California historically has set its own standards, and the issue of whether it can continue to do so is being litigated in the courts. (California Office of the Attorney General 2009) The problem here is a political one. The procedures for settling the dispute are agreed on by all, even if some are not happy at the outcome.

But at the transnational level, problems are much worse. At the national level, we can have disagreements about what policies contribute most to national well-being. But there is no dispute at the national

DOI: 10.4018/978-1-60566-922-9.ch005

level about what societies are affected, about who the relevant stakeholders are, and what legal and political authority applies for a given problem. All of these are up for grabs at the transnational level. For example, at least in the short run, offshoring jobs results in lost jobs in developed countries (a burden for those countries) and in increased numbers of lower wage jobs in developing countries (a benefit for those countries). But the countries involved are not part of the same economy or the same society. India and the US do not share benefits or burdens and cannot regard themselves as part of the same cooperative scheme. There may be ways to extend domestic justice to handle cases like these, but they are far from self-evident. In the following chapters in Section 2, **Theories of Globalized Ethics,** we will examine several proposals for principles of globalized justice.

Ethics for individuals and ethics for a particular society depend upon each other. This is not surprising. As we saw in the previous chapter, ethical principles for individuals are principles which override self-interest in order that we can realize cooperative benefits. Thus they make it possible for us to live peaceably and productively with each other in society.[1] An individual ethical principle is thus implicitly a social rule.

At the level of a society, there are additional ethical considerations contained in the concept of justice. People, say the employees of a firm or the citizens of a state, can do the right thing as individuals and yet keep in motion institutions of great evil. Thus justice--the ethics of a society--requires principles for institutions over and above individual ethical principles. And conversely, a just society must respect the rights of the individuals in that society. Individual ethical principles are not simply engulfed by principles of justice. There is a name for societies for which observance and enforcement of laws and social rules is more important than individual rights. Such societies are called totalitarian.

In this chapter I will deal mostly with the two most popular theories of what a just society is: Utilitarianism[2] and the social contract theory of justice of John Rawls. (Rawls 1999a) Much discussion of the structure of social institutions is done by economists, and most economists almost invariably assume some version of utilitarianism: The set of institutions for society is just if it produces the greatest value for the greatest number.[3] Utilitarianism does not *directly* concern itself with how value is distributed. (Indirectly, a very uneven distribution of value could lead to a lower overall amount, and thus could be ruled out on utilitarian grounds.) The social contract theory of John Rawls does concern itself directly with the distribution of value, and has become a viable alternative since its introduction in the 1970s.

OTHER THEORIES OF JUSTICE

A few other theories of justice besides utilitarianism and the social contract theory have some popularity and are worth mentioning. They are *meritocracy, libertarianism, perfectionism, egalitarianism,* and *pluralism*:

- Meritocracy holds that a just distribution of goods is allocation according to the merit of the person. Merit is determined by the individual's achievement through the use of his or her ability and talent.
- Libertarianism holds that a just distribution of goods is any distribution that started from an initially just position and resulted from transactions which are, roughly, honest ones. Libertarianism calls for minimal interference with people's transactions in maintaining a just distribution. (This is the version of Robert Nozick (1974))

- Perfectionism is the view that a just society promotes the realization of human excellence.
- Egalitarianism is the view that all goods produced by society should be distributed equally.

I will not consider any of these theories as candidates for a theory of justice because they would not likely be freely chosen by people agreeing on principles to regulate their society. Following Rawls, I regard the correct principles of justice as those that would be chosen as a social contract. For Rawls, the *original position* is the situation in which the social contract is made and the principles of justice are chosen. (1999a) I will return shortly to a discussion of why the less likely theories would not be chosen.

The fifth theory, *pluralism*, is the view that there are many principles of justice which conflict, but there is no higher-level principle to settle these conflicts.[4] This theory basically rejects using a social contract to determine the highest-level principles of justice. Pluralism claims instead that we have a bundle of intuitive principles of justice which have to be balanced against each other, but we do this balancing without the aid of any higher-level principle or principles of justice. The only reply to pluralism is to show that there is a higher-level principle which is in reflective equilibrium[5] with our judgements concerning justice. So pluralism is the default theory if no more comprehensive theory is plausible.

THE SOCIAL CONTRACT

The basic idea of a social contract is that a justly ordered society is one to which individuals can freely decide to obligate themselves. This idea is clearly expressed by the Declaration of Independence of the United States of 1776. Influential early versions of the social contract include Thomas Hobbes (1651), John Locke (1690), and Jean-Jacques Rousseau (1762). Locke in particular had great influence on the founding fathers of the US. The idea of a social contract is attractive because it provides a non-coercive ethical basis for social rules. Of course there is no actual social contract, either written or oral, that members of societies agree to. But we can determine whether our social rules are ones that *could have been* chosen in appropriate decision circumstances. It was the insight of the 20th century philosopher John Rawls (1999a) that this procedure was the appropriate one to determine the principles of justice, the ethical principles governing society and its institutions.

The features of this hypothetical original position are ones that express ethical constraints. Thus our decision on principles will be biased in favor of our own interests if we base it on our current situation. So in the original position, the decision must be made prior to being in society, without knowledge of what our particular position will be in society. We will know general facts about societies and how they function. It will also be a decision we will be obligated to stick to and expect others to make and stick to as well. When we are deciding on the principles of justice, we are deciding on principles to govern the basic structure of society, the institutions that determine our life prospects. (Rawls 1999a sec. 4) This original position is never actually a position we are in, because we are all born into some society or other. Yet it is a position we can return to in order to evaluate our principles and institutions.[6]

Rawls believes that there are two major candidates for principles of justice, rule utilitarianism and his own principles of justice as fairness. We will return to these candidates shortly. But first to give an illustration of how the social contract and the original position can be used to decide on ethical principles, I will consider how the less likely candidates for principles of justice fare. These were meritocracy, libertarianism, perfectionism, and egalitarianism.

Meritocracy is very often used in company settings. Employees are compensated in accordance with their achievements. As a principle of justice within companies, it is hard to think of a good alternative. For example, rewarding employees on the basis of their kinship to the boss, or on the basis of sexual favors provided to the managers, are clearly unjust. But in the original position we are considering principles to govern the basic structure of society. And meritocracy as the basic principle of justice for society would be unacceptable. The social contract must be one that any member of society could agree to *regardless of his position in society.* Achievement depends on effort, talent and luck. Talent and luck are out of the control of the individual and thus should not be taken into account in the original position.[7]

Suppose under meritocracy as the main principle of justice, you end up as the worst off person in society because of bad luck or not much talent. Will it be OK with you that your life was worse than it could be because others are reaping the rewards of effort, talent, and luck? Recall that in the original position, as far as you know, you could be this person. Also recall that we are considering the basic structure of society. In effect, meritocracy says that if you end up at the bottom through no fault of your own, that's just tough. We are going to reward the talented ones, the lucky ones, the ones who made the effort, and not care about what happens to anyone else. Even in our own society, which has meritocratic elements, the most successful such as Warren Buffett and Bill Gates feel an ethical obligation to give away large sums of money to the disadvantaged.[8] One of Rawls' alternative principles of justice, *the Difference Principle*, makes more sense: To arrange society to make the worst off as well off as possible.

Libertarianism as a principle of justice was developed by the late philosopher Robert Nozick. (1977) His idea was that the distribution of goods in society is just if it starts from a just distribution and all transactions changing the distribution are, in effect, honest ones. Thus society does not have to monitor how things are distributed, merely that transactions are honest. Rawls observes that this libertarian theory amounts to no social contract. (1996, 265) There are merely a number of private agreements which individuals can choose to make or not to make. But the whole point of principles of justice is to establish a social space in which everyone can share. Patchwork private agreements would not be enough to guarantee the level of social cooperation we take for granted in civilization. Almost every single object in the human physical environment is a result of cooperative activity. Likewise virtually all social institutions require a background of cooperation which does not resolve into a number of private agreements. The whole idea of being a member of a society sharing cooperative benefits and burdens is missing. It is to guarantee a fair basis for that cooperation that we look to a social contract agreed to by all.

Perfectionism is related to meritocracy. It holds that the goal of society is to promote human excellence. Major proponents of this view have been the ancient Greeks, notably Aristotle, and the 19th-century German philosopher Nietzsche. "Human excellence" is often thought of as manifesting itself in achievements in the arts, sciences, and culture. Perfectionism seems reasonable as a secondary aim for a society, but the difficulty is that there are likely to be different opinions about what constitutes excellence and those differences cannot be resolved within perfectionism itself. Some prior background principles of justice are required.

Consider, for example, those who would want to promote the sciences versus those who would want to promote the arts. It's not that opinions in each area are "subjective;" on the contrary, there are clear accepted standards of what constitutes excellence in scientific inquiry and what constitutes excellence in creation and performance in the various arts.[9] Rather, different individuals have different conceptions of excellence and so there is no conception that everyone can agree on as the basic structure of society.

The discussion of perfectionism uncovers another feature of the original position. Each of the individuals (the "parties") involved is assumed to have their own conception of the good, that is, their ends in life and their values and priorities. In the original position, they don't know what their values are, but they know that they have some, and they know, in general terms, how values would be important in their lives. Further, they know that they believe different comprehensive doctrines, whether religious, philosophical, or moral.[10] Within those conditions, they consider which of the likely candidates for principles of justice to adopt.

Rawls does not regard egalitarianism as a plausible theory, because division of labor makes it possible for all to do better if some receive greater resources. Michael Bell, for example, has shown himself to be better than most at building computers. So society gives him a greater unequal share of resources enabling him to do so, and everyone is better off. Egalitarianism would be a plausible theory only if massive amounts of envy were pervasive in society, so that no one could stand to see others do better than themselves.

As I indicated earlier, pluralism is pretty much a default backup theory: If no higher-level principle capable of adjudicating conflicts between principles of justice would be chosen in the original position, then pluralism would be chosen. As a result, in some cases we would allocate in accordance with merit. In other cases we would choose the alternative producing the greatest expected utility. And so on. We would have no principled basis for deciding between these different principles. We therefore need to examine the case for choosing either utilitarianism or Rawls' principles of justice as fairness as highest-level principles of justice.

THEORIES OF JUSTICE

So, what principles of justice would be chosen by individuals to govern them? *Rule utilitarianism* is a plausible candidate: Act on the set of rules likely to produce the greatest amount of good for the greatest number. Or, even more simply stated: Maximize utility. Either statement of utilitarianism immediately raises a question: How to define the good (also called "utility") for each individual in such a way that the good (or utility) can be summed over all individuals. In economics, a fiscal (dollar) value is put on everything and indifference curves can indicate the value an individual puts on different goods. However, there are theoretical limits to whether it is possible to derive a social preference for goods from individual goods.[11] In practice, however, it is often clear that other alternatives in a situation are much worse in utility for everyone than the one recommended by utilitarianism. So utilitarianism may still be a workable theory of justice. As we will see in Chapter 7, **Cosmopolitanism**, it extends easily to transnational contexts. I will have more to say about utilitarianism after we examine Rawls' two principles of justice as fairness.

From the point of view of the social contract, however, there is a more serious objection to utilitarianism. It does not care directly about how goods are distributed so long as the sum is increased. It also does not care directly about freedom. So what if you are in a society which, at the time, is arranged to produce the greatest good for the greatest number? But it also includes slaves. From a social contract view, what if in such a society you end up as a slave? Parties to a social contract would instead insist that each individual has basic liberties which are not to be compromised or traded off for other benefits. This is Rawls' social contract first principle of justice, *Greatest Equal Liberty*:

Society is to be arranged so that all members have the greatest equal liberty possible for all, including fair equality of opportunity.

Table 1. Maximin Payoff Matrix

	Get caught	Don't get caught
Rob bank	Shot to death	Get $1,000,000
Don't rob bank	Security guard waves to you	Life as usual

Besides the basic freedoms such as freedom of speech, assembly, religion, and so on, it includes equality of opportunity. Thus society's rules are not biased against anyone in it and allow all to pursue their interests and realize their abilities.[12] Freedom is to be limited only for the sake of another freedom. (Rawls 1999a)

Rawls' second principle of justice is *the Difference Principle*:

Economic inequalities in society are justified insofar as they make members of the least advantaged social class, better off than if there were no inequality.

"Better off" is to be measured against enabling values affected by the social structure reflecting an individual's life prospects. Rawls cites authority, income, and wealth as those enabling values. (Rawls 1999a, 78) The social contract basis for the Difference Principle is straightforward: If you are entering a society with no knowledge of your specific place in that society, the Difference Principle guarantees that you will be no worse off than you need be to keep the society functioning.

The principle of rational choice which gives this result is called the *maximin* principle. It directs that you choose the alternative which yields the best payoff when the worst happens. Suppose you decide to forget about ethics and rob a bank. Your payoff matrix is shown in Table 1.

Don't rob the bank gives you the best payoff if the worst happens. Note that if your principle is the utilitarian one of greatest expected utility, there will be some dollar amount large enough to give you the greatest sum of utility even if the other alternative is death. The maximin principle is very conservative, however, and is rational only when the choices make a major difference in your life. For more usual choices, expected utility is usually the most rational choice. If the choice is between a restaurant with highly variable quality of food and one that always has decent but unexciting food, your payoff matrix might be as shown in Table 2.

The maximin rule would say always to choose the decent restaurant--you come off best if the worst happens. Expected utility would allow you to pick the uneven restaurant if the spectacular meal has higher utility for you than the decent meal. With the numbers above, the expected utility of the uneven restaurant would be

$$(20\% \times 80) + (60\% \times 20) + (20\% \times (-10)) = 16 + 12 - 2 = 26$$

Table 2. Expected Utility Matrix

	Best happens (20%)	Ordinary (60%)	Worst happens (20%)
Uneven restaurant	Great meal (80)	Decent meal (20)	Inedible meal (-10)
Decent restaurant	Decent meal (20)	Decent meal (20)	Decent Meal (20)

The expected utility of the decent restaurant would be 100% x 20 = 20. Thus the choice of the uneven restaurant has greater expected utility.

The choice of principles of justice in the original position is not a trivial choice. One is choosing principles which will have a major impact on how one's entire life unfolds. Rawls claims that in this situation, the maximin principle would be the right one to use, and the result is that the Difference Principle--make the least advantaged as well off as possible--would be chosen over the principle to maximize expected utility.

The two principles of justice apply within a society whose members share cooperative benefits and burdens. So they are principles of *domestic* justice. Rawls indicates we should apply the Difference Principle to the background institutions, the major institutions that determine people's life prospects. When applying the Difference Principle, we consider the effects of the background structure on the life prospects of representatives from each relevant socioeconomic class--for example laborers, white-collar workers, managers, employers, corporate officers, investors, and so on. Then, of efficient background structures, choose the one that makes the worst-off class best off. (Rawls 1999a, secs. 2, 16)

The first principle of Greatest Equal Liberty always has priority over the Difference Principle. Justice requires that liberty cannot be traded off for greater economic benefit. In an actual society with very limited resources and a very low income level, it may be necessary to restrict freedom temporarily for the sake of development. But any such restriction should have its own removal as a goal. The Nobel Prize winning economist Amartya Sen titled one of his books *Development as Freedom*, and in that book he argues that development is justified because it increases freedom, and not merely because it improves Gross National Product (GNP). The improvement of GNP should be thought of as a means to increased freedom rather than as an end in itself. (Sen 1999)

In an oversimplified example, giving slaves their freedom would be an advance in the justness of society--a serious violation of the Greatest Equal Freedom Principle would be corrected. But if the slaves are kept in the same, or worse, economic situation, then the Difference Principle may be violated. We can understand ongoing debates in terms of these principles: Affirmative action, for example, can be seen both as a violation of the basic freedoms of some (those denied admission in order to allow minorities to attend law school, for example) or an attempt to create fair equality of opportunity for others (minorities denied good public education are given compensatory treatment). Even though there is bitter disagreement, one can see how both sides of this debate can be framed in terms of the two principles of justice.

A market economy's efficiency-- no one is able to be better off without someone else being worse off --goes a long way toward satisfying the Difference Principle. Efficiency in a market economy means that there is no slack. And no administrative overhead means that there are more resources to distribute. But efficiency is not all there is to the Difference Principle. Economists and social theorists accept that justice (their term for justice is equity) is more than efficiency.[13] As Rawls points out, there can be many efficient distributions, even including absurd ones where someone has all the economic goods and every-one else has nothing. If Rupert Murdoch were to achieve this situation (he seems to be trying), it would be efficient--he would lose if any economic goods were transferred to anyone else. American society is not based upon a market economy as the primary ethical justification for social rules, even in economic matters. As noted, a market economy is a good candidate to be an institution in a just society because of its efficiency and its compatibility with the Principle of Greatest Equal Freedom. But without some social constraints, an unregulated market economy can allow monopolies, which have no competitive pressure to be efficient or to respond to the needs of customers or to price goods in a fair way.

For example, for many years now Microsoft has had a near-monopoly over PC operating systems and office applications. (This situation may be changing with the greater adoption of Linux and Unix-based alternatives.) Microsoft has had no incentive to improve its products in any other ways except those determined by internal decisions. Thus very annoying features of Word formatting remain completely unchanged since the mid-90s, and the superior formatting controls of WordPerfect (user access to all formatting markers in the text) remain implemented in that product. Help messages in Microsoft products remain rudimentary: The text of a draft of this book unexpectedly printed out at 75% of expected size. Help for MS Word revealed the probable cause to be the shrink-to-fit command, but commented that if the document had been saved, it would be very hard to reverse the change. No further comments or instructions. Competition is essential for a market economy to work for the benefit of all.

Some progressives maintain that economic decisions in a truly just society must be made by citizen participation rather than the market. (Bello 2008) Exactly how this is supposed to happen is not clear. From the work of Kenneth Arrow, we know there is no just way of combining citizen preferences. (Arrow 1951) On the other hand, as we just saw, properly functioning markets are provably efficient (Pareto optimal). That is, there is no slack: No one can be made better off without making someone else worse off. Any "participatory" alternative would make people worse off, probably a lot worse off if the market is replaced by central planning, however democratically agreed to.[14] Progressives may have confused political principles such as participatory decision making with economic ones. There is no excuse for making large numbers of people worse off for the sake of political ideology.

IT AND THE LEAST ADVANTAGED

I will consider another application of the Difference Principle in connection with IT's effects on the well being of the least advantaged. There are two questions to consider: First, how does the use of IT by the least advantaged affect their life prospects? Second, how does the use of IT by other sectors of the economy contribute to the life prospects of the least advantaged?

The use (or lack of use) of IT by the least advantaged is partially addressed in discussions of what is called the Digital Divide:

There has always been a gap between those people and communities who can make effective use of information technology and those who cannot. Now, more than ever, unequal adoption of technology excludes many from reaping the fruits of the economy. We use the term "digital divide" to refer to this gap between those who can effectively use new information and communication tools, such as the Internet, and those who cannot. (www.digitaldividenetwork.org, Digital Divide Basics)

One concern is that the more advantaged are getting the benefits of their own use of IT added to their previous advantages, whereas the least advantaged are not using IT and therefore falling farther behind the more advantaged. This concern assumes that the use of IT leads to increases in personal productivity. For the present discussion, we will simply assume that this is so, that the use of IT, especially by the more advantaged, provides the advantaged with significant benefits. Attempts to ameliorate this problem are framed in terms of increasing the skills to use technology rather than directly in terms of improvement of life prospects. From the point of view of justice, the assumption that increase in IT skills will improve a person's ability to "reap the fruits of the economy," while reasonable, really needs to be examined through some research. It could very well be that some improvements in IT skills are much better at improving the prospects of the less well off than other possible improvements. In any case, justice embodied in the Difference Principle requires us to try to find out.

Another justice-related concern has to do with equality of opportunity, which is part of the first principle of justice of Greatest Equal Liberty: Society is to be arranged so that all members have the greatest equal liberty possible for all, including fair equality of opportunity.

As of 2000, the U.S. Department of Commerce found that white (46.1%) and Asian American & Pacific Islander (56.8%) households continued to have Internet access at levels more than double those of Black (23.5%) and Hispanic (23.6%) households. They also found that 86.3% of households earning $75,000 and above per year had Internet access compared to 12.7% of households earning less than $15,000 per year. In addition, nearly 65% of college graduates have home Internet access; only 11.7% of households headed by persons with less than a high school education have Internet access. (US Dept of Commerce 2000) A 2004 update by the Kaiser Family Foundation found that lower-income and minority youth were still much less likely to use computers or the Internet. In 2004, 92% of households earning $75,000 and above had computers at home compared to 45% of households earning less than $20,000. Internet access was available at home to 80% of whites compared to 67% of Hispanics and 61% of African-Americans. (Kaiser Family Foundation 2004)

So, while there has been improvement, there is still no question that attempting to improve the IT skills of those who lack them, will also end up targeting the less well off. The question remains, though, about how the improvement in IT skills improves the prospects of the less advantaged. Fair equality of opportunity by itself may justify efforts to ameliorate the Digital Divide. Insofar as it is difficult or impossible even to apply for higher-status jobs without email capability, justice would require making this capability available even to the least advantaged.[15]

A related concern is the contribution of IT use in other sectors of the economy to the life prospects of the least advantaged. In the United States, the homeless are a good candidate for least advantaged. So the question is: Are the homeless better off because of the use of IT in some sectors of the economy? We assume that the use of IT has impact for all groups across the board. If government is internally more efficient because of IT, for example in processing paperwork, that frees up resources to be used by anyone. The same applies if corporations or other organizations become more internally efficient because of IT. But none of that has a special impact on the homeless.

When we apply the Difference Principle and consider the IT usage of the least advantaged, we need to consider both the impact of their own usage as well as the indirect effects of increased productivity on their prospects. Even those less well off benefit from efficiency brought about by IT even if they themselves do not use it. Wal-mart's Guaranteed Low Price strategy benefits the less well off. Significant low-end consumer cost savings are brought about in part by IT-enabled efficiency in the supply chain.[16] But from the point of view of the principles of justice, increased IT skills for the less advantaged are not valuable just for their own sake. Increased skills must contribute either to the first principle of justice by implementing fair equality of opportunity, or to the second principle of justice by improving the prospects of the least advantaged. Although it is very likely that increased IT skills for the less advantaged work to fulfill both principles, ethics and justice require us to maintain the proper focus in this area.

Rawls' Difference Principle seems to be accepted as a basis for the discussion of public policy by both conservatives and liberals in the United States. Liberal attempts to improve the lot of those worst off are usually challenged by conservatives on the basis that these attempts will make the worst off even less well off. Two examples: Attempts to raise the minimum wage are challenged with the claim that employers will want to hire less people. And attempts to require home developers to build a certain percentage of low-income housing are challenged on the grounds that developers will decide not to develop rather than cut their profits.[17] In both cases, the conservative argument is that proposals intended to make the worst off better off will instead make them still worse off. Regardless of whether these claims are true, both conservatives and liberals in these debates are implicitly accepting the Difference Principle as a basis for discussion.

So there is a good case that Rawls' two principles of justice are indeed the ones most Americans accept as higher-level principles. Recall that most Americans are very unwilling to trade off freedom for economic or other benefits. Also, even defenders of offshoring don't simply defend it on the ground that it raises average utility; rather, the argument is that everyone will be better off. So I believe some version of the Difference Principle, making the worst off best off, is being appealed to.

Rawls made a critically important change to his original statement of the principles of justice during the 1980s. (Rawls 1993, 12-15) It is that in a constitutional democracy such as the United States with freedom of opinion and religion, we can't expect agreement on what Rawls calls *comprehensive doctrines,* that is, doctrines about the ultimate nature of man, or even moral doctrines. Such a society must be pluralistic in these matters. Effectively, the First Principle of Justice, Greatest Equal Freedom, requires that we don't demand agreement on comprehensive doctrines. Consequently, attempts by religions to embed their own comprehensive doctrines in the constitution are a serious danger to a free society. For example, a constitutional amendment to prohibit gay marriage, presumably proposed on religious grounds, is a serious a threat to the basis of American society. A society that recognizes that comprehensive doctrines cannot be socially enforced requires toleration of all religions, but on the condition that those religions acknowledge that tolerance of other comprehensive doctrines is a condition of they themselves being tolerated.[18]

In this book, Rawls' comprehensive doctrines are called *moral* doctrines. By contrast, principles of justice are *ethical* principles, a type of principle enabling cooperation. As principles of justice, I believe those under them must agree to them. Rawls allows that principles of justice can be agreed to from *within* comprehensive doctrines and thus people could have different reasons for agreeing (for example, God commands us to obey or Allah commands us to obey). Any agreement on principles will be by what Rawls calls an *overlapping consensus.* (Rawls 2001, section 11) When the principles of justice are regarded as ethical principles of cooperation, I don't see the necessity for this added complexity. Overlapping consensus would in any case be completely inappropriate in a global context. Even in a domestic context, I believe comprehensive religious doctrines should have much less of a say in public policy than Rawls apparently wants to allow.

UTILITARIANISM RECONSIDERED

I claimed that utilitarianism should be rejected because it would not be chosen as the highest-level principle of justice in the original position. Two points suggest reconsideration: (1) If the apparatus of the social contract and the original position is rejected, utilitarianism may be a better direct fit to our intuitive judgements about justice. (2) The quick rejection of Utilitarianism was on the grounds that it could not handle the inalienable freedoms guaranteed by the First Principle of Greatest Equal Freedom. But it is possible to accept that First Principle of Justice and to propose Utilitarianism as a principle of distributive justice instead of the Second Principle, the Difference Principle.

The 18th century philosopher David Hume found the social contract proposals of John Locke and other contemporaries unacceptable. He points out at great length that there is very little evidence of any *actual* social contract as the basis of social authority. And if the social contract is said to be *tacit* or *implied*, Hume thinks it adds nothing to the justification of legitimate authority. Suppose we say that we acknowledge and apply the principles of justice because we have made a tacit agreement to do so. Then Hume asks, why do we keep that agreement? What is the basis for sticking to the social contract? Hume says that the basis must be that to do so is "in the general interests and necessities of society"--that is, it has great utility for all. Then Hume concludes, why bother with the social contract at all? Why not say that the principles of justice contribute to greater utility and that is their justification? (Hume 1777)

Hume's objection illuminates the distinctive role of the original position in Rawls' version of the social contract. Hume's objection would be valid if it were exactly the same people with exactly the same properties they have in the society that decided on the principles of justice.[19] I will later use the description of the original position in producing a transnational social contract in Section 3, **A Social Contract for Globalized Institutions**. So it is important to understand just how the original position contributes to the choice of principles in the social contract.

The most important difference in the parties when they assume the original position is that they don't know what their own interests are. They know that they *have* interests and will want to pursue them; in the original position they just don't know what they are. Why do we impose this condition? We want principles that best serve the "general interests and necessities of society" (to use Hume's phrase), in a way that is fair to everyone. By eliminating knowledge of particular interests, we insure that principles chosen will not be biased in favor of anyone in society. We don't know in advance of this exercise what principles will be chosen, although we (and the people in the original position) have some idea of the possibilities. Thus we use agreement in the original position to find out what principles best serve "the general interests and necessities of society." The social contract is thus not an unnecessary runaround.

Rawls says that knowledge of one's own interests is behind the *veil of ignorance* in the original position. This includes one's natural assets and abilities, one's values, and one's place in society. Further, all that is known about the society are general facts. For example, that some principles of justice are needed. That is, the society is not so badly off that cooperative benefits are not possible, nor so well off that cooperation is not necessary. In other words, social cooperation is possible and necessary for those in the society to have a decent life. Finally, knowledge that one has certain psychological peculiarities is also excluded. These are a high propensity to choose very risky alternatives[20] and the propensity to destructive envy. The tendency to go for extreme risk is not appropriate when the choice will affect one's entire life prospects. This exclusion reflects the seriousness of the choice. Also, a person experiencing destructive envy will prefer himself being worse off provided the envied person also does badly. "If I can't have it, neither can he or she," regardless of how much it hurts me or hurts us all. The reason for excluding destructive envy is that if it is in operation, it prevents choices that would be better for all.

We can think of the Second Principle of justice as having been arrived at in the following way: If we don't know who we are in society, then let's have everyone get equal amounts. (This position is *egalitarianism*.) But we know that some inequalities can make everyone better off, for example giving someone really good at making computers (like Michael Dell) the resources to produce them, with the result of better, cheaper computers for everyone. Thus we arrive at the second principle, the Difference Principle: Allow inequalities when they make everyone better off, demonstrated by the fact that the least advantaged person is better off. If destructive envy were allowed in the original position, we could not take advantage of social benefits produced by inequality.[21]

One good way to think about the knowledge restrictions of the original position is to compare them to the knowledge restrictions on jurors in a trial. In both cases we are aiming for a just outcome: In the original position, principles of justice, and in the trial, a just verdict. Bias in the trial situation is minimized by questioning prospective jurors and dismissing those likely to be prejudiced. That is, those likely not to decide on the basis of the evidence presented at the trial are dismissed. During the trial, certain evidence can be excluded if obtained or presented in an unfair way. Note that judges regularly instruct juries to ignore certain statements and evidence if objections to them have been sustained. Juries regularly have no trouble doing this. Therefore, asking us all to ignore certain kinds of knowledge when we are considering what would happen in the original position is not asking us to do something unusual. Most jurors have no trouble with this, and their only qualification is being citizens.

We could object to jury trials in a way parallel to Hume's objection to a social contract. Both sides have the evidence, so why don't we just look at the evidence on both sides and decide on a verdict? The problem with a shortcut in both cases is that the more involved procedures insure that the conclusion is arrived at fairly.

I will take it as given that the first principle of justice, the Greatest Equal Freedom principle, would be chosen as the first priority principle of domestic justice.[22] We next turn to the choice of the Difference Principle as a principle for the distribution of economic goods, over some version of utilitarianism.

For utilitarianism, a clarification is necessary in "the greatest good for the greatest number." The simplest rule would be to take the utility for each person and add them together. However, this simple version has the consequence that society is better if it has more people with the same utility. Even worse, since more people can easily result in less utility for all (traffic jams, air pollution, less food, etc.), this rule could easily result in a larger total utility but somewhat less for each person.[23] The solution is to switch to greatest average utility. The average utility principle would choose the distribution of goods which results in the greatest average utility.[24]

Someone in the original position would choose the average utility principle over the Difference Principle if they considered all possible positions in society equally likely. But there is no reason to assume this, and it could easily have the result that, back in society, many people would be worse off than if the Difference Principle were chosen. If the less advantaged positions were very numerous, many people would not benefit from the higher average.

One significant difference between utilitarianism and Rawls' principles of justice is that utilitarianism does not take individuals seriously and the principles of justice do. Utilitarianism sums utility without considering whose utility it is. In some ways, this is impartial, but it ignores the fact that utility is utility for a person. People aren't indifferent to the fact that someone else gets the utility for no good reason.

Rawls considers the possibility of replacing the second principle with rule utilitarianism with a minimum; in other words, not any value-maximizing economic distribution would be allowed, but only those with an acceptable minimum. For example, the minimum could be "meeting the basic human needs essential for a decent life."[25] (Rawls 2001, 127-128n) Minimum wage legislation might be an example of this approach. Rawls feels that the "social minimum" cannot be clearly enough specified to provide a workable basis for assessing the justice of institutions, and therefore the Difference Principle without a minimum will yield better results. (Rawls 2001, 129-130) But in practice, it is hard to see how it will be any easier to determine whether specific policies have the result that the least well off is made as well off as possible, or whether the social minimum is one that allows an individual to meet basic human needs.

If the acceptable minimum is set by appealing to the Difference Principle, i.e., to make the worst off as well off as possible, then this proposal is merely an application of that principle. It will give the same results, and therefore there is no choice here. If the acceptable minimum is set by considerations independent of those within the Principles of Justice, there are two possible cases: Either the Difference Principle leads to a better outcome for the least advantaged than adopting a minimum, or adopting the Difference Principle leads to a worse outcome for the least advantaged than adopting a minimum. In the first case, clearly one will choose the results of the Difference Principle. And in the second case, where the Difference Principle leads to a worse result than the minimum, the Difference Principle itself requires us to go with the minimum. So there seems to be no harm in implementing the Difference Principle by setting an acceptable minimum. It is in the spirit of the second principle itself, which is to guarantee that no one is worse off than they need be to permit society to function.[26]

Various anti-poverty provisions suggest that the minimum approach may not work as well in practice as the Difference Principle. For example, if a social minimum is implemented by a guaranteed minimum income given as welfare, there may be a disincentive to work as one comes to make more than the minimum. Milton Friedman's negative income tax eliminates this problem, but requires a flat tax on taxpayers of all income. It seems hard to justify not taxing more those with greater ability to pay. The benefit of efficiency in the tax code does not make up for violating the Difference Principle. Earned income credits ameliorate the welfare problem and are more in accord with the Difference Principle than a minimum.[27]

As an illustration, here is how the two main theories of justice might apply to the case of intellectual property within a nation. Suppose the issue is whether to permit noncommercial copying of CDs and videos. A utilitarian would consider the parties involved: The music and video companies on the one hand, and their customers on the other. Then the average greatest expected utility would have to be calculated. At first sight, the less copying permitted, the greater utility received by the entertainment companies. However, if there is less copying, then there is less distribution of a given CD or video, and this can result in lower sales. (When VCRs were introduced and copying was legal, the result was growing sales. With restricted noncommercial sales, and restricted online access to music, sales have fallen.) Then there is the utility for the customer. Directly, utility is a little greater with noncommercial copying in that copies don't have to be bought. Less directly, the customer loses by less available access to music and videos. So for the utilitarian, the issue depends on how much the restricted availability of CDs and video reduces sales for the companies and accessibility for the customer. If restricted availability does not reduce overall utility much, then the greater utility for the companies outweighs the minor extra cost borne by each customer.

To apply the two principles of justice to this case, we first have to remember that they apply to basic institutions. In this case, the basic institution is intellectual property, and the issue of justice is whether the least advantaged is better off with which one of the following rules:

1.   The creator has permanent rights to restrict copying of his creation.
2.   The creator has exclusive rights to copying of his creation for enough time to make it worthwhile for him to create it.
3.   The creator has no exclusive rights to copying of his creation; the novelty of the item should be enough to allow him to gain sufficient reward.[28]

Now we can ask, which of these policies would result in the worst off being best off? Rule 1 will clearly not improve the lot of the worst off, especially compared to the remaining two rules. Rule 2 is probably the choice that would most improve the lot of the worst off. Rule 3 makes it a lot more risky for the creator and would probably discourage creation. Supposing that new creations, especially inventions, tend to improve the lot of all, rule 2 is then the choice.

To complete the analysis using the principles of justice, we ask: Under rule 2, how do we handle noncommercial copying? The US Supreme Court held in 1984 that noncommercial copying was not copyright infringement.[29] Given the purpose of copyright, noncommercial copying does not interfere with the (limited) right to profit from one's creation. Of course, the music companies justify their pogrom against noncommercial copiers strictly on the basis of impact on their profits. Corporations are by their very definition utilitarian. Their stated goal is to maximize value in the form of profits. We will return to this issue in Chapter 8, **The Ethical Status of Globalized Institutions.**

BEYOND DOMESTIC JUSTICE

The principles of justice just discussed apply within a society whose members share cooperative benefits and burdens. These days, they are referred to as principles of *domestic* justice. But what about *transnational* or *global* justice?

There are four basic possibilities for transnational or global justice:

1. *Political realism*, which holds that nations can be just internally (or domestically), but the only ethical principle that applies to and between states is acting in their own self-interest;
2. *Society of societies*, which holds that societies can be bound by agreements of mutual self-interest. Rawls' *Law of Peoples* is a social contract version of this view. (1999b) Rawls allows for some ethical constraints—societies refrain from making war on each other and help each other to achieve stability.
3. *Cosmopolitanism* holds that all humans are essentially one society, and thus principles of justice applying within societies also apply globally. [30] There are utilitarian cosmopolitans such as Peter Singer (2004), who extends utilitarianism within a society to global scope. Social contract cosmopolitans such as Charles Beitz (1979,1999) apply Rawls' two principles of justice globally. Pluralist cosmopolitans such as Thomas Pogge (2002) claim that the same intuitive ethical principles hold at all levels, individual, societal, and global.
4. *Transnational social contracts* both for political international principles between nations and to regulate the global economy. The International Social Contract is akin to Rawls' Law of Peoples. The Global Economic Social Contract is between participants in the global economy.

I will next consider each of these possibilities in turn, noting their suitability for handling ethical issues concerning ethically global institutions. In considering these ethical positions, which apply primarily to institutions, it is worth noting that there is a parallel progression with the development of individual ethics. Individuals accept reasons of self-interest except when following self-interest conflicts with self-interest, allowing the possibility of mutual advantage. For this to happen, a higher-order principle regarded as overriding self-interest must be mutually adopted. This is the basis for individual ethics.

Similarly, when conflicts arise between nations and transnational institutions, higher-order principles need to be adopted to secure mutual advantage.

Here is a brief example of how each of these theories would handle labor standards:

1. A *realist* would hold that each nation has its own labor standards and there are no grounds for interfering with those standards. The economist Jagdish Bhagwati argues that workers prefer working in harsh conditions because it is better than their alternatives, and that labor standards cannot be enforced transnationally. "It will produce chaos," he says. (2007, 178) This observation concerns the practicality of the enforcement of ethical principles. But it could be grounds for no transnational ethical standards, especially in the area of labor standards.

2. A believer in *society of societies*, in particular Rawls in his *Law of Peoples,* holds that members of another society have rather limited ethical duties to aid worse off people in other societies. Because people in different societies don't share benefits and burdens, one society only has the ethical responsibility to help it become a democratic just society. One society doesn't have an ethical responsibility to redistribute its goods to a society which is worse off. Thus, unless labor standards interfere with the ability of a society to become just and democratic, there are no grounds for criticism and certainly grounds only for aid to that country and not intervention.

3. *Cosmopolitans* (from the Greek 'kosmopolites' or citizens of the world) claim that there are transnational ethical standards. Labor standards should accord with global principles of justice. Depending on the particular cosmopolitan theory, these principles will be intuitive, or utilitarian, or make the worst off globally as well off as possible. In any case, the labor standards will apply to all human beings on the planet.

4. *Transnational social contracts* would derive labor standards from principles of justice applying to participants in the global economy, rather than all human beings on the planet.

Finally, there are ethical principles concerning conflicts between human needs and the environment. Many of the relevant issues are discussed in Chapter 14, **IT-enabled globalization and the environment**. There is again a choice of principles, and which are chosen depends on high-level beliefs about human technology and its relation to nature. If one believes that technology can correct its own errors in a timely manner and that a policy of unregulated technological progress is most conducive to overall human progress, then technological progress becomes the ultimate value and touchstone for policy. If one believes human technology has built-in unanticipated conflicts with the ecosystem, then a policy of minimum mutilation of the ecosystem is called for. The relevant point here is that the principles governing the overall utilization of technology, because of the far-reaching nature of that utilization, have to be on a higher level even than principles of justice and even those of principles of transnational justice

REFERENCES

Arrow, K. (1951). *Social choice and individual values.* New York: John Wiley & Sons.

Beitz, C. (1999). *Political theory and international relations.* Princeton, NJ: Princeton University Press.

Bello, W. (2008, December 24). The coming capitalist consensus. *Foreign Policy in Focus.*

Binmore, K. (1994). *Playing fair: Game theory and the social contract.* Cambridge, MA: The MIT Press.

California Office of the Attorney General. (2009). *Improved fuel economy standards.* Retrieved March 26, 2009 from http://www.ag.ca.gov/globalwarming/fuelstandards.php

Digital Divide Network Staff. (2003). *Benton foundation.* Retrieved June 19, 2004 from http://www. digitaldividenetwork.org

Hobbes, T. (1999). *Leviathan.* Retrieved May 12, 2004 from http://darkwing.uoregon.edu/~rbear/hobbes/leviathan.html

Hume, D. (1985). Of the original contract. In E.F. Miller (Ed.), *Essays moral and political.* Indianapolis, IN: Liberty Classics.

Kaiser Family Foundation. (2004). *Children, the digital divide, and federal policy.* Retrieved July 7, 2008, from www.kff.org/entmedia/upload/Children-The-Digital-Divide-And-Federal-Policy-Issue-Brief.pdf

Locke, J. (2002). *The second treatise of government.* Retrieved from http://www.constitution.org/jl/2ndtreat.htm

Mill, J. S. (2004). *Utilitarianism.* Retrieved May 20, 2004 from http://etext.library.adelaide.edu.au/m/mill/john_stuart/m645u/

Pogge, T. (2002). *World poverty and human rights.* Cambridge, England: Polity Press.

Rawls, J. (1993). *Political liberalism.* New York: Columbia University Press.

Rawls, J. (1999a). *A theory of justice* (rev. ed.). Cambridge, MA: Harvard University Press

Rawls, J. (1999b). *The law of peoples.* Cambridge, MA: Harvard University Press.

Rawls, J. (1999c). Outline of a decision procedure for ethics. In S. Freeman (ed.), *Collected papers.* Cambridge, MA: Harvard University Press.

Rawls, J. (2001). *Justice as fairness: A restatement.* Cambridge, MA: Harvard University Press.

Rousseau, J. (2004). *The social contract.* Retrieved May 10, 2004 from http://www.constitution.org/jjr/socon_01.htm

Sen, A. (1999). *Development as freedom.* New York: Random House.

Singer, P. (2004). *One world* (2nd ed.) New Haven, CT: Yale University Press.

Taglang, K. (2001). A low-tech, low-cost tool for the homeless. *Digital Divide Network.* Retrieved June 6, 2004, from http://www.digitaldividenetwork.org/content/stories/

U.S. Department of Commerce. (2000). *Falling through the Net.* Retrieved June 19, 2004, from http://www.ntia.gov/ntiahome/fftn00/confer

Waldron, J. (1986). John Rawls and the social minimum. *Journal of Applied Philosophy*, 3.

Walzer, M. (2007). *Thinking politically.* New Haven, CT: Yale University Press.

Wikipedia. (2008). *Negative income tax*. Retrieved June 20, 2008, from http://en.wikipedia.com/Negative_Income_Tax

ENDNOTES

[1]   It would be an *academic* exercise (i.e., pointless) to try to determine whether a human being completely outside of any society would need ethics. So much of what defines us as human beings would be missing (especially language) that it would be hard even to imagine such an individual's life. If this individual had cooperative interactions with anything else (plants, animals), there would be a possibility for something like ethical principles. Castaways like Robinson Crusoe aren't exceptions because they were raised in society and thoroughly socialized.

[2]   Mill 1868 is the classic reference.

[3]   Two recent Nobel-prize-winning economists are exceptions: Amartya Sen, who worked with Rawls. Joseph Stiglitz mentions Rawls' theory approvingly. (Stiglitz 2007)

[4]   Rawls calls this theory *intuitionism* but says that pluralism would also be a good name. See Rawls 1999b sec 7.

[5]   See **Chapter 4**, "Reflective Equilibrium"

[6]   The original position is like other positions in which some of our knowledge and interests are deliberately disregarded, for example, being a juror.

[7]   Others disagree. Political theorist Michael Walzer calls the view that talent and luck should not influence the principles of justice "[a]great mistake" but unfortunately does not say why. (Walzer 2007, 304)

[8]   Top executives in corporations getting enormous salaries justify it by achievement. However, observers such as Warren Buffett and the late management guru Peter Drucker disagree. They feel these people are giving themselves large salaries because they can. Certainly top executives in Japan and Europe have made comparable achievements without huge salaries.

[9]   This insight is from Rawls' discussion of perfectionism. See Rawls 1999a, 288-289.

[10]   Rawls makes this clarification in his later *Justice as Fairness* (2001, 14). He explicitly denies that his theory of justice is a part of ethics; it is rather, he claims, political philosophy. My distinction between ethics and morality makes Rawls' denial unnecessary. The theory of justice is part of ethics as principles of cooperation. However, it is not part of morality.

[11]   The Arrow Theorem of Kenneth Arrow (1951) shows that under reasonable conditions, it is impossible to derive a social preference from individual preferences.

[12]   Rawls includes fair equality of opportunity under the second principle, although he himself includes it with the freedoms of the first principle when discussing how to apply the Difference Principle. See Rawls 1999a, 82.

[13]   This condition is known by economists as *Pareto optimality.* For Rawls' discussion of Pareto optimality and the Difference Principle, see Rawls 1999a, sections 12 and 13.

[14]   The experiences of Soviet Russian and China before its economic revolution should make clear that central planning as an economic policy is a disaster.

[15]   The Community Voice Mail project discussed by Taglang 2001 would be a step in this direction. In Community Voice Mail (CVM), a CVM Director distributes the voicemail boxes to hundreds

of agencies across a community; the agencies in turn provide [homeless] clients with personalized, 7-digit phone numbers that can be accessed from any touch-tone phone, 24 hours a day.

[16]   The savings may also be due to coerced pricing agreements with suppliers and substandard wages for employees.

[17]   See Shirley Svorny, "'Inclusionary Zoning' Will Not Work."(San Fernando Valley) *Daily News*, April 21, 2004.

[18]   Rawls 1999a, **Section 35**, "Toleration of the Intolerant."

[19]   Ken Binmore (1994) requires the social contract to be between actual people and so Hume's objection applies to him. By having the social contract be between actual people, he also eliminates the use of maximin reasoning as the basis for Rawls' Principles of Justice.

[20]   This is probably an addiction to adrenaline rushes.

[21]   Although destructive envy is not uncommon in society as it is, I don't think it is pervasive enough to require us to accept worse results for members of society.

[22]   In the US constitution, the Bill of Rights contains much of the content of the Greatest Equal Freedom principle. So the first principle should be noncontroversial.

[23]   This may have happened in Los Angeles and other southwestern cities.

[24]   Measuring the well-being of a society by gross national product (GNP) per capita would be an application of the average utility principle.

[25]   Rawls attributes this formulation to Jeremy Waldron (1986).

[26]   Rawls (2001) argues that people will be more committed in terms of justice if the difference principle is adopted without a minimum, but I don't find his argument convincing.

[27]   See Wikipedia, "Negative Income Tax."

[28]   This was actually the popular conservative position in England in the 19th century.

[29]   U.S. Supreme Court SONY CORP. v. UNIVERSAL CITY STUDIOS, INC., 464 U.S. 417 (1984) (FindLaw Legal News http://news.findlaw.com)

[30]   This account is based on one given in Wikipedia, "Global Justice."

Chapter 6
Political Realism and the Society of Societies

In this chapter, I examine two theories of transnational ethics: Political Realism and the Society of Societies. The first theory, Political Realism, denies the meaningfulness of transnational ethics. Proponents of Political Realism note that states act in their own interest, and there is no order or principle governing those states other than their own self-interest. I will discuss the views of an important proponent of Political Realism of this kind, the late political theorist Hans Morgenthau. (1993) An interesting variant, which I will call Relativist Realism, holds that there are no transnational principles which supersede the principles of any given society because the different principles of different societies ought to be respected. This version of Political Realism has been developed extensively by the political theorist Michael Walzer. (2007) I will discuss the pros and cons of these two views shortly.

Our second theory, which I call the Society of Societies, is John Rawls' social contract version of transnational ethics. Rawls calls his version "the Law of Peoples" to avoid the implication that the parties to a transnational social contract are states or nations.[1] (1999b) The name "the Law of Peoples" itself makes Rawls' point that the participants in a transnational social contract are not states or nations, but *peoples.* From the perspective of a social contract, states or nations gain their authority from the consent of the people under that contract and have no ethical authority without it.

The final theory of transnational ethics we will examine, *cosmopolitanism,* will be discussed in the next chapter. I will discuss three versions of cosmopolitanism, a pluralist version with a set of principles

DOI: 10.4018/978-1-60566-922-9.ch006

justified by intuition, a social contract version, and a utilitarian version. All three have as their starting point the idea that for ethical purposes all human beings belong to one global society.

These cosmopolitan theories, and to a lesser extent Rawls' theory, unfortunately almost totally discount any ethical relevance for nations or nation-states. At very least, this makes these theories almost impossible to apply until current nation-states fade away. The omission of nation states also betrays a serious misunderstanding of the social structure to which transnational ethics must apply. When I began examining these theories, I had not expected to find these inadequacies. Consequently, they may be less helpful than originally expected in formulating a viable theory of transnational ethics.

POLITICAL REALISM

Political Realism maintains that states act in their own interest, and there is no order or principle governing those states other than their own self-interest. Thus states are in a state of nature with respect to each other, in the terminology of the early social contract philosopher Thomas Hobbes. (1651) Hobbes describes the state of nature as a war of all against all. Clearly considerations of mutual advantage do occur to states, and agreements called *treaties* occur often in the dealing of states with each other. But realists hold that when a state's interests are no longer served, a treaty can be ignored. It has to be conceded that the actual behavior of states does closely approximate Political Realism. And there also is currently no principle acknowledged by states that prevents them from making war at their sole discretion, as recently demonstrated in Vietnam and Iraq. Although ethical principles, unlike legal principles, do not have to have punishments attached, there should at least be an ethical community which can at least register disapproval of the behavior. And there does not seem to be.

Political Realism is not a skeptical or relativist doctrine. Political Realists from Machiavelli (1515) in the Renaissance to Hans Morgenthau in the 20th century believe that the correct ethical thing for rulers to do is to be guardians of the interests of the states they govern, and that in order to serve those interests, they need to set aside conventional individual morality. Morgenthau states

. . . the state has no right to let its moral disapprobation of the infringement of liberty get in the way of successful political action, itself inspired by the moral principle of national survival. (1993, 12)

Although nation-states are to be judged on the ways in which they create and use power, there are ethical elements:

In the last analysis, then, the power of a nation . . . resides in the quality of its government. A government that is truly representative . . . in the sense of being able to translate the inarticulate convictions and aspirations of the people into international objectives and policies, has the best chance to marshal the national energies in support of those objectives and policies. . . free men fight better than slaves. . . (Morgenthau 1993, 154)

And there are ethical constraints in the relations of nations with other nations. Nations agree to protect human life in times of peace. Assassination is no longer a common political tool, as it was in Renaissance Venice.[2] Mass extermination is not acceptable as a tool of policy, as in Nazi Germany and for the Romans with Carthage,[3] even if necessary for a "higher purpose."

Around 1650, war went from being a contest between all inhabitants to a contest between armed forces of states. From about 1875, international treaties including the Hague conventions required prisoners of war to be treated humanely, with the Red Cross as guarantor. Protest within countries began to be treated as evidence of moral conscience rather than criminal acts. From about 1900, avoidance of war itself became an aim of international policy, as in the Hague Peace Conferences, the League of Nations, the Briand-Kellogg pact of 1928, and the United Nations. War came to be regarded as a natural catastrophe or evil deed of another, not as an instrument of policy.[4] (Morgenthau 1993, 224)

Morgenthau finds that this international morality has weakened since the end of the First World War. Aerial weapons have made the mass destruction of civilian productivity and morale acceptable war aims. Opposition of nations is no longer within a shared framework but instead between each nation's claims to universal validity. Morgenthau feels that what he calls *nationalistic universalism* has done serious damage to previous international morality. Nationalistic universalism is the view that the ideology and principles of your nation ought to be adopted by all countries. Even Woodrow Wilson's desire to "make the world safe for democracy" (now continued in grotesque fashion by using aggressive force supposedly to turn countries into democracies) are instances of this tendency. Morgenthau notes

The problem at the heart of this issue is …[whether] it is morally just and intellectually tenable to apply liberal democratic principles to states that, for a number of reasons, are impervious to them." (1993, 246)

So, although Morgenthau believes that relations between states need to be analyzed in terms of power, he also believes there are transnational moral principles. Not only that, but he also believes that the only way war can be prevented is through a supranational power having sovereignty over existing states. Morgenthau notes that there are a number of existing transnational institutions, but that they do not have the ability to enforce significant transnational ethical principles. There is an inherent contradiction between national sovereignty and the effectiveness of an international organization, (1993, 325) as I noted at the beginning of Chapter 2, **Current Ethically Globalized Institutions.**

Peace and order are relatively stable within states and unstable in relations between states, Morgenthau claims. As Hobbes noted, supreme power within a state is responsible for peace and order within the state. So international peace and order seem to require supreme power wielded by a world state. In the domestic case, all people are "embedded within the densely woven fabric of the national community." (1993, 336) This fabric includes loyalties to the state/nation above other groups, an expectation of justice in adjudicating claims, and protection of nation from destruction without and disruption within as overriding lesser loyalties.

Morgenthau has an extensive and subtle discussion of the differences between domestic and international justice in attempts to leave the state of nature for stability and peace. Some relevant aspects of domestic states as compared to an international state are:

1. Although justice in the abstract is no problem in either domestic or international circumstances, when conflicting claims arise, there need to be mechanisms of what Rawls calls "public reason," such mechanisms as public opinion, elections, lobbying, review boards, and a mutually accepted legal system. These mechanisms exist in the domestic but not the international case.
2. In domestic society, organized violence is usually against individuals. Even then social pressures usually render police violence infrequent.
3. The domestic state is a compulsory organization of society, that is, a legal order determining when society can employ violence to preserve order. It provides legal continuity, is a source of benefits and burdens, and is the object of loyalty as important as family or church.

4.   The domestic state is necessary but not sufficient for peace. This is shown by the existence of civil wars, revolutions, and coups d'etat, when factors enabling peace disintegrate. (1993, 340).

How would a world government handle these aspects? Morgenthau notes that no society exists with the same extent as a possible world state. It is hard to see, for example, how states would acquiesce in decisions by a world state, however justly arrived at, to radically alter immigration quotas. (A world state would have to regulate immigration.) Would Americans accept an edict requiring acceptance of two million Mexican immigrants? Or would they acquiesce in agricultural subsidy policies detrimental to US farm interests? The inability of the US to eliminate agricultural subsidies which have severely damaged agriculture and society in developing countries, even when the WTO demands their elimination, shows how far we are from a world state. Morgenthau holds that there can be no world state or society without a world community willing and able to accept and support it. (1993, 343)

There are some successful transnational institutions such as agreements on internationally handling mail (the Universal Postal Union) and airline flights. But there is no international legal system with a memory of case precedents. The international courts do not consider previous decisions as precedents. The assumption of UN organizations such as UNESCO that greater understanding and familiarity of nations will build a world community is, Morgenthau believes, wrong. Wars have often been fought with very clear understanding of both sides of the other.

Morgenthau believes that a world state is essential for preventing war. He is especially concerned about the necessity of avoiding nuclear holocaust. Although nuclear holocaust has not been a prominent issue since the disintegration of the Soviet Union in 1991, it is still a problem. Nuclear stockpiles are still many times larger than they need be for any recognizable national purpose. And scientists point out that it is a theorem of probability that, given that there is a finite chance that nuclear weapons will be used, they will go off some day.[5] (Lyttle 2005)

Yet Morgenthau notes that the essentials for a world state are simply lacking. The peoples of the world are currently unwilling to accept a world government.[6] They would be unwilling to maintain it, because that would entail eliminating the sovereignty of the nation state.

Morgenthau finally hopes that these conditions can be changed. He believes the essential world state can come to be through the "peace-preserving and community-building processes of diplomacy. For the world state to be more than a dim vision, the accommodating processes of diplomacy, mitigating and minimizing conflicts, must be revived." (1993, 389) Thus for Morgenthau diplomacy is the international substitute for domestic mechanisms for resolving conflicts.

For Morgenthau, what rulers of nations ought to do is to best serve the interests of the nation. The best interest of nations is not always achieved by getting one's own way regardless of what the other person is doing. Cooperative benefits are possible for nations as well as individuals. In addition to such international cooperative benefits as an international postage system and an international airline system, there have been conventions to make war more humane. But such agreements are fragile because there is no mechanism for dealing with violators or enforcing penalties.

For Morgenthau, transnational ethics is largely determined by the nature of the state and its power with respect to other states.. As I mentioned earlier, cosmopolitan theories--and to a lesser extent Rawls' theory--discount any constructive ethical relevance for nations or nation-states. There are reasons for taking a negative ethical view of states and their actions. The French philosopher Blaise Pascal wrote the following:

Why do you kill me? What! Do you not live on the other side of the water? If you lived on this side, my friend, I should be an assassin, and it would be unjust to slay you in this manner. But since you live on the other side, I am a hero, and it is just. . . . A strange justice that is bounded by a river! Truth on this side of the Pyrenees, error in the other side. (Pascal 1670, sec. V)

In any case, Political Realism is clearly not a workable theory for ethically globalized institutions. Political Realism is a theory of the relation between *states,* not globalized institutions. And we have already seen that globalized institutions impact the well-being of those who live in states. It remains to be seen, however, whether principles higher than self-interest can be formulated which govern these institutions, and whether there is an appropriate community which accepts them. The contribution of Political Realism to an ethical theory of ethically globalized institutions lies in its clear account of the role of states in international ethics.

RELATIVIST REALISM

Michael Walzer's variant of Political Realism holds that ethical principles should not take priority over state power because societies have different ethical standards and those standards should be respected. Walzer states that there is ultimately no

...one law, one justice, one correct understanding of the good life or the good society or the good regime ... If we think of justice as a social invention, variously made, one more product of human creativity, ... What reasons do we have to expect a singular and universal justice?" (Walzer 2007, 184-5)

Walzer thus accords justice exactly the same status as what Rawls calls *comprehensive* doctrines, such as religious doctrines and individual moral principles. In Rawls' theory of (domestic) justice, people in the original position or in society are not expected to be in agreement about such matters--everyone expects there to be a plurality of religious, philosophical, and ethical views. (Rawls 2001, section 11) Additionally, for Rawls the conditions of social cooperation giving rise to justice very definitely include complete individual freedom to define one's own conception of the good life.

Rawls' justification of the principles of justice is what would be chosen--universally--as the best solution of principles to govern fair social cooperation. Walzer clearly denies that such principles exist, and the best we can have is a diversity of principles suited to different societies. But it is not clear what it can even mean to say that a set of principles of justice is suited or not suited to that society. That would involve a judgement from outside the society. And, on Walzer's view, the notion of *progress* or *development* of a society in becoming more just is empty. We believe that our own US society became more just when slavery was abolished or women were given the right to vote. Or that South African society became more just when apartheid was abolished. These claims no longer have meaning unless there is a transnational concept of justice which applies across societies.

Walzer's relativist views may stem in part from modish postmodernism.[7] But the problem with postmodernism is that it attenuates meaning and truth to such a degree that it is hard to understand why postmodernists themselves are even still speaking or writing. Discourse is degraded to the level of a flock of seagulls, as the ethologist Konrad Lorenz describes them. All gulls make a certain sound when they fly in a specific direction. A few gulls make a different sound, and if it catches on, the flock changes direction. (Lorenz 1952) The various possible directions and signals for them are fixed, presumably, by evolution. Our more varied signals are the result of social practice, but on a postmodern view, their employment, mainly to change the direction of academic discourse, has no more meaning.

Walzer's relativism is not merely descriptive--he is not just pointing out the fact that different societies have different standards. He is in effect saying that we ought to allow them to have different standards. His view is therefore itself a theory of transnational ethics and therefore self-contradictory. It is difficult for relativists to avoid self-contradiction if they attempt to say anything. Insofar as there is a blanket acceptance of selected anti-Western principles, I don't think they are in reflective equilibrium[8] with our judgements of social judgements. For example, to say that it is cultural imperialism for women be treated equally makes realist relativism itself an immoral theory. And when postmodernists sometimes claim equal rights and democracy are "Western values," it is hard to understand what is wrong with this, given their own principles.

Does the fact that some societies have inhumane labor standards exempt them from criticism or change?[9] It may very well be true for a variety of reasons that sweatshop workers have no better alternative. But do the employing companies really require conditions that harsh in order to survive and prosper? And, ethically, should they? It needs to be remembered that decent working conditions came about in the developed countries only after great strife with corporations--which survived quite well.

Rather than take Walzer's theory as a blanket theory applying to all customs in all societies, it would be better to recognize that there may be an ethical case for preserving some differing cultural standards. The question is which cultural standards, and what principles to apply. Walzer himself suggests there are "minimal" standards which apply across societies, but it is impossible to tell what they are, because he attaches qualifications to every potential standard. (209) Walzer is impressed with what he terms the "sheer heterogeneity" of human experience and feels that ethical principles are constantly being created and revised. Both claims are dubious. How consistent with "sheer heterogeneity" is the fact that the social life and ethics of stone-age people in New Guinea are completely understandable to us? (See *Living with the Kombai,* Anstice and Steeds, 2008) And basic principles of trust and keeping agreements are "constantly being created and revised" only by criminal sociopaths.

Walzer rejects an attempt by Stuart Hampshire (1983) to make a distinction between ethics rooted in principles for cooperative behavior and morality located in particular cultural customs. (My very similar distinction in Chapter 4 between ethics and morality is the basis for much of this book.) But without such a distinction, he cannot even specify the society which is supposedly free to create its own morality.

As we will see in the next chapter, cosmopolitans reject any ethical significance for nations or national societies. Of course, for Walzer, this is completely wrong because ethics occurs only within a society. But his horror of universal principles makes him wary even of giving a definition of nation: "There is no universal model for a national culture." (212) Yet he finally does give one: "A nation is a historic community, connected to a meaningful place, enacting and revising a way of life, aiming at political and cultural self-determination." (214) Of course, *self*-determination presupposes that we know what the "self" is, whether nation or community or culture. And Walzer is loath to say anything general about what a community or culture is.

In Walzer's own terms, there is probably no way out of the self-referential bog he has landed himself in. But there is a useful concept here which figures in our ethical judgements. It does matter to us that we have a nationality and Walzer is right in assigning some significance to groups that share "a wide range of cultural artifacts: language, religion, historical memory, the calendar and its holidays, the sense of place, a specific experience of art and music." (203) But most of these are cultural interest groups and it is hard to put much ethical weight on them.[10] Our economic ties and the social and political institutions implementing them are instead the characteristics with ethical consequences. We regard our well-being and freedom as bound up with the well-being and freedom of our countrymen. The other cultural artifacts often accompany these economic and political ties, but they don't have the ethical weight of those ties.

We will return to the issue of the ethical status of nationhood in a global society in Chapter 8, **The Ethical Status of Globalized Institutions**. It is a central thesis of the cosmopolitan theories of global justice we will discuss in the next chapter that belonging to a nation has little or no ethical significance.

For Walzer, there can be no transnational ethics--except for the completely self-contradictory transnational principle that it is wrong to have transnational ethical principles. For Walzer, there can also be no international society. If it did exist, it would require a universal state. And this state would be imposed, to the detriment of all national societies. It would require us to "disregard or repress patterns of cultural creativity and patterns of mutual attachment which we ought to value." (215) So ultimately the unit which Walzer wants to value seems to be the "culture," an abstract pattern of traits and behaviors. Why this particular entity should be the basis of what we value is not obvious.

In any case, contrary to Walzer, since there are principles which allow us to judge whether a society is just or manifestly unjust, there seems to be no reason to respect all standards in other societies just because they are different societies.

SOCIETY OF SOCIETIES

The society of societies position holds that there is an ethical community of societies. Rawls in his later work *The Law of Peoples* (Rawls 1999b), develops a social contract for international justice which differs from the social contract for domestic justice. Principles of international justice are chosen, not by the political officials of each nation or nation state, but by *peoples*. On a social contract view, members of a given social group are the source of state and national authority, not the other way around. (Rawls 1999b, 25-27) Rawls constructs a second social contract to govern relations between peoples. The principles chosen he calls the Law of Peoples. The basis for the second social contract is that the representatives of any society must be able to agree to principles without knowing how their society would be favored or disfavored by those principles. Many principles that Rawls claims would be chosen to regulate relations between societies are analogous to principles that would be chosen by individuals to regulate their own societies. First, they honor human rights, respect each others freedom, and respect cooperative agreements made between them. Second, peoples do not intervene in each others affairs and only make war in self-defense. (These principles are parallel to the Greatest Equal Freedom Principle). Third, peoples have a duty to assist other people living under unfavorable conditions.[11] (This principle is parallel to the Difference Principle) (Rawls 1999b, 37)

The Law of Peoples, as Rawls formulates it, respects the integrity of individual societies. Not only is there to be no authority over all peoples; but the analogue of the Difference Principle, the duty to assist "burdened societies" (Rawls' term for people living under unfavorable conditions) is much more limited than the Difference Principle. One society is permitted to be a lot better off than another. The only duty is to help less fortunate societies to attain what is necessary to maintain a just democratic society. Justice between societies does not require redistribution to make to least well off society as well off as possible.

(Rawls 1999b sections 15 and 16) Rawls argues that the peoples' representatives will not choose to trade off economic benefits and burdens between peoples. Rawls says:

... no people organized by its government is prepared to count, as a first principle, the benefits for another people as outweighing the hardships imposed on itself. (Rawls 1999b, 40. Emphasis in original.)

In other words, although we can have agreements between societies (and parties within those societies) which redistribute benefits and burdens, we must first be assured that the internal arrangements within those societies are just. It doesn't count toward the justice of institutions in the U.S. to point to our good work in Afghanistan. And conversely, it doesn't ameliorate injustice in Afghanistan to point to our contribution to improving the lot of the least advantaged in the U. S. So the justice of transnational redistribution of benefits and burdens is necessarily a *secondary* matter, to be considered against a background of justly functioning institutions on the home front.

Cosmopolitans find this replacement for the difference principle too weak. They claim that ethics requires massive redistribution of wealth to end poverty in the poorest nations. Merely giving limited aid to poor societies is just not enough, ethically speaking. As we will see, they are treating a world society as something that already exists.

Although the United States was a model for the Principles of Justice as a social contract of free and equal people within a society, it unfortunately fails as a model for the Law of Peoples as a social contract of free and equal societies. In the case of the recent war with Iraq, it has abandoned the principle of the Law of Peoples concerning war. If we accept the principles contained in the Law of Peoples as ethical principles, then war is justified only in self-defense. It follows that the Iraq War is unethical. It is grotesque to propose that destroying the infrastructure of a country, as in Iraq, has much to do with helping them. In any case, helping a country cannot be an excuse for violating the first two principles of respecting freedom and only making war in self-defense.

TYPES OF SOCIETIES

The social contract establishing the Law of Peoples initially assumes that the societies taking part in the society of societies are just or nearly just societies committed to the principles of domestic justice. Rawls thinks that the second social contract among peoples would hold even for some types of societies that do not accept the domestic principles of justice. These societies are capable of participating in undertakings for the mutual benefit of theirs and other societies, even though they do not fully comply with the principles of justice. Obviously this is right--we don't want to give up the potential benefit of dealing with other societies even if they don't fully meet our domestic standards of justice. A current example would be China. We would hardly expect it to be unethical to deal with China.

Rawls distinguishes several types of non-just societies: Decent peoples, outlaw states, burdened societies, and benevolent absolutisms. It is not easy to understand what Rawls means by "decent peoples." He defines them by a complex and detailed set of conditions, but refuses to give any further basis for those conditions. He regards the concept of "decent" as applied to a people as parallel to the concept of "reasonable." Further, it is not clear why he needs the concept of a decent people for his overall theory. The best I can make of it is that decent peoples are multiethnic or multireligious states with a dominant group which accords lesser rights of public participation to non-dominant groups. Possibly an Islamic republic respecting the human rights of non-Muslims, such as Pakistan. Or Israel: Non-Jews cannot be married in Israel, although they can vote. Holding public office is restricted to those who affirm the Jewish state. (Israel - Basic Law 1987)

The other types of non-just societies are outlaw states, burdened societies, and benevolent absolutisms. Outlaw states are states that refuse to comply with the Law of Peoples, especially with respect to waging war. Societies acknowledging the Law of Peoples do not tolerate outlaw states. Burdened states are those whose historical, economic, and/or social circumstances make it impossible for them to be just or decent. Just societies have a duty to help these societies become just. Benevolent absolutisms honor the human rights of their citizens, but give them no participation in political decisions. They have a right to war in self-defense. Rawls is silent on how they are otherwise to be treated by those in the Law of Peoples, but the same reasoning for decent societies should apply. As long as they respect the Law of People, cooperative arrangements for mutual benefit seem both possible and desirable.

These distinctions between types of states are clearly intended to determine which states are candidates for full or partial participation in the Society of Peoples. That is, they agree to abide by the Law of Peoples in order to avail themselves of the benefits of cooperation between states such as trade. The society of peoples is set up by a different social contract than the social contract that establishes the internal domestic principles of justice. So, thinking only of cooperative benefits from relations between states, it should be only the behavior of states in relating to each other (their international relations and foreign policy) that matters for the Society of Peoples, and not how just they are internally.

One of Rawls' types of states, the outlaw state, is defined by its international behavior. It rejects the principles of the Law of Peoples, themselves mainly concerned with international behavior. The one principle which is both internal and external is to respect human rights. The other types of states are defined by features of their internal organization: Decent peoples do not fully honor human rights or allow full political participation to all groups. Burdened societies have internal social and economic problems which prevent them from being internally just. And benevolent absolutisms honor human rights but do not allow full political participation.

So, still thinking in terms of cooperative benefits between states, what is the basis for including the principle of honoring human rights in the Law of Peoples and requiring it for membership in the Society of Peoples? In practice, countries such as China that do not honor human rights are granted full rights in the international community. Rawls has an extensive discussion of how reality differs from the precepts of the Law of Peoples, which I will return to shortly. The answer to the question of the role of human rights in the Law of Peoples is different. Honoring human rights would be chosen in the original position for the Law of Peoples because the parties choosing are representatives of *peoples* not states. Obviously if representatives of dictatorships or Islamic theocracies or communist states had a voice, the principle of respecting human rights would not be chosen.

A *people,* as Rawls defines it, is the group that gives the state its authority. In practice, it would be governed by a nearly just constitutional democracy, share common goals and feelings, and be committed to justice. A state is concerned with power. A people is concerned with security and preserving the freedom of their institutions. (1999b, 29) For a social contract theory based on consent, something like Rawls' conception of peoples must be the basis. Consent of despots or dictators would be meaningless.

Nevertheless, Rawls' way of proceeding seems to give just constitutional democracies, or at least societies that honor human rights, privileged places in actual international society. Rawls notes that states exist which are not almost just and which do not honor human rights. They may not suffer from unfavorable conditions and they may not intend to attack their neighbors. For Rawls, they are nevertheless outlaw states because they violate human rights. They may be subject to intervention "in severe cases." (1999b, 90n1) Rawls' example of a severe case would be a society driven by slavery and human sacrifice. Even though they are no threat internationally, he would exclude them from the international cooperative benefits of the Society of Peoples. He suggests appealing to the benefits they could receive if they honored human rights. If this doesn't work, sanctions could be imposed. And, in "egregious" cases, if sanctions don't work, intervention by force would be justified. (1999b, 93-94n6)

Rawls recognizes that in practice, there is and has been intervention by democracies in other countries. National security can be a subterfuge for "monopolistic and oligarchic interests" seeking economic expansion. But according to Rawls, a people (or its state) has no claim of justice for non-intervention unless it honors human rights. (1999b 92) This seems incorrect. Even though a commitment to human rights is not just another Western comprehensive doctrine, and even though such a commitment is rightly enshrined in Article I of the Universal Declaration of Human Rights, yet as Hans Morgenthau notes,

[to] know that nations are subject to the moral law is one thing, while to pretend to know with certainty what is good and evil in the relations among nations is quite another. There is a world of difference between the belief that all nations stand under [ethical] judgement . . . ., and the blasphemous conviction that God is always on one's side and that what one wills oneself cannot fail to be [right]. (1993, 13)

In other words, who is to judge that intervention is called for in unjust states? Given the real possibility of duplicitous or egregiously incorrect judgements on the part of the most developed states, a casual and blanket permission for intervention does not seem ethically appropriate. Given the history of past and current US intervention, it seems best to me to limit intervention in another state to self-defense and genocidal behavior. The war in Iraq has killed as of this writing in 2008 perhaps one million Iraqis, created two million refugees, and wreaked untold havoc on the physical and social infrastructure of the country. How can this possibly be an improvement over the admittedly brutal dictatorship of Saddam Hussein? Yet Rawls' views on intervention would allow the possibility of such intervention.

US military men have told me that they think their higher ethical purpose is to spread democracy around the world by force. Such people regard the Iraq war as entirely justified, as well as the numerous American military interventions over the years. Rawls' position that intervention can be justified to rectify injustice allows such claims. It is not only the empire-building neoconservatives of the Project for a New American Century[12] who want America to dominate the world by military force. It is the American military on a crusade to bring democracy to the rest of the world by whatever means necessary.

Rawls discusses a number of American interventions unfavorably including the US overthrow of democracies in Chile, Guatemala, Iran, and Nicaragua. He notes that the covert economic reasons behind these actions did not justify intervention. (1999b, 53-54) But, given that it has proven so easy to invoke promoting democracy as a subterfuge for invasion, and in the absence of a neutral international institution to judge the justice of particular proposed interventions, it would be best to limit ethically justified intervention to self-defense or genocidal activity.

Also, Rawls' exclusion of states which do not honor human rights from the Society of Peoples, although well-motivated, has unrealistic consequences in the present world. The anomaly is, of course, China. Rawls seems to have expected less-developed states to be lured into the circle of human-rights-respecting nations by the prospect of improved economic conditions. China, instead, kept its authoritarian communist political structure while granting great economic freedom. In effect, it followed the Difference Principle in making the worst off better off, but without adopting the Greatest Equal Liberty

Principle. China has achieved the greatest reduction in poverty in history in a short time span. (Stiglitz 2003, 182-3) The 2008 demonstrations in connection with the Olympics may be the right course of action, to hold Chinese violations of human rights up for scrutiny. But no one is thinking about economic sanctions on China or sending soldiers to Tibet, nor should they be.

In another country with human rights deficits, namely Cuba, sanctions have been in place for over 40 years. Although (to some extent because of the US sanctions) economic growth has not been very good, some quality of life indicators are very positive. Cubans have a significantly greater life expectancy than US citizens and the infant mortality rate is lower than in the US. (World Health Organization 2005) There doesn't seem any consistent reason for applying sanctions to one communist country and not to another, except for tradition.

The case from Chapter 1 of Yahoo's releasing information about Chinese dissidents to the Chinese government illustrates the incompleteness of Rawls' approach. China, because of persistent failures to honor human rights, is an outlaw state in Rawls' typology. Therefore, members of the Society of Peoples should not be having economic relations with China. The ethical fault lies with Yahoo and all those other companies that do business with China, with fault to be shared by those states in the Society of Peoples who permitted and enabled relations with China. And what about the dissidents? They sued Yahoo in US Courts and Yahoo settled. The dissidents and Yahoo's policies are simply completely outside the range of ethical considerations of Rawls' Law of Peoples.

For Rawls, the Society of States is an ethical ideal. As such, it has two connected major limitations: It deals only with relations between peoples as represented by states; and it deals only with the actions of peoples that respect human rights. Samuel Freeman notes that

... global capitalism has created ways to elude political controls by the world's governments. ... part of the problem is that there is no global structure to deal with it. Perhaps some additions need to be made to Rawls' Law of Peoples to deal with this .... (2006, 258)

But tacking on principles on a nation by nation basis will not help. There is a *de facto* global transnational economic and political structure. The problem is that there are no settled ethical principles or principles of justice governing the entities that belong to this structure, most importantly transnational corporations. Further, the relations between all states (or their peoples) must be considered in formulating any transnational principles. The cosmopolitan theories discussed in the next chapter are one attempt to provide such principles.

REFERENCES

Anstice, M., & Steeds, O. (2008). *The lost tribes: Living with the Kombai.* Retrieved July 5, 2008, from http://www.travelchannel.com/tv/kombai/kombai.html

Dawkins, R. (2008). *The god delusion.* New York: Houghton Mifflin.

Freeman, S. (2006). Distributive justice and the law of peoples. In R. Martin & D. Reidy (Eds.), *Rawl's law of peoples: A realistic utopia?* Oxford, UK: Blackwell.

Hampshire, S. (1983). Morality and convention. In *Morality and conflict*. Cambridge, MA: Harvard University Press.

Hobbes, T. (2004). *Leviathan*. Retrieved May 6, 2004, from http://darkwing.uoregon.edu/~rbear/hobbes/leviathan.html

Israel - Basic Law. *The Knesset*. (1987). Retrieved May 24, 2008, from http://www.servat.unibe.ch/icl/is02000_.html

Lorenz, K. (1952). *King Solomon's ring*. New York: Thomas Y. Crowell.

Loven, J., & Hurst, S. (2009, April 1). US, Russia call for nuke cuts in sweeping agenda. *Associated Press*. Retrieved April 1, 2009, from http://news.yahoo.com

Lyttle, B. (2005). Clock strikes 12. *University of Chicago Magazine, 98*(2).

Machiavelli, N. (2008). *The prince*. Retrieved May 24, 2008 from http://www.constitution.org/mac/prince00.htm

Martin, R., & Reidy, D. (Eds.). (2006). *Rawl's law of peoples: A realistic utopia?* Oxford, UK: Blackwell.

Morgenthau, H. (1993). *Politics among nations, brief edition*. New York: McGraw-Hill

Pascal, B. (2008). *Pensees*. Retrieved June 6, 2008, from http://www.gutenberg.org/etext/18269

Rawls, J. (1999a). *A theory of justice* (rev. ed.). Cambridge, MA: Harvard University Press.

Rawls, J. (1999b). *The law of peoples*. Cambridge, MA: Harvard University Press.

Rawls, J. (2001). *Justice as fairness: A restatement*. Cambridge, MA: Harvard University Press.

Stiglitz, J. (2003). *Globalization and its discontents*. New York: W. W. Norton.

Walzer, M. (2007). *Thinking politically*. New Haven, CT: Yale University Press.

World Health Organization. (2005). *Cuba*. Retrieved March 27, 2009, from http://www.who.int/countries/cub/en

ENDNOTES

[1]   The Wikipedia article on global ethics characterizes Rawls' theory as a "society of states" theory, which is somewhat misleading.

[2]   The CIA apparently still regards assassination as a method of public policy, but has not always had notable success, for example with major world leaders such as Fidel Castro.

[3]   Rome handled its rival, Carthage, by utterly destroying the city and killing all its inhabitants. The general responsible reported back to Rome with the famous saying, "Carthago delenda est."

[4]   Thus US behavior in Vietnam and, especially, Iraq makes it impossible for the US to be a moral or ethical world leader. It leads by military domination.

5　　After years of inattention to the problem of nuclear proliferation, the Obama administration has begun talks with the Russians about reducing nuclear stockpiles and preventing nuclear proliferation. Obama's stated goal is to eliminate nuclear weapons from the planet. (Loven & Hurst 2009)

6　　The US does not accept the jurisdiction of the World Courts.

7　　French thinkers such as Derrida, Foucault, and Kristeva are often thought of as central figures of postmodernism. The biologist Richard Dawkins coined the term "Francophonies" to describe them. (Dawkins 2008)

8　　See Chapter 4, **The Basis of Ethical Principles,** "Reflective Equilibrium."

9　　Interestingly, Jagdish Bhagwati, a conservative economist explicitly opposed to postmodern relativism, resorts to it to defend inhumane labor conditions. (2007)

10　　Culture clearly has value, however. This issue will be addressed in Chapter 15, **The Value of IT-Enabled Globalization.**

11　　In *Law of Peoples*, Rawls states eight principles. "No World State" is not itself regarded as a principle, and I have condensed a few others. The one omission I find striking is agreement that there be a mechanism for dealing with violations of the principles.

12　　See Chapter 2, **Current Ethically Globalized Institutions,** "Superpowers."

Chapter 7
Cosmopolitanism

Cosmopolitanism is the view that the relevant ethical community is all of humanity. In this chapter, I will examine three somewhat different cosmopolitan theories: The pluralist theory of Thomas Pogge (2002), the social contract theory of Charles Beitz (1979 and 1999), and the utilitarian theory of Peter Singer (2004). All theories hold that humanity as a whole is the relevant ethical community for global ethics. All theories also hold that ethical principles are essentially principles for individuals.

Taking the individual as ethically primary may be what makes cosmopolitanism plausible. Human reality for these theorists is just individual human beings endowed with moral principles. But it is not an accidental fact that human beings live in society. Like ants, termites, lions and chimpanzees, they have evolved so that living in groups is not optional for them. The many benefits produced by social institutions, whether formal or informal, depend on our human ability to forgo self-interest in the interest of the relevant group. The group principles—ethical, political, economic—allowing us to do this are not optional either, especially those having to do with nations. So to begin with it seems that cosmopolitan theories may have too limited a view of human reality.

However, I will give these theories a chance. The main questions I will ask of each theory are: The rationale for basing ethics on individuals as members of the group all of humanity; and the plausibility of each theory as a basis for transnational ethics.

DOI: 10.4018/978-1-60566-922-9.ch007

COSMOPOLITAN PLURALISM

In the Introduction to his *World Poverty and Human Rights*, Thomas Pogge presents a persuasive and emotionally compelling case that world poverty could be dramatically reduced at little cost to ourselves. It is worth summarizing his presentation of the nature and extent of world poverty. As of 2002, 2.8 billion people—46% of the world's population—lived below the $2 a day line the World Bank uses to define poverty. Each year, 18 million people die prematurely from poverty-related causes, including 12 million children under the age of 5. Shifting about 1 per cent of the income of those in high income economies (about $312 billion per year) to those in poverty would, says Pogge, "eradicate poverty." (Pogge 2002, 2-3)

However, Pogge recognizes that many of the inhabitants of the better-off countries don't regard it as an ethical duty or obligation to help those in need in other countries. We certainly regard it as a good thing to do, but maybe not an ethical requirement. Pogge argues to the contrary, that ameliorating poverty is an ethical requirement. We don't need some dramatic new transnational principle for this. The individual ethical principle of benevolence,[1] to help another when the cost to ourselves would not be great, could apply to this case. This principle can easily be justified on either utilitarian or universal principle grounds.[2] Unlike Rawls, who regards transnational ethics as a definite *extension* beyond domestic justice requiring new principles, Pogge argues that the ethical principles that apply within a society must also apply transnationally. Rather than special principles for a transnational context, Pogge appeals to a preexisting universal morality which grounds both domestic and transnational principles of justice.

Thus his ethical theory is not a social contract theory at all. (Pogge 2007, 41) It is grounded in what Rawls calls *comprehensive* beliefs, religious, philosophical, or moral beliefs which the participants in a just society know they disagree on. Thus for a social contract theory such beliefs cannot be the basis for principles of justice.[3] They lie outside what can be required of us as a consequence of our being participants in a system of social cooperation. Thus, using the distinction made in Chapter 4, **The Basis of Ethical Principles**, his theory is a *moral* theory rather than an *ethical* theory.

Pogge's analysis may provide grounds for adopting moral or ethical principles furthering the reduction of poverty in poor nations, perhaps even ethical requirements to do so. Perhaps one will give money to NGOs working to ameliorate poverty in poor nations, or even travel to those nations to help, or even adopt a child. But these will be *personal* moral requirements. Thus, when Pogge argues that we have a moral obligation to reduce poverty, the question is who exactly is the "we" being addressed? It is in the first instance individuals in the developed nations, meaning the US, Europe, Japan, and Australia, who share our moral beliefs. As we will see shortly, Pogge's attempts to extend his conclusion to institutions have some serious drawbacks.

Pogge does think there is a universal criterion of justice which all persons can accept as grounds for judgements about the global order and international relations. (Pogge 2002, 33-34) He notes that it is "unfortunately rather complicated," (44) thus making it what I call a *pluralist* theory of justice.[4] And, as I noted in Chapter 5, a pluralist theory of justice should be adopted only if no theory based on a few prioritized principles is acceptable. Instead, Pogge insists that a theory of justice must deal with the *particular* relation of social institutions to human goods. This suggests a rather extreme version of pluralism: We cannot make ethical generalizations about how institutions are to function justly, but must depend on our moral intuitions.

His examples of cases which he claims more general theories of justice cannot handle seem to confirm this. He claims that most theories of just distribution (such as Rawls' theory or utilitarianism) cannot handle cases where, for example, blacks or women disproportionately suffer hardship. This is because those theories have to regard the distribution as being anonymous. (2002, 44) But equal treatment (anonymity) is an ideal of justice! It is obtuse to claim equal treatment requires that departures from equal treatment have to be ignored. Further, there have to be reasons of justice to believe the departure from equal treatment was deliberate, the result of unjust prejudice. If it turned out that people with "insie" belly buttons were disproportionately sent to jail, but that was purely coincidental, there would be no reason of justice for redress. Similarly, Pogge's other cases don't warrant making a theory of justice relative to particular institutions in any way that a general theory can't handle.[5]

As Rawls correctly observes, the principles of justice have to be understood and acknowledged, not only in the original position, but back in society. A complex set of multiple principles backed only by multiple moral intuitions are not a good candidate to accomplish this.

Pogge may have these views because he does not regard the foundation of ethics or even justice as principles which supply the conditions for social cooperation. For him, what makes a group of people into a morally relevant social unit—a society—is their feelings of closeness and concern for one another.[6] This may be part of the reason why he sees no ethical difference between justice in one society and global justice. As long as one has the relevant moral feelings, that's all there is to it. Whereas, the differences in the ways benefits and burdens are shared within a society and globally are critical for a plausible global ethical theory.

POGGE'S THEORY OF GLOBAL INSTITUTIONS

All versions of cosmopolitanism call for radical changes in the structure of nations and international institutions. Pogge's changes are more radical than those called for by either social contract cosmopolitanism or by utilitarian cosmopolitanism. His cosmopolitanism could be negatively described as "rootless cosmopolitanism," the belief of a human with no ties to anyone or anything, drifting aimlessly around the world. This rather alienated figure is probably not a good candidate for the ideal ethical subject on which to base transnational ethics.

Pogge wants to replace the current system of states, not with a universal state but with a nested series of political units, each with its own powers, with no dominant power. (2008, 178) Such an arrangement, claims Pogge, will help prevent oppression. And it will prevent arrangements like the current one, where dominant powers fail to provide the help Pogge thinks they should to those living in poverty. Anyone who has had any experience with entrenched hierarchical bureaucracy knows that this arrangement is completely unworkable. If power is dispersed enough to prevent the bad consequences Pogge is so anxious to avoid, it will be because the hierarchy is unable to act for good or ill. Life would become a nightmare of trying to determine who is responsible for what.

The main point of political and social institutions is to determine how to distribute social benefits fairly. For Pogge, this is irrelevant. Distributive justice, on his view, does not have to do primarily with distribution. It concerns "how to choose or design the economic ground rules that regulate property, cooperation, and exchange and thereby condition production and distribution." (2007, 176) The ethical constraint is that everyone is guaranteed a minimum that would meet basic needs. But without cooperation, the other institutions of property, exchange, production, and distribution are impossible. For Pogge, social goods are a given, like natural resources. His ethical constraint of a social minimum is similar to Rawls' Difference Principle, but without a contract situation in which to design social and economic institutions. Instead, we have ethical intuitions which may or may not be shared within any society, let alone in an as-yet nonexistent global society.[7]

There really are no good reasons for accepting Pogge's pluralist cosmopolitanism as a basis for transnational ethics. The institutional proposals just discussed seem unworkable and implausible. He also discusses another institutional proposal, called the Global Resource Dividend (GRD), which has more plausibility. It goes beyond just saying that we have more goods than those in poverty, so we should give them some.[8] The GRD is basically a tax on resources removed from poor countries, to be used to improve the lot of those in poverty. Unfortunately questions about how the GRD is to be administered and distributed get schematic answers. Pogge says this should be "easy to understand," (2007, 206) but provides only schematic answers such as: The distribution scheme should be effective, understandable, and not cost much. But what currently nonexistent global institutions will enable and enforce this scheme?

Perhaps there is a clue in another observation. Pogge also says distribution of funds should be maximally effective in ensuring all can meet basic needs. He then says that it is up to "economists and international lawyers" to figure out how to accomplish this. (2007, 206) So this proposal suffers from the same problems as his other proposals. It is grounded in an implausible transnational ethical theory and a very sketchy account of global institutions necessary to implement the theory. However, this institutional suggestion—the GRD—may be of value within the context of another transnational ethical theory. Pogge's theory leaves the details of a new global institution order to be worked out without benefit of ethical guidance. All we have is a general ethical theory which applies only to individuals. The dangers involved in this approach will become clearer when we next consider social contract cosmopolitanism. We will return to the issue of globalized institutions in Chapter 11, **New Globalized Institutions.**

SOCIAL CONTRACT COSMOPOLITANISM

In 1979, some years after Rawls published his *Theory of Justice* but before Rawls formulated his Law of Peoples, Charles Beitz in his *Political Theory and International Relations,* sketched a social contract version of transnational ethics. Beitz argues that Rawls' domestic principles of justice can be applied transnationally without change. His argument takes the form of demolishing objections to applying Rawls' Difference Principle to the entire globe. Like Pogge, he is certain that ethics requires massive redistribution of goods between richer and poorer countries. He is somewhat more sensitive to potential differences between the contexts of domestic and international justice. Nevertheless, in the end he claims the differences don't matter ethically.

Unfortunately it is hard to have much confidence in his conclusion that the Difference Principle should be applied globally. His strategy is to mount complex, rather legalistic, arguments against hypothetical objectors. People in the (appropriate) original position need to have confidence that they have made the right decision, and not that they have been talked into it by a sharp lawyer. Beitz would be a good choice of defense lawyer for someone who knew they were guilty of a serious crime.

In a way, implementing the globalized Difference Principle would seem to some like committing a serious crime. It would mean that, *regardless of whatever society an individual belonged to,* justice requires making the worst off person as well off as possible. Some years ago, I saw an ad noting that distributing then-Disney-CEO Michael Eisner's annual salary to Haitians would enable raising hundreds of thousands out of poverty. But is this how to implement global justice? Our uncertainty here is due to several differences in application between the domestic Difference Principle and the Global Difference Principle:

1. In the domestic situation, everyone is part of the same society and economy, but not in the global situation.
2. In the global situation, there is currently no set of institutions to enforce global rules.
3. In the global situation, principles for individuals are not appropriate.

Cosmopolitans deny all three of these. Also, all our cosmopolitans hold that:

4. Ethical standards or principles of justice at the global level are justified through individual moral standards.

Beitz argues that 1 through 3 do not provide reasons for rejecting the Global Difference Principle. Assumption 4 is made by all the cosmopolitans I am examining. Beitz developed his globalization of Rawls' principles of justice before Rawls made the crucial change to his theory of justice that we discussed earlier. The change was that accepting the Principles of Justice did NOT involve agreement on moral principles. In fact, the principle of Greatest Equal Freedom should include freedom of thought and conscience and therefore agreement on what Rawls termed *comprehensive doctrines* should not be expected in a just society, nor as the basis for such a society.[9] Comprehensive doctrines include religious, moral, and philosophical beliefs. It may seem as though grounding justice directly on moral principles is a firmer basis than grounding justice on principles for social cooperation. But Rawls' wisdom here is that people have wildly different moral principles. The Nazis, for example, thought the elimination of Jews was ethically required. And if such moral principles, whatever they are, are the basis for social policies, the only basis we have for criticism is the conviction that ours are correct and theirs are wrong. To repeat Hans Morgenthau's observation:

To know that nations are subject to the moral law is one thing, while to pretend to know with certainty what is good and evil in the relations among nations is quite another. There is a world of difference between the belief that all nations stand under the judgement of God, inscrutable to the human mind, and the blasphemous conviction that God is always on one's side and that what one wills oneself cannot fail to be willed by God also. (1993, 13)

Why is basing justice on principles of social cooperation better? Recall Chapter 4 and the Prisoner's Dilemma example.[10] Most people tacitly recognize that overriding immediate self-interest is necessary to achieve cooperative benefits. It is not a matter of sharing moral beliefs, but rather believing that the benefits and burdens of belonging to one's society are for the most part fairly distributed, and that most people in the society believe this and believe each other believes this. This mutual belief is characteristic of any tacit agreement. Thus it would be more accurate to call a social contract "tacit" rather than "hypothetical."

So what happens if we give up the moral foundation for principles of justice that both Pogge and Beitz rely on? For Rawls, the fact that we can't rely on moral agreement to ground principles of justice caused him to call his principles *political* principles rather than moral principles. Principles of justice are then agreed to as ground rules for social and political cooperation, rather than as part of a moral theory.[11]

Both Pogge and Beitz regard this fact as unimportant, but I believe it is because they see principles of justice at any level as derived from individual moral beliefs.

Beitz thinks that "enough" background global social and political institutions exist so that there can be global principles of justice. He mentions extensive trade between nations and "a global regulative structure" consisting of financial and monetary institutions, international property rights, treaties, and a rule of nonintervention. (1979, 148-149) But how do these institutions become vehicles for a global difference principle? There is clearly room for and need for principles of international justice. As we saw in chapter 1, there are lots of major unresolved transnational problems. Current institutions do not address them. And simply extending domestic justice for individuals is not a good way of addressing them.

Consider, for example Yahoo's problem with Chinese law. If we just "go global" with the principles of justice, we would have to say that Chinese law is irrelevant; it conflicts with the principle of Greatest Equal Freedom, which is for Beitz a priority principle of global justice. Of course *we* know that it is a correct principle of justice, and if the Chinese don't accept it, that is their problem. "We" can require China not to censor the internet or impose sanctions as executors of global justice.[12] All social contract theory is based on consent of those subject to the agreement. But instead Beitz's Global Social Contract requires us to impose our own beliefs on others. And it is far from clear who should be doing the imposition.

Some other suggestions for reforming present global institutions present similar disconnects from global principles of justice. Who, for example, proposes and enforces World Bank reforms to make it more responsive to the needs of developing countries? And what globalized institution can see to it that multinational corporations obey antitrust principles? Or that they don't engage in tax shifting?[13] The domestic principles of justice, globalized, provide almost no guidance. We need instead principles of justice for the structure of transnational institutions that recognize and build on the justice of societies. That is what I will consider in Section 3, **A Social Contract for Globalized Institutions.**

Beitz believes that the global principles of justice (equal liberty and the global difference principle) have priority over any domestic considerations of justice or any ethical claims of sovereign states. Thus a principle of nonintervention in the affairs of sovereign states is, for Beitz, completely subordinate to the global principles of justice. Only just states (or states in the process of becoming just) have any right not to be interfered with. Presumably, since the United States has behaved very poorly with respect to redistributing its wealth, it would for Beitz be a candidate for intervention. Beitz recognizes there are many cases that intervention (whether violent or nonviolent) would not be productive. But his transnational theory has the result that intervention in US affairs would be *ethically justified,* even if for practical reasons it would not be advised. (1979, 91) Consider the 2003 US war in Iraq. After the collapse of the justification of self-defense against weapons of mass destruction, the US justification became destroying an unjust regime and building a democracy. Leaving aside the impossibility of establishing a democracy by force, Beitz's views would regard this war as ethically justified.

With Beitz's theory, the amount of justified intervention would be very great because any ethical significance of boundaries has vanished. We can turn his argument on its head about there being no difference between domestic and international justice. If national boundaries are not ethically relevant, we could justify as much economic and social intervention between countries as we now see internally within states. Just imagine Scandinavia imposing their fuel efficiency standards on the US. Or the EU jailing the CEOs of American health care corporations.[14] Or Islamic states requiring all French women to wear scarves and long pants. Beitz cannot properly factor in the disruption caused by intervention in other states, because for him there is no ethically relevant disruption other than individual harms.

In *The Law of Peoples*, Rawls notes three differences between domestic and international justice. He then criticizes Beitz's global difference principle. (1999b, 115-120) The differences Rawls cites are these:

1. Within a society, justice requires that the worst off has sufficient means to make use of their freedom and lead a worthwhile life. No redistribution is called for to better the worst off, even if there are great inequalities. Among societies, as long as the society has the means to maintain a just government, no redistribution is called for to improve the justice of its institutions.
2. If there is justified resentment on the part of the less well off because of their being treated as inferior, redistribution is called for, domestically. Internationally, as long as aid to improve justice has been provided, the society should consider saving or borrowing to improve the lot of the less advantaged.
3. Domestically, fairness in procedures and in opportunity is required. Internationally, fairness would require guidelines for cooperative organizations and standards for trade.

Beitz believes natural resources are analogous to talents of the individual and thus should be subject to redistribution by principles of justice. Rawls notes that a country's well being is determined more by its political culture than by the presence or absence of resources. Think of Singapore, very successful with no natural resources, and the Congo Republic (Zimbabwe), not very successful with loads of natural resources. Rawls' point seems to be correct, and so redistribution of resources may not help in creating just states.

In criticizing Beitz's global difference principle, Rawls asks us to imagine two societies. Both start in the same place, both are just and economically secure. Society A decides to industrialize and succeeds in increasing the wealth of all its citizens. Society B decides to retain a leisurely pastoral society. In a few decades society A is twice as wealthy in all respects as society B. Is there any ethical requirement for society A to transfer the extra wealth to society B? Rawls thinks not, and I agree. Although the cases are hypothetical, they include a feature that cosmopolitans ignore, namely the benefits are the result of shared burdens and plans that were agreed to by the participants in that society. (Rawls 1999b, 117-118) Suppose, within our society, my friend Ahab and I embark on two different investment plans. My plan is to reinvest all profits I receive. My friend Ahab's plan is to invest only half the profits he receives. The other half he spends as he goes along on plasma TVs, wireless cards, etc., whereas I live reasonably well but frugally on my salary. When Ahab retires, unfortunately, he does not have enough for day to day expenses and is eating dog food. I, on the other hand, can take trips to Italy. If the difference principle applied to us as individuals (which it does not), would I be ethically required to contribute to his welfare? I think not. In the situation as imagined, I would have an ethical duty of benevolence, which would be help Ahab out as long as the cost to myself were not great.

If both of us are placed in (a just) society, then I do have an ethical requirement to support policies and institutions which assure that the worst off can live a decent life, even if their investment skills are not so hot. These policies and institutions might include taxes, welfare, Medicaid, minimum wage laws, educational opportunities, and so on. But suppose further that we live in different societies, say, Ahab lives in Italy and I live in the US. I am not in a position to evaluate how Ahab has contributed to his society, nor how Italy's institutions have helped or hindered him. I could directly help him out through the individual ethical duty of benevolence, just mentioned. But it is hard to see the application of a global difference principle. That principle would require my helping Ahab. The correct ethical considerations seem to be through the institutions of one's nation or economic group, rather than in terms of individuals. Thus it would be at the level of states or global institutions that one would address transnational inequalities.

In Rawls' Law of Peoples, Rawls thinks the relevant obligation on states toward less advantaged states would be only to bring them to the point where they are capable of becoming just societies. Rawls believes in the optimistic assumption that if a country's internal institutions are just, a decent economy will follow, or at least an economy decent enough to enable satisfaction of the Difference Principle. For Rawls, the ethical requirement would only be to contribute toward the establishment of a just state. But so long as there are countries who behave like Ahab and fall on hard times, benevolence at the country level seems to be ethically required—more than simply contributing to the establishment of a just state.

How much more? The Global Difference Principle requires too much and in the wrong way. Perhaps the duty of benevolence extended to countries would be enough. This would require helping countries suffering from poverty when the cost to ones' own country was not too great.[15] But countries are not ethical individuals, although they are composed of them. In actual practice, the US gave 0.1% of its gross national product for development aid. Most other developed countries gave from two to seven times as much percentage wise. (Singer 2004, 180-181) Even worse, the US, the wealthiest country in the world, allows 36.5 million people to live in poverty, the highest percentage among developed countries. (Notten & Neuborg 2007) About 3.5 million people in the US are homeless in any given year. So currently the US is doing a poor job not only with its international ethical duties, but in fulfilling even the most basic obligations of domestic justice. The previous US administration that provided massive tax cuts for the wealthiest individuals and corporations, while vetoing legislation for children's health insurance did not have much in the way of ethics going for it.[16][17]

The question of how to formulate the international analogues of the difference principle and the principle of benevolence will be taken up again in Section III, **A Social Contract for Globalized Institutions.**

UTILITARIAN COSMOPOLITANISM

Cosmopolitans claim that there is no difference between individual ethical principles and transnational principles. Peter Singer, in his *One World* (2004), argues for this conclusion. Singer is also more sensitive than our previous cosmopolitans to the role of cooperation in formulating transnational ethical principles and to the current lack of institutions to support ethical globalization.

Singer argues that the basic unit for our ethical thinking must now be the entire planet. Problems such as global warming, environmental protection, economic development and redistribution, and genocide cannot be addressed on a state-by-state basis. Singer provides utilitarian grounds for a cosmopolitan approach to these problems. However, he is sometimes willing to consider a social contract approach as equally good. In discussing World Trade Organization (WTO) reform, he suggests that:

Just as in the philosophy of social contract theorists like Rousseau, people forming a political community give up some of their individual freedom in order to gain a voice in the running of the whole community, so nations entering the WTO would give up some of their national sovereignty in order to gain a voice in the running of the global economy. (Singer 2004, 74-75)

This social contract justification for limiting national sovereignty would also require democratization of the WTO to give all nations a meaningful voice.

In fact, in spite of Singer's announced utilitarian basis for transnational ethics, cosmopolitanism is more important to him than utilitarianism. He believes that nationality has derivative ethical importance. But unlike Pogge and Beitz, his discussion of the global institutional background is much more circumspect and realistic:

To rush into world federalism would be too risky, but we could accept the diminishing significance of national boundaries and take a pragmatic, step-by-step approach to greater global governance. (Singer 2004, 200)

I believe that a social contract approach may be better than a utilitarian approach, even for some of Singer's cosmopolitan conclusions. After all, utilitarianism is concerned with maximizing value or average value. It doesn't care very much about how any specific individuals (especially the worst-off) make out, so long as the overall sum is better. Under utilitarian principles a loss in one society can be outweighed by a gain in another. So the losing society can end up, on its own terms, much worse off. An example is corn production in the U. S. and Mexico after NAFTA. Subsidized U.S. corn drove small Mexican corn producers out of business. Overall, economic benefits increased. But since we are separate societies, most such out-of-work Mexicans who come to the U.S. to raise corn now shipped to Mexico, often come as illegal aliens. (Bensinger 2003) So far, none of our global ethical theories can deal with this kind of situation.

Another problem is that the institutions needed to implement a cosmopolitan ethical view are as yet very imperfect, and a social contract for globalized institutions does not exist. Singer concedes that the appropriate global institutions do not exist, but thinks current ones such as the United Nations are a good start. (Singer 2004, 134-135) Singer discusses the World Trade Organization as a global institution with the subsidiary goal of improving the lot of poor countries through increasing free trade. Singer thinks the jury is still out on whether free trade does make things better for the poorer countries, but notes:

. . . we can still ask if there are ways of making [economic globalization] work better, or at least less badly. Even those who accept . . . the economic benefits of a global free market should ask themselves how well a global free market can work in the absence of any global authority to set minimum standards on issues like child labor, worker safety, [unionization], and environmental protection. (2004, 92)

Thus Singer, like Morgenthau and Stiglitz, requires a global authority to enforce at least some global ethical requirements.

Although Singer believes that "national sovereignty has no *intrinsic* moral weight," (2004, 148) this belief is part of "the ethical foundations of the coming era of a single world community." (2004, 198) Unlike Pogge and Beitz, he does not think that this world community already exists. His views on intervention in the affairs of other states and on global redistribution are more sensible than their views (or indeed Rawls' views). Short of actual invasion of another country, there are the possibilities of trade restrictions and criminal prosecution of the country's leaders.

The issue of the legitimacy of a government is important in determining whether a government has the right to trade in a country's resources. Singer proposes that what he calls a *minimalist democracy* has that right. A minimalist democracy is one that has been ruling for a long time with the apparent acquiescence of its people, without severe restrictions on civil liberties, and without using repression to maintain its power.[18] (2004, 101) But a refusal to deal with a repressive dictator in selling resources should not normally be a boycott of all trade with the country. (2004, 105) The World Trade Organization does exactly the opposite: It prohibits refusing to trade with nondemocratic members. Thus the WTO gives free trade a higher priority than democracy. By contrast, the EU puts democracy and human rights conditions on membership, thus putting those values above free trade. (2004, 102)

In international criminal law an unresolved issue is "universal jurisdiction." Universal jurisdiction is the doctrine that any state has the right to try someone accused of war crimes or crimes against humanity. Israel used this doctrine in trying Adolf Eichmann for the genocide committed by the Nazis, but did not allow its own officials to be tried for crimes against the Palestinians. The doctrine has the potential to be misused politically by states to try leaders of other states for sham crimes. It would be better to have war crimes and crimes against humanity tried solely by international courts. However, as of 2008 the US does not recognize the International Criminal Court and would recognize it only on condition that its officials and military personnel be exempt from prosecution. Since this condition obviously rejects the jurisdiction of the court, the US is saying that it will recognize the jurisdiction of the court only if the court has no jurisdiction over it.

Singer believes that intervention is justified when a government causes large-scale loss of life and/ or large-scale ethnic cleansing. If these conditions obtain, intervention is justified whether the government is minimally democratic or not. However, there are utilitarian limits to intervention. Predictable bad consequences can make it wrong to intervene. This is why intervention in Kosovo was justified but intervention in Chechyna or Tibet would not be. The predictable costs of war with Russia or China would outweigh any benefits. There is no point to "destroy[ing] a village in order to save it." (2004, 137-139)

Ultimately, national sovereignty has value for its consequences: It promotes peace between states. "The limits of the state's ability and willingness to protect its people are also the limits of its sovereignty." (2004, 148) When the state is unable to protect its people from mass killing or ethnic cleansing, it no longer has the right to sovereignty. Only the UN should intervene, however, as protector of last resort, because if nations undertake this responsibility, national interests will conflict and "plunge the world into international conflict." (2004, 149)

Singer's conclusions about the ethics of ameliorating world poverty are perhaps more utilitarian than the rest of his discussion. Singer cites statistics similar to those of Pogge to show the enormous disparities between those in the richest countries and those in the poorest countries. But the ethical issue is, what are we required to do about this disparity? I believe everyone would agree that the standard ethical principle of benevolence applies, that we are required to help those in need when we can do so at little cost to ourselves.[19] Singer does well to point out that we are not even doing this. The US government, as of this writing in 2008 the richest country in the world,[20] budgets less than 1 percent for foreign aid. It is striking that, when polled, Americans thought the figure was 15 to 20 percent! (2004, 183-184) The UN some years ago set a target of 0.7 percent of a nation's gross national product for state aid to poor nations. (This target is called the Millennium Development Goal.) Several northern European nations meet this target. In the most recent year figures were available, the US gave 0.1 percent, or $10 billion. It also gave $4 billion in private contributions. In the same year, the US spent $26 billion on soft drinks. Also, much US government aid is allocated to strategically important countries and does not go to ameliorate poverty. (2004, 180-181)

So, just on the basis of the ethical principle of benevolence for individuals, we are ethically required to do a lot more for poor countries than we are now doing. We can, as individuals, contribute to organizations we know will be helping to ameliorate global poverty. Or we can tell our elected representatives to increase aid to poor countries. The question raised by Singer and the cosmopolitans is, how much more are we ethically required to do? Pogge and Beitz say that, since we are all ethically part of one society, we should apply Rawls' Difference Principle globally, and arrange our institutions to make the worst off globally as well off as possible.

Singer, unlike Pogge and Beitz, does not think we are already in a global society, although he thinks ethics requires that we move in that direction. Also, unlike Pogge, Singer thinks environmental problems which cannot be handled on a state by state basis require global institutions for their solution. Singer thinks that it is an ethical requirement to reduce inequality between nations. He does make two important qualifications. One is that it is also important to reduce inequality *within* nations, but reducing inequality *between* nations should still be given priority. (2004, 174-175) Second, utilitarianism requires us to consider the consequences of adopting an ethical policy with demanding requirements that people will not follow. It may then lead people to do even less to ameliorate poverty in poor countries. If so, we need to make the requirements less demanding. Singer concedes this point, and proposes a minimum 1% contribution from personal income of those with discretionary income. Not to honor this "global responsibility" would be "seriously morally wrong." (2004, 194)

But what is the source of this global responsibility? Recall that Rawls concluded that the only ethical requirement of one state for another was aid to disadvantaged states to help them become just societies. Singer mentions Rawls' discussion of two societies which end up with different levels of resources through their own preferences and decisions. Rawls concluded that no redistribution was called for. Singer replies that if no redistribution is called for in this case of two societies, redistribution should also not be called for within a society when someone has made choices which lead him to get lower levels of resources. (2004, 178)

Singer's reply misses the point. Benefits to be distributed are the result of shared burdens and plans that were in effect agreed to by the participants in that society. (Rawls 1999b, 117-118) Let us return to my previous example from this chapter. Suppose I execute a different investment plan from my friend Ahab and when we retire, Ahab must eat dog food but I can take trips to Italy. Redistribution is not called for. My only ethical duty to Ahab would be benevolence, to help Ahab out as long as the cost to myself was not excessive.[21] I also have an ethical requirement to support policies and institutions which assure that the worst off can live a decent life, such as taxes, welfare, Medicaid, minimum wage laws, educational opportunities, and so on.

But if I live in the US and Ahab lives in Italy, I am not in a position to evaluate how Ahab has contributed to his society, nor how Italy's institutions have helped or hindered him. The correct ethical considerations seem to be through the institutions of one's nation or economic group, rather than in terms of individuals. Thus it would be at the level of states or global institutions that one would address transnational inequalities.

We can turn Singer's argument against him: If it is not morally required to redistribute resources domestically just because there are inequalities, then it is not morally required to redistribute resources transnationally just because there are inequalities. Rawls' argument for the Difference Principle in the original position shows when inequalities are justified. We depart from giving everyone equal resources because we know that, given our social and economic institutions, giving people unequal resources will produce better results for all, even the least advantaged. The production of value[22] within a shared social

Table 1. Distribution of resources between two countries

	Needia	Desperia	Aggregate value
Distribution 1	A lot→ really good lives	Little→ Abject poverty	
Distribution 2	Small→hard but decent lives	Small→hard but decent lives	

context is essential to justify inequality. Now, what is the analog in the transnational situation? When (some) value is produced with the aid of another country, should we then regard both countries as the same society? This is essentially Beitz's unacceptable conclusion. Should we simply ignore the ways in which the transnational distribution of resources came about and the different contributions of the different nations involved? This is essentially Singer's approach, and if it was unacceptable for domestic justice, there is no reason to accept his approach for transnational justice.

Actually, in spite of the great concern of cosmopolitans with the welfare of the global poor, cosmopolitan utilitarianism has problems similar to domestic utilitarianism. Aggregate total value is what matters to utilitarianism; distribution is irrelevant. This leads to ethically unacceptable conclusions. Consider two possible transnational distributions of resources, which could take the form of World Bank loans. Distribution 1 gives a lot to one country, Needia, but very little to a second country, Desperia. Distribution 2 gives both Needia and Desperia equal small amounts. A utilitarian must use *consequences* to decide between the distributions. The consequences are: With Distribution 1, Needia would be able to use the increased resources to provide really good lives for everyone in the country, but Desperia would be sunk in abject poverty (short lives, poor health, etc.). With Distribution 2, people in both countries have hard lives but decent ones. The possibilities can be summarized in the matrix of Table 1.

A utilitarian must be able to give numerical utility values to the consequences in order to decide between the distributions. Here are some possible values. As discussed earlier, average utility in each country is probably the most reasonable choice of value. In Table 2 I have simply averaged the averages. One might also weight the averages for the number of people in each country for aggregate value.[23]

These values are arbitrary, but it is plausible that there could be distributions with the same pattern. And so there will be cases where a utilitarian has to choose Distribution 1, even though that choice leaves people in the abject poverty cosmopolitans were trying to avoid. By contrast, for a social contract theory, distribution by itself is not decisive. We need to consider the institutions within those countries producing the benefits. Any sort of social contract will very likely include an analogue of Rawls' Difference Principle, to make the worst off as well off as possible. If so, in the example above, Distribution 2 would be the more likely choice.[24]

In Section III, I will construct a new global social contract to govern the distribution of benefits from globalized institutions. It should be clear from the discussion of the various transnational theories in this

Table 2. Value results of distribution

	Needia	Desperia	Aggregate value
Distribution 1	really good lives = 75 average	abject poverty = -5 average	35 average
Distribution 2	hard but decent = 20 average	hard but decent = 20 average	20 average

chapter that it is not a given that transnational economic inequalities are in themselves ethically wrong. The purpose of constructing a new social contract is to provide a sound basis for determining when they are ethically justified and when they are not.

UTILITARIAN SOLUTIONS TO IT-ENABLED GLOBALIZED ETHICAL PROBLEMS

How would cosmopolitan utilitarianism handle cases like Yahoo in China? We would need to consider what policies would produce the greatest (average) value across the globe. Obviously, unless we consider average value rather than overall value, the Chinese will always win because of their much greater numbers. Even with this condition, it is open to question whether freedom of speech is more valuable than economic gain. Could China have achieved its breathtaking economic growth without restriction of personal liberty? If China's restriction of personal liberty is justified on utilitarian grounds, then Yahoo was justified in turning over dissidents to the Chinese government to be tortured. Questions of transnational justice don't even arise.

Also, Yahoo's stockholders may have had good utilitarian justification for voting against any prohibition of censorship. Letting each country enforce its own censorship laws on the internet would likely produce more profits for Yahoo. And a utilitarian could argue that having corporations stick to their purpose of maximizing profits is the policy that will produce the best results for everyone.[25]

The World Trade Organization, which Singer discusses extensively, is not directly related to the World Bank. The WTO sets trade rules which, as Singer notes, make it impossible to enforce transnational ethical and environmental restrictions. In addition, its governance cannot be regarded as based on the consent of its members. These are not in themselves utilitarian criticisms. On the question of whether globalization (that is, the free trade promoted by the WTO) helps ameliorate global poverty, Singer concludes that it is not possible to be sure whether it has helped more people than it has harmed, or vice versa. (2004, 89-90) For a utilitarian consequentialist theory, that is the bottom line judgement. For social contract theory, the non-democratic governance of the WTO would prevent it from being ethically legitimate. The WTO would also need an institutional way of addressing clear egregious injustices.

A utilitarian view of the World Bank would ask whether its policies (together with those of the IMF) produce more harm than good for poor countries. In this case I think most commentators would agree that World Bank policies of fiscal austerity and privatization have produced more harm than good as implemented in the actual world. But World Bank defenders would claim that the harm was produced by not following the policies thoroughly enough. Since such claims are based more on free market ideology than experience, the utilitarian conclusion would be to adopt changes in these policies. Economists such as Joseph Stiglitz and Ha-Joon Chang have made sensible suggestions. (Stiglitz 2007, Chang 2008) (By contrast, a social contract theory would look at the nature of World Bank policies and consider whether they are in accordance with transnational principles of justice.)

WHEN ARE SINGER'S CONCLUSIONS UTILITARIAN?

'Consequentialism' is another name Singer and others employ for 'utilitarianism.' The name consequentialism emphasizes that utilitarianism evaluates actions or policies by their consequences. In Chapter 4, I used the shorter term 'end-based.' The alternative to consequentialism—universal principle—is to evaluate actions and policies by the type of action or policy they are. I argued above and in Chapter 4 that consequentialism is not as good an ethical theory as universal principle theory. I believe consequentialism has led Peter Singer into some untenable conclusions. But I also believe some of his conclusions are sound and much better founded than those of the other transnational theorists we have examined. I will now consider whether those valuable conclusions—which I will make use of later—depend upon consequentialism.

On national sovereignty and intervention, Singer's notion of minimalist democracy as the basis for nonintervention is, I believe, more in reflective equilibrium with our ethical judgements than the views of Rawls or Beitz. As we saw, Rawls simply excludes states which do not honor human rights from any dealings with just states. Further, excluded states can be interfered with pretty much at the discretion of the just states. Beitz also holds that unjust states forfeit any claim to noninterference. In contrast, Singer's minimalist democracy is stable, has apparent popular support, does not severely restrict human rights nor maintain power by repression. Minimalist democracies earn the right to nonintervention and cooperation with other states. China would probably count. China may not honor human rights, but it currently seems inaccurate to say that China severely restricts human rights. The net difference is that Singer's account of nonintervention would, if followed, lead to much more peaceable relations between nations.

Does Singer's account of nonintervention depend upon consequentialism? He does indeed justify it in exactly those terms: National sovereignty is justified only in terms of its consequences of promoting peace between nations. (2004, 148) So national sovereignty would not be ethically justified for nations making or threatening war. But Singer also claims that minimalist democracies have the right not to be interfered with. Being a minimalist democrary is another reason which justifies respect of national sovereignty. The *type* of government (minimalist democracy) as a reason to justify national sovereignty ethically is not a consequentialist reason. This may be why Singer ignores it. But taking promoting peace as a justification for nation's respecting each other's sovereignty is almost circular. Why do we even have entities (nation states) capable of peace and war? If nation states didn't exist, there would be no issues of peace and war. So nation states can't exist only to promote peace.

Thus I will adopt Singer's account of minimalist democracy as a criterion for a state ethically entitled to nonintervention, whether by force or by trade restrictions or economic sanctions. I will also adopt his criterion of genocide or other mass murder as the only ethical reason for invading another state by force. Both of these criteria do not require consequentialist justifications; at this point, they are justified because they are a better match to our judgements about intervention in other states.[26]

On dealing with poor nations, Singer's conclusions and reasoning is explicitly consequentialist. How wealth is produced is irrelevant. Transnational inequalities are simply unjust, and whenever they exist, they should be eliminated—unless more harm would be done thereby. Singer (and, earlier, Pogge) produce compelling accounts of the bad consequences of unequal global distribution of wealth. But Singer's consequentialism leads him to ignore the institutional structure that produces the wealth and any requirements of justice for those institutions beyond eliminating transnational inequalities in distribution. All three cosmopolitans regard questions of the justice of transnational institutions as secondary to the problem of redistributing wealth. Unlike Pogge and Beitz, Singer does think it important to discuss the justice of transnational institutions such as the WTO. But in the end, it is redistribution of wealth that matters.

Focusing solely on the distribution of wealth leads one to focus on the wrong ethical issues. If wealth is produced for the most part from resources entirely within one country, there seems no ethical reason to require transnational redistribution of that wealth. A principle of benevolence at the national level could apply, which would require a country to give to those countries in need if the cost to itself is not excessive.[27] But if wealth is produced transnationally, with contributions of effort and resources from many countries, then there is a reason of justice to insure that benefits are distributed fairly between those contributing in those countries. For this to happen would require attention to principles governing not only states but multinational corporations. I believe it will turn out that social contract reasons of justice for altering the global distribution of wealth will be more compelling to states, multinationals, and transnational institutions. Social contract reasons are, I believe, more compelling than consequentialist or intuitive reasons to make the lot of the suffering poor better. Why more compelling? I believe people will be much more willing to follow principles that they themselves could have adopted. This is the whole point of a social contract justification, and why I believe it will prove to be superior to the alternatives we have just considered.

IMPLICATIONS FOR GLOBAL ETHICS

I previously quoted Samuel Freeman's remark about globalized ethics:

Finally, I think what bothers many cosmopolitans is that global capitalism has created ways to elude political controls by the world's governments. ... part of the problem is that there is no global structure to deal with it. Perhaps some additions need to be made to Rawls' Law of Peoples to deal with this... (2006, 258)

Freeman adds that the common cosmopolitan solution of redistribution is clearly not the way to deal with ethically globalized problems. But neither will tacking on principles on a nation by nation basis. There is a *de facto* global transnational economic and political structure. The problem is that there are no settled ethical principles or principles of justice governing the entities that belong to this structure, most importantly transnational corporations. The problem is not only transnationality, but also the fact that corporations do not seem to be ethical entities at all. We turn to this issue in the next chapter.

REFERENCES

Beitz, C. (1999). *Political theory and international relations.* Princeton, NJ: Princeton University Press.

Chang, H. (2008). *Bad Samaritans.* New York: Bloomsbury Press.

Freeman, S. (2006). Distributive justice and the law of peoples. In R. Martin & D. Reidy (Eds.), *Rawl's law of peoples: A realistic utopia?* Oxford, UK: Blackwell.

Kovalik, D. (2008, July 31). Rand Corp — war on terror is a failure. *Politico.* Retrieved March 28, 2009 from http://www.huffingtonpost.com/dan-kovalik/rand-corp——war-on-terro_b_116107.html

Martin, R., & Reidy, D. (Eds.). (2006). *Rawl's law of peoples: A realistic utopia?* Oxford, UK: Blackwell.

Notten, G., & de Neubourg, C. (2007). *Poverty in Europe and the USA: Exchanging official measurement methods* (Paper 4669). Germany: University Library of Munich.

Pogge, T. (2002). *World poverty and human rights.* Cambridge, England: Polity Press.

Rawls, J. (1993). *Political liberalism.* New York: Columbia University Press.

Rawls, J. (1999a). *A theory of justice* (rev. ed.). Cambridge, MA: Harvard University Press

Rawls, J. (1999b). *The law of peoples.* Cambridge, MA: Harvard University Press.

Rawls, J. (1999c). Outline of a decision procedure for ethics. In S. Freeman (ed.), *Collected papers.* Cambridge, MA: Harvard University Press.

Rawls, J. (2001). *Justice as fairness: A restatement.* Cambridge, MA: Harvard University Press.

Singer, P. (2004). *One world* (2nd ed.) New Haven, CT: Yale University Press.

Stiglitz, J. (2007). *Making globalization work.* New York: W. W. Norton.

ENDNOTES

[1]   As mentioned in Chapter 4, I follow common usage in using 'benevolence' to mean both willing good and doing good.

[2]   For a utilitarian, if the cost to yourself is less than the benefit to the person being helped, you should do the benevolent deed. For a universal principle theorist, the question is whether you could make it a principle to help for this much cost to yourself, or whether regularly incurring this cost will damage yourself more.

[3]   And therefore specific comprehensive beliefs are excluded from the original position. The parties in the original position know that they will *have* comprehensive beliefs which they will try to realize, they have general knowledge of the role comprehensive beliefs will play in their lives, but when deciding on principles of justice, they don't know *which* comprehensive beliefs they have.

[4]   See Chapter 5, **Domestic Theories of Justice,** "Other theories of justice."

[5]   The other main complication is requiring justice to consider how particular institutions contribute to human good. Pogge claims that neither social contract nor utilitarian theories can take into account differential social costs of remediating injustices such as excessive traffic deaths. (2007, 43) His example is the differential cost between lowering the speed limit or building extensive overpasses. But utilitarian cost/benefit calculations are regularly used in deciding on priorities for public works projects. So there is no reason why an ethical utilitarian could not incorporate such calculations into his overall judgement of what policies would produce the greatest average net benefit. And for a social contract theorist, this determination would depend on what policy or policies for public works made the worst off as well off as possible. This could very likely be the utilitarian policy often used for such decisions.

[6]   Later, Pogge attempts to define a (cosmopolitanly ethical) nation in terms of spatial proximity and claims that (cosmopolitan) justice must ignore totally any claims of family, ethnic group, culture, religious, or national membership. (2007, 169)

[7]   Pogge also has a discussion of ecology and ethics in which he implausibly grounds ethical responsibility for the environment in a person's having the right to participate in decisions that affect him. I discuss this position further in chapter 15, **IT-Enabled Globalization and the Environment**.

[8]   Redistribution in accordance with Rawls' Difference Principle must produce better results for the least advantage rather than just evening things out for its own sake.

[9]   See Chapter 5, **Domestic Theories of Justice,** "Theories of Justice."

[10]   Chapter 4, **The Basis of Ethical Principles,** "The Rational Basis of Ethics."

[11]   Using the definitions of Chapter 4, principles of justice belong to *ethical* rather than *moral* theory.

[12]   Perhaps with a superhero chest insignia emblazoned with the letters GJ.

[13]   See Chapter 2, **Current Ethically Globalized Institutions, "**World financial and economic institutions" and "Multinational Corporations (MNCs)"

[14]   Both probably not inherently bad ideas, but perhaps chaos is the right word if such interventions were common.

[15]   The Millennium Development Goal of 0.7% of a country's gross national product going to poor countries could be regarded as benevolence at the country level.

[16]   Not to mention the war crimes committed in Iraq. When the self-defense justification became inoperative and the war was continued, the G.W. Bush administration became guilty of the same war crimes as the German generals executed after World War II.

[17]   The Obama administration reversed these Bush-era policies, at least in principle. Notice was given that the Iraq war was to be terminated. The continuing Afghanistan war is still ethically problematic. A substantial RAND corporation report has demonstrated that a full-bore military campaign is neither necessary nor desirable for self-defense against stateless terrorist groups such as al-Qaeda. (Kovalik 2009)

[18]   Singer's conditions are more plausible than Rawls' more stringent ones.

[19]   It would be good but more than ethically required to help when there is some or great cost to oneself. The precise term is "supererogatory" or heroic or noble.

[20]   But not, as of this writing in 2008, the world's largest economy. The EU is.

[21]   On a universal principle theory, the cost level would be determined by what level I could handle if I made it a principle to sustain that level.

[22]   Surplus value in Marx's terminology.

[23]   Since my purpose with the example is to discredit utilitarianism, I see no point in pursuing refinements. Any alternative here has problems. As pointed out in Chapter 4, **The Basis of Ethical Principles**, considering average utility makes more sense than just adding all utilities. Otherwise an increased population with lower utility would be chosen. Simply adding the average utilities of the two countries seems somewhat arbitrary. But weighting the averages by population has the same problem. In terms of the countries in the example, if Desperia has four times as many people as Needia, the result would still be the same provided that Needia's inhabitants had really *really* good lives averaging a value of 145. The weighted aggregate value is then $(1 * 145 + 4 * -5)/5 = 25$ average. The difficulty occurs because values must be summed across countries.

[24]   On a social contract theory, the choice would depend on the institutions producing these results rather than just on the distribution itself. So we can't declare Distribution 2 the winner just on the basis of these numbers.

25 This claim is probably incorrect. There will be more discussion in the following Chapter 8, **The Ethical Status of Globalized Institutions.**

26 In Section 3, **A Social Contract for Globalized Institutions,** a social contract justification will be given for these criteria.

27 For a utilitarian, if harm to your country is less than the benefit to the country being helped, you should help. For a universal principle theorist, the question is whether it could be a principle to help at this cost level, or whether regularly incurring this cost will damage the country more.

Chapter 8
The Ethical Status of Globalized Institutions

The purpose of this chapter is to determine where ethically globalized institutions need ethical principles and what kind of ethical principles are needed. Two preliminary discussions are needed: First, global or trans*nation*al ethics clearly depends on the ethical status of *nations*. The transnational ethical theories we have just examined differ markedly on this issue, and we need to reach a conclusion about the ethical status of a country or nation. Second, I need to summarize what is right and what is deficient in the transnational ethical theories examined in the two previous chapters.

After these rather extensive preliminary discussions, I will examine the ethical requirements of current ethically globalized institutions.

THE ETHICAL STATUS OF NATIONAL SOVEREIGNTY

In this section, I want to determine the ethical significance of national sovereignty in a way that avoids the biases of the transnational ethical theories we have just examined—that is, without Walzer's assumption that the internal ethics of a society mostly can't be questioned, or without Rawls' assumption that

DOI: 10.4018/978-1-60566-922-9.ch008

sovereignty is ethically justified only for just societies, or without the cosmopolitan assumption that national sovereignty has only derivative value and will soon disappear.

The cosmopolitan assumption would require a radical departure from the ways in which human beings have defined themselves since the founding of nations and states since about 4000 BC in the Fertile Crescent, China, and Mexico. Patriots have died for their countries in battle ever since. Were they all simply mistaken? There has also been self-sacrifice in battles between smaller groups not organized into states from the dawn of humanity up to now. Seeing the intensity of national groups at sports competitions such as the European Cup, World Cup, the Olympic Games or other international athletic competitions make it seem even less likely that a true cosmopolitan attitude of indifference toward group identity will take over anytime soon.

In fact, one of the complaints of social activists against transnational economic institutions such as the World Bank and World Trade Organization is that they don't respect the sovereignty of developing nations. "What right," observes William Tabb, "do rich Westerners have to impose their preferences on other countries?" (Tabb 2004, 335) Even within the US in the 1996 Presidential campaign, conservatives such as Buchanan and Dole denounced the WTO for nullifying American laws. (Tabb 2004, 315-316) So if sovereignty has no ethical status, a cosmopolitan must dismiss such complaints as ethically irrelevant. The problem, of course, is that economic activity is largely organized within states and the governments of those states are currently largely responsible for whether their economies are doing well or badly. Whether this ultimately should be changed cannot be decided on cosmopolitan grounds, because that would beg the question. It might be possible to make a case that a total global organization of economies would ultimately be better for satisfying a global difference principle. But there is no evidence for this now. Until the case is made and an integrated stateless economy is the world consensus goal, we need to deal with nations as sovereign.

Wars—organized violence—have been a way of resolving conflicts between national groups. One hopes, of course, that war is a last resort. That is, war is waged only as a defense against aggression by another state or to intervene in a state whose government is practicing genocide. But members of all states at war are willing to give their lives to promote their country's survival. Even in totalitarian states like the former Soviet Union, soldiers were willing to defend their country when threatened from without. Is all this ethically indefensible? Were all those willing deaths in vain? Could it be that giving your life for your country was once ethically justified, but will not be necessary in the coming world community where states have no power?[1]

Rawls discussed international ethics in terms of *peoples.* Other terms covering similar ground are *nation, state, government,* and *country.* A *nation* is a self-defined cultural and social community with a common identity, and usually a common origin, in history or ancestry, usually with its own territory or homeland. A *state* is a political association with effective sovereignty over a geographic area, often a nation but sometimes part of a nation or many nations. *Government* is the institution or institutions that exercise sovereignty, both at the national level and at regional or local levels. A *country* is similar to nation. (Wikipedia 2008a) The martyred American Revolutionary patriot Nathan Hale might have said "I only regret that I have but one life to give my nation." But he would not have said, "I only regret that I have but one life to give my state." Or "I only regret that I have but one life to give my government." "Country," even more than "nation," suggests a community one owes personal allegiance to. "My nation, 'tis of thee," just does not have the ring of "my country, 'tis of thee."

Ethical requirements attach in different ways to countries or nations, on the one hand, and states or governments, on the other. Duties to countries or nations arise out of one's free acceptance of being a subject of the country.[2] Obligations to states or governments arise when they are lawful exercises of the authority of the government or state of the country one is a subject or citizen of. In what follows, I will use whichever of country, nation, state, or government seems most appropriate for the context.

What Rawls calls a *people* is like a nation or a country (as opposed to a state or government) with two additional characteristics: It has a nearly just government, and acknowledges principles of justice. (Rawls 1999b, 23-25) As we saw, the additional characteristics added to this definition make it of limited usefulness in transnational ethics. But the notion of the people, the individuals, of a nation or country can be important in formulating transnational social contracts. I will therefore define a *people* differently from Rawls, to be just the individuals in a nation or country.

Nations are, of course, economic units. Nations may no longer be as self-sufficient as they once were, but any economic activity, even if it takes place transnationally, is still reported as taking place in some nation or another. Economic regulation and management takes place in the first instance within nations, even if these days it can be changed by the actions of the WTO. And much economic activity can still be meaningfully described as taking place within one country, with activities which generate exports to other countries or which utilize imports from other countries engaging in the activity. Within the economy of each country, benefits and burdens are shared and regarded as the product of cooperative activity of all in the country.

Yet the fact that a country provides economic benefits, however good, is usually not a reason for killing or dying for it. People sacrifice their lives for their countries, but it would be insane to die for one's corporation or football team. The (justifiable ethical) reason must be that the freedom of my countrymen is seriously threatened. Why should the freedom of others matter to me? If I were a cosmopolitan citizen of the world, I would attach no special value to the freedom of someone in one country as opposed to another country. Yet we think of freedom as freedom within a particular country.

Freedom is the right not to be interfered with or prevented from doing something. It would be a meaningless term for a solitary person. It is others who could interfere with you or prevent you from doing things. If you are free, then they cannot or should not interfere with you. An absolute ruler like Ivan the Terrible could interfere with other people to his heart's content. Yet we do not consider him to be free or, for that matter, not free. To be free is to be a member of a community whose members are also free to determine their own fates. The social contract philosopher Hobbes (1651) noted that since some members of a community can try to interfere with others by force, a sovereign (or government) with the ability to use force is necessary. People cede their right to use force to a sovereign in order to gain freedom from interference by others.[3] The sovereign (government) also has the right to use force against other communities that threaten the freedom of its citizens. Thus the state or government is the guarantor of individual freedom and self-determination in a nation or country. It cannot be abolished until there is little or no threat of aggression from other countries. Unfortunately, the aggressive[4] US war on Iraq by the strongest power on the planet makes it impossible to discount a threat of aggression for the foreseeable future.[5] The cosmopolitan world where there are no longer national boundaries is a world very far in the future.

WHAT IS A COUNTRY?

Civil wars, revolutions and secessionist groups present circumstances where governments may not be identical to countries or nations. In a civil war or revolution, a group within a country attempts to overthrow and replace the current government by force. In secession, an ethnic group (or other organized minority) attempts to secede from the original country and set up a separate nation with its own government in a part of the original country. Civil wars and revolutions can be ethically justified when the current government is committing acts of grave injustice or when the current government denies representation to the people of the country, as with colonial governments.[6]

Secession raises ethical questions which are not easily settled. There is no ethical requirement that every ethnic group must have its own country. Many stable nations contain many ethnicities. In the early 20th century, Greece and Turkey engaged in forced repatriation to prevent the existence of a destabilizing Greek minority in Turkey and a destabilizing Turkish minority in Greece. This repatriation caused a great deal of harm to individuals. (Blanchard 1925) In the late 20th century, the breakup of the former Yugoslavia indicates the force of the desire of different ethnic groups to be their own nations with their own governments. If the rights of secessionists have been systematically violated, then it is understandable why they should want to secede. The ethical question here is whether the mere desire for self-rule by an ethnic or cultural or religious group within a country justifies the creation of a new country and government. A people certainly have the right to self-determination, but the question is whether a given ethnic (or cultural or religious) group constitutes a country or nation. Wikipedia lists 114 secessionist movements in all continents but Australia! (Wikipedia 2008b) This question often comes up when national boundaries were drawn by colonial powers without regard for differences in ethnic or cultural or religious groups. The result has been unstable regimes without a clear national identity to support the state. Examples include Iraq and Niger. Partitions of larger countries to separate ethnic, cultural, religious or political groups have also been a main cause of war in the 20th and 21st centuries.[7]

Two examples of ethnic groups split between more than one country include the Kurds in Turkey, Iraq, Iran and Syria, and the Basques in southwestern France and northern Spain. Both groups have suffered severe oppression over centuries. Both have mounted their own terrorist groups. Both have had their languages and cultures suppressed. France suppressed the Basque language and culture because of its policy of assimilating ethnic minorities. Turkey provided token relaxation on prohibition of the Kurdish language and culture, presumably to meet EU requirements.[8] (Wikipedia 2008c)

So when is secession ethically justified? It clearly is justified if both the entire state and the part that wants to secede vote to approve the secession. But how far does the right to self-determination go? Who or what is the *self* in self-determination? If the seceding part approves, but the entire state does not, then secession is normally not justified.[9]

If a separate area of the state is being significantly oppressed by the rest of the state, even if the majority of the state does not want secession, then we can say with Peter Singer that government in the oppressed area is not a minimalist democracy and does not have legitimacy.[10] So a separate state or nation is then ethically justified. Even if the larger state uses oppression only to counter the separatist movement, that means there is no longer a minimalist democracy in the separatist area. Thus Kosovo, with a history of oppression of the Albanian majority by Serbia as part of Serbia, is clearly a case of justified secession. If more than one state is involved, with one state being oppressive and the other not, a possible choice would be for the oppressed area to join the other non-oppressive state. I don't believe this has ever actually happened.

Even before cosmopolitan ethical theories were elaborated, negative features of nations were widely noticed. In Chapter 6, **Political Realism and the Society of Societies,** I noted that Pascal, the French philosopher, compared people living on the same and on different sides of national boundaries of warring nations. If we are on the same side and I shoot you, I am a murderer. If we are on different sides and I shoot you, I am a hero. (Pascal 1670, sec. V) Others who have commented on the irrationality of loyalty to country include G. B. Shaw, Emma Goldman, and Einstein.

So what is the ethical status of a country? Countries that are not minimalist democracies have no ethical legitimacy. (Recall that a minimalist democracy has been ruling indefinitely with the apparent acquiescence of its people, without severe restrictions on civil liberties, and without using repression to maintain its power.) Even if a government is repressive, individuals may still obey its orders to avoid punishment. And they may still owe allegiance to the (internally) repressive government in its dealings with other countries. If the security of one's country is threatened from without, one may have a duty to obey government policies to deal with the threat, possibly conscription into the military. It is important to recognize that one's duty here is to the country rather than the different governments the country may have over time. These governments may be more or less representative of the people of that country.

Conscientious objectors to military service can hold the (comprehensive) moral view that all war is wrong, often on religious grounds. A society accepting the principle of Greatest Equal Liberty should honor such sincere claims. Likewise, if the particular war or orders within a war are unjust, sincere refusal to obey should be honored.[11] A full discussion of these issues would be lengthy and is not directly relevant here.

Let me note that reasonable ethical judgements in this area appeal not only to the (domestic) principles of justice but also to recognized principles holding between nations. Both Morgenthau and Rawls summarize these principles. They include the rights of self-defense and self-determination, and the obligation to honor treaties. Most importantly for the current issue, there are ethical constraints on waging war and on treating combatants codified in the Hague Conventions of 1899 and 1907 and the Geneva Conventions. (Morgenthau 1993, 229) Morgenthau notes that the prohibition on deliberately killing noncombatants is unfortunately increasingly ignored. And the prohibition against torture has recently been dropped by the United States for no clear reason. The former Soviet Communist states employed torture to obtain false confessions; no one has ever claimed that torture is effective in getting the truth. One can only conclude that obtaining the truth was not the aim of the US government under Bush. Since most other nations at least acknowledge these principles, that would be a basis for ethical refusal to participate in unjust wars or unjust conduct within a war.

To conclude, the basis for the ethical status of countries is that their institutions (states, governments) provide security for their inhabitants. 'Security' means protection of their freedom to live their lives as they see fit and work toward goals of their own choosing. Inhabitants of countries have duties to help protect that security when threatened externally, whether the governments of those countries are just or minimalist democracies or not. However, there is no ethical requirement to obey a government that is not a minimal democracy, although it may be wise to do so to avoid retribution. Also, other countries may restrict trade or employ sanctions against governments that are not minimalist democracies. Actually intervening in other countries (by war) is ethically justified only in self-defense or when the country is engaged in some version of genocide. Even in case of genocide, it might be better for an international organization to handle the intervention to prevent muddying the waters with national self-interest.

Much of what I have concluded is the same as Peter Singer's recommendations. His different conclusion is that "national sovereignty has no *intrinsic* moral weight" (Singer 2004, 148) and that its only moral purpose is to protect its people. His examples (Cambodia, Rwanda, Indonesia) make it clear that he is thinking of *internal* protection. *External* protection from other nations is still very much needed, and since justice is still administered *internally,* a government (a country's political and economic institutions) still has many ethical responsibilities.

Singer quotes approvingly from John Lennon's song *Imagine*: "Imagine there's no countries . . . Imagine all the people/Sharing all the world." (1971) But do we want that world to be one homogenized culture? We may not want to follow Michael Walzer in declaring each culture or society sacrosanct and ethically justified on its own terms. But surely there is some value in cultural differences, in different ways of doing things. One of the functions of countries has explicitly been to preserve those differences, sometimes at great cost. This question of value will be addressed in **Chapter 15. The Value of IT-Enabled Globalization.** The nature of the value of diversity needs to be assessed and balanced against the likelihood of preventing war by eliminating such differences.

TRANSNATIONAL ETHICS AND LOVE

One difference between cosmopolitan ethical theories and theories that give some ethical status to membership in a country is that each exemplifies a different kind of love. There are three kinds of love, each with a different Greek name: *Eros* (ἔρως), romantic or sexual love; *philia* (φιλια), brotherly love; and *agapē* (αζαπη pronounced AH-gah-pay), unconditional love.[12] The first two have traces in our current usage. *Eros* is the source of our word 'erotic.' And *philia* contributed to the name of Philadelphia, the city of brotherly love. *Agapē* remains a Greek word but it figures prominently in parts of the New Testament originally in Greek. In the commandment to "love thy neighbor as thyself" (Matthew 19:19), *agapē* is the word used for love in the original Greek.[13] Cosmopolitanism clearly is calling for us to practice *agapē*, while theories giving ethical status to country or other group membership are calling for *philia.*

The ethical question here is, can having a feeling (especially love) be an ethical requirement? The philosopher Kant thought not. He remarked that "love is a matter of feeling, and I cannot love because I *will* to, still less because I *ought* to. . . . So a *duty to love* is logically impossible. (1797b, 401) However, Kant did think that it was a duty to help others, regardless of one's feelings.

But if one did have feelings of *philia*, would one's ethical intuitions be to give ethical status to countrymen and other groups one belonged to? And would having feelings of *agapē* lead one toward cosmopolitan ethical intuitions? Perhaps so. But I believe Kant is right about feelings. They can't be the basis for ethical requirements. So the real ethical issue is to what extent we are ethically required to help others. In Christian thought, *agapē* is an ideal, not a requirement. I believe the same is true of the cosmopolitan principle of treating all humanity as equal subjects of our ethical concern. Cosmopolitanism might be a requirement for a saint, but we are not ethically required to be saints. The word for this requirement is *supererogatory*, above what is required. Heroic and saintly acts are supererogatory: Such acts are laudable and praiseworthy, but not ethically required. So too for cosmopolitanism.

Peter Singer does raise the issue of whether cosmopolitan economic redistribution— giving to other countries because we have more than they do—might be too demanding as an ethical requirement, with the result that less people will observe it. For him, the issue is that the consequences of advocating such an ethical position may be counterproductive. He concedes that this may be true, but he claims it does not affect the correctness of the cosmopolitan position. He suggests that publicly we could advocate a less stringent ethical position while privately we observe the (correct) cosmopolitan position. (2004, 191-192) I think this is where consequentialism gives the wrong ethical answer. Universal principle ethics require that our ethical principles be public, that is, we be willing to let everyone know what they are.[14] Thus announcing a principle you do not believe because it will have better results is simply not ethical. It destroys the basis for trusting what people say. But on universal principle grounds, there would be no ethical problem with cosmopolitan economic redistribution as a saintly ideal and not an ethical requirement. The more limited ethical requirement is to help those in poor countries up to some reasonable amount to be determined by principles of global justice.

Peter Singer's case for cosmopolitanism is that there is no ethical basis for any special status for (his phrase) "our own kind." (2004, 155) If we give any preference to family and friends, it is because those feelings are ingrained and it would cause more difficulty and harm to eradicate those feelings than to accept them. The fact that others are close to you is ethically relevant only insofar as it gives you more opportunity to deal with them ethically. And there is no special obligation to one's countrymen (Singer frames the issue in terms of 'nation-state') because the needs of others outside are so great! Singer thinks these needs make being part of a country as a community with shared benefits and burdens irrelevant. He does not consider economic and social interdependence within communities.

Singer's final consideration is that our current problems such as the environment and world poverty are transnational and therefore nation-states are irrelevant to their solution. (2004, 171) Of course this does not follow. All three of our cosmopolitans require us to give up any allegiance to any group or institution short of the whole human race. Yet it is not necessary to take all human beings impartially as the scope of one's ethical concern and exclude all concerns of lesser scope. We can address transnational ethical problems without making countries, multinational corporations, and other groups ethically irrelevant. Indeed, exclusive cosmopolitanism makes it impossible to formulate the ethical principles essential to handle transnational problems just because the institutions involved in those problems become ethically irrelevant.

AN ASSESSMENT OF GLOBALIZED ETHICAL THEORIES

All three cosmopolitan theories I examined give no ethical weight to any group short of all of humanity, and a more correct theory of globalized ethics will have to take into account the ethical status of the countries, nations, and societies people belong to. Principles of justice are principles of social cooperation for people sharing economic and social benefits and burdens.

The other theories of global ethics I examined were political realism and Rawls' international social contract. Political realism is a theory of the relation between *states,* not globalized institutions. Rawls' international social contract suffers from same defect: Also, it can't be directly extended because the guidance it provides for less-than-just states makes it too utopian to be usable. For example, it would require us to have no trade relations with China until China's human rights deficiencies are corrected.

Thus an alternative to existing transnational ethical theories must take into account the actual institutions of social cooperation among states and in the global economy. Additional new transnational institutions will almost certainly be needed to implement globalized ethics, as well as changes to current institutions. We can now turn to current institutions, see where ethical principles are needed, and get a preliminary idea of the nature of those principles.

ETHICALLY GLOBALIZED INSTITUTIONS

The list of ethically globalized institutions from Chapter 2 is:

- Superpowers
- Multinational Corporations
- The United Nations and its agencies; the World Court
- World financial and economic institutions such as the World Bank, International Trade Organization (ITO), and the International Monetary Fund (IMF)
- Non-Governmental Organizations (NGOs) without ties to existing states.
- Websites with international presence
- New global institutions

The last item, new global institutions, did not appear in Chapter 2. In this chapter, I will note possible new global institutions which have emerged in the discussion so far. In Chapter 12, **New Globalized Institutions,** I will discuss these institutions and possible additional new global institutions in the context of implementing a new global social contract.

SUPERPOWERS

As Peter Singer disapprovingly points out, the record of the United States in giving up any of its sovereignty to any sort of world community is very poor. The US has refused to endorse the Kyoto protocol to reduce greenhouse gases. The US has refused to participate in an International Criminal Court to try crimes against humanity and genocide unless its own citizens were exempted. The US often refuses to pay its dues to the UN. Singer says "One can only hope that . . . the United States will eventually be shamed into joining in [with the rest of the world]." (Singer 2002, 198-199) [15]

But neither shame nor Hans Morgenthau's inexorable logic for a world state to prevent nuclear holocaust seem likely to dissuade the US from a policy of world domination enabled by military force.[16] Previous empires employing this strategy have collapsed under the sheer economic weight of maintaining military dominance or military parity. [17] The (late) Soviet Union collapsed under the economic weight of maintaining military parity with the US. As of 2008, there are signs that this could happen to the US. The US dollar has dramatically lost value against other major currencies as most of its expenditures go into maintaining military operations in the Middle East. The domestic economy is worsening in part as a result. It is not out of the question that something like the dramatic loss of economic power that destroyed the Soviet Union could happen to the United States. This may not be a good thing, especially for the well-being of US citizens, but neither would it be all bad.[18]

For the problem as of the time of this writing is that the United States recognizes no ethical boundaries on its ability to wage war and invade countries when it deems that doing so serves its own purposes. It recognizes no international obligations to deal with climate change[19] or war crimes. As Peter Singer demonstrates, it contributes only minimally to ameliorating conditions in poor countries. (Singer 2006, 180-185) There is nothing in principle ethically wrong with a country's being a superpower, but when it uses that power with no regard for ethics, it qualifies as a 'rogue state.' Thus the US as a superpower is part of the transnational ethical problem and not part of the solution.

It is worth recalling Hans Morgenthau's views on preventing war. Morgenthau believed that the only way war can be prevented is through a supranational power having sovereignty over existing states. Existing transnational institutions do not have the ability to enforce significant transnational ethical principles. Morgenthau believes that it is essential to prevent war to avoid nuclear holocaust.[20] We still have large nuclear stockpiles. And probability theory guarantees that as long as nuclear weapons are around, they will go off some day. (Lyttle 2005) Morgenthau reportedly once said that the nation state has now become the enemy of the human race.

Yet Morgenthau noted that the essentials for a world state are simply lacking. The peoples of the world are currently unwilling to accept a world government if the interests of their own state were harmed. Morgenthau believed the world state can come to be through the "processes of diplomacy." (1993, 389) It is hard to see how international diplomacy will be able to get nations to reduce their power in a fairly radical way. Diplomacy, after all, lacks transnational power.

So a world state does not seem to be likely. But transnational institutions with some power over nations already exist. The World Trade Organization has considerable say over the economies of individual countries. And the World Bank and International Monetary Fund can effectively put pressure on sovereign states to adopt economic and social policies. But the WTO and the IMF do not always act ethically. We will examine their transnational ethical status shortly.

But even if there came to be a world state with sovereignty over existing states, multinational corporations raise complications. Multinationals even now can escape the sovereignty of any one country by shifting actions and consequences between states. If existing states simply ceded some portion of their sovereignty to a world state, it does not automatically follow that the world state would have control of multinational corporations. More needs to be said about an institutional structure that would enable them to operate in accordance with transnational justice.

MULTINATIONAL CORPORATIONS

Because multinational corporations can override the authority of individual nations, they have transnational authority. But what is the source of this authority? On a social contract theory, any ethically legitimate authority stems from some social contract. And an appropriate social contract does not seem to exist. So multinational corporations currently exercise their power without benefit of ethical constraints.

When social contract cosmopolitans merely extend Rawlsian domestic justice to the entire world, they do not take seriously the fact that much global economic production (about 60%) is already largely in the hands of multinational corporations. The word 'corporation' does not even appear in the index to Rawls' *Law of Peoples* or in the index to Singer's *One World*. Charles Beitz mentions multinational corporations but argues that they present no issues that current political arrangements can't handle. (Beitz 1979, 146)

But there is a severe ethical problem. Corporations, whether domestic or multinational, are *legally* individuals but not *ethically* individuals. Commentators as diverse as activist Michael Lerner and former Labor Secretary Robert Reich agree that corporations are not going to sacrifice profits for social or ethical goals. (Reich 2007) Lerner notes "Even the corporate executives with the highest level of spiritual sensitivity . . . have no choice but to accept corporate profits as the absolute bottom line." (Lerner 2000, 311) Corporations are concerned about their reputations because that can affect the bottom line. But this concern is a very limited and primitive form of ethics.[21] Corporations are not individuals with an ethical point of view. [22] Therefore *they cannot be regarded as parties to the social contract.*[23] So we have the spectacle of tobacco corporations contributing predictably to the deaths of millions over the years—and still staying profitably in business even after paying millions to settle lawsuits.

Some commentators simply extend individual ethics to corporations. Thomas White (2007) asserts that the 'job' of business is to make life better for everyone in society. Michael Hopkins (2003) describes a "planetary bargain" in which corporations undertake to be socially responsible. Both of these commentators assume that we have a good idea of what globally ethical behavior would be for corporations and that corporations will behave if we call ethics to their attention. More realistic is the case of FedEx, which, though officially committed to minimizing greenhouse gases, has decided not to implement more than a token replacement of dirty trucks. The reason, says their environmental director Mitch Jackson, "We have a fiduciary duty to our stockholders." There are better uses of company capital. Even worse, FedEx even won an environmental award for its plan, which it never carried out. This case is a graphic illustration of appearing to be ethical rather than being ethical. (Elgin 2007)

Consultancies for corporate ethics deal with a predictably limited range of ethical concerns. LRN Corporation, a consultancy for corporate ethics, states its procedure as follows:

"We use a business process approach to actively manage ethics and compliance risks throughout the organization. We offer everyone involved at all levels of a global organization – employees, managers, executives, board members – the knowledge, tools and solutions they need to make better decisions and achieve higher standards of conduct. Our offerings not only help mitigate the risk of costly ethics lapses and compliance failures, but more importantly, they also help companies earn a reputation for responsible conduct that drives long-term business success." (LRN Corporation 2008)

LRN's concern is initially with costly failures to adhere to external standards, and ultimately with reputation. Appearing so, but not necessarily being so is what is ultimately important for corporations.

I will consider in Chapter 11, **Globalized Ethics and Current Institutions**, the claims of those who believe that voluntary corporate social responsibility (CSR) can harmonize corporate goals and ethical requirements. A commentator such as David Vogel in his *The Market for Virtue* (2004) argues that evidence shows that corporations will work toward their business goals whenever there is a conflict. This is what we just saw in the case of Fed Ex. In fact, corporate response to criticism of their environmental ethics often makes clear that corporations have more interest in seeming to be ethical than in actually being ethical. Christian Aid, a UK-based religious nongovernmental organization (NGO) that fights global poverty, issued a report critical of the social responsibility efforts of three major corporations. The corporate response through a public relations firm promoting CSR was vituperative and argued that Christian Aid had not done sufficient academic studies to draw conclusions. Of course the public relations firm had also not done any such studies showing that CSR was in fact effective in the cases discussed. (Baue 2004) Christian Aid had observed in its report that corporations wanted to keep ethical compliance voluntary to preserve their own power. This observation may have been what prompted the all-out attack.

Many of the problems raised by multinational corporations are simply extensions of domestic socially irresponsible behavior of corporations. Corporations are unique because they are legally individuals—and must be to fulfill their legal function. But they are not subject to the ethical constraints of individuals.[24] For other groups such as governments and voluntary associations, ethical responsibility lies with the leaders of those organizations. And for governments, the principles of justice provide a whole extra level of ethical constraints. But for corporations, individual leaders are *legally protected* from being personally liable for the damages caused by their leadership. Therefore the solution has to be a new set of legal requirements for corporations which serve the function of providing ethical accountability.[25]

The first step is the minimal one of having corporations not act like sociopathic monsters: No killing people, no deliberately not telling the truth, no thwarting the legitimate rights of your employees through union-busting, complying with accepted accounting standards for truthfulness in financial reporting. Even meeting these four requirements for a corporate ethical evaluation would be an enormous improvement in corporate behavior in the worst cases. Some further steps would be outside periodic ethical review by an authority with the power to dismantle the corporation and sell off its assets.[26] In any case, corporations should be prohibited from attempting to influence public policy by advertising or campaign contributions or by financing electoral initiatives.[27] Remember that corporations are only *legal* individuals. They do not inherit rights from nor are they participants in a domestic social contract.

These suggested regulations on corporations are necessary within a domestically just society in order to preserve the justice of the society. We would expect analogues of them to be necessary to prevent multinational corporations from damaging or distorting global justice. But, as we just saw, corporations resist any attempt to limit their power, so it will not be easy to implement restrictions as draconian as those just suggested.[28 29] The UN's Global Compact sets voluntary standards for multinationals. The Global Compact for the most part does not address the ethical gap between individuals and corporations. Its principles are those of a global social contract, with the addition of an anti-corruption principle. I will discuss the content of the Global Compact together with my proposed Global Economy Social Contract in Chapter 10, **Elements of a Global Contract.** The Global Compact's added principle for business to work against corruption, including bribery and extortion, is certainly a welcome and sound ethical principle. But again the Global Compact is only voluntary.

The economist Joseph Stiglitz takes a more balanced view of corporate ethics. In his *Making Globalization Work* (2007, ch. 7) he notes myriad abuses of corporate power, many of them involving corporations playing off one state against another: Bribery or political contributions to overlook environmental regulations, monopolization accompanied by threats simply to pull out if the country tries to regulate them (Microsoft did this in South Korea), monopolistic price fixing. As he sees it, the problem is that the corporate goal of maximizing profits very often conflicts with social and ethical goals. Stiglitz makes a number of suggestions to improve matters, among them: Allowing more legal transparency between countries when corporations act transnationally; a global competition law and a global authority to enforce it; enlarging liability of corporate officers when egregious violations of environmental protection laws occur; a common carbon tax.

Stiglitz's suggestions begin to address the issue raised by ethically globalized institutions, especially multinational corporations. Solutions within a society and principles dealing with how societies relate to each other often don't touch the problems. Some of his suggestions require overriding state sovereignty. Others may require global authority above states (competition laws, common carbon tax). As I mentioned, one problem is the source of authority for these transnational institutions. On my view, we need a transnational social contract to provide this authority. Two related difficulties then present themselves: Corporations cannot be parties to the social contract. But at the same time they need to be subject to the authority of institutions derived from a transnational social contract.

It is not too hard to deal with corporations not being parties to a global social contract. This contract has to be between all classes of individuals contributing to or benefiting from the global economy. Parties to the contract must therefore include corporate stakeholders such as stockholders, customers, executives, and other employees. Thus corporate interests as reflected in individuals will be taken into account. Obviously to include corporations as entities would repeat the mistake of treating them as ethical individuals when they are so clearly not.

The second difficulty is how corporations come to recognize the authority of institutions derived from a global social contract. This is actually not a difficulty with a global social contract, but rather with the fact that corporations are currently under no social contract and no authority. Thus multinationals can evade requirements of the various states they do business in by strategies mentioned above. To be brutally honest, this problem is insoluble on its own terms. Once the genie was let out of the bottle of giving corporations virtually all the rights of individuals, it is impossible to put that genie back. Corporations have both motivation and the overwhelming resources to prevent any restriction of their powers.[30] And, in accordance with their primary goal, that is what they will do. So even the domestic legal analogues of ethics for corporations just suggested will not be easy to implement, let alone their transnational versions.

I will suggest now a few possible directions for a way out of this difficulty. We will discuss these more fully in Chapter 12, **New Globalized Institutions.** One possible way out is the *social business* developed by Mohammed Yunus, 2006 Nobel Peace Prize Laureate. A social business is run as a business, but the goal of profit maximization is removed. Investors or shareholders receive no profits from the business; they receive (at most) their money back. All profits are plowed back into the business. This arrangement allows the business to pursue its social goals without conflicting with the aim of profit maximization. It differs from a nonprofit organization (such as most NGOs) because it does not have to spend large amounts of time and resources raising money. As long as expenses are covered, it can continue operations indefinitely. (Yunus 2003)

In later discussion, I will explore the question of how widely such a model could be applied to corporations. Obviously, getting a social business off the ground requires investors who are committed to the social goals without expecting any financial return. If social businesses can be transnational, they may have a different status for the global economic social contract than corporations.

Here is a completely different approach to the problem of authority over multinational corporations. Let us ask why we are concerned with the unlimited power of (especially multinational) corporations. One obvious answer is that corporations tend to treat their impact on the environment as an externality. The *corporation* doesn't suffer the effects of pollution or environmental degradation; only various human beings and other living things contingently connected to the corporation suffer those effects.

But the human agents behind corporations may come to realize that their security and survival depends on their limiting the power of the corporation to damage the environment.[31] The motivation for such limits would be similar to individuals' motivation to enter a social contract ceding some of their authority to the state in order to gain greater security for all. Since the environment is an externality for corporations acting as corporations, the predictable result is an environment unable to support human life. If humans disappear, so does the meaning of their corporate financial transactions. If there are still any computers left running on their own power, the actions of corporations and their ultimate goal of increased profits, will become completely meaningless, abstract patterns like frost on a windowpane.[32]

Thus when I come to design the global social contract and the institutions expressing it in Section 3, **A Social Contract For Globalized Institutions**, these observations about corporate power will need to be kept in mind. Corporations are not parties to the global social contract and they do not have a direct motivation to obey institutions derived from it. Yet possible alternative organizations and the possible environmental motivation just sketched must be kept in mind. Because without some plausible motivation for corporations to limit their power, any global social contract will be completely meaningless.

THE UNITED NATIONS AND RELATED AGENCIES

The United Nations (UN) was founded 1945 just after World War II, with the hope that it would settle conflicts between states and thereby avoid war. As we saw in Chapter 2, these aims were not fulfilled. UN peacekeeping forces have succeeded in reducing the level of violence many times in conflicts such as between Israel and its Arab neighbors, between Greece and Turkey on Cyprus, and between India and Pakistan over Kashmir. But the UN has not been able to prevent the use of aggressive military force by superpowers, such as the former Soviet Union in Afghanistan, Hungary, and the former Czechoslovakia, and the United States in Vietnam, Iraq, Somalia, Panama, and Grenada. Aggressive military force in Kosovo/Serbia was used under NATO auspices, not through the UN.

Also, the UN has not done well in acting against genocides such as those in Rwanda, Kosovo, and Darfur. There was a UN peacekeeping force in Rwanda to deal with a civil war between Tutus and Hutsis. But when the long-planned and publicized mass killings began in 1994, the UN Security Council and then-Head of Peacekeeping Operations Kofi Annan failed to act. The Canadian commander of UN peacekeeping operations Romeo Dallaire was denied reinforcement. He refused to obey orders to withdraw and heroically helped save thousands of lives. Other peacekeepers such as the Ghanians "abandoned many leading Tutsis to death squads during the genocide, in one instance physically handing Rwandan chief justice (Joseph Kovaruganda) over to a Hutu death squad, then sharing drinks with the killers while they assaulted Kovaruganda's wife and two young daughters." (Wikipedia 2008d) Both the UN Security Council and Belgium (which withdrew its peacekeeping forces during the genocide) have publicly apologized for their actions.

Although it's good that the UN has admitted its mistakes, it is not clear whether the failures of governance which allowed a highly publicized genocide to occur have been addressed. In 1995, similar problems emerged in Bosnia. The Human Rights Watch reported that:

The fall of the town of Srebrenica and its environs to Bosnian Serb forces in early July 1995 made a mockery of... United Nations protection. United Nations peacekeeping officials were unwilling to heed requests for support from their own forces... thus allowing Bosnian Serb forces to easily overrun it and—without interference from U.N. soldiers—to carry out systematic, mass executions of hundreds, possibly thousands, of civilian men and boys and to terrorize, rape, beat, execute, rob and otherwise abuse civilians... (Human Rights Watch 1995)

There were numerous other Serbian atrocities before and after Srebrenica. With no follow up action by the UN, NATO began activity on its own. After a successful Croatian military operation with US help,[33] the Dayton accords of 1995 under US auspices divided Bosnia into Muslim-Croat and Serbian areas. Current tourist guides warn about omnipresent land mines and booby-trapped houses in Bosnia. Over ten years later, the masterminds of the genocide by Serbians are still being brought to justice. Some Serbians still vehemently defend the genocide.

A 2008 UN report quotes the head of the UN force in Darfur as saying that the operation faces critical shortages in troops, personnel, equipment and logistics. (UN News Centre 2008) So what else is new? A UN commander at Srebrenica noted that he was part of a peacekeeping force where there was no peace. Genocide is mass criminal violence against part of the population of the same country. To stop it requires mass military force, not a peacekeeping operation. The UN has in fact never itself employed mass military force. The possible exception, the UN-authorized Korean action, was 90 per cent American.

The UN as presently constituted is an extensive humanitarian NGO and is not in a position to take effective action against genocide. Clearly some transnational institution is needed to take such action. The UN currently has no significant power over any nation state, so its current ethical status is the same as any nongovernmental humanitarian organization. That is, it needs to do what it says it will do and provide an accounting to its supporters. Its scope is larger than most other humanitarian NGOs and that makes it more important. Some, including Peter Singer, would like to see the transnational authority of the UN increased, possibly along with some organizational changes. These issues will be discussed in Chapter 11, **Globalized Ethics and Current Institutions.**

WORLD FINANCIAL AND ECONOMIC INSTITUTIONS

The World Bank, the International Monetary Fund (IMF), and the World Trade Organization (WTO), have transnational power. The declared aim of the World Bank and the IMF is to provide support to developing countries. The World Trade Organization's aims are to reduce trade restrictions and to adjudicate trade disputes between members. The IMF's power resides in its approval of a country's economic situation being a condition for the World Bank granting a loan. In practice, IMF requirements include opening a country's financial markets together with privatization of government-controlled enterprises. These policies have had very mixed results for the countries complying with them. For example, they contributed substantially to the collapse of Argentina's economy in 2001.[34] (Stiglitz 2003, 70) (Klein 2007)

So the aims of the World Bank and IMF are clearly ethical ones. The question is how they are implemented, in particular who has a say in their policies and what accountability mechanisms are available. Right now, the answer is that the developed countries set policy. Also, the IMF has incurred ethical criticism because it supports repressive military dictatorships. Its defense that it has no power to enforce democratization is disingenuous. Together with the World Bank, it has the power to aid or fail to aid a country. Its power can, after all, pressure a country into privatizing important institutions. The ethical point is that, even if a substantial number of countries wanted a policy of no aid to repressive dictatorships, currently the IMF would not have to take this into account.

Thus the IMF (and World Bank) with their current structures are ethically globalized but not responsive to ethical considerations. The nature of the changes necessary to make them responsive will be discussed in Chapter 11, **Globalized Ethics and Current Institutions**. The WTO has similar ethical problems. Unlike the other two, its aim is explicitly to reduce trade restrictions. Its power stems from its ability to impose significant trade sanctions for noncompliance. Other WTO members—which is nearly all countries—must cooperate in enforcing sanctions or be subject to sanctions themselves. Free trade may or may not always be ethically desirable. There is also some question on how even-handed the WTO is in enforcing the removal of barriers to free trade. The US has maintained massive agricultural subsidies for many years.[35] There is no question that the WTO is not responsive to ethical considerations. I noted that the WTO forbids trade restriction based on whether a country is repressive. It also forbids almost all environmental restrictions. And its intellectual property policies cause drug accessibility problems in poor countries.

One might not agree with all the ethical judgements behind these criticisms, but that is not the point. For an institution to be ethical or just, it must include a mechanism for considering claims of ethics and justice. For these institutions, there is currently no mechanism short of violent demonstrations. In Chapter 11, **Globalized Ethics and Current Institutions**, I will consider whether there are changes to these institutions that will make them ethical, or whether entirely new institutions are required. The aims of the World Bank and IMF are ethical aims, so changes to insure that they fulfill those aims would make them ethical. The aim of the WTO is more neutrally economic, so it may make more sense to leave it as it is and develop another institution to handle global economic justice.

The Organisation for Economic Cooperation and Development (OECD) is also an ethically globalized institution. Its aim of improving the functioning of the international economy is not entirely an ethical one. But it has taken upon itself a number of clearly ethical issues, such as corporate tax shifting, corruption, educational assessment, and environmental issues. However, one of its projects, the MAI (Multilateral Agreement on Investment), was scuttled after great opposition by a group of NGOs. The agreement, although it would have simplified and facilitated transnational business, would have eliminated any state control over business and investment, as well as labor and environmental standards. Thus it was very much in the (short-term) interests of multinational corporations. (Tabb 2004) The fact that the OECD was able to consider claims of ethics and justice in this case, as well as its work on transnational ethical issues, is in its favor as an ethical institution. The fact that it promoted a principle so clearly biased in favor of the profitability of multinationals shows that it can't be trusted to be ethical, although its work deserves attention by other transnational institutions.

NON-GOVERNMENTAL ORGANIZATIONS (NGOS)

I am specifically concerned with humanitarian and social activist NGOs acting on transnational issues such as human rights, the environment, social programs, and women's rights. The World Bank, IMF, WTO, and OECD do not technically qualify because they have governments as members. And substantively, some governments have greater power in setting their policies. Additionally, the World Bank, IMF, and WTO have some power to compel compliance with their policies, but typically NGOs only have persuasion and influencing public opinion as their tools.

In discussing the ethical status of the UN, I earlier said that any NGO has the ethical obligation to do what it says it will do and provide an accounting to its contributors. Jagdish Bhagwati, in discussing NGOs, proposes extending to NGOs the standards of oversight which apply to governments, corporations, and transnational organizations. (2007, 43) One problem with this good suggestion is that standards of transparency and regulation are very unevenly present in the institutions he cites. One problem is: Who oversees the oversight? The failed US Department of Justice in the Bush administration regularly fought tooth and nail against releasing information, not only to individual citizens, but to the US Congress itself. Joseph Stiglitz documents an almost complete lack of transparency at the IMF. In one case, the US Congress was itself unable to obtain information. Even participants in IMF projects were unable to obtain relevant information, with no institutional recourse. (Stiglitz 2003, 33-34, 51-52) Transparency (and accountability) is clearly an area in which new institutions or policies are needed, both for NGOs and governments, multinationals, and other transnational organizations.

In addition, governments, especially ones that do not honor human rights, sometimes unjustly restrict the activities of NGOs. A Russian 2006 law restricts NGOs on moral or national security grounds. China's refusal to permit even the web presence of NGOs such as Amnesty International is well known. Unjust restriction of NGOs is an ethically globalized issue which needs to be addressed by globalized institutions or policies.

WEBSITES WITH INTERNATIONAL PRESENCE

In my earlier Chapter 2 discussion, I noted that websites operating transnationally raised the global ethical issue of the applicability of the laws and customs of particular countries. The US has effectively shut down music file sharing servers operating from outside its borders. China's Great Firewall attempts to obstruct access to China from outside. And the whistleblower site Wikileaks was unsuccessful in arguing that the US did not have jurisdiction and could not be shut down by the US. Wikileaks was able to resume operations after a US Court ruled that shutting it down was a (US) violation of free speech (prior restraint) (Elias 2008, Kravets 2008) So there is an ethically globalized issue of how to handle routine legal disputes difficult or impossible to locate in a specific national jurisdiction. A new institution may be necessary to handle such disputes.

If websites exist to contribute to public policy on behalf of multinational corporations, then, as I indicated earlier, they should not have free speech rights, either domestically or globally. But a for-profit corporation or business with the purpose of facilitating non-corporate free speech might be entitled to global free speech rights. This issue might be within the scope of a new institution.

NEW GLOBAL INSTITUTIONS

In this chapter, we have uncovered the need for a number of new global institutions or policies. Regardless of what institutions are proposed, there remains the problem of the authority of such institutions over existing states or multinational corporations. In this chapter, I will consider in a preliminary way proposals for global institutions or policies to implement global justice. In Chapter 11, **Globalized Ethics and Current Institutions** and Chapter 12, **New Global Institutions,** I will address issues of feasibility more thoroughly.

A world state is perhaps one of the more problematic suggestions. Morgenthau believed that the creation of a world state was the only way war and nuclear holocaust can be prevented. Yet he also could not see how a supranational power having sovereignty over existing states could come into being. Both Kant and Rawls have also remarked on the unfeasibility of a world state. As I remarked in Chapter 2, Rawls asserts, following Kant, that any global sovereign will either be a "global despotism or. . . a fragile empire torn by frequent civil strife. . ." (Rawls 1999b, 36) Kant, however, thought a federation of states ceding part of their sovereignty to a global association was possible. (Kant 1795, 113)

The question is, how much sovereignty must a nation give away to a world sovereign to enable the world sovereign to prevent war? Experience suggests that the UN currently does not have enough authority. But actually the UN has been somewhat effective in preventing war between states or mitigating the consequences of war, except in Korea and in wars started by the superpowers. The Korean War, the only aggressive war mounted under UN auspices, was approved only because Russia, one of the superpowers, was not party to the decision.[36] So, with suitable changes in membership, the UN Security Council could be an effective institution for preventing war and mitigating its consequences. However, this excludes wars started by superpowers and also internal disturbances such as genocide.

A world state with the power to force superpowers to abandon their plans could easily abuse its power. The problem is that a further institution with effective oversight over the world state would have to have yet more power. Thus the only possible way to keep superpowers ethical would be to reduce their power. It might be effective to have trade sanctions for states that maintained military power for more than defense. But multinational corporations might also make it possible for a superpower to evade such sanctions.

As we saw, the UN has not done well in acting against genocides. The UN, as a humanitarian NGO, is not in a position to take effective action in such cases. Clearly some transnational institution is needed to take such action. The US, as superpower and the "world's policeman" has been able to act effectively in the past. But the US, as of 2008, having abandoned all principles of justice both domestically and transnationally, cannot fulfill this role. This development shows why having a superpower as a guarantor of transnational justice is probably not a good idea. Governments can change and a government that was formerly an agent of justice can become merely an agent of power.

The example of the United States in 2008 also makes it clear that superpowers cannot police themselves in observing ethical constraints on waging war and on treating combatants. These constraints were codified in the Hague Conventions of 1899 and 1907 and the Geneva Conventions. (Morgenthau 1993, 229) However, the US up to 2008 was engaged in an aggressive war, redefined 'combatant' as it pleases, and engaged in torture of detainees.[37] An institution like the International Criminal Court could police abuses. Even though the US does not accept the jurisdiction of this court, it would be interesting to see what would happen if former Attorney General Alberto Gonzales were arrested and tried during a vacation trip, say, to the Netherlands.

Unlike the UN, existing transnational institutions do have some power to enforce transnational principles. The World Bank, IMF, and WTO can enforce constraints on government's internal economic and trade policies. In order for these institutions to become ethical or just, changes in governance to allow broader influence in setting policies are necessary. For these organizations, and especially for the WTO, a body with oversight of these agencies is probably necessary. Such a body would also handle other global economic functions require new global responsibilities. Stiglitz's suggestions of a global competition law and a global authority to enforce it would fall under such a global economic authority. If global warming (which is by definition global) is going to be addressed effectively, globally enforced policies are necessary. Stiglitz's common carbon tax would be such a policy. Additionally, a global economic authority could handle problems such as corporate transnational transfers to avoid compliance with national tax and other regulations. It would probably be the appropriate institution to oversee corporate ethical behavior. The oversight of such an authority would raise the same problem as that for a world state.

Other institutions with less impact may not raise sovereignty or oversight problems. There is currently not an institution to handle routine legal disputes not located in a specific national jurisdiction. A new institution may be necessary to handle such disputes. A related issue is unjust restriction of NGOs or websites. The question is to what extent human rights (the First Principle of Justice) should be enforced globally and through what institutions? The rights of NGOs or websites are primarily individual rights. These questions come up repeatedly in connection with China and the right to freedom of speech.

Global distributive justice is another related issue. I concluded that the issue was how far our duty to help others extends. The familiar (individual) principle of benevolence—to help others in need when the cost to ourselves is not excessive—would require us to do more than we do now for those in poor nations. But it is clearly excessive to say that we should give to others in other countries *just because* we have more than they do. As I pointed out, that much giving would be saintly (supererogatory) rather than required. I believe more than benevolence is at issue. Global justice requires that we share our benefits when they result from someone else's burdens. Any such redistribution would best be accomplished through the current market economic system, constrained by principles of global justice.

For any global institutions, transparency (and accountability) is clearly a requirement. This is true for NGOs and governments, multinationals, and other transnational organizations. The difficult question is, who oversees the oversight? To avoid an infinite regress (an overseer of the oversight, and overseer of the overseer of the oversight, and so on), something like the checks and balances of the branches of the US government might work. Effectively, each branch checks on the other. As I will conclude in Chapter 12, **New Globalized Institutions,** three seems to be the right number of branches—two branches would fight, and more than three would overly dilute oversight.

The preceding has been a preliminary discussion of globalized institutions needed to implement global ethics and global justice. Section 3, **A Social Contract for Globalized Institutions**, will continue this discussion. The next chapter Chapter 9, **IT and Globalized Ethics,** examines the impact of transnational ethics on IT, for IT professionals, other individuals involved in IT, and for IT companies.

REFERENCES

Achbar, M., Abbott, J., & Bakan, J. (2004). *The corporation* [Motion Picture]. USA: Zeitgeist Films Ltd. (Available from http://www.zeitgeistvideo.com)

America.gov. (2008). *Economy: USA facts in brief.* Retrieved from http://www.america.gov/st/educ-english/2008/April/20080407160413myleen7.712954e-02.html

Baue, W. (2004, February 26). Critics challenge Christian aid report as biased, cynical, and inaccurate. *Sustainability Investment News.* Retrieved July 29, 2008, from http://www.socialfunds.com

Beatty, J. (2007). *The age of betrayal.* New York: Knopf.

Beitz, C. (1999). *Political theory and international relations.* Princeton, NJ: Princeton University Press.

Blanchard, R. (1925). The exchange of populations between Greece and Turkey. *Geographical Review, 15*(3), 449-456. Retrieved December 15, 2008, from http://www.jstor.org/pss/208566

Center for Corporate Policy. (2008). Retrieved on October 15, 2008 from http://www.corporatepolicy.org

Chang, H. (2008). *Bad Samaritans.* New York: Bloomsbury Press.

Elgin, B. (2007, October 29). Little green lies. *BusinessWeek.*

Hobbes, T. (1999). *Leviathan.* Retrieved May 12, 2004 from http://darkwing.uoregon.edu/~rbear/hobbes/leviathan.html

Hopkins, M. (2003). *The planetary bargain.* London: Earthscan Publications Human Rights Watch. (1995 October). *The fall of Srebrenica and the failure of U.N. peacekeeping.* Retrieved August 1, 2008, from http://www.hrw.org/summaries/s.bosnia9510.html

Kant, I. (1797b). *The doctrine of virtue. Metaphysics of morals, part II.* Koenigsberg: Friedrich Nicolovius

Kant, I. (1970). Perpetual peace. In H. Reiss (Ed.), *Kant's political writings*. Cambridge, UK: Cambridge University Press.

Klein, N. (2007). *The shock doctrine*. New York: Henry Holt.

Lerner, M. (2000). *Spirit matters*. Charlottesville, VA: Hampton Roads Publishing Co.

Locke, J. (2004). *The second treatise on government*. Retrieved May 10, 2004 from http://www.constitution.org/jl/2ndtreat.htm

LRN Corporation. (2008). Retrieved June 15, 2008 from http://www.LRN.com

Lyttle, B. (2005). Clock strikes 12. *University of Chicago Magazine, 98*(2).

Morgenthau, H. (1993). *Politics among nations, brief edition*. New York: McGraw-Hill

OECD. (2004). *Principles of corporate governance*. Retrieved September 22, 2008 from http://www.oecd.com

Pascal, B. (1670). *Pensees*. Retrieved June 6, 2008 from http://www.gutenberg.org/etext/18269

Pogge, T. (2002). *World poverty and human rights*. Cambridge, England: Polity Press.

Rawls, J. (1999a). *A theory of justice* (rev. ed.). Cambridge, MA: Harvard University Press

Rawls, J. (1999b). *The law of peoples*. Cambridge, MA: Harvard University Press.

Reich, R. (2007). It's not business' business. *Business Week*, (September): 10.

Singer, P. (2004). *One world* (2nd ed.) New Haven, CT: Yale University Press.

Stiglitz, J. (2007). *Making globalization work*. New York: W. W. Norton.

Tabb, W. 2004. *Economic governance in the age of globalization*. New York: Columbia University Press.

Teach, E. (2005). Two views of virtue: the corporate social responsibility movement is picking up steam. Should you worry about it? *CFO: Magazine for Senior Financial Executives*. Retrieved July 29, 2008, from http://findarticles.com/p/articles/mi_m3870/is_17_21/ai_n15999730

Vogel, D. (2005). *The market for virtue*. Baltimore, MD: The Brookings Institution Press.

White, T. (2007). *Data, dollars, and the unintentional subversion of human rights in the IT industry*. Waltham, MA: Center for Business Ethics.

Wikipedia. (2008a). *Nation*. Retrieved July 5, 2008, from http://en.wikipedia.org/wiki/nation

Wikipedia. (2008b). *Secession*. Retrieved July 12, 2008, from http://en.wikipedia.org/wiki/secession

Wikipedia. (2008c). *Kurdish people*. Retrieved July 18, 2008 from http://en.wikipedia.org/wiki/Kurdish_people

Wikipedia. (2008d). *United Nations assistance mission for Rwanda*. Retrieved August 1, 2008 from http://en.wikipedia.org/wiki/UNAMIR

Yunus, M. (2003). *Banker to the poor.* New York: Public Affairs.

ENDNOTES

1. Compare Marx's prediction that under Communism the state will "wither away."
2. John Locke's notion of tacit consent is close to correct here. (Locke 2004) People born and brought up in a country don't often have a meaningful option to leave when they become adults, but most willingly behave as though their country was chosen.
3. Thus the June 2008 US Supreme Court decision to allow anyone to carry firearms destroys the basis of not only government but civil society.
4. As mentioned before in note 13 of Chapter 7, **Cosmopolitanism**, continuing the war after reasons of self-defense proved false makes it an aggressive war.
5. It would require the trial and conviction of G. W. Bush and his administration for war crimes to reduce the threat of aggression.
6. These were the justifications for the French and American Revolutions.
7. A specialty of the British: India/Pakistan, Northern Ireland/Ireland, North and South Vietnam, Israel/Palestine. My thanks to Otto Seeman for this point.
8. Turkey seems to be a country even more incapable of any kind of self-criticism than the United States. When in 2007 Nelson Mandela refused a Turkish peace prize because of Turkey's treatment of the Kurds, the Turkish press mounted a campaign of vilification against Mandela. Not to mention Turkey's refusal to acknowledge the Armenian genocide.
9. In the early 2000s, a part of the city of Los Angeles attempted to secede from the city. California law required both the entire city and the seceding part to approve. Only the seceding part approved, and the secession failed.
10. The Jews in Germany were not trying to secede. Genocide always justifies intervening in a country.
11. See Rawls 1999a, sections 55-59 for an extensive discussion of these issues.
12. I was first made aware of this distinction by the late philosopher Rogers Albritton.
13. A person could love his neighbor as a brother, with *philia*. Loving your neighbor with *eros* suggests having an affair with your neighbor's wife or husband.
14. Also called the Golden Rule or Categorical Imperative—see Chapter 4, "Ethical Principles for Individuals."
15. The new US Obama administration has announced its intention to participate in an international agreement to reduce greenhouse gases. As of early 2009, that administration has not addressed the other issues mentioned here.
16. There are very cogent and clear dissenters from this policy such as US Congressman Ron Paul in the 2008 Presidential campaign, but Paul consistently received only about 10% of the vote. As of April 2009, the new Obama administration has neither clearly accepted nor clearly rejected the policy of US world domination by military force. Continuation of the war in Afghanistan suggests they have so far not rejected that policy.

17   The US is technically not an empire. It achieves world power without formally acquiring other states. The Roman Empire is a notable example of collapse under the weight of military expenditures necessary to maintain its hegemony.

18   The US was the origin of the practices that led to the massive financial collapse of late 2008, but the effects were definitely globalized. It is not possible at this time to predict longer-term differential effects on the US.

19   The new Obama administration has recognized an obligation to deal with climate change.

20   The group Beyond War has been actively promulgating this view since the early 1980s.

21   See Kohlberg (1976) for a discussion of stages of ethical development. His views are summarized in Chapter 4, **The Basis of Ethical Principles,** "Ethical Development."

22   The townships of Licking, PA and Porter, PA have passed ordinances declaring that corporations are not individuals. (Achbar, Abbott, Bakan 2004) The National Lawyers Guild sued to have the state of California dismantle Union Oil (UNOCAL) for alleged misdeeds. They wanted the corporate charter revoked and all its assets redistributed. The state did not dismantle UNOCAL, although they acknowledged that they did have the power to do so. (Achbar, Abbott, Bakan 2004)

23   This might be the most important sentence in this book.

24   See Beatty 2007 for a discussion of how corporate personhood came into being.

25   Insofar as Limited Partnerships and sole proprietorships have the overriding aim of profit maximization, they have the same ethical status as corporations. In any case, they account for a tiny proportion of business revenue, under 5% in 2003. (America.gov 2008)

26   See Center for Corporate Policy (2008) for additional suggestions.

27   In California, corporations routinely distort the initiative process by fielding several initiatives similar to the one they want to defeat, solely to confuse the public.

28   The OECD's Principles of Corporate Governance (OECD 2004) mainly concern responsibilities to shareholders and do not address any of the issues just raised.

29   Nobel Peace Prize winner Mohammed Yunus' social businesses may be an alternative. They are not currently multinational. I will discuss them further in Chapter 11, **Globalized Ethics and Current Institutions.**

30   The Christian Aid case discussed just above is an illustration.

31   Some corporate CEOs have come to this realization. Ray Anderson, CEO of Interface, Inc., details his epiphany in the film *The Corporation.* (Achbar, Abbott,Bakan, 2004)

32   The ethical priority of principles concerning the environment is separate from other ethical issues and will be discussed in Chapter 15, **IT-Enabled Globalization And The Environment**.

33   The Croats themselves also apparently carried out mass executions of unarmed Serbs

34   In Argentina, the combination of opening financial markets and privatization resulted in a mass exodus of funds such as the entire Argentine social security system.

35   US corn subsidies, when combined with NAFTA, caused the collapse of small scale corn farming in Mexico.

36   See Chapter 2, **Current Ethically Globalized Institutions, "The United Nations."**

37   The Obama administration as of early 2009 had eliminated the use of 'combatant' for anyone detained, renounced torture, and announced the end of the Iraq War. The war of Afghanistan was officially proclaimed to be a war of self-defense, which, if correct, would make it ethical.

Chapter 9
IT and Globalized Ethics

In this chapter I will first discuss the individual ethical principles an IT professional is likely to encounter. Then I will consider the impact of the ethics of globalized institutions on the ethics of IT professional. Finally, I will discuss the role of IT professionals in the global social contract to be formulated in Part III, **A Social Contract for Globalized Institutions.** IT professionals are parties to the global social contract because of their essential role in making globalized institutions possible. So we need to determine how they will participate in this social contract.

IT PROFESSIONAL ETHICS

As an individual, An IT professional has ethical principles and moral principles. In this book, *ethical* principles are those grounded in social cooperation, as opposed to *moral, religious, and philosophical* principles, which not everyone shares.[1] Principles of professional ethics have to be ethical rather than moral principles, because IT always appears in the context of an organization, whether business or non-profit. Organizations are cooperative enterprises. Thus IT is always concerned with the development or maintenance of systems in some context of social cooperation.

DOI: 10.4018/978-1-60566-922-9.ch009

The different types of IT professional ethical requirements are as follows:[2]

1. Ethical duties as citizens and as human beings.
2. Duties and obligations to employers as employees or contractors.
3. Enabling professional duties, done to maintain their capability as professionals.
4. Substantive duties to system users.
5. Substantive system duties (infrastructure and application).

Each type of requirement has a different ethical basis. Some of these are *enabling* duties, for example, things one does in order to maintain one's capability in a profession--in IT, by staying current. Some are *substantive* duties, requirements of the practice of the profession.

The first two--duties as citizens or human beings and ethical requirements as employees--are not specific to IT professionals and demand attention only when the IT context requires it. For example, conflicts of interest and using employer's resources for one's own purposes occur perhaps with some frequency in IT contexts. Broader social or ethical implications of IT development also need to be considered. Most duties and obligations as employees are also not specifically IT professional duties, although their performance is important to maintaining the integrity of the profession. Confidentiality and not misusing resources are employee duties of special importance in an IT context.

Enabling professional duties need to be performed either to keep one's own place in working toward the goals of the profession, or enhancing the profession itself. Knowledge-related duties are especially important for IT. Keeping up with the rapid changes in IT is a daunting proposition. IT professionals often have to spend significant portions of their free time "keeping current." "Keeping current" is essential for being able to fulfill the goals of the profession, as well as doing one's job well. Also, an IT professional needs to work at making the existence of the profession and its special expertise and goals known to the public as well as to managers and employers. Quality work within IT and cooperation between fellow professionals toward reaching professional goals are also important. In this area, there are potentially difficult and destructive conflicts between proprietary information and the needs of the profession. An important function of patent and copyright is to provide legitimate protection for the originator of the idea to make it possible to recoup development costs and exploit legitimate competitive advantage. But keeping some information proprietary can stifle growth and make everyone worse off. This is how problems of intellectual property rights play out in an IT context.

Finally, there are substantive IT professional duties. To users, IT professionals have the duty to include all affected by a system in requirements design and implementation. They also have a duty not to misuse their technical expertise in dealing with those less knowledgeable. To management, IT professionals have the duty to provide whatever information and expertise they can toward keeping projects on time and on budget. I would count this as a substantive professional IT duty just because the track record of IT projects being on time and on budget is so poor.[3] If an IT professional needs to be reminded of anything, it is this track record. Substantive system duties include helping to maintain data integrity, being responsible for appropriate maintenance standards, and more generally ensuring appropriate ongoing support for systems implemented.[4] These are duties that an IT professional needs to aware of even when management may not have much understanding of their importance. Management failure to support data integrity and provide for appropriate support may require protest if management chooses to ignore them to the possible detriment of the entire system.

But are any of these substantive professional considerations ethical requirements at all? How can keeping projects on time and on budget be an ethical duty? I believe once an IT professional accepts the goal of providing the best functioning IT systems possible in the organizational context, then the duties and obligations just discussed become ethical requirements for him. These ethical requirements will help determine the role of the IT professional in the global social contract.

THE INDIVIDUAL WITHIN THE ORGANIZATION

Since the IT professional is always working within an organization, the ethical status of that organization is ethically relevant. In the Chapter 1 case of the World Bank, I noted that transnational ethical principles were needed to determine the ethical status of the World Bank. In the next subsection, I will consider how well the transnational ethical theories we have examined work in doing this. In this subsection I will consider the background ethical issue of the ethical responsibility of an individual when the organization he works for is less than ethical. The difference between the case of a transnational organization and the case of a local organization is the difference in the principles used for judging the ethical status of the organization.

In the Chapter 1 discussion of the World Bank case, I offered a preliminary account of the ethical status of an individual working for less than ethical organizations. The ethically flawed organizations I considered were tobacco manufacturers and distributors of child pornography. But are these ethical flaws derived from principles of social cooperation or moral flaws derived from comprehensive[5] doctrines which we cannot expect all to share?

Tobacco manufacturers are unethical because the product they produce kills people. For many years, tobacco manufacturers fought this conclusion, advancing skeptical theories of cause and effect.[6] False or misleading communication is unethical from the point of view of social cooperation because it damages the aims of communication. And when tobacco companies came to admit the serious health risks of smoking but continued to offer an addictive product, they were knowingly killing or making people seriously ill. Killing or making people ill is wrong from the point of view of social cooperation because it kills some of those cooperating for the benefit of the manufacturers.

Are child pornographers immoral rather than unethical? Sex related issues are very often matters of moral or religious comprehensive beliefs rather than ethical principles of social cooperation. I believe there are both moral and ethical components to the wrongness of child pornography. The ethical component has to do with sex with children, who cannot give meaningful consent to the activity. Harming children, who are people, violates principles of social cooperation. Depictions of such sexual activity would fall under the same principle, especially since the depiction would have to be staged by adults. And others viewing the pornography would be complicit in the same unethical activity.

There may be a moral component as well as an ethical component. If no children are involved in the production of pornographic images, as when the images are drawn or computer generated, what is the ethical objection to someone viewing them? If someone's viewing pornography would make it more likely that they would act out sexually with children, then that would be grounds for its being unethical under the same ethical principles. But research on public health effects of pornography, though inconclusive, suggests that availability of pornography reduces rather than encourages sex crimes. (Diamond 1999) So the objection would be moral or religious rather than ethical. An Internet search on 'harm from pornography' confirms that almost all objectors are religious groups.

Of course, applying any ethical principle about child pornography requires a criterion for when someone is a child. This may involve moral or religious beliefs about the innocence of children rather than ethical principles. In the United States, children are sexually active by the age of thirteen. The age of consent in the US is sixteen, but jail terms for 16 year olds for having consenting sex with other 16 year olds have little to do with protecting children.[7] Twenty European countries have ages of consent lower than 16. The minimum age is effectively 12 in the Netherlands, Spain, Portugal and Malta. It is 14 in Slovenia, Iceland, Montenegro, Serbia, Italy, San Marino, Albania and, in certain circumstances, Germany. (Tatchell 2008)

So if an IT professional were to produce a first rate website and back office system for an outfit distributing child pornography involving photographs of actual children, the question about the ethical status of his activity would be ethical, not moral. Since the activity of the organization is unethical, it is not ethical for an IT professional to aid its implementation. If the website did not use children in producing its content, any objection would be moral rather than ethical. The participation of the IT professional would then depend on his or her moral or religious beliefs.

Tobacco may be ethically somewhat like child pornography with no children. The IT professional enabling the sale of tobacco can say "I only work here." Producing and developing tobacco products is legal. It is another question whether distributing a product which tends to kill people in large numbers should be legal. But so long as it is legal, it is a matter of personal moral preference whether or not to aid and abet the production and distribution of tobacco. It may be ethically *better* not to aid and abet the tobacco industry but it is not ethically required.

But "I only work here. I'm only following orders" is not always an acceptable ethical defense. Clearly it matters how directly implicated people are in ethically questionable activities. The IT professional enabling unethical child pornography clearly cannot say "I only work here" to establish that he is acting ethically. We expect him to recognize that the activity he is enabling is both illegal and unethical. But why was Adolf Eichmann, in charge of administering the Holocaust, unsuccessful in using "I only work here" as a defense? (Arendt 1965) As in the tobacco example, he was legally OK-- following German laws implementing the "final solution."[8] What's the difference? If it is ethical to aid a tobacco company in its operations, it can only be because we regard the legality of the tobacco company as at least ethically neutral. On the other hand, laws mandating genocide are not ethically neutral.

FROM INDIVIDUAL ETHICS TO GLOBAL ETHICS

What ethical standards are appropriate for the World Bank as a globalized organization? Ought the IT professionals who did such a good job for the World Bank consider the Bank's negative impact on developing countries? Or do ethical standards of international banking take precedence? Is the ethical situation of the IT staff at the World Bank more like the situation at the child pornography website or at the tobacco company? As a globalized institution, what is legal for the institution is not determined by the laws of any one state. And the ethical status of its operations is not determined by the ethical standards of any one nation.

Thus neither political realism nor the society of societies theory have anything to say about the ethical principles we should use to evaluate the World Bank, because they deal only with relations between nations and principles governing relations between nations. Of the three cosmopolitan theories, the only one with much plausibility is Peter Singer's consequentialist utilitarian theory, so it is the only cosmopolitan theory I will consider. A cosmopolitan view of the World Bank would ask whether its policies (together with those of the IMF) produce more harm than good for poor countries. In this case I think virtually all commentators would agree that World Bank policies of fiscal austerity and privatization have produced more harm than good as implemented in the actual world. So the cosmopolitan conclusion would be that the policies as they stand are unethical and that they need to be changed to increase the benefits to poor countries. Economists such as Joseph Stiglitz and Ha-Joon Chang have made sensible suggestions for changes. (Stiglitz 2007, Chang 2008)

By contrast, a social contract theory would look at the nature of World Bank policies and consider whether they are in accordance with transnational principles of justice. The aims of the World Bank and IMF are to provide support to developing countries. Principles of transnational ethics determine when support is ethical-- what the ethical bottom line is, so to speak. The World Bank and IMF may think that a policy of privatizing institutions is in itself support for poor countries. But clearly the test is how those in poor countries are benefited. And cosmopolitan and social contract theories differ on how benefit is to be assessed.

Other ethical considerations included in a social contract approach would be who has a say in the policies of the World Bank and what accountability measures exist. Right now, the answer is that the developed countries set policy. The IMF also incurs ethical criticism because it supports repressive military dictatorships. The IMF shrugs off this criticism. For an institution to be ethical or just, it must include a mechanism for considering claims of ethics and justice. For the World Bank and IMF, there is currently no mechanism besides sometimes violent demonstrations.

The next chapters will develop and justify a global social contract, but I will present a sketch now so that we can begin to compare how the global social contract approach differs from the cosmopolitan approach when applied to IT. Recall that a social contract approach requires that any ethically enforceable authority must rest on a contract agreed to by those under that authority. The parties to the contract must be individuals, but not all human beings just because they are human. The purpose of a social contract is to allocate socially produced goods fairly, so the parties must be those benefiting from or contributing to globally produced benefits. Multinational corporations cannot be parties to any social contract because they are not ethical individuals.

Parties to the contract could be representatives of stockholders, of societies, and of individuals involved in the global economy. To insure fairness in the agreement and that the principles they choose will be principles of justice, they should not know whom they represent. I will argue in the next chapter that they will choose principles analogous to Rawls' two principles of (domestic) justice:

Global Economy Difference Principle: Institutions implement rules to make the worst off participating in the global economy, as well off as possible.

- But not rules which cripple the productivity of institutions to the extent of making everyone, even the worst-off person in the global economy, still worse off.

Global Economy Greatest Equal Freedom Principle: All individuals in the global economy have an equal claim to basic liberties.

- But for individuals, not corporations, states, or other global institutions.

This is a preliminary statement of the principles of a global social contract. There will be more detailed clarification and explanation in the following chapters. Right now I want to give a general idea of how globalized ethical problems would be handled by a social contract approach, especially those involving IT.

The application of the global social contract to the World Bank would be this: Ethically globalized institutions are bound by the principles of justice for a global economy. So their policies must make those in the worst off societies, as well off as possible. Adopting policies of fiscally responsible international banking does not seem to do this. The global social contract differs from cosmopolitanism. Cosmopolitanism maximizes good consequences for all humanity and the global social contract instead aims to distribute benefits fairly for participants in the global economy.

How does this impact the ethics of an IT professional working for the World Bank? First, when the World Bank loans money to a country, that country is a participant in the global economy for that very reason. For a cosmopolitan, it is ethically irrelevant whether a country is a participant in the global economy or not. The cosmopolitan is concerned only with the gap between those in rich countries and those in poor countries. As we saw in Chapter 7, **Cosmopolitanism,** the requirement to assess total aggregate value leads cosmopolitan utilitarians to ignore global poverty in some cases.[9] By contrast, for a social contract theory, total aggregate value is not decisive. Instead, we must make the worst off as well off as possible.

Thus, in assessing the ethics of his ethically globalized institution, an IT professional at the World Bank should consider principles derived from a global social contract. He would consider whether the policies of the World Bank tended to make those in the worst off country participating in the global economy, as well off as possible. As things stand right now, the answer is probably no. As demonstrated by economists such as Joseph Stiglitz (2003, 2007), World Bank (and IMF) policies reflect the interests and ethics of international banking instead of the goal of reducing world poverty. So what is the ethical responsibility of the IT professional working at such a globalized institution? When it comes to global responsibility, is "I only work here" a defense? Is the ethical situation of the IT staff at the World Bank more like the situation at the child pornography website or at the tobacco company?

In the case of the World Bank, the social contract answer is that "I only work here" is an acceptable defense. The World Bank, unlike tobacco companies, has an ethical aim of reducing world poverty instead of the aim of making profits from an addictive product that sickens and kills people. So "I only work here" is an even more acceptable defense in this case. And even more than the tobacco case, it is strictly a personal decision--not even an ethical one--whether to continue facilitating an organization whose ethical flaw is not realizing its goals. There may be opportunities to provide input to improve matters, but when the scope of one's job does not include making policy, being circumspect may be a good idea.

GLOBAL INSTITUTIONAL ETHICS

The ethical situation is different when one's position does include input into the institutional policy of an ethically globalized institution. In the case of Yahoo, shareholders and customers, as participants in the global social contract, are in a position to make or influence global ethical policy. Executives and employees can provide ethical input as individuals but not as agents furthering the interests of a profit-maximizing corporation. In the case from Chapter 1, China demanded information from Yahoo which Yahoo supplied and which led to the violation of the human rights of dissidents. There was also a subsequent vote of the shareholders not to uphold a ban on censorship. Yahoo claimed that it was merely following Chinese law in providing the information but subsequently lost a lawsuit to the Chinese dissidents. Yahoo subsequently established a human rights fund to provide humanitarian and legal aid to dissidents.

I think we have to say in this case that, without some transnational legal rules or policies, Yahoo has no good ethical alternative. The Internet, as a transnational institution *par excellence,* deserves transnational regulation. Perhaps transnational postal or airline regulations might be a model, so that transnational regulation of the Internet could take place without having to implement some sort of new transnational authority. But without some acknowledged transnational policy, Yahoo is stuck with obeying the law of one state (China) and getting punished (successfully sued) in another (the US).[10]

The shareholder's vote against a ban on censorship is another ethical matter. Yahoo's shareholders have equal rights, but not the right to deny equal rights to participants in the global economy including Internet users. Thus they do not have the right to prevent Yahoo from enforcing equal rights (that is, banning censorship). This follows from the global social contract principle of Greatest Equal Liberty.

IT'S CONTRIBUTION TO THE GLOBAL SOCIAL CONTRACT

Do IT professionals actually deserve a role in deciding on a social contract for the global economy? As we saw in Chapter 3, **IT's Contribution to Globalization**, both IT and logistics are major enablers of this economy. But economic enablers (such as logistics) don't have seats at the table for deciding on the domestic social contract for the principles of justice. What is the difference between the global and the domestic case?

Recall that domestic principles of justice were chosen to enable social cooperation and to insure that its benefits were distributed fairly.[11] The parties to the domestic social contract were individuals representing the main different starting points in the system of cooperation.[12] They know general facts about human society, and in particular they regard themselves as belonging to the society for which they are choosing principles of justice. It follows that they are part of the same economic system and share benefits and burdens.

The global economy is instead superimposed on the economies of a number of different societies. Almost as long as there have been human groups, there has been economic exchange or trade between groups--certainly as long as there has been civilization and states. Charles Beitz incorrectly concludes that any interdependence--that is, any trade--makes the economy a global one.[13] Most benefits and burdens are still shared within societies, and individual countries still pursue their own economic policies. Even in Thomas Friedman's "flat" or globalized world, the US is still an economic actor competing against other countries who are also economic actors.[14]

So the global social contract necessary to ground authority to regulate the global economy is also superimposed on the social contracts of the separate societies.[15] The parties are not part of the same underlying economic system, but they do share the benefits and burdens enabled by global cooperation. It is these benefits and burdens which are the subject of the global social contract. Their existence depends upon IT. By contrast, no single component of any particular domestic society is a requirement for the benefits and burdens of that society to exist. But IT must function well for the global economic system to exist. So IT needs to be at the table to ensure that whatever principles are chosen do not undermine the basis of the system of global cooperation. As part of this responsibility, IT must ensure that it can fulfill its own ethical duties.

Does logistics also deserve a seat at the global social contract table? I don't think so. Logistics is a different kind of enabler than IT, and becoming clearer about the differences will make us clearer about IT's unique role in the global social contract. The difference is this: Without improved logistics--containerization--much global trade would not have been feasible because it would have cost too much. We could have shipped Spider Man action figures from China by older methods, but it would have been pointless because they would not have been cost competitive at US destinations. By contrast, multinational corporations, especially those with complex transnational supply chains, could not exist without IT. Recall Friedman's example of the typical Dell Inspiron notebook, co-designed in Texas and Taiwan, and assembled in Malaysia with parts from the Philippines, Japan, Korea, Costa Rica, Mexico, Taiwan, Israel, or China. (Friedman 2005, 415-417) Even without such supply chains, it is impossible to manage a transnationally distributed company as an integrated whole without an excellent integrated transnational company-wide IT system to handle operations, financials, and management.

Our current economic arrangements--and the global social contract built upon them--may turn out to be provisional. I think it is unlikely that a single world economy completely integrating all separate national economies will emerge. According to cosmopolitans, this either has happened or is in process. But such global integration may not be desirable, both for ethical and economic reasons. This issue will be discussed further in Chapter 15, **The Value of IT-Enabled Globalization.** But there is no reason social contracts cannot change when the social structure of benefits and burdens changes. It is appropriate to formulate a new social contract or change an old one whenever principles and authority are needed to insure the fair distribution of benefits and burdens from some new system of social cooperation.

IT ISSUES IN A GLOBAL SOCIAL CONTRACT

As essential enablers of the scheme of social cooperation embodied in the global economy, IT professionals have a special place in the construction of the global social contract. There are two kinds of considerations: First, the principles chosen must provide a place for the enabling and substantive duties of the IT professional. If any candidate principles actually conflicted with fulfilling these duties, they would have to be rejected. Second, the principles chosen must not undermine the basis for the global system of cooperation they apply to. It may turn out that cosmopolitan principles, for example, require an unfeasible extra amount of information gathering and reporting.

Similar issues for the domestic social contract are discussed by Rawls as concerns of *stability*: Principles chosen for the social contract must not, when applied, generate conditions which make it difficult to observe them.[16] Rawls was concerned with tendencies in principles of justice encouraging non-observance, either by encouraging self-interested behavior at the expense of cooperative behavior or encouraging why-should-I-when-others-aren't-behavior. These are problems of the stability of a particular theory of justice. Rawls presupposes to begin with that the system of social cooperation itself is stable, although he notes that its stability depends in complex ways on the principles of justice operative in the society. (Rawls 1999a p. 6)

I think the role of IT in the global economy is more than just providing stability, although the stability of the global economy depends upon the smooth and reliable operation of the global IT infrastructure. The communications theorist Marshall McLuhan had the important insight back in the 1960s that electronic technology moved the human nervous system outside the skin. (McLuhan 1962) In the global economy, IT takes over functions normally performed by people in close physical proximity. Thus there are global supply chains utilizing parts from all over the globe. The equivalent for domestic justice might be if a pervasive feature of the environment was a disorder that would cripple communication between people in the same enterprise. Any domestic social contract would have to deal with such a disorder.

How might any principles chosen allow appropriately for the enabling and substantive duties of the IT professional? The IT professional does not have the role of guaranteeing background justice in choosing the principles to govern global social cooperation. His or her role is to ensure that whatever principles are chosen will not interfere with the ability of the IT profession to maintain its professional duties or to maintain the ability to carry out its duties to system users, for system development and for system maintenance.

The IT professional must also ensure that principles chosen do not undermine the basis for the global system of cooperation they apply to. Cosmopolitan transnational theories require massive financial transfers to implement global redistribution. If a complete reworking of all systems involved in global finance is required, it may require dismantling current systems of global finance. The important professional IT question is whether implementing such a redistribution would seriously damage the global system producing the benefits being redistributed.

These are preliminary thoughts about the IT professional's role in the global economy social contract. As I fill in the details in the following chapters, a fuller account will emerge. But I hope to have established that the IT professional must have a role in formulating this global economy social contract.

REFERENCES

Arendt, H. (1965). *Eichmann in Jerusalem.* New York: Viking Press.

Chang, H. (2008). *Bad Samaritans.* New York: Bloomsbury Press.

Diamond, M. (1999). The effects of pornography: An international perspective. In J. Elias et al. (Eds.), *Porn 101: Eroticism, pornography, and the first amendment.* Retrieved March 29, 2009, from http://www.hawaii.edu/PCSS/online_artcls/pornography/prngrphy_ovrvw.html

Friedman, T. (2005). *The world is flat.* New York: Farrar, Straus and Giroux.

Gibbs, W. W. (1994, September). Software's chronic crisis. *Scientific American*, September, 86–100.

McLuhan, M. (1962). *The Gutenberg galaxy.* Toronto: University of Toronto Press.

Rawls, J. (1999a). *A theory of justice* (rev. ed.). Cambridge, MA: Harvard University Press

Rawls, J. (1999b). *The law of peoples.* Cambridge, MA: Harvard University Press.

Satzinger, J. W., Jackson, R. B., & Burd, S. D. (2004). *Systems analysis and design in a changing world.* Boston, MA: Thomson Course Technology.

Schultz, R. A. (2006). *Contemporary issues in ethics and information technology.* Hershey, PA: IRM Press.

Stiglitz, J. (2003). *Globalization and its discontents.* New York: W. W. Norton.

Stiglitz, J. (2007). *Making globalization work*. New York: W. W. Norton.

Tatchell, P. (2008). *Consent at 14*. Retrieved August 8, 2008 from http://www.petertatchell.net/age%20 of%20consent/consent%20at%2014.htm

ENDNOTES

[1] See Chapter 4, **The Basis of Ethical Principles,** "Ethical principles for individuals."

[2] See Schultz (2006), Chapter 4, **Professional Duties.**

[3] Numerous commentators have made this observation throughout the years, for example Gibbs 1994 and Satzinger et al. 2004.

[4] My thanks to David Mill for pointing out that ensuring appropriate system support should be a duty.

[5] 'Comprehensive belief' is Rawls' term for beliefs not shared by all parties to the social contract. See Chapter 5, **Domestic Theories of Justice,** "Theories of Justice."

[6] It is a serious ethical failing of corporations, especially large ones, that they will deliberately promote falsehoods when truth would harm their profits. Oil corporations promoted the idea that human responsibility for global warming was scientifically controversial when scientific consensus was overwhelming.

[7] There was a well-publicized case in 2008 in Georgia, USA.

[8] My thanks to a reviewer for the 2008 Informing Sciences conference in Bulgaria for pointing this out.

[9] See Chapter 7, **Cosmopolitanism,** "Utilitarian cosmopolitanism."

[10] The Global Network Initiative of October 2008 may be an ethical solution. This alternative is discussed in Chapter 13, **Ethical Implications for IT,** "Transnational policies and the Internet."

[11] See Chapter 5, **Domestic Theories of Justice**

[12] See Rawls 1999a, section 24, "The Veil of Ignorance."

[13] See Chapter 7, **Cosmopolitanism,** "Social Contract Cosmopolitanism."

[14] See Chapter 3, **IT's Contribution to Globalization,** "Globalization and 'Flattening.'"

[15] A separate social contract for relations between states of the same kind as Rawls' Law of Peoples (1999b) is also required. This will be discussed in Chapter 10, **Elements of a Global Contract.**

[16] See Rawls 1999a, section 76, "The Problem of Relative Stability."

Section 3
A Social Contract for Globalized Institutions

Chapter 10
Elements of a Global Contract

We saw in Section 2, **Theories of Globalized Ethics,** that there is a need for institutions with transnational ethical authority. Such authority would be needed for: Preventing war; dealing with genocides; dealing with transnational legal problems; and a global economic authority would be needed to deal with problems such as fairness in transnational economic distribution, transnational competition, multinational tax avoidance, and common tax policies to deal with global warming.

Without ethical oversight, transnational authority can easily be misused. Thus the World Trade Organization prevents effective environmental regulation of transnational trade and economic action against repressive states, and there are no channels to consider changing these policies other than street demonstrations. But just creating another authority with enough power to oversee transnational institutions effectively will also create the same oversight problem. That is, who oversees the new, more powerful authority? One way around this apparent paradox is a social contract. A social contract is a way for parties to acknowledge that they need to limit their own interests in order to achieve greater cooperative benefits, and can assume that others will do so.[1] Oversight may still be necessary if a social contract exists, but the bulk of compliance will rest with observance of the contract for mutual benefit. So much less oversight will be required, and the overseeing institution will need that much less power.

DOI: 10.4018/978-1-60566-922-9.ch010

THE INTERNATIONAL SOCIAL CONTRACT

Because I recognize the ethical status of nations, another social contract for relations between nations is required. I will first consider the International Social Contract and then turn to the Global Economy Social Contract.

There are acknowledged principles of international ethics, and we clearly need a second social contract to justify authority in connection with ethical principles for nation-states. My original intention was to rely of Rawls' Law of Peoples for this contract, but as I noted in Chapter 6, **Political Realism and the Society of Societies,** there are problems which make Rawls' international contract unworkable for my purposes. It applies only when states are nearly just. As we saw, this limitation made the contract and its principles very difficult to apply in anything like current international circumstances. For example, Rawls' Law of Peoples would call for us not to have any dealings with China until China improved its human rights record. The problem is the relevance of injustice *within* a country to ethical behavior *between* countries.

The main subject of this book is globalized ethics and not international relations. Yet any account of globalized ethics which completely omitted the contribution of nations would be seriously incomplete. A thorough account of an International Social Contract would require at least another book. So I will use Rawls' account of the International Social Contract as a basis for my discussion and indicate the revisions necessary to make it useful for the ethics of globalization. The Global Economy Social Contract will receive more complete treatment.

Rawls' Law of Peoples--the social contract establishing ethical principles between societies--is decided by *peoples*. We will keep part of Rawls definition: A *people* is the inhabitants of a nation or a country. Rawls adds that the nation or country also has a nearly just government and acknowledges the principles of justice. But then the decision to honor human rights domestically is automatic--that's what they do, or they wouldn't be a *people*. And then the society of peoples is too limited in membership. Rawls did not want states (rather than peoples) to decide on ethical principles between countries because making any old rulers--perhaps dictators or despots--parties to the social contract between nations would not produce ethical results. But his restrictions make the law of peoples virtually unusable under current conditions.

So, for what I will call the *International Social Contract*, we need to stay with peoples as the parties deciding on principles. But we don't want to incorporate into the definition of *people* the conditions that the society is nearly just and that Rawls' principles of justice are acknowledged. This has two consequences: First, there are changes to Rawls' principles of international ethics and the argument for those principles; and second, it becomes possible to include countries in the International Social Contract that are not nearly just.

Peter Singer's condition of being a minimalist democracy is a better condition for participation in an International Social Contract. A minimalist democracy is one that has been ruling for a long time with the apparent acquiescence of its people, without severe restrictions on civil liberties, and without using repression to maintain its power. (Singer 2004, 101) If these conditions are satisfied, it would be ethical for us to deal with such nations, and it would be reasonable to expect them to honor agreements between nations. So such nations would be good candidates to be parties to the International Social Contract, and to abide by principles decided in the contract. Lack of domestic justice other than what is required to be a minimalist democracy can no longer disqualify a nation from participation in the International Social Contract.

Here are the principles (modified from Rawls' Law of Peoples) that would be adopted as an International Social Contract. As in Rawls' contract, the representatives of any society must be able to agree to principles without knowing how their society would be favored or disfavored by those principles.

1. Their governments maintain a minimalist democracy and respect cooperative agreements made between them.
2. Peoples do not intervene in each others affairs and only make war in self-defense.
3. Peoples have a duty to assist other people living under unfavorable conditions.
4. They agree to have a procedure for dealing with violations of these principles. [2]

Some comments on each of the principles of the International Social Contract:

*   **Principle 1:** 'Maintain a minimalist democracy' means the government continues to get the continued approval of its people, the government does not severely restrict civil liberties, and it does not use repression to maintain its power. This condition replaces Rawls' stronger condition of respecting human rights. 'Respecting cooperative agreements' would include respecting treaties as well as recognized international ethical constraints such as the Hague and Geneva Conventions on waging war and on treating combatants.
*   **Principle 2:** Both Rawls and some cosmopolitans allow broad exceptions to this principle of non-intervention to correct injustice in another nation. Peter Singer has the better policy of allowing exceptions only in case of human rights violations as severe as genocide. (Singer 2004, 143) All cosmopolitans believe that national sovereignty is more-or-less an outmoded concept. I would be willing to give more credence to this belief if and when all nations have eliminated their military forces.[3]
*   **Principle 3:** How far does the "duty to assist" extend? Rawls interprets this principle as requiring only the support of burdened nations up to the point that they can become functioning democracies. My view was that a principle of benevolence applies at the country level, that a society has a duty to help people in other societies when the cost to itself is not excessive. This principle applies to benefits generated within a country. Benefits generated transnationally are handled by the Global Economy Social Contract. Then the question is how to coordinate economic distributions required by the two social contracts. If there are benefits from the Global Economy Social Contract due to a country or people in that country, then those benefits should not be reduced because another country is willing to be benevolent. That is, the (national) duty to assist applies after any transnational benefits are allocated.
*   **Principle 4:** This is an addition to Rawls' principles in the *Law of Peoples*. The history of international politics is strewn with agreements and principles honored only with lip service. Important institutions dealing with violations of international ethics already exist, namely the International Court of Justice and the International Criminal Court. Some changes to these institutions would be necessary to deal fully with violations and thus to satisfy Principle 4 fully. Procedurally, neither court is bound to honor its own precedents, and this makes it difficult to regard their decisions as binding. (Morgenthau 1993, 262-265) Another major problem with the International Criminal Court is that the US does not accept its jurisdiction and will do so only if US personnel are exempted from any penalties.

This is an instance of a more general enforcement problem: Sovereign states (especially superpowers and other major powers) tend to be unwilling to compromise their sovereignty. As I pointed out in Chapter 8, **The Ethical Status of Globalized Institutions,** political theorist Hans Morgenthau thought a world state with sovereignty over existing states was essential to prevent war in general, and nuclear war in particular. Yet Morgenthau also noted that the peoples of the world are currently unwilling to accept a world government if the interests of their own state were harmed. So such a world state is not likely.[4] I will postpone further discussion of the problem of enforcement of the International Social Contract to Chapter 11, **Globalized Ethics and Current Institutions,** and Chapter 12, **New Globalized Institutions**.

But even if there were an effective institution to enforce the principles of the International Social Contract between nations, multinational corporations raise complications. Multinationals even now can escape the sovereignty of any one country by shifting actions and consequences between states.[5] If existing states simply ceded some portion of their sovereignty to a global authority, it does not automatically follow that this global authority would also have authority over multinational corporations. Thus there is a need for a second social contract, the Global Economy Social Contract, to justify such authority. I will now return to the elements for this contract.

THE GLOBAL ECONOMY SOCIAL CONTRACT

Any enforceable ethical authority should rest on a contract agreed to by those under that authority. The elements for a full definition of a social contract are as follows:

1.   Conditions requiring a contract
2.   Relation to other social contracts.
3.   The parties agreeing to the contract
4.   Knowledge constraints in choosing principles
5.   Conditions on the psychology of the parties
6.   The type of principles agreed to
7.   The general conditions of application of the principles

   After the contract is defined, two further elements can be specified:

8.   The principles and their justification
9.   General requirements of institutions implementing the principles

   I will deal with all of these elements in defining the Global Economy Social Contract.

CONDITIONS REQUIRING A CONTRACT

A social contract is appropriate when there are cooperatively produced benefits and burdens to be distributed fairly. Further, a contract is appropriate when institutions with ethically justified authority are needed to implement a fair distribution of these benefits and burdens. The global economy, as we have seen, consists of cooperatively produced benefits and burdens currently under no effective ethical authority. Institutions to implement transnational ethical principles either do not have enough power (the United Nations), fall short of their own ethical goals (the US, the World Bank, and the IMF), or are unable to implement ethical policies (the WTO). So the global economy meets the conditions calling for a social contract.

It must also be true that the parties to the contract do regard themselves as being part of a single scheme of social cooperation. Interestingly enough, corporate and state beneficiaries of economic globalization apparently believe this. Offshoring is defended on the grounds that increased wages to lower-wage offshored countries offset decreased wages to higher-wage developed countries.

RELATION TO OTHER SOCIAL CONTRACTS

I accept Rawls' reasoning for his Principles of Justice as a social contract within a society. These principles, the Greatest Equal Freedom Principle and the Difference Principle, would be chosen as principles of justice for domestic societies. I also accept Rawls' derivation of these principles from the conditions of the domestic social contract.[6] A domestic society is a people in a country sharing substantial cooperative benefits and burdens. There are two aspects to a domestic society, the political and the economic. The fundamental political structure of a just domestic society will be a democracy honoring human rights. The economic institutions of such a just society will tend to make the worst off member of that society as well off as possible. In our current world, domestic societies are nation-states. Federal arrangements such as the US and EU add some complexity: In some respects they are single societies and in some respects they are multiple societies.

The two transnational social contracts--the International Social Contract between countries and the Global Economy Social Contract between participants in the global economy--operate in different areas. The international contract is primarily a *political* contract concerned with the ethics of relations between nations. The global economy contract is primarily an *economic* contract concerned with the benefits and burdens of those involved in the global economy. Each contract should include a principle to respect the principles of the other contract. (I will formulate these below in element 8, "The principles and their justification.")

Although the international contract is primarily political, it has a secondary transnational economic aim expressed in its <u>principle 3</u>: A society has a duty to help needy people in other societies when the cost to itself is not excessive.[7] And although the Global Economy contract is primarily economic, transnational legal and political institutions or policies will be required to enforce its principles of economic justice.

There are still going to be conflicts in the inevitable areas of overlap. Nation states making war on each other can disrupt segments of the global economy. Unfortunately, the institutions of the global economy don't seem to have great influence on the behavior of nation-states. At the beginning of the Iraq War, commentators including the editors of BusinessWeek expressed great concern about the impact of the war on the global economy. (2003) Regrettably, the global economy did not turn out to be a sufficient force for peace. But the economic impact of the global economy on nation states is one of the main reasons for considering a Global Economy Social Contract.

There already are transnational institutions with economic power over nations: The World Trade Organization has considerable say over the economies of individual countries. And the World Bank and International Monetary Fund can effectively put pressure on sovereign states to adopt economic and social policies. But the WTO, World Bank, and the IMF do not always act ethically. As agents in the global economy, the principles of a Global Economy Social Contract will apply to them.

Some issues of overlap between the International Social Contract and the Global Economy Social Contract may prove difficult to resolve. But some will not be. As we saw above, the question of priority between global redistribution and international ethics had a clear answer: Don't reduce global economy benefits just because individual countries are willing to give. Questions of priority are not always so clear cut. At each stage of the construction of the global economy contract and its accompanying institutions, we need to consider how the global economy contract aligns with the international contract.

PARTIES AGREEING TO THE CONTRACT

On a social contract view, any enforceable authority must rest on a contract agreed to by those under that authority. Multinational corporations need to be under that authority. But they can't be parties to the contract because they are not ethical individuals.[8] The parties must be individuals—but not representatives of societies, as in Rawls' *Law of Peoples*. The global economy contract is not another agreement between societies. But neither should we include all human beings on the basis of their humanity, as the cosmopolitans would have it. For two reasons: (1) It is hardly an ethical requirement that all inhabitants of the planet take part in technologically intense Western Civilization. We want to allow indigenous peoples who don't want to become part of Western Civilization to do so.[9] (2) The major function of a social contract is to allocate socially produced goods fairly. So the individual parties must be restricted to those benefiting from or contributing to globally produced benefits.

Therefore, the contract should be between parties involved in the multinational economy, representative of individuals contributing to or benefiting from a global economy. Corporations produce benefits for themselves, their stockholders, and other stakeholders such as societies and individuals. So the parties to the contract should be representatives of stockholders, of societies involved in the global economy, and of other individuals involved in the global economy such as managers, employees, suppliers and customers.[10] Each of these parties represents the interests of a class involved in the global economy.[11] It would not be appropriate to grant different numbers of representatives of each class mirroring their actual numbers. As with the domestic social contract, we want the parties deciding on principles to be able to assess their effects on different classes of individuals. They then have to decide on principles without knowing which class they will in fact belong to.

I proposed in Chapter 9 making IT professionals one of the parties to the global social contract.[12] We will see that their participation is essential in the design of the institutions implementing the principles of justice for the global economic order, but that their role in the actual choice of principles is the same as those in other classes such as managers or employees.

KNOWLEDGE CONSTRAINTS IN CHOOSING THE PRINCIPLES

As just mentioned, for the purposes of the agreement, the parties should not know what class they belong to. This guarantees fairness in the same way as for the domestic social contract. As in the domestic social contract, knowledge of one's own interests is behind the *veil of ignorance* for the decision on a social contract. This includes one's natural assets and abilities, one's values, and one's place in the global economy. All that is known about the global economy and its participating societies are general facts. For example, that some ethical principles are needed to regulate global economic activity. Also, social cooperation is possible and necessary for those participating in the global economy to have decent lives.[13]

They also need to know general facts about the place of IT in the global economy. For example, they need to know that participants (including societies) have sufficient resources to underpin the IT infrastructure necessary for the global economy.

As I noted in Chapter 5, **Domestic Theories of Justice,** a social contract is a pointless runaround unless those agreeing to the contract are in a different position with respect to their knowledge than those obeying it. The conditions imposed on those making decisions--especially the veil of ignorance--enables their decision to express what Hume called 'the common interest' rather than just their individual interests.[14]

CONDITIONS ON THE PSYCHOLOGY OF THE PARTIES

The same knowledge of certain psychological peculiarities that was excluded in the domestic social contract is also excluded for the Global Economy Social Contract. These psychological traits are a high propensity to choose very risky alternatives and the propensity to destructive envy. The tendency to go for extreme risk is not appropriate when the choice could affect one's entire life prospects. The global economy has different impacts on different countries and may not impact some classes of people at all. But when there is an impact, it often changes the life prospects of those affected. The parties have to recognize that they could be sweatshop workers for life in Indonesia. I believe this consideration is sufficient to exclude a propensity to take extreme risks.

Excluding the propensity to destructive envy also carries over from the domestic social contract. A person motivated by destructive envy will prefer himself (or his class) being worse off provided the envied person or class also does badly. For example, he might want to deny health care benefits that he lacks to welfare recipients. The reason for excluding destructive envy is that it prevents choices that would be better for all, whether for the domestic or the Global Economy Social Contract.

Some of the parties to the Global Economy Social Contract will be involved in corporations, either as shareholders, or managers, or workers. What will they know about their motivation? If they know that corporations exist to maximize profits, how will that affect their decision on principles impacting corporations? Here again, it is important to realize that, although the parties have general knowledge, they don't know which of the classes of people in the global social contract they belong to. They know that shareholders in corporations expect corporate profit to be maximized.[15] But they don't know whether they will be a major shareholder in a wealthy country or an impoverished wage earner in a sweatshop in a poor country. When they decide on principles, they will have to consider the impact on corporations. But the corporate point of view on the economy will be expressed entirely through its impact on individuals.

THE TYPE OF PRINCIPLES AGREED TO

They will agree on principles of justice for the global economy, which serve the function of regulating the distribution of benefits and burdens in that economy. These principles will be the most general and highest order ethical principles applying to the global economy. Since similar considerations apply as for the domestic social contract, the principles will be similar. I have already discussed the alternatives for the principles in Section 2, **Theories of Globalized Ethics.** The alternatives, political realism and cosmopolitanism, had serious defects which will prevent their choice as principles.

Political realism and Rawls' Law of Peoples do not supply alternatives for the Global Economy Social Contract because they apply only to relations between countries or nations or states. Global economic considerations are simply not relevant. For political realist Michael Walzer, ethics is by definition within a society, so transnational ethics is not even possible.

Cosmopolitanism is a transnational ethical theory. So it is a possible choice of principle. For cosmopolitans, the parties for a global social contract must include all human beings as individual human beings. Since they ignore the role of social cooperation in ethics, their ethical conclusions don't have much to do with current institutions. I will shortly consider cosmopolitanism as a possible choice of principle supposing that the parties to the contract are participants in the global economy.

The three cosmopolitans discussed in Chapter 7, **Cosmopolitanism,** employed three different methods for choosing ethical principles: Thomas Pogge used *pluralism,* Charles Beitz used *social contract,* and Peter Singer used *consequentialism* (or utilitarianism). Pluralism is the view that there are a lot of ethical principles and principles of justice which cannot be reduced to a few prioritized principles. Pluralism is almost a non-theory; it gives us almost no guidance with difficult decisions and should be accepted only when attempts at a more useful theory have failed. Charles Beitz combined a global social contract with a cosmopolitan view of its parties, namely all humanity. The results are: There is no clue about how to implement a global difference principle other than to shift economic goods from those who have them to those who don't; and considerations about nations or countries are ethically irrelevant. Despite Peter Singer's many insights, his use of consequentialism to make global economic decisions has severe ethical problems. I noted two important problems: (1) A consequentialist can lie about what ethical principles he is following if that would produce the best overall results. (2) A general problem of consequentialism is that it does not care about how goods are distributed. I showed that a consequentialist has to prefer a distribution which makes some people more miserable when the overall sum is better.[16]

The alternative reasoning for choosing the principles is Rawls' maximin reasoning, and that turns out also to be appropriate for the Global Economy Social Contract.[17]

Both political and economic principles will be chosen. As I stated before, for the Global Economy Social Contract, economic principles are primary, but political principles also need to be chosen to implement the economic ones. In addition, a principle will be chosen outlining how respect for the International Social Contract is to be implemented. Since the international contract includes respect for the domestic arrangements of different societies, we could regard the global social economic contract as including respect for justice within a society by default. But multinational corporations have been known to destabilize just regimes and abet unjust ones, to serve their own ends. So it would be better also to include respect for domestically just regimes (or perhaps minimalist democracies) as a principle for the Global Economy Social Contract.

THE GENERAL CONDITIONS OF APPLICATION OF THE PRINCIPLES

The major consideration here is what institutions are subject to these principles. As with the domestic social contract, principles apply to institutions affected by them and able to implement them. The institutions responsible for distribution of benefits and burdens in the global economy are the ones discussed in Chapters 2 and 8. Those with the most impact are multinational corporations, governments (especially superpowers), world financial and economic institutions (such as the World Bank, the WTO, and the IMF). Institutions with subsidiary influence include the United Nations and its agencies, the World Court, and NGOs. New institutions capable of dealing with the issues for which a global economic contract is needed would definitely have an impact on the global economy. These were of two types: First, institutions dealing in a transnational way with governments, to prevent war and deal with genocides. These will be under the international contract, but global economic institutions will need to respect transnational political authority dealing with these problems. Global political institutions are needed to deal with transnational legal problems of individuals. Finally, a global economic authority will need to deal with fairness in transnational economic distribution, transnational competition, multinational tax avoidance, and common tax policies to deal with global warming.

Individuals will be impacted when these principles are applied by institutions. It is ultimately the impact on individuals that determines whether the institutional application of the principles chosen to regulate the global economy are just or not.

THE PRINCIPLES AND THEIR JUSTIFICATION

I will first restate the principles that would be chosen for institutions with authority in the global economy. Then I will consider the justification of these principles.

Global Economy Greatest Equal Freedom Principle: All individuals in the global economy have an equal claim to basic liberties.

- But individuals, not corporations, states, or other global institutions

Global Economy Difference Principle: Globalized institutions implement rules arranged to make the worst off participating in the global economy, as well off as possible.

- But not rules which diminish the productivity of institutions to the extent of making everyone, even the worst-off person in the global economy, still worse off.

Principle of Respect for Other Social Contracts:

- The actions of global institutions must not impair the application of the (domestic) principles of justice in just societies, or growth toward justice in other societies.
- The actions of global institutions must not impair the application of international principles of justice in societies complying with the International Social Contract.

Before discussing the justification of these principles, some comments of clarification are in order. The Global Economy Greatest Equal Freedom principle is intended to guarantee basic human rights. Like the Greatest Equal Freedom Principle for domestic justice, it is intended to guarantee an equal starting point for all participants. So it includes fair equal opportunity.[18]

The Bill of Rights (BR) of the US constitution is a model for many important human rights. (US Constitution 2002) The UN's Universal Declaration of Human Rights (UDHR) has a similar list. (Office of the High Commissioner on Human Rights 1948). Both list freedoms of the person, legal and economic equal rights, and freedom of association including participation in government. Both are therefore candidates for rights to be guaranteed under the Global Economy Greatest Equal Freedom Principle.

One major substantive difference between the two documents is that the Bill of Rights includes a right to own and bear arms, which is not included in the Universal Declaration of Human Rights. This right has until recently been interpreted as facilitating military training. A recent (2007) US Supreme Court decision interpreted this right as forbidding government regulation of guns. The ruling destroys the basis of civil society, which is for citizens to give up their right to use legal force to the sovereign in exchange for a civil society with law enforcement.[19] Current levels of gun violence in the US are on average from *four times to ten times* greater than other developed countries. (Coalition for Gun Control 2001) There is therefore no basis for the current court interpretation, nor is there reason for considering bearing arms a fundamental right.

The two documents spell out different details. Most details are worth including so that they don't get evaded. Under freedoms of the person, the UDHR includes prohibitions against slavery, torture, and inhuman punishment. Under legal and economic rights, the BR includes prohibitions against self-incrimination, double jeopardy, and requires grand jury indictment for serious crimes. The UDHR includes an enabling principle that people have the right to a domestic order permitting realization of these rights, whereas the BR has a clause reserving rights not enumerated to the citizens or the states.

The UDHR includes economic rights which belong under the Difference Principle. These are: Economic, social, and cultural rights enabling free personal development. The social rights include right to a free education at the elementary and secondary level. Economic rights include the right to work for equal pay for equal work, and pay adequate for human dignity and well-being. Included are the right to form labor unions and no discrimination against motherhood. These rights actually specify a floor for the worst off. As discussed in Chapter 5, **Domestic Theories of Justice**, "Utilitarianism Reconsidered," a Difference Principle calling for making the worst off as well off as possible can be implemented by specifying a minimum floor. It just needs to be recognized that if implementing that particular floor actually makes things worse, the Difference Principle requires one to change it.

The (separate) UN Global Compact in effect applies the principles of the UDHR to multinational corporations. Since the Global Compact is voluntary, it is difficult to see much motivation for businesses to follow it when their profitability is impacted. The content is to support human rights (as enumerated in the UDHR), to uphold just labor standards (as enumerated in the UDHR), to show concern for the environment (a concern I will discuss in Chapter 14, **IT-Enabled Globalization and the Environment**), and an anti-corruption principle. Thus the Global Compact mostly elaborates concerns included in the Global Economy Principles of Justice. Although making the Global Compact voluntary removes any enforcement problem, the fact that it is voluntary underscores the fact that multinational corporations are not parties to the Global Social Contract. I believe the actual parties to the contract--basically all the global players besides corporations--will need to work out an institutional structure to keep the inherent lack of ethics in corporations in check.

The Global Economy Difference Principle, when applied, will be impacted by domestic economic policies and decisions as well as international economic agreements between states. The principle would apply directly to benefits and burdens generated solely by global economic activity. If, as is much more likely, benefits and burdens are generated by both domestic institutions and state policies as well as global economic activity, the requirement would be that the portion of that activity attributable to the global economy satisfy the Global Economy Difference Principle.

Because of the many economic layers and because of differences of opinion in assessing economic benefits and burdens, application of the principle will often be difficult and contentious. But there are similar difficulties with applying the domestic principles of justice. The important thing is that a just ideal is formulated and accepted.

Thus, as an immediate consequence, the justice of the World Trade Organization's emphasis on free trade depends on whether free trade tends to make those worst off in the global economy, better off. There is good evidence that some modifications to unrestricted free trade would yield better results.[20] So the global difference principle would require adopting those modifications.

Ethically globalized institutions are bound by the global economy principles of justice, so their policies must make those in the worst off societies, as well off as possible. The World Bank, by adopting policies of fiscally responsible international banking, does not seem to do this. Thus its actions are not in accordance with the Global Economy Difference Principle.

But domestic national policies may impact transnational benefits and burdens. NAFTA--the North American Free Trade Agreement--was intended to improve the lot of everyone in the three countries involved, namely Canada, Mexico, and the US. The implementation of NAFTA resulted in widespread agricultural unemployment in Mexico. Applying the Global Economy Difference Principle, it is not enough to say, so what? Efficiency is not justice. In this case, the US, the primary beneficiary of NAFTA, needs to provide some compensation to those losing in Mexico. Worse, the loss of agricultural jobs in Mexico was not due solely to greater US agricultural efficiency. US farmers (mainly agribusinesses) received massive agricultural subsidies for corn. Domestic US political influences make it virtually impossible to eliminate these subsidies. The point of the story is that even if economic practices can be made just, domestic national politics may still produce results not in accordance with the Global Difference Principle.

This brings up the question: To what extent are domestic national policies and international agreements to be respected by the global economy principles of justice? I will consider first economic policies and then human rights under the Global Economy Greatest Equal Freedom Principle.

Since the global economy depends on a stable international order, the limits to intervention should be the same as for states against each other. That is, serious human rights violations such as genocide are required for intervention in a state. Since agents of the global economy do not have military force, possible intervention would be withdrawing business, imposing cooperative sanctions, or cooperating with states and transnational authorities who are employing military force.

An important related issue is ownership of natural resources by repressive governments. As Thomas Pogge points out, repressive governments in less developed countries are often supported by selling raw materials into the global economy. He correctly points out that corporations or states dealing with those government legitimize the ethically illegitimate appropriation of those countries' national resources. As currently practiced, he calls it the "international resource privilege." (Pogge 2002, 112-116) Since there is abundant evidence that this privilege contributes to making people in underdeveloped countries worse off, the Global economy Difference Principle requires restrictions. I will discuss this issue further in

Chapter 12, **Globalized Ethics and Current Institutions.** In that chapter, I will also discuss whether there are positive ethical actions that agents in the global economy may be required to take against repressive states.

There is one source of conflict which is more than potential. The global economy principles of justice honor human rights, as expressed in the Global Economy Greatest Equal Freedom Principle: All individuals in the global economy have an equal claim to basic liberties. So what should a global economic agent do when human rights are violated in a country? The Yahoo in China case previously discussed in several chapters is an example. Violation of labor rights in sweatshops and in using child labor is another.

China demanded information from Yahoo which Yahoo supplied and which led to the violation of the human rights of dissidents. There was also a subsequent vote of the shareholders not to uphold a ban on censorship on the Internet. Yahoo claimed that it was merely following Chinese law in providing the information but subsequently lost a lawsuit to the Chinese dissidents who were tortured as a result of their releasing information. I concluded in Chapter 9 that, without some acknowledged transnational policy, Yahoo is stuck with obeying the law of one state (China) and getting punished (successfully sued) in another (the US). We can conclude that the Global Greatest Equal Liberty principle requires the establishment of some such transnational policy or institution guaranteeing freedom of speech on the Internet.[21] The Global Network Initiative, to be discussed in Chapter 13, **Ethical Implications for IT**, may be such a policy.

The shareholder's vote against a ban on censorship is another ethical matter. Yahoo's shareholders have equal rights, but not the right to deny equal rights to participants in the global economy including Internet users. Thus they do not have the right to prevent Yahoo from enforcing equal rights (that is, banning censorship). This follows from the Global Economy Principle of Greatest Equal Liberty.

Multinational corporations are often very concerned about violation of labor standards in less developed countries. Companies selling products produced by contractors in less developed countries who use inhumane working conditions and child labor, get lots of very unfavorable publicity. As noted earlier, companies such as Nike, Ikea, and Apple, have taken elaborate precautions to prevent such things from happening.[22] As also noted earlier, conservative apologists for economic exploitation argue either that there has always been child labor (Friedman 1999) or that transnational labor standards cannot be enforced. (Bhagwati 2007, 178)

On this issue especially it seems that conservatives are arguing about efficiency rather than justice. Friedman's observation that child labor has always existed, even if correct, is irrelevant for the issue of what ethical standards should be. And Bhagwati's point is not credible. We are, after all, talking about a global economy in which strict standards of production, including details of work, have to be met to enable global production. To claim that ethical work standards would "produce chaos" (Bhagwati 2007, 178) is simply unbelievable in the context of a functioning global economy.

Also, since there is a functioning global economy with extensive communication, it is disingenuous to claim anything like priority for local standards in this area. Conservatives always argue (as they do here) that improving standards will make things worse off. Raising the minimum wage will cost jobs. Eliminating child labor will force girls into prostitution. For conservatives, there is often no way to improve the justice of a situation.

Fortunately, many multinationals think better. Labor standards follow from the principle of Global Greatest Equal Freedom. And some multinationals are ready to move their business if it will improve adherence to just labor standards. Although, for a corporation, reputation is all that counts, it is important what the reputation is *for*, and that is for humane labor standards. Thus they are implicitly acknowledging a transnational standard of justice.

JUSTIFICATION OF THE PRINCIPLES

The parties will choose principles not on utilitarian grounds but rather on maximin grounds. (Maximin is choosing the alternative that will make you best off in the worst case.) [23] Thus they have to adopt rules for institutions which will maximize the benefits of individuals participating in the global economy, but not rules which may cripple the productivity of institutions in such a way as to make everyone, even the worst-off person, still worse off. They will also choose an analog of Rawls' greatest equal freedom principle, but for individuals, not institutions such as corporations or states.

We saw that the alternatives for principles of justice for the global economy had serious defects.[24] Rawls established that the maximin rule (choose the alternative which makes you the best off should the worst happen) should be used in making the choice of domestic principles of justice. The maximin rule better reflects the social contract conditions for making the choice than does utilitarianism.[25] The same reasoning applies to the Global Economy Social Contract, primarily because the parties to this contract also do not know what position they will occupy in the global economy. To illustrate how this works, I will compare the choice of the maximin rule versus the choice of the cosmopolitan utilitarian (consequentialist) rule.

As discussed above, we will assume that the parties to the global economy contract are those sharing benefits and burdens in the global economy, rather than the full-blown cosmopolitan assumption of all of humanity. So the restricted cosmopolitan utilitarian position we will consider is that institutions should be arranged to maximize average utility over all participants in the global economy.

As we have already noted, the parties to the global social contract, like the parties to the domestic contract, have no basis for knowing what position they will occupy in the global economy. This position will be a complex combination of what society they are a member of as well as their actual position in the global economy itself. But they won't gamble on being in the US rather than Niger. They won't take extreme risks with their life prospects. So they will choose to use the maximin rule rather than the cosmopolitan utilitarian rule to maximize utility.[26]

How would these principles apply to the practice of offshoring? The main point of international labor offshoring is to take advantage of lower wage rates in developing countries. In such offshoring, economic benefits and burdens are experienced by different societies with different economic and political arrangements.

If cosmopolitan utilitarianism were the standard by which the justice of offshoring is decided, offshoring would be justified by its increasing the total amount of value across the world. For cosmopolitan utilitarians, the distribution of value doesn't matter. So it wouldn't matter that employees in the higher-wage economy were losing jobs. It also wouldn't matter that there is no connection between the wage structures of the countries involved in offshoring. So there is no pressure for wage differentials to even out. For cosmopolitan utilitarians it doesn't matter that there are different economies. Thus the apparent benefits of offshoring for the US, for example, may be illusory. Because the US needs to buy back goods produced in the offshored countries, there is a loss to the US economy not reflected in increased corporate profits. The loss is reflected in increased debt. In the economic meltdown of late 2008, the illusory nature of gains to the US economy became evident. I quoted *BusinessWeek* Chief Economist Michael Mandel in Chapter 1 as saying:

U.S. companies [will] *have to pay more attention to sustaining productivity growth and innovation at home rather than resorting to outsourcing as their main source of cost savings. That would boost wages and incomes for U.S. workers and reduce the need for... huge debts* [for the US] *to pay for foreign-made goods.* (Mandel 2008)

Because of the negative economic impact of offshoring on the domestic economy, an excess profits tax on corporate profits due to offshoring could be in order to internalize what is now an externality for corporations. (Reubens 2008)

Such an excess profits tax is one example of the background institutions and policies needed to make offshoring a just practice. But these are considerations not available to the cosmopolitan utilitarian. So long as the sum of value is increased, it does not matter what country gets the value.

For the cosmopolitan utilitarian, offshoring is probably currently a just practice. Because of the difficulties I have brought up, offshoring would not currently be a just practice under the Global Economy Social Contract. Offshoring may become a just practice under the Global Economy Social Contract when institutions and policies are able to regulate the sharing of benefits and burdens within the global economy. This would include all workers having the rights guaranteed by the Global Economy Greatest Equal Freedom Principle. In those circumstances raising the well-being of a programmer in India may be just even though the well-being of an American is consequently reduced to the extent that we are all part of one economic system sharing benefits and burdens. However, it must also be shown that members of the society losing positions are not being treated unjustly.

Offshoring might be defended as an application of the Global Difference Principle: We are making the (somewhat) worse off, namely programmers or factory workers in India or China, better off. However, the loss of a higher paid job is not compensated for within the US economy. It does not make the worst off in the US economy better off. So it conflicts with respect for domestic justice. In any case, the social cost to the United States of I.T. personnel losing skilled jobs needs to compensated for in some way.

Offshoring is an example of the different results given by choosing cosmopolitan utilitarianism and the Global Economy Social Contract. I believe that the results of the Global Economy Social Contract are more in reflective equilibrium with our judgements about the justice of offshoring. The same kinds of considerations--that is, the fact that cosmopolitan utilitarianism ignores distribution and separate national economies--make cosmopolitan utilitarianism an inferior choice for a principle of global justice.

GENERAL REQUIREMENTS OF INSTITUTIONS IMPLEMENTING THE PRINCIPLES

Current transnational institutions, both governmental and nongovernmental, are sometimes not equipped to insure that the global economy principles of justice are followed. There will be a fuller discussion of new institutions in the following chapters. But a complete discussion is well beyond the scope of this book. Here I will list some constraints any institutions will have to satisfy. We are talking here *only* about new institutions (or policies for old institutions) which are necessary to implement the principles of justice of the global economy.

These institutions need to be:

- Democratic: Their members are chosen by the people they are responsible to, and their policies must be revisable by their constituents.
- Transparent: All proceedings are open to all they affect.
- Implement Global Economy Principles of Justice: Difference Principle, Equal Freedom Principle, Principles of Respect for Other Social Contracts.
- Authoritative: They have the means of enforcing their decisions concerning those they have authority over in accordance with the Global Economy Social Contract.

These conditions express the conditions of the Global Economy Social Contract. The principles arrived at were a free decision of equal participants. Hence any non-democratic and non-transparent implementation would violate the very conditions of the contract. Their purpose is to implement the Global Economy Principles of Justice, and any implementation must itself comply with those principles. Also, the purpose of the contract was to set conditions on legitimate authority in the area of the Global Economy. So they have the authority to enforce decisions taken in accordance with the principles and these constraints.

IT professionals must have a role in making sure that these conditions on institutions are fulfilled. Their role in choosing the principles themselves is no different from any other employee or manager; they must consider how the principles will affect their life prospects. But especially to guarantee democracy and transparency of institutions in the context of the IT-enabled global economy, their input is essential at all stages.

Looking back at the International Social Contract, these conditions on institutions also apply there. The principles of the ISC were:

1. Their governments maintain a minimalist democracy and respect cooperative agreements made between them.
2. Peoples do not intervene in each others affairs and only make war in self-defense.
3. Peoples have a duty to assist other people living under unfavorable conditions.
4. They agree to have a procedure for dealing with violations of these principles. [27]

The Democratic institution condition is reflected in principle 1, the requirement for members of the contract to be minimalist democracies. The Transparency condition would ensure that institutions under the International Social Contract comply with the conditions of that contract, and so it would be adopted under the ISC. Transparency would thus be a mechanism for insuring compliance under principle 4. The Authoritative condition, that is, having the means of enforcement, is also explicit in principle 4 of the International Social Contract.

CONCLUSION

I have now set out the principles of justice for the global economy and the general conditions for their application to institutions. I believe it would be best first to consider the impact of global justice on current institutions and then consider what new institutions would be necessary to implement global justice. This order will minimize the necessity for creating new institutions wielding authority. We first see how much current institutions can handle, and then add new institutions only when necessary. This is not for conservative ideological reasons, that non-market institutions must be bad. Rather I want to minimize problems of oversight. Indeed, it makes sense to use market-based institutions whenever possible within the principles of justice because of their greater efficiency and potential lesser administrative overhead.

In the next chapters, I will continue to see how well the principles of the Global Social Contracts agree with accepted intuitive principles of global justice. This process is *reflective equilibrium*--we want our theoretical principles to match our intuitive judgements in particular cases.[28] I believe that the principles of the Global Social Contracts match our intuitive global justice judgements much better than cosmopolitanism.

So the following Chapter 11, **Globalized Ethics and Current Institutions,** will deal with the extent to which the principles of justice of the global social contracts can be realized within current institutions. Then Chapter 12, **New Global Institutions,** will discuss additional new institutions necessary to realize the principles of justice of the global social contracts.

REFERENCES

Beitz, C. (1999). *Political theory and international relations.* Princeton, NJ: Princeton University Press.

Bhagwati, J. (2007). *In defense of globalization.* Oxford, UK: Oxford University Press.

Coalition for Gun Control. (2001). *Access to small arms/firearms and death rates.* Retrieved October 25, 2008 from http://www.guncontrol.ca/Content/international.html#access

Constitution, U. S. (2002). *Bill of rights.* Retrieved October 25, 2008 from http://www.constitution.org/billofr_.htm

(Ed.). *BusinessWeek.* (2003, April 14). *BusinessWeek,* 96.

Friedman, M. (1999). *Take it to the limits: Milton Friedman on libertarianism.* Interview filmed on February 10, 1999. Retrieved February 11, 2008 from http://www.hoover.org/multimedia/uk/3411401.html

Hobbes, T. (1999). *Leviathan.* Retrieved May 12, 2004 from http://darkwing.uoregon.edu/~rbear/hobbes/leviathan.html

Hopkins, M. (2003). *The planetary bargain.* London: Earthscan Publications

Jesdanun, A. (2008, July 6). 'Public' online spaces don't carry speech, rights. *Associated Press.* Retrieved July 7, 2008 from http://news.yahoo.com

Mandel, M. (2008, October 27). How to get growth back on track. *BusinessWeek.*

Morgenthau, H. (1993). *Politics among nations, brief edition.* New York: McGraw-Hill Office of the High Commissioner on Human Rights. (1948). Universal declaration of human rights. *Office of the High Commissioner on Human Rights.* Retrieved October 25, 2008 from http://www.unhchr.ch/udhr/

Pogge, T. (2002). *World poverty and human rights.* Cambridge, England: Polity Press.

Rawls, J. (1999a). *A theory of justice* (rev. ed.). Cambridge, MA: Harvard University Press

Rawls, J. (1999b). *The law of peoples.* Cambridge, MA: Harvard University Press.

Reubens, E. (2008, March 31). The wages of offshoring. *BusinessWeek.*

Singer, P. (2004). *One world* (2nd ed.) New Haven, CT: Yale University Press.

Summers, L. (2008). The economic agenda. *Harvard Magazine, 111*(1).

Yunus, M. (2003). *Banker to the poor.* New York: Public Affairs.

ENDNOTES

[1] This is another application of the discussion in Chapter 4, **The Basis of Ethical Principles,** "The Rationality of Cooperative Principles."

[2] This is a new addition to Rawls' principles in the *Law of Peoples.* (Rawls 1999b, 37)

[3] Costa Rica may be the only country which has never had a military.

[4] Morgenthau believed a world state can come to be through the "processes of diplomacy." (Morgenthau 1993, 389) But it is hard to see how international diplomacy can get nations to reduce their power, because diplomacy lacks transnational power.

[5] Economist Lawrence Summers calls this shifting to avoid state regulation "corporate arbitrage" and notes that it needs to be prevented. (Summers 2008)

[6] See Rawls 1999a, Part One, "Theory."

[7] Recall that this was an alternative to the cosmopolitan solution of eliminating any differences in resources between people in different countries.

[8] Mohammed Yunus' social businesses may have social goals, but as businesses, they are also not ethical individuals. So they are also not parties to the social contract. See also note 11 below.

[9] Even if it is difficult for them to stay apart from Western Civilization, we have to allow them the chance.

[10] This list is the same as Michael Hopkins' list of stakeholders in the "planetary bargain." (Hopkins 2003, 49.)

[11] Mohammed Yunus' social businesses have the same structure as a regular business but their shareholders are not allowed to take profits from the business and the goal of the business is specific social goals rather than profit maximization. These differences do not make them different enough from corporations to require adding them as an additional party to the contract, but all parties must have the general knowledge that there are alternatives to profit maximization as the goal for a business.

[12] Chapter 9, **IT and Globalized Ethics,** "IT's contribution to the global social contract"

[13] See the discussion in Chapter 5, **Domestic Theories of Justice,** "Utilitarianism reconsidered." See also Rawls 1999a, section 24, "The Veil of Ignorance."

[14] See Chapter 5, **Domestic Theories of Justice,** "Utilitarianism reconsidered."

[15] They also know that social businesses are possible. See notes 8 and 11 above.

16   See Chapter 7, **Cosmopolitanism, "**Utilitarian Cosmpolitanism."

17   See Chapter 5, **Domestic Theories of Justice, "**Theories of Justice."

18   Although Rawls (1999a) places equality of opportunity under the Difference Principle rather than the Equal Freedom Principle, it makes more sense to me to include it with other considerations guaranteeing an unbiased starting place in society--or in the global economy.

19   This has been the view of all political theorists since Hobbes. (1651)

20   See Chapter 2, **Current Ethically Globalized Institutions,** "World financial and economic institutions,"and Chapter 8, **The Ethical Status Of Globalized Institutions** "World financial and economic institutions."

21   Actually, the right of freedom of speech does not extend to the Internet in the US. See Jesdanun 2008.

22   See Chapter 1, **IT-Enabled Global Ethical Problems**, "Labor Standards/Child Labor."

23   See Chapter 5, **Domestic Theories of Justice,** "Theories of Justice."

24   See Chapters 6, 7, and 8, summarized in the discussion of element 6 above.

25   The reasoning occupies sections 26 through 30 of Rawls' *Theory of Justice.* (1999a)

26   Yunus' argument that per capita GNP is not a good measure of how well off people are in a society is a similar argument against average utilitarianism. See Yunus 2003, 211-212.

27   This is a new addition to Rawls' principles in the *Law of Peoples.* (Rawls 1999b, 37)

28   See Chapter 4, **The Basis of Ethical Principles,** "Reflective Equilibrium."

Chapter 11
Globalized Ethics and Current Institutions

In this chapter, I will examine the extent to which current institutions might be able to implement the principles of global justice. I will begin with a few remarks about a market economy and continue with the two major institutions involved in the global economy--states and multinational corporations. Then I will consider other current transnational institutions such as world financial and economic institutions (World Bank, IMF, WTO), the United Nations and World Court, and other transnational NGOs. Finally, a number of practices have transnational impacts, and the Global Principles of Justice require changes to those practices. These are: Property and intellectual property, taxes, and Internet regulation.

JUSTICE AND THE MARKET ECONOMY

Any economic arrangement satisfying the principles of justice at any level will almost always include the market economy as a starting point. A properly functioning market will produce the most efficient results, without administrative costs. Economists say that markets produce *Pareto optimal* results. This means that no one's outcome can be improved without making someone else worse off--everyone is as well off as they could be. The similarity to the Difference Principles of domestic justice and global

DOI: 10.4018/978-1-60566-922-9.ch011

economic justice is not accidental. The additional requirement of the Difference Principle is that justice requires choosing from among many Pareto optimal results, the one that makes the worst off as well off as possible. (Rawls 1999a section 12)

For a market economy to be just, it needs to be functioning "properly." The market needs to be competitive. So monopolies or oligarchies will prevent everyone's being as well off as they could be. The monopolist (for example Microsoft) makes huge profits at the expense of the consumer. It requires external regulation by some institution (the government is the likely candidate) to break up monopolies and otherwise ensure that the market is functioning honestly.[1] Some authority external to the market is also required to handle environmental problems, since the environment's interests are not directly represented in the market. The environment is neither producer nor consumer.

If the market is more-or-less functioning properly, it will usually be unjust not to use the market for economic allocation. Central planning is rarely Pareto optimal, and thus a centrally planned economy will make some worse off than they need to be. The extra administrative costs tend to fall on everyone, and when this happens, the Difference Principle is violated. These conclusions of economic theory have been dramatically corroborated by the experience of China in the past few decades. However, the Chinese experience shows that however much markets help in implementing the Difference Principle, implementing the first principle of Greatest Equal Freedom is another matter.

Similar observations apply when the market is extended globally. In Chapter 3, I characterized global institutions as those with transnational properties enabled by IT or transportation technology. I will add to this characterization and define *economic globalization* to mean global institutions participating in a global market economy. Realistically, that is what we are dealing with. There may be other possible ethical economic arrangements, but there is good reason to believe that a market economy suitably constrained will turn out to satisfy the Global Principles of Justice. Considering other economic arrangements would have to be the subject of one or more additional books.

STATES, SUPERPOWERS, AND GLOBAL JUSTICE

Any transnational authority raises a major issue for nation-states: Is their own sovereignty compromised? As we have seen, the US has refused to accept the authority of the World Court because its decisions would override decisions made by US personnel. There are, however, some cases in which it would be to the advantage of nation states to accede to a transnational authority with the power to enforce transnational edicts. Nation-states by themselves cannot easily deal with tax-shifting by multinationals precisely because they have economic authority only within their own states.

A global institution able to deal with tax-shifting could be to the cooperative advantage of all states. Even states currently receiving reduced taxes from multinationals would have the advantage of having their own tax structures honored transnationally. The authority of the World Court is a different story, however. As a superpower, the US can simply ignore international law and get the benefits of a non-cooperative solution.[2] A cooperative (ethical) solution involves a loss in self-interested benefits in exchange for a gain in cooperative benefits. Accepting the authority of the world court would mean that US personnel would no longer be able to violate principles of international justice with impunity. Apparently it is not a concern that other countries following the example of the US could also violate principles of international justice, for example concerning treatment of US prisoners and the use of torture on US prisoners.

If states recognize that there is cooperative benefit in transnational authority but no way to realize this benefit within the bounds of national authority, as in an international economic authority to deal with tax shifting, then there is no practical barrier to creating such an authority. International postal and air traffic authorities could be starting points for such an authority. There would, however, likely be serious opposition from multinational corporations, the beneficiaries of tax shifting.

But on the other hand, if principles of cooperative benefit can be violated with impunity, it is unlikely that any nation-state will voluntarily give up any self-interested benefits it receives through non-compliance. The immediate thought in such a case is to establish a transnational institution, a world state, with enough power to *make* the nation-state comply. But how are we going to guarantee that this super-super powerful transnational institution won't simply enforce its own arbitrary will just because it can? I will postpone further discussion of the viability of a world state to the next chapter, Chapter 12, **New Global Institutions.** For now, it is enough to recognize that this problem of effective ethical limits to state sovereignty cannot be solved within the framework of current transnational institutions.

MULTINATIONAL CORPORATIONS AND GLOBAL JUSTICE

There is a problem with the ethics of corporations because corporations have the goal of maximizing profits. As we saw in Chapter 8, **The Ethical Status of Globalized Institutions,** corporations are not individuals with an ethical point of view. [3] Therefore they cannot be regarded as parties to the social contract. And the goal of profit maximization can require corporations to adopt unethical solutions when that would benefit the bottom line.

It is standard practice in California for large corporations to mount extensive advertising campaigns with false or highly misleading claims against ballot propositions which they believe are against corporate interests. Power company advertisements against a 2008 renewable energy proposition claimed that power rates will be raised, when the proposition itself has safeguards against this. Some green groups found the proposition to be flawed, but for much different reasons.

Multinational corporations inherit the socially irresponsible behavior of corporations. Corporations must legally be individuals to fulfill their function.[4] But they are not subject to the ethical considerations of individuals. Indeed, individual corporate leaders are *legally protected* from being personally liable for the damages caused by their leadership. Therefore, as I previously pointed out, a new set of legal requirements is needed for corporations in order to serve the function of providing ethical accountability. These are: No killing people, no deliberately not telling the truth, no thwarting the legitimate rights of your employees through union-busting, complying with accepted accounting standards for truthfulness in financial reporting. Further steps would be outside periodic ethical review by an authority with the power to dismantle the corporation and sell off its assets. Corporations should also be prohibited from attempting to influence public policy by advertising or campaign contributions or by financing electoral initiatives.[5] Remember that corporations are only *legal* individuals. They do not inherit rights from individuals nor are they participants in a domestic social contract.

These suggested (domestic) regulations on corporations are necessary to preserve the justice of a domestic society. The same requirements would be necessary to prevent multinational corporations from damaging or distorting global justice. But since corporations resist any attempt to limit their power, it may not be easy to implement these restrictions. Although the governments of states would be responsible for implementing corporate requirements domestically, a new transnational institution is needed to implement corporate ethical requirements transnationally. I will consider the viability of this authority in the next chapter, Chapter 12, **New Global Institutions.**

Corporations have developed their own transnational organizations to further their own interests. These organizations do not get their authority from states. They promulgate informal or "soft" law for industrial codes. For example, the Global Business Dialogue on Electronic Commerce developed standards for electronic commerce. These standards are explicitly formulated to increase benefits to multinational corporations, so they do not directly have to do with global justice. Sometimes, as we will see shortly, they work against global justice. Enforcement by "international arbitration," and not the laws of any state, is often written into contracts. The standards for arbitration are the standards of the international business community. (Tabb 2004, 166-168)

CORPORATE SOCIAL RESPONSIBILITY

Some commentators simply extend individual ethics to corporations. Thomas White (2007) asserts that the 'job' of business is to make life better for everyone in society. He believes that corporations will behave ethically if we call ethics to their attention. More realistic is the case of FedEx described in Chapter 8, **The Ethical Status of Globalized Institutions**. FedEx, though officially committed to a plan to minimize greenhouse gases, implemented only a token replacement of dirty trucks. Their reason was their fiduciary duty to our stockholders; there were better uses of company capital. FedEx even won an environmental award for the plan it never carried out. This case is a graphic illustration of appearing to be ethical rather than being ethical. (Elgin 2007) Appearing so, but not necessarily being so, is what is ultimately important for corporations. It is good public relations for a company to promote its reputation for social responsibility. This motivation has always been a part of business life, and companies routinely budget for it: Christmas gifts for the poor, donations to inner city schools, and so on.

Many writers also believe that voluntary corporate social responsibility (CSR) can harmonize corporate goals and ethical requirements. However, the business theorist David Vogel in his *The Market for Virtue* (2004) argues to the contrary that evidence shows that corporations will work toward their business goals whenever there is a conflict. This is what we just saw in the case of Fed Ex scuttling its plans for a greener fleet of truck when the bottom line would be affected.[6]

So what is the case for CSR as a driver for corporate ethics? I will next consider a few spokespersons for CSR. Ira Jackson and Jane Nelson, in their *Profits with Principles* (2004) attempt to show that social responsibility belongs "at the core of business." Christine Arena, in her *Cause for Success* (2004), presents several cases where putting social concerns first has been best for the company. Michael Hopkins, in his *The Planetary Bargain* (2003), describes a "bargain" in which corporations undertake to be socially responsible. Jeffrey Sachs in his *Common Wealth (2008)* believes that voluntary partnerships between NGOs and multinationals are possible that are both socially responsible and serve profitability. All four authors are able to point out numerous opportunities for corporations to improve their ethical behavior and at the same time improve their bottom lines. Many of their suggestions would definitely improve matters. But the real test of genuine ethical resolve is pursuing ethical behavior even when one's own interests are not served. Obviously a conflict between ethical behavior and corporate interests can happen, and we will see how our authors handle such a conflict.

Jackson and Nelson make some excellent points. They note that "successful and sustainable companies need the existence of prosperous and just societies." (Jackson and Nelson 2004, xi) Thus companies should promote and help societies to be prosperous and just and not undercut justice and prosperity in societies. But when it comes to the bottom line, there is still a conflict. It is worth pointing out, as Jackson and Nelson do, that there are numerous cases in which pursuing social goals is *compatible* with profit maximization. Indeed they describe numerous cases in which pursuing social goals enhances profitability, either directly or indirectly through enhancing reputation and good will. But for an individual, the test is whether he or she persists in being ethical even when that is not in the individual's interest.

According to a 2003 survey, 82 percent of businesses said that social responsibility helps their bottom line.[7] Since a negative response would be bad PR, it is hard to trust this figure. Jackson and Nelson also state that many studies show a "positive relation between a company's financial performance and its social and environmental performance," and that "many . . . research findings debunk the view that suggests the inevitable tradeoff: Profits against principles, and shareholders against other stakeholders." (Jackson and Nelson 2004, 51-53) Unfortunately, they do not actually cite a single research finding and instead refer the reader to an appendix with about 100 citations on numerous topics. There is no question about the value of showing many ways in which profits and ethics are compatible, but Jackson and Nelson say nothing to show that profits and principles are nearly always compatible, nor to show that companies will give up profits to observe principles.

This is exactly what Christine Arena sets out to do in her *Cause for Success.* (2004) Part of the title is "10 Companies That Put Profits Second and Came in First." As it turns out, the ethical concern of some of these companies was to reduce damage to the environment. They also managed to do it in ways that added to their profits. This is entirely laudable. But the basis for ethical environmental principles is different from the ethical principles of social cooperation, and it is social principles we are considering now. I will consider ethical principles for the environment in Chapter 14, **IT-Enabled Globalization and the Environment.** One indication that there may be less incompatibility between principles and profits in the case of the environment is that environmentally unsound practices almost always involve waste. And eliminating waste almost always improves productivity and hence profits. The first case in *Cause for Success* is the carpet manufacturer Interface. Eliminating waste was a large part of their becoming a sustainable operation, and also in making sustainability profitable. But this case and environmental aspects of cases will need to wait until Chapter 14 for a more extensive discussion.

The companies in *Cause for Success* that focused on social ethical goals did so in a variety of ways. Green Mountain Coffee, the pioneer of fair trade coffee, made a large contribution to global justice by adopting and promoting price standards for coffee growers in impoverished countries. These standards allow poor farmers to make a living wage. Thus they are a direct application of the Global Economy Difference Principle. NGOs such as Fairtrade Labeling Organizations International (founded in 1997 for coffee production) also require production to come from democratically organized cooperative groups, thus helping to insure compliance with the Global Economy Greatest Equal Liberty Principle. Another fair trade certification organization TransFair (founded 1992) works with coffee and a number of other products from poorer countries. Ten thousand US companies and thirty-five thousand European companies participate, and over 800,000 producer families have improved their economic status. (Arena 2004, 102) In 2008, eBay announced a marketplace, WorldofGood.com, for fair trade goods and recycled items. (agence France Presse 2008)

It is important to recognize how social goals and profits are reconciled in these cases. The goal of maximizing profits is constrained by publicly announced trade standards, and competition is on the product differentiation of observing those standards. Thus the market itself is constrained by global principles of justice. Those standards are observed because observing them supplies a competitive advantage. So profits and social ethical principles become compatible.

Two cautions: First, if competition is on the differentiation of obeying the standards, then if everyone obeyed no one would have a competitive advantage. Of course, from the point of view of global justice, this would be an entirely desirable state of affairs.

Second, not all companies may choose to compete on these terms. They can continue to maximize profits by squeezing poor suppliers. And corporations like Wal-Mart which traditionally operate in this way are defended by Jason Furman, one of the economic advisers to the US Democratic 2008 Presidential Campaign, because they improve the well-being of poor people in the US by supplying lower prices. (Gerstein 2008) Here we see a potential conflict between the domestic difference principle and the global difference principle: Poor domestic people are made better off by Wal-Mart's lower prices, but poor global producers are made worse off. In this case, the Global Economy Social Contract gives an ethical answer: Insofar as the lower Wal-Mart price is due to making a worker in the global economy worse off, even to below a living income, improving the lot of a poor American does not make it just. (I assume that the poorest American is still making a living wage.) Of course, the low Wal-Mart price includes plenty of American profit, and the interests of the poor domestic consumers and of the poor global suppliers could be reconciled by less corporate profits. But then the corporation would need to have other motivations besides profit maximization. This remains a problem for corporate social responsibility as a means for insuring global justice across the board.

Anita Roddick, the founder and owner of The Body Shop, a bath-and-beauty English company, expresses her individual ethical convictions within the framework of her business. In addition to implementing fair trade practices within the company, she has mounted an extensive human rights media campaign, in collaboration with Amnesty International, and a media campaign against corporate injustice. She notes that:

...companies still commit human rights violations [because] they are allowed to... If [there were laws to protect human rights], many big companies would have been penalized out of existence long ago. But they're too busy maximizing profits and offering the poorer communities in America a cheaper and cheaper product... on the backs of slaves... [T]he press doesn't want to open up these cans of worms to the public, especially in America, because the media is controlled by the ...advertisers committing these violations in the first place... [G]overnments are in bed with the corporations... The only possible hope for change is that enough consumers will stand together and demand it... They have hundreds of organizations on their side... Issues like child slavery are becoming high profile, and that is the key to change. (Arena 2004, 131-2)

Roddick's large-scale media campaigns are clearly a positive step toward achieving global justice. But how realistic is her faith in consumers as the agent for realizing global justice? Fair trade labeling and social businesses are successful instruments for social justice because they alter the very structure of profit maximization. Fair trade labeling supplants price as the basis of consumer choice. And social businesses explicitly replace profit maximization with achieving social goals. But it is hard to see how consumer pressure can actually force corporations to modify their basic structure.[8] This is not to say that consumer pressure cannot force valuable changes to realize global justice, especially in the area of trade practices. And even within the structure of profit maximization, there is room for much positive change.

The computer company Hewlett-Packard (HP) has a long tradition of philanthropy. In 2000, it decided to increase its efforts to bring IT to poorer communities which lacked it. Its motivation was that "the most prosperous IT markets of the future will come from the world's most underserved, underaccessed, and underprivileged communities." (Arena 2004, 154) The community of Kuppan, India, served as a pilot. The company was clear that its aim for the community was to help community members "overcome economic barriers such as illiteracy, insufficient access to new jobs, and limited ability to partake of global trade." (Arena 2004, 155) But there is an obvious conflict of interest with HP's aims as a technology producer. Indeed this conflict arises in many "digital divide" projects. HP wants to increase IT skills and access. But IT skills and access are relevant to social justice only if they contribute to how well off community members are. That may have happened, but it is not clear that HP paid as much attention to the impact on community well-being as to the increase in utilization of technology.[9]

From the point of view of the Global Social Contract, there are other aims which HP seems to have considered only tangentially. Participants in the Global Social Contract need to have skills and access to IT that equip them to participate fairly in the global economy. Were the villagers participating in the global economy in any ways? Could they have benefited by such participation? In a rural village, improving access to agricultural market information and availability would likely be helpful. Not mentioned. Starting new businesses with technological equipment is mentioned, and is fine. But it is a bit disheartening to read about the outcome: "Scattered along its dusty streets are bustling government offices, community centers, schools, service organizations, and community Internet centers -- *all powered by HP technology* [my emphasis]." (Arena 2004, 164) Then there is a list of things the villagers can now do. This is absolutely typical of an equipment-driven IT development project. Maybe the fault is only in the description and these services are actually being used by the villagers and their well-being is actually being improved. HP talks a lot about their methodology of learning the villager's needs, but it is very suspicious that they don't think of the project in those terms. A good contrast is the Grameen Phone project.[10] Grameen Phone was done in a social business context (although see the discussion below), so social goals took precedence over enhancing the company business.

Rob Preston, the editor in chief of *informationweek,* argues for compatibility between CSR and profitability for IT companies. IT companies, when surveyed by IBM's Institute for Business Value, had similar views. Two thirds demanded that CSR activities drive revenue, and half said these activities were delivering competitive advantage. CSR activities for IT firms include training, software donations, and (unspecified) green initiatives. Preston notes, however, that "it would be irresponsible for public companies to get behind economic, environmental, and social causes that don't serve shareholders interests in some way." (Preston 2008) Thus for Preston social responsibility is secondary to profits.

The EICC (Electronic Industry Citizenship Coalition) has promulgated a voluntary set of ethical standards for electronics companies, including IT companies. Its standards cover worker rights, the environment, management implementation of the standards, and ethics. The worker rights include standards drawn from other transnational labor NGOs. The environmental standards call for reducing pollution and waste and complying with environmental regulations. The ethical standards call for no corrupt practices and upholding standards of fair business and competition, protecting whistleblowers, transparency as required by regulations, respecting intellectual property, and encouraging community involvement. (EICC 2007) These aims are good as far as they go, but they are reactive and to a large extent depend on the lead of government regulation. The ethics requirement of respect for intellectual property regardless of what regulations actually are betrays a corporate bias. In any case, they are no help with transnational problems arising from conflicting national regulations.

THE PLANETARY BARGAIN

The name of the book *Planetary Bargain* (2003) has echoes of the Global Social Contract, and there are similarities. Its author, Michael Hopkins, was familiar with Rawls' social contract theory, but only in the context of setting a code of ethics for participants within corporations. When it comes to the global or planetary context, Hopkins says:

It would be nice to imagine... a planetary bargain that arises from all of the major companies of the world sitting around a table and horse trading, eventually producing a final document. (Hopkins 2003, 43)

The first difference between his Planetary Bargain and the Global Social Contract is that it is an agreement between all *actual* parties. The second difference is that it is between multinational corporations. The social contract objection is that the Planetary Bargain doesn't abstract from individual interests and hence won't result in agreement on principles for cooperative benefit. That's why in any social contract we don't allow parties to know what their own particular interests are. And for the Global Social Contract in particular, we don't allow corporations (or more generally non-individuals) to be parties deciding on the contract. From the discussion just preceding, we can see why: Profit-maximization is not an ethical principle, and yet that is what corporations may even be required to do. The parties to a global social contract have to be individuals with the capability of devising ethical principles.

Indeed, Hopkins seems to realize this. Stakeholder pressure by consumers, employees, campaigners, and shareholders on corporations is necessary to make corporations socially responsible. The actual content of CSR for Hopkins is a given, imported from other discussions. There are four areas: (1) Good corporate governance, including no corrupt practices and open, transparent finances; (2) Treating employees fairly; (3) Community and social fund involvement, philanthropy, and paying appropriate taxes; (4) Care of the environment. (Hopkins 2003, 27-28) Although the content is plausible, there are significant omissions such as global distributive justice.[11]

PUBLIC/PRIVATE PARTNERSHIPS

Jeffrey Sachs, an economist active on the international stage, has the credentials to speak about public/private partnerships. He was one of the prime movers of the successful public/private effort to get antiretroviral drugs for AIDS distributed in Africa beginning in 2000-2001. The problem was the patent-protected cost of the drugs, about $10,000 per patient per year. The actual cost of production of the drugs was $350 per year. The drug companies were persuaded to segment their markets and charge $10,000 per year in developed countries and $350 per year in Africa. Since there was no African market for $10,000 per year drugs, they would not lose any money, especially with enforceable restrictions on selling back to wealthy countries. (Sachs 2008, 316-319)

However, there were still gaps: Africans typically could not afford even as much as $10 per year; delivery infrastructure including basic health services were lacking; and people often didn't have enough food to allow the drugs to work well. All these problems were undertaken by NGOs governments, and business philanthropy. The gaps were not covered by businesses working in markets. (Sachs 2008, 316-319)

Sachs proposes this accomplishment as a template for achieving other social goals. Sachs acknowledges that "the overriding job of business is to make money for the owners, but that in no way precludes an active role for business in solving nonmarket problems..." (Sachs 2008, 319) Two features of the AIDS drug case need to be singled out: First, the drug companies were not making money on the reduced-price drugs for Africa, they were simply not losing money. So why did they do this when they were supposed to be making money? This brings us to the second distinctive feature: The drug companies sued to stop production of low-cost AIDS drugs; this produced a firestorm of negative consumer response. Sachs attaches great importance to reputational consequences for businesses, and this was a strong motivating force for the drug companies in this case. But more generally, there are companies that don't care that much about their reputation. Exxon-Mobil, the world's largest oil company, stonewalled victims of the ExxonValdez disaster for years. Some corporations manifest their concern for reputation by continuing to act badly and spreading disinformation, as the tobacco companies did for years about the link of their product to lung cancer. Coal companies market "clean coal," which currently does not exist, and it is far from clear whether it will ever exist. (Elgin 2008)[12] Conversely, a pharmaceutical company needs to have the reputation for being ethical and caring.

When companies are motivated (primarily by reputation) to become part of ethically responsible projects, Sachs does have an important and innovative proposal. The idea is for corporations to contribute part of the effort toward a solution of social problems, with philanthropy, NGOs, and governments contributing the rest. The assets a business might be able to contribute include its proprietary technologies, supplier and customer networks, workforce, and reputation.

The contribution of Sachs' proposals to ethical goals notwithstanding, there is nothing which leads me to alter my conclusions about the ethical status of corporations. Corporations are still not ethical individuals, corporations are not part of the Global Social Contract, and corporations need both domestic and transnational regulation to close the ethical gap.

GLOBALIZATION AND SOCIAL BUSINESSES

Jackson and Nelson cite Grameen Phone in Bangladesh as a success story for "profits with principles." (2004, 79) Grameen Phone was founded by Mohammed Yunus, whose concept of "social business" I previously described: A social business has the primary aim of realizing stipulated social goals, and its investors do not take profits out of the business.[13] Grameen Phone was successful in getting cell phone service to the poorest and enabling communication which has significantly improved the well being of villagers. Norwegian telecom operation Telenor has 62% ownership. Yunus is threatening legal proceedings against Telenor to force it to transform their joint Bangladeshi subsidiary into a "social business" aimed at helping the poor.

Yunus wants Telenor to honor a deal dating back to 1996 that would hand control of GrameenPhone to his Grameen Bank, a social business. Profits would go only to social projects. Grameen Bank already has a similar arrangement with Danone for yogurt made in Bangladesh. Profits have been used to build a new, local factory.

Yunus points out that Telenor in 1996 agreed to transfer majority control of the subsidiary to the Bangladeshis within a six-year period, but never did. With more than 20 million subscribers, GrameenPhone has become a lucrative business for Telenor, which now insists that the 1996 agreement was not legally binding. Yunus said he remained hopeful that "legal action will prove unnecessary because the owners of Telenor will require the company to honour the intention it expressed in 1996 to transfer ownership and control of GrameenPhone to the poor of Bangladesh." (Deshayes 2008). Telenor wants to rectify the poor working conditions among suppliers which was the trigger for Yunus's claim, but is planning to hold onto majority control.

Clearly one of the trickiest aspect of social business is control of the business by investors. Telenor is actually majority-owned by the Norwegian government, which has refused to intervene in this case. So it is a conflict between the profit-maximizing Telenor and the social business Grameen Bank. In the absence of a transnational legal authority to enforce the agreement between Grameen Bank and Telenor, suit must be brought in some country. Offhand, Telenor's claim that the agreement is not *legally* binding seems only an excuse to take profits out of the business: The agreement was not legally binding but was binding in some other unspecified way? It was an agreement. The main point is that social businesses face an uphill battle in remaining social businesses in the face of investment from profit-maximizing institutions. So I don't see that they are going to be able to provide a great proportion of multinational corporate ethical observance.

WORLD FINANCIAL AND ECONOMIC INSTITUTIONS

As I noted, the World Trade Organization, the World Bank and the IMF are institutions of the right kind to implement a global social contract. The WTO would be in a position to formulate policies regulating competition and the use and regulation of IT amongst different states. However, the WTO's mission is to promote trade whether or not the consequences are ethical or not. The WTO is completely insensitive to such clear issues of global justice as trading with repressive or genocidal governments. (Its de facto prohibition on environmental restrictions to trade will be discussed later.) In addition, its governance shows a clear bias toward the desires of the major powers. So the WTO probably cannot be reformed, and a new and different transnational economic authority implementing the Global Principles of Justice will be needed. Trying to tack ethics onto the WTO would be like making the World Coal Institute responsible for measures to reduce carbon emissions.

Is this also true of the World Bank and IMF? One difference is that, unlike the WTO, the World Bank and IMF include in their mission the ethical aim of improving the lot of those less well off. But the governance of these institutions is also biased toward input from the major powers. In fact, major policy changes for the World Bank and IMF closely track ideological changes in US governments. (Tabb 2004) So bringing the World Bank and IMF under ethical principles would be a radical change in their nature. It would be necessary to reduce the influence of the major powers on these institutions and to reconceive their goals. And it is not clear how to make this happen.

The current policy of the World Bank and IMF involve particular elements of free market ideology that are impervious to evidence. The spectacular success of Malawi's subsidies to small farmers--Malawi went from major food importer to major food exporter--simply doesn't register with World Bank authorities. When asked about Malawi's program, one official said success was produced by the World Bank's program of providing infrastructure in the form of roads and water supplies. Another World Bank official was very concerned there was no target date for ending the subsidies. President Mathariki of Malawi countered that he would set a target date as soon as the US set a target date for ending its agricultural subsidies. The US and Britain refused to subsidize Malawi's program. (Masina 2008)

If, instead, new institutions are initiated to regulate transnational trade and provide financial services to the poorer countries, then the new institutions must have some authority over the WTO, World Bank, and IMF. If so, those current institutions would have to acquiesce to that authority. Social activist NGOs have been able in recent times to alter the policies of the WTO, World Bank, and IMF. But the main policies of these institutions may be impervious to change, as the Malawi example shows.

THE UNITED NATIONS, THE WORLD COURT, AND OTHER TRANSNATIONAL NGOS

The UN has more to do with the International Social Contract than with the Global Economy Social Contract. We noted previously that the UN has very limited powers in dealing with aggression by superpowers or genocide, two gross violations of the International Social Contract. So long as the UN has to depend on the agreement of the most powerful states even to prevent war, any ethical problems involving its member states have to be resolved with those states. The UN as presently constituted is an extensive humanitarian NGO and is not in a position to take effective action against genocide. Clearly some transnational institution is needed to take such action.

Can the UN be reformed to change its current ethical status? To do so, the UN would need to acquire significant power over nation states, especially major powers. The UN Security Council's oversight over peace and war has been severely limited by the veto power given in 1945 to the five permanent Security Council members, the US, Russia, France, England, and China. But even if the Security Council were made more democratic, there is still the problem of enforcing any decisions, especially against the major powers. Also, in cases of genocide, the UN has regularly not been able to mount sufficient force, even for peacekeeping purposes.[14] Peter Singer proposes somehow generating sufficient revenue for the UN to have its own military force. (Singer 2004, 144) UN Secretary-General Kofi Annan's suggestion of an international tariff on arms manufacturers worldwide would be an especially appropriate way to acquire such funding. (Wikipedia 2008)

Other reforms suggested by Peter Singer include a world assembly, each nation electing delegates in proportion to its population. Rather than exclude nations with undemocratic regimes, elections would be supervised, and if UN supervision was refused, that country would get just one delegate. (Singer 2004, 147-148) The suggestion for elections is a good one, but Singer's suggestion for a world assembly with delegates apportioned by population requires accepting his cosmopolitan globalized ethical theory. I gave a number of reasons for rejecting cosmopolitanism in Chapters 7 and 8. We note that since cosmopolitans reject any ethical status for nations or countries, apportioning by population is the only option open to cosmopolitans. Since I do recognize that nation states are repositories of legitimate ethical interests of their citizens, they also deserve representation. One possible model would be the two houses of the US Congress, a new world assembly apportioned by population (the House of Representatives) and the current General Assembly with one or two representatives from each nation (the Senate).

I rejected cosmopolitan "justice" because it is not justice. So the question becomes, how can we structure the UN so that it helps in promoting and preserving the International Social Contract? The International Social Contract requires that nations be minimalist democracies, that nations not interfere in each others affairs except to help each other on request when feasible, and that there are procedures for dealing with violations of these principles.

Obviously the UN and World Court are potential institutions for dealing with violations of the International Social Contract. The World Court could determine whether violations have occurred. Adding the use of precedents to World Court procedure would make its judgements more plausible. Suitably democratizing the UN's deliberative body would give it more authority on policy, and a suitably democratized Security Council could make executive decisions on matters of war and egregious human rights violations such as genocide.

The barrier to these reforms is primarily the hegemony of the government of the United States. The US is able to back up its positions with overwhelming military force deployed world wide. Over half its national budget is devoted to military expenditure and it spends about as much on its military as all other nations of the world combined. (GlobalSecurity.org 2009) In history, countries whose hegemony has been based on military force have never given up hegemony voluntarily. However, all previous military hegemons have fallen either to stronger military powers or have collapsed under the economic burden of maintaining sufficient military power--for example, Rome. This may be happening to the US right now. Leaving aside ethical problems with the war in Iraq, its staggering cost with not much apparent benefit for anyone suggests that the US may be in a downward economic spiral. Certainly the collapse of the other recent superpower, the Soviet Union, was facilitated by the enormous military expenditures it was forced to make to match the US. If US power is diminished, it may be more amenable to measures restricting its sovereignty. Measures promoting the International Social Contract would in fact be in its cooperative interest with other nations. What it would give up is the greater individual interest it could maintain only as a superpower. This is once again an example of the prisoner's dilemma configuration for ethical cooperative benefits.[15]

There are transnational NGOs which wield authority in restricted areas. The Universal Postal Union allows the postal systems of different nations to honor each others' stamps and sets standards for international mail. It is now a UN agency, and all UN member nations are its members. Thus it makes possible transnational mail without separate agreements between each country. We can contrast this NGO with the Global Business Dialogue on Electronic Commerce. This is an initiative to set policy governing transnational electronic business. Its members are corporations. It considers policy in a number of e-commerce related areas such as transnational payments, privacy and security, taxation on the internet, and intellectual property. It does consider the public good to some extent. For example, it acknowledges that governments have a legitimate need to collect taxes to fund infrastructure. But it also requires that no taxes be levied beyond those levied on conventional transactions. This policy is clearly in the interests of practitioners of e-commerce. Is the policy ethical? Also, its recommendations on intellectual property follow the Digital Millennium Copyright Act, which I argued elsewhere was biased in favor of content providers.[16] We will further consider in an internet context both the issues of taxation and intellectual property in Chapter 13, **Ethical Implications for IT.** The ethics of intellectual property as a global institution will be discussed shortly.

Perhaps the most dramatic successful action of the NGOs was the scuttling of the MAI (Multilateral Agreement on Investment) in 1998. The agreement was written by the OECD. The agreement was to "encourage . . . investment, job creation, consumer choice, and lower prices" (Tabb 2004, 398-399) by undercutting monopolies in protected local markets. The MAI contained "clear" definitions of property rights and effective dispute settlement procedures. It removed basically all barriers to outside investment in a country. Its proponents such as the US Council for International Business successfully opposed any mention of labor or environmental standards in the agreement. Nations would have no ability to oppose international investment. Attempts to reserve any segment of the market for local business would become illegal, even including state provision of low-cost health care against private transnational health providers. (Tabb 2004, 398-406)

A collection of NGOs informally calling themselves Civil Society widely distributed and criticized the draft agreement. One member, Lori Wallach, said they were implementing a "Dracula Strategy," because exposing the MAI to the light would kill it. This proved to be the case. France withdrew, primarily because the agreement had insufficient protections for national and especially cultural sovereignty. (Global Issues 2000) Catherine Lalumiere, the Frenchwoman who authored the report which caused France to withdraw, made the following comment:

For the first time, one is seeing the emergence of a *global civil society* represented by NGOs [from] several states . . . Furthermore, the development of the internet . . . allows the instant diffusion of the texts under discussion, whose confidentiality becomes more and more theoretical. It permits, beyond national boundaries, the sharing of knowledge and expertise. . . . the representatives of civil society seemed to us perfectly well informed, and their criticisms well argued on a legal level. (Lalumiere 1998)

It is important to realize that the NGOs were working from what they took to be generally accepted principles of globalized ethics when they mounted their attack on the MAI. These principles are protection of human rights, labor and environmental standards, and aid to the least developed countries. We can see that they are in reflective equilibrium[17] with the Global Economy Social Contract and the International Social Contract. Some of them such as fair labor standards are clearly required by the Global Equal Rights Principle. I have put conditions on other principles such as nonintervention in the economic affairs of a state, namely that the state be a minimalist democracy. Speaking of reflective equilibrium, it is worth noticing that the NGOs of civil society give much ethical significance to the sovereignty of nations. They would not be in reflective equilibrium with cosmopolitan ethical theories. (Civil Society International 2003)

It is also important to recognize that the NGOs of civil society have shown that a great deal of ethical compliance can be achieved without formal mechanisms of authority. But notwithstanding the great importance of these institutions, their function is remedial and preventative. It may be that this is enough, in the context of a society in which what Rawls calls *public reason* is in force. The idea of public reason is that the reasoned deliberation of all persons under the social contract is the final authority over questions of basic justice.[18] Civil society is well named as an agent of public reason. But the MIA could have been adopted with devastating consequences for poorer countries, were it not for France's qualms about cultural sovereignty. And these qualms were about issues that were not central to the injustice of the MIA. So it would be desirable to have ongoing institutions with responsibility and the authority to safeguard the crucial features of global justice.

OTHER INSTITUTIONS WITH GLOBALIZED DIFFERENCES

I will consider three current institutions which function differently in a transnational context. Hence these institutions need to be revised, and I will consider how those revisions need to be done to be consistent with the Global Economy Principles of Justice. The institutions are: Property and intellectual property, taxes, and internet regulation.

PROPERTY AND INTELLECTUAL PROPERTY

Property rights can only exist with a background of social cooperation. Therefore property rights are ethically justified only under the principles of justice of a society sharing benefits and burdens, typically a country or nation. So, transnational property rights are ethically justified only under the Global Economy Principles of Justice.

Recall that a person has a *right* to do something or have something when it would be wrong to prevent him from doing the action or having the object.[19] So a person would have a right to property when it would be wrong to interfere with his use of the property. Property rights can easily conflict with other rights or other ethical requirements, so balancing is necessary. I may not want messy firemen trampling my garden, but if they need access to get control of a wildfire threatening my neighborhood, my property rights do not take priority.

A number of people (notably anarchists and libertarians) have attempted to derive property rights from scarcity. This is partially right, because it is the general fact that social cooperation is both possible and necessary that makes a social contract possible. That is, if nature were so bountiful that we were supplied with all our needs without working together, principles of justice would be unnecessary. And if conditions were so harsh that we could not gain from social cooperation, principles of justice would also be unnecessary.[20] So a certain overall scarcity gives rise to the need for a social contract to govern the distribution of benefits and burdens within a society. But the idea that the institution of property is created to solve disputes engendered by scarcity is not credible. There would simply be another dispute over ownership of the thing rather than over the thing itself. The justification of property is quite different.

The important point is that property rights are relative to a society and its social contract and exist because they are useful in a just society. Rawls notes that the ultimate justification for property is that a property owner will tend to take better care and make better use of something he owns. (Rawls 1999b, 39) Also, however great a contribution an individual makes to the development of an asset, his actions can succeed only if many things go smoothly in the social context as a result of many people cooperating. Indeed, his actions may not even be possible without a functioning complex infrastructure to support them. This is especially true in the global economy. Consider outsourcing a call center to India. Or consider the IT infrastructure that must function properly in order for the acquisition of one multinational company by another to happen. Or consider what is necessary for the existence of the logistic chain involved in getting Spider Man action figures from China to the US. Even at a domestic level, a business decision to implement a new product requires a complex chain of cooperation for the decision to be implemented. The institution of property within a society is governed by the Difference Principle. It is a departure from equality justified by its increasing the well being of all, including the worst off. The current Chinese economic change from state ownership to private property is an example of how well this can work. The Chinese have achieved rates of economic growth unparalleled in modern history.

Repressive governments currently can claim ownership of natural resources. This is called the *international resource privilege*. Since there is abundant evidence that this privilege contributes to making people in underdeveloped countries worse off, the Global Economy Difference Principle requires restrictions.[21] The question is, what positive ethical actions are agents in the global economy required to take against repressive states. It will typically be corporations who will be acquiring these resources, so whatever institution is regulating corporations will need to ensure that repressive governments are not receiving this kind of trade. Of course, it needs to be considered whether preventing trade of natural resources will make life much worse for the poor in that country.

The international resource privilege is one example of the impact of the Global Economy Social Contract on the institution of property. In general, transnational property, property whose rights are ethically global, needs to be justified under the Global Economy Difference Principle. Increased productivity is good, but if this productivity does not tend to make those worst off in the global economy better off, then it is not ethically justified.

Intellectual property is an especially important global case of property. The social function of a copyright or patent is to give the artist or creator of intellectual property the exclusive right to reproduce it, but not just for the artist or creator to be able to reap suitable rewards for his creation, but rather to encourage the development of ideas within the society in which they were created. Thus, the various US legal extensions of copyright or patent work against the social purpose of copyright or patent.[22] From the point of view of global ethics, domestic drug patents and copyrights are not automatically valid transnationally. Corporations and drug companies mistakenly claim their property rights are absolute. The WTO's 1995 TRIPS (Trade Related Intellectual Property) Agreement strengthens copyright and patent protection. But this practice can clearly work against ability of poor nations to build on the copyright or patented material. Chang points out numerous ways in which the strong protection of intellectual property rights work against poor countries. Even the necessary books to get the knowledge to develop are economically beyond the reach of those in poor economies. Chang emphatically does *not* want to abolish global intellectual property rights. Rather, there needs to be less protection: Shortening the period of protection, increasing originality requirements, making licensing and parallel imports easier. (Chang 2008. 142-143)

The important ethical point here is that the TRIPS agreement is not ethically justified. Simply extending domestic property rights to a global context clearly violates the Global Economy Difference Principle. This is a case in which intuitive judgements are in reflective equilibrium with social contract theory. In fact, the Global Economy Difference Principle can give us guidance on how much and where to weaken the TRIPs agreement so that it does not work to make things worse for developing countries. A rough beginning would be to set royalties and fees in developing countries at a level that would allow those in developing countries to build on those items.

TAXES

The ethical function of any tax is to support the infrastructure necessary for the taxed thing to exist. Thus a sales tax is collected to support the infrastructure needed for the sales transaction to take place. A value added tax seems to have a fairer connection to infrastructure, since it is collected when the value is added rather when the object is sold. Other taxes such as corporate income taxes support the infrastructure more broadly. One of the definite ethical problems of global ethics is corporate tax shifting. In this case, everyone recognizes what corporations are doing and that it is unethical. It does, however, improve the bottom line. In Chapter 8, **The Ethical Status of Globalized Institutions,** I suggested a global economic authority to handle such problems. Could current states cooperate in ending these practices, possibly by international treaty? There would at least have to be agencies (probably UN) to monitor transnational taxes and to administer gathering the requisite information. The problem of determining compliance and enforcement would, however, still be unsolved. So a new institution, to be discussed in the next chapter, is definitely required.

Because fair taxation is based on the location of the infrastructure of the taxed entity, e-commerce raises interesting questions. The state of California currently has what is called a "use tax" on internet transactions. This tax, the same amount as sales tax, is collected along with the state income tax. But how can this be a fair tax for a typical Dell Inspiron notebook . . . codesigned in Austin, TX, and Taiwan, assembled in Malaysia with parts from the Philippines, Japan, Korea, Costa Rica, Mexico, Taiwan, Israel, or China? (Friedman 2005, 415-417) Calling this a "use tax" is California's unjust attempt to get around the Supreme Court's Sales Tax Locality Principle, that:

Only firms with a physical presence in the jurisdiction are required to collect that jurisdiction's sales taxes. (Institute for Local Self-Reliance 2004)

California has no ethical basis for its use tax. At the very most, only that portion of the transaction requiring California infrastructure should be taxed.

Following this line of reasoning, any institutions supplying the infrastructure for global commerce are entitled to payment by those using the infrastructure. However, the Internet is supported in a distributed manner. Not only is there no central computer, there is nothing that is not maintained either by commercial ISPs charging for services, or companies whose contribution to the Internet is a business expense, or nonprofits like universities which are funded in other ways. So with the present Internet architecture, there is no need for any additional support and hence no need for a transnational Internet tax.

INTERNET REGULATION

The Yahoo case in Chapter 1 raised the issue that different jurisdictions have very different laws concerning such human rights as freedom of speech. Indeed, it came as a shock to me to discover that in the US, the right of freedom of speech does not apply on the Internet. (Jesdanun 2008) It was clear that the parties to the Global Economy Social Contract would agree to a Global Principle of Greatest Equal Freedom. So how can this principle be enforced over the various national jurisdictions? Any jurisdiction (like China or the US) that found it important to restrict human rights such as freedom of speech would probably not be willing to enter into an international treaty not to restrict speech or other rights. An international agreement to end tax shifting is more-or-less in the cooperative self-interest of all nations. But an agreement on human rights impacts only individuals. It is actually not clear that a transnational human rights authority would make things better, because an authority with enough power to override laws concerning rights within a country could easily become the "global despotism" of Kant and Rawls. We will discuss this issue further in the next chapter in connection with a proposed world state. For now, it looks as though the appropriate institution to improve the status of human rights under the Global Economy Greatest Equal Freedom Principle is an institution like the civil society of NGOs.

Indeed, the various transnational Internet companies have reached a similar conclusion. In October 2008, a number of Internet companies including Yahoo, Google, and Microsoft launched the Global Network Initiative, which provides guidelines for communications technology companies to follow in response to laws in various countries that may interfere with an Internet user's privacy or freedom of expression. The initiative is supported by a number of human rights NGOs and was facilitated by the Center for Democracy and Technology and Business for Social Responsibility. (Condon 2008)

The Global Network Initiative acknowledges that global internet and communication companies are committed to respecting freedom of expression and privacy. These companies will respect these rights even when confronted with countries which do not obey international standards. (Global Network Initiative 2008) These companies in effect acknowledge freedom of expression and privacy, the part of the Greatest Equal Freedom Principle applicable to their dealings in electronic communication.

SUMMARY OF WHAT'S MISSING

Here are the possible new institutions mentioned in this chapter that might be needed to implement the Global Economy Principles of Justice:

- A world state
- A global economic authority
- World court with universal jurisdiction
- A global corporate ethics commission
- Impartial democratic institutions to regulate global trade and global finance
- International police to deal with war and genocide
- A world assembly

We will consider their necessity and viability in the next chapter.

REFERENCES

Achbar, M., Abbott, J., & Bakan, J. (2004). *The corporation* [Motion Picture]. USA: Zeitgeist Films Ltd. (Available from http://www.zeitgeistvideo.com)

Agence France Presse. (2008, September 3). *eBay launches 'ethical' online marketplace*. Retrieved September 3, 2008, from http://www.yahoo.com

Arena, C. (2004). *Cause for success*. Novato, CA: New World Library.

Bater, P., Hondius, F., & Lieber, P. K. (2004). *The tax treatment of NGOs*. The Hague, Netherlands: Kluwer Law International.

Chang, H. (2008). *Bad Samaritans*. New York: Bloomsbury Press.

Civil Society International. (2003). *What is civil society?* Retrieved March 31, 2009, from http://www.civilsoc.org/whatisCS.htm

Condon, S. (2008, October 28). Tech initiative aims to protect privacy, free speech online. *Yahoo! News*. Retrieved November 11, 2008 from http://news.yahoo.com

Deshayes, P. (2008). Nobel laureate threatens lawsuit against telecom operator. *Agence France Presse.* Retrieved September 5, 2008 from http://news.yahoo.com

EICC. (2007). *Electronic industry code of conduct.* Retrieved February 11, 2008, from http://www.eicc.info on 2/11/08.

Elgin, B. (2008, June 30). The dirty truth about clean coal. *BusinessWeek.*

Gerstein, J. (2008, June 10). Wal-Mart defender to direct Obama's economic policy. *The New York Sun.* Retrieved on September 12, 2008, from http://www.commondreams.org/archive/2008/06/10/9534/

Global Issues. (2000). *Multilateral agreement on investment.* Retrieved March 31, 2009, from http://www.globalissues.org/article/48/multilateral-agreement-on-investment

Global Network Initiative. (2008). *Global network initiative.* Retrieved November 11, 2008, from http://www.globalnetworkinitiative.org/

GlobalSecurity.org. (2009). *World wide military expenditures.* Retrieved March 31, 2009 from http://www.globalsecurity.org/military/world/spending.htm

Hopkins, M. (2003). *The planetary bargain.* London: Earthscan Publications

Hume, D. (1739). *A treatise of human nature.* London: John Noon.

Institute for Local Self-Reliance. (2004). Internet sales tax fairness. *The New Rules Project.* Retrieved from http://www.newrules.org/

Jackson, I., & Nelson, J. (2004). *Profits with principles.* New York: Doubleday.

Jesdanun, A. (2008, July 6). 'Public' online spaces don't carry speech, rights. *Associated Press.* Retrieved July 7, 2008 from http://news.yahoo.com

Lalumiere, C. (1998). *Report on the multilateral agreement on investment, intermediary report.* Trans. by C. Dumonteil. Retrieved on September 19, 2008 from http://www.geocities.com/w_trouble_o/lumier.htm

Masina, L. (2008, December 8). Malawi president Mutharika honored for food security policies. *VOANews.com.* Retrieved December 18, 2008 from http://www.voanews.com/english/Africa/2008-12-02-voa35.cfm

Preston, R. (2008, August 11). When good corporate deeds yield good returns. *InformationWeek.*

Rawls, J. (1996). *Political liberalism.* New York: Columbia University Press.

Rawls, J. (1999a). *A theory of justice* (rev. ed.). Cambridge, MA: Harvard University Press

Rawls, J. (1999b). *The law of peoples.* Cambridge, MA: Harvard University Press.

Sachs, J. (2008). *Common wealth.* New York: Penguin Press.

Schultz, R. (2006). *Contemporary issues in ethics and information technology.* Hershey, PA: IRM Press.

Singer, P. (2004). *One world* (2nd ed.) New Haven, CT: Yale University Press.

Tabb, W. (2004). *Economic governance in the age of globalization.* New York: Columbia University Press.

Vogel, D. (2005). *The market for virtue.* Baltimore, MD: The Brookings Institution Press.

White, T. (2007). *Data, dollars, and the unintentional subversion of human rights in the IT industry.* Waltham, MA: Center for Business Ethics.

Wikipedia. (2008). *The United Nations.* Retrieved September 13, 2008 from http://en.wikipedia.org/wiki/United_Nations

Yunus, M. (2003). *Banker to the poor.* New York: Public Affairs.

ENDNOTES

[1] Microsoft's successful efforts to avoid dismantling its monopoly show the power of corporations to distort the functioning of markets. See Schultz 2006, Chapter 5. Recent inappropriate removal of outside regulation produced the California power crisis in 2000-2001 and the mortgage-related financial meltdown of 2008.

[2] See the discussion of cooperative solutions and the prisoner's dilemma in Chapter 4, **The Basis of Ethical Principles,** "The Rationality of Cooperative Principles."

[3] The townships of Licking, PA and Porter, PA have passed ordinances declaring that corporations are not individuals. (Achbar, Abbott, Bakan 2004)

[4] Corporations came into being to allow individuals to engage in cooperative enterprises without having to deal constantly with transfers of individual property.

[5] NGOs are sometimes organized as nonprofit corporations, which obviously do not have the same ethical problems as for-profit corporations, especially with respect to participating in public policy. Nonprofit organizations are normally required to serve some social purpose and to comply with that purpose to receive tax and other benefits from governments. In many states including the US, nonprofit organizations must refrain from participating in political campaigns in order to receive these benefits. See Bater et al. 2004 for details.

[6] See Chapter 8, **The Ethical Status of Globalized Institutions,** "Multinational Corporations."

[7] The survey was done by the US Chamber of Commerce, Boston College, and the Hitachi Foundation. It included small and medium sized businesses as well as corporations.

[8] Indeed, in the US, corporations can be *legally required* to have maximizing profits as their goal.

[9] See Schultz 2006, Chapter 5, **Justice in a Market Economy,** "IT and the Least Advantaged."

[10] See Yunus 2003, Chapter 12.

[11] See especially Chapter 7, **Cosmopolitanism.**

[12] Coal is made clean by sequestering carbon from burning it underground. The technology to do this in an economically viable way is "decades away" and even then would be incredibly expensive. (Elgin 2008)

[13] See Chapter 8, **The Ethical Status of Globalized Institutions,** "Multinational Corporations."

[14]   See Chapter 8, **The Ethical Status of Globalized Institutions,** "The United Nations and related agencies."

[15]   See Chapter 4, **The Basis of Ethical Principles,** "The rationality of cooperative principles."

[16]   See Schultz 2006, Chapter 9, **Copyright and Piracy.**

[17]   See Chapter 4, **The Basis of Ethical Principles,** "Reflective equilibrium."

[18]   See Rawls 1996, Lecture 6, "The Idea of Public Reason."

[19]   See Chapter 4, **The Basis of Ethical Principles,** "Duties, Rights, Obligations."

[20]   These Rawls calls the *circumstances of justice.* (1999a, section 22). Hume has a similar account (1739, Book 3, Part 2, Section 2.

[21]   See Pogge 2002, 112-116.

[22]   See Schultz 2006, Chapter 9, **Copyright and Piracy.**

Chapter 12
New Global Institutions

How do we decide which new global institutions should be created to implement the Global Economy Principles of Justice? It would be tempting to create authorities whenever wrongs and injustices need to be prevented or corrected. As I noted in Chapter 8, **The Ethical Status of Globalized Institutions**, the difficult question is, who oversees that an authority is using its power appropriately? We don't want to create institutions with unchecked power, yet we don't want to create any more authorities than absolutely necessary for the implementation of the Global Economy Principles of Justice. For if each new institution requires oversight, we apparently create an infinite regress: We need someone to oversee the oversight, and someone else to oversee whoever is overseeing the oversight, and so on.

There are two possible ways to avoid this infinite regress. As I suggested in Chapter 10, public recognition of the existence of a social contract itself lessens the need for oversight and enforcement activity. Most people obey the law even when they are sure a policeman is not watching. The other way to avoid the regress, as I suggested in Chapter 8, was to use the checks and balances system of the branches of the US government. Effectively, each branch has oversight on the others. Three seems to be the right number of branches,[1] and executive, judicial, and legislative branches are plausible. I use these branches in Table 1 to exhibit possible new global institutions:

"Mainly political" institutions chiefly implement the International Social Contract. "Mainly economic" institutions chiefly implement the Global Economy Social Contract. "Both political and economic in-

DOI: 10.4018/978-1-60566-922-9.ch012

Table 1. Possible new global institutions

	Executive	Legislative	Judicial
Mainly Political	International police		International criminal court
Mainly Economic	Global economic authority	Global economic authority	Global economic authority
Both Political & Economic		World state (assembly)	
Both Political & Economic	Global corporate ethics	Global corporate ethics	Global corporate ethics

stitutions are involved with both social contracts. For any global institutions under any social contract, transparency and accountability are requirements. This is true for NGOs and governments, multinational corporations, and any other transnational organizations.

MAINLY POLITICAL INSTITUTIONS

Institutions designated as 'mainly political' chiefly implement the International Social Contract rather than the Global Economy Social Contract. Thus they are not within the primary scope of this book. But since they definitely interact with the institutions of the Global Economy Social Contract, some discussion is necessary. As long as there is generally recognized international law and ethical principles prohibiting aggressive war and genocide, we will need a judicial world court to determine violations and an executive institution to enforce the court's judgements. Current institutions partially fulfill these functions. The judicial function is partially fulfilled by the International Criminal Court. The jurisdiction of the current International Criminal Court has not been accepted by the US, Russia, China, and India. It currently does not hear cases of aggressive war. These limitations need to be removed. Also, its judgements need to count as precedents for further judgments. For the executive function, the UN can mount peacekeeping forces but these have not been effective against genocide. Also, it currently does not have sufficient authority or military power to intervene in unjust wars. Beefing up military forces would help the UN in dealing with genocide. But for dealing effectively both with war and genocide, changes in governance to make the UN more responsive and more independent of major powers would be necessary. Regardless of what institutions are proposed, there remains the problem of the authority of such institutions over existing states or multinational corporations.

The World State

The remaining question is whether an international legislative authority is possible, desirable, or necessary as part of the International Social Contract or the Global Economy Social Contract. As discussed previously, Rawls quotes Kant as saying a global state would either be a "despotism or riven with dissension." (Kant 1795, Ak: VIII:367) Kant's reason is that there can't be a sovereign with power over sovereigns. But both he and Rawls think a federation of sovereigns, or a society of societies, is possible.

One proposal for how to handle global governance is called *democratic globalization.* (Wikipedia 2008) Democratic globalization is intended to give world citizens a say in world organizations. Proponents want to bypass nation-states, corporate entities, and ideological NGOs in favor of a new political organization of all humanity. As proposed, existing national sovereignty is to be shared with a Federal

World Authority, Federal World Government and Federal World Court. "Federal" may or may not be an appropriate term, depending on how the sharing is implemented. The Authority serves a legislative function, intended to deal with such problems as hunger, water, war, peace-keeping, pollution and energy--essentially globalized problems. The World Government serves an executive function. Proponents of the plan want this branch to have a single chief executive President elected by citizens by a direct vote. (Wikipedia 2008)

Supporters of the democratic globalization movement want to provide political institutions devoid of any substantive political or economic content. This is problematic from a social contract point of view. Would just any political or economic decisions be OK? How about a majority decision to commit genocide on a minority? Unconstrained majority rule is not a just institution. Also, since there are no principles to constrain the interests of the more powerful countries, the result would likely be very similar to the current arrangement of superpowers and transnational corporate economic organizations. From a social contract point of view, democratic institutions are required by the principles of justice. But although democratic institutions are necessary for justice, they are not sufficient. Democratic institutions by themselves can't produce global justice. All the former Soviet republics had elections, but were hardly models of democracy and justice.

The proponents of democratic globalization make the same mistake as the US Bush administration in Iraq. A democracy is not created only by creating a voting mechanism. Without *public reason,* voting is meaningless. The idea of public reason is that the reasoned deliberation of all persons under the social contract is the final authority over questions of basic justice.[2] Thus the expressed opinions of ordinary citizens have to count for something. And without observance of the Greatest Equal Liberty principle, this cannot happen.

These problems are by themselves enough to show that the global democracy proposal is an empty shell. There are additional difficulties with the account of how global democracy is to be implemented. I will discuss these because they raise important issues about implementing transnational institutions. The (empty) institutions previously mentioned would be created, a few at a time, with authority over "a few crucial fields of common interest." These institutions would later "federate" into "a full-fledged democratic world government" administering world civil defense and emergency management." The proponents of this plan seem to be thinking that the function of government is to provide services to its citizens, and this could be done better if it were done globally. (Wikipedia 2008) Also, it is not clear how these parallel institutions then come to have authority over the globalized problems (war, resources, environment) they were created to solve.

This implementation plan is untenable as it stands. The function of government is not to provide services. Its function is to provide economic and social infrastructure. Non-infrastructure services are usually best provided by companies in a competitive market. Most infrastructure (roads, utilities, economic oversight) is in the form of natural monopolies. So either the government or closely regulated private firms should provide those services. Less obvious infrastructure institutions are health care and insurance. Although they are not natural monopolies, for-profit health care and insurance companies have severe built-in conflicts of interest which prevent them from delivering services effectively.[3] A health care company improves its profitability by denying as much care as possible to its patients, just as insurance companies do best by collecting as much premium as possible and paying out the fewest claims.[4] Governments or social businesses should provide these services because the profit motive is incompatible with providing them in an ethical way.

The other untenable idea is that the problem of globalization is simply to spread control of services to an elected global entity. The thought seems to be that current governments just don't have enough scope. For one thing, the global entity has absolutely no expertise in the logistics of delivering such services. Multinational corporations have worked out such logistics very well. For another thing, some services are better delivered locally, taking into account local conditions, than having an unspecified elected someone trying to manage a whole world's worth of (say) flood protection. Finally, the authority of the World Authority over globalized problems -- environment, poverty, war -- comes from nowhere. It "gradually" happens. The stratagem of explaining a hard-to-understand transition by saying it happens "gradually" explains nothing.

The faults of this conception of global democracy underline what we are looking for in global political institutions. It is neither necessary nor desirable to *replace* the current international political structure (the various nations), nor is it necessary or desirable to *replace* the current global economic structure with something else. Instead, we need institutions to handle global political and economic problems of ethics and justice which are not being handled by current institutions.

A somewhat more plausible account of the evolution of global institutions is provided by Kimon Valaskakis, former Canadian ambassador to the OECD, in his "Westphalia II." (2000) Valaskakis contends that the right way to approach the problems of global governance is through the realization that globalization has weakened the sovereignty of nation states, leaving a gap. Now multinational corporations, NGOs, and IGOs (his term for organizations such as the World Bank, IMF, WTO, and OECD) wield significant power. Globalization has made production transnational. There is a governance vacuum. Valaskakis feels that if globalization proceeds "unchecked and unregulated, the breakdown of the rule of law will lead to a global mafia economy," (2000, 19) not a desirable state of affairs.

According to Valaskakis, it is necessary to redefine and redistribute sovereignty to make it both efficient and legitimate. We must: "Allow the benefits of economic expansion to accrue to all;" balance *market-based decisions* and *political decisions;* define new principles of enforceable international law, containing a minimum set of globally accepted values such as democracy, human rights, the management of interdependence, the maintenance of cultural specificity; and reform the IGOs in the ways previously discussed here.

Valaskakis notes that a summit meeting of the world's leaders would probably not work, and that the IGOs aren't structured to implement principles of this kind. He proposes instead informal meetings of opinion makers to work out the details of governance, the Club of Athens being a pilot. The Club would convene meetings of former heads of government and international organizations, CEOs of leading global corporations, labor leaders and representatives of Civil Society, supported by a permanent think-tank of world class academics. This group meets regularly for conferences as the global governance group. (www.globalgovgroup.com)

Unlike democratic globalization, Valaskakis is very much aware of the need to transform current institutions. I believe splitting concerns into two social contracts, one for the relations of nations and the other for the global economy is a better starting place for designing new institutions than Valaskakis' pluralist set of principles. For instance, balancing market considerations and political considerations is easier said than done in the absence of any principle either has to satisfy.

Valaskakis' principles don't tell us whether we need a world legislative body or what it should do. Keeping in mind the previous discussion, the question is, what global political (and economic) problems of ethics and justice require legislation to provide global infrastructure for their solution? I don't really see that a new set of global laws is needed. Policy in a few areas needs attention, especially in the matter of rights on the Internet in conflict with national policies. But current international institutions seem adequate to set and maintain standards for ethics and justice between nations.[5] Hence a world legislative body is not necessary to implement the International Social Contract. On the other hand, I have already indicated that world political executive and judicial institutions are necessary.

But would having only two of the three branches provide sufficient oversight? In this case, I think so. Treaties and cooperative agreements between nations provide a suitable basis of international law of ethics. If there are disagreements, they are not over the principles of international law and ethics, but whether a superpower such as the US is required to comply with them. Describing the actions and policies of the US Bush administration as "unilateral," that is, one-sided, acknowledges this point. In the following discussion, the use of multilateral cooperative agreements between states to solve globalized problems plays an important part.

GLOBAL ECONOMIC INSTITUTIONS

I just concluded that a global legislative authority is not necessary to implement the International Social Contract. Do we need a global economic authority for economic infrastructure policies: Insuring competition, regulating trade and finance, dealing with tax shifting? These are all concerned with infrastructure for the global market economy. They are extensions of regulations within nations. Do they have to be handled by a transnational authority?

Let us consider competition as an example. In 2007, Thomas Barnett, of the Antitrust Division of the U.S. Department of Justice, outlined a number of ways in which the antitrust agencies of various countries were cooperating to detect and eliminate global anticompetitive behavior. (Barnett 2007) Their efforts were in three areas: Preventing *cartels* (a *cartel* is a group of companies producing the same product who agree to fix prices on that product), evaluating *mergers* for anticompetitive effects, and detecting *unilateral conduct* (a company's abusing its dominant position in an anticompetitive way). Barnett reports increasing awareness and cooperation among the antitrust agencies in numerous countries. In the area of cartels, especially, coordinated investigations, extraditions, and prosecutions of companies for price fixing were common and increasing. A transnational agency, the International Competition Network (ICN), as of 2007 includes antitrust agencies from ninety countries. (Barnett 2007, 6) Its major task is to promote convergence on standards for evaluating the anticompetitive effects of mergers. Most transnational disagreement is about what constitutes unilateral conduct.

As one would expect, the Department of Justice of the 2007 Bush administration tends to take the side of business. Thus the merger review process is designed to absolve mergers of anticompetitiveness as quickly as possible. (2007, 6) Similarly, unilateral conduct is defined as narrowly as possible. (2007, 9) In effect, evidence of unilateral conduct is not unilateral conduct. The European Union has had stricter enforcement of anticompetitive actions, both with the proposed Honeywell/GE merger and with Microsoft's unilateral conduct with its web browser. Thus there can be a beneficial transnational effect: The EU's rejection of the Honeywell/GE merger killed the deal because the company could not afford not to operate in the EU, which was the world's largest market as of 2008. The merger's approval in the US was not sufficient.

Another problem with globalized distributed antitrust enforcement is the US Supreme Court's recognition that antitrust enforcement dealing with harm outside a country's borders "creates a serious risk of interference with a foreign nation's independent ability to regulate its own commercial affairs."

(F. Hoffman-La Roche Ltd. vs. Empagran S.A, 2004) But this Supreme Court statement raises exactly the problem of dealing with transnational issues on a nation-by-nation basis. Global antitrust enforcement raises similar problems because, even though there is broad agreement between nations (called convergence) on the nature of antitrust violations, there are differences in penalty structure and in the use of leniency to obtain evidence. So, there will be conflicts for which there are no current procedures to resolve. (Buxbaum 2004)

The question therefore is: Is it necessary to have a new world economic authority regulating anti-competitive behavior? There has come to be a great deal of effective cooperation between nations in dealing with anti-competitive behavior. The remaining areas of difficulty are largely legal issues of jurisdiction rather than conceptual or ethical issues about anti-competitiveness itself. For example, allowing private lawsuits by foreign plaintiffs in US courts for antitrust violations both prevents gaps in the application of antitrust laws but creates enforcement conflicts because the US is unique in specifying treble damages in those cases. (Buxbaum 2004) But such conflicts seem resolvable within the present transnational framework.

There are similar underlying common interests between nations in dealing with tax avoidance by multinational corporations. But a current transnational institutional framework for tax avoidance like that for anti-competitive behavior is lacking. If the various governments took corporate tax shifting as seriously as they take anti-competitive behavior, there would be international cooperation on detection of and enforcement against corporate tax shifting. A GAO report shows that two-thirds of US corporations paid no income tax at all from 1998 to 2005. It was not clear how much the tax burden had been reduced because of transfer pricing. (Hughes 2008) The OECD has provided transfer price guidelines, implementing an arms-length principle to price products at different subsidiaries of a multinational corporation as though they were independent companies. (Neighbor 2008) Perhaps it is the influence of multinational corporations which make governments not as willing to pursue possible tax shifting violations. But there don't seem to be any barriers to treating transfer pricing tax abuse in a similar way to anticompetitive behavior, that is, through cooperation among the various nations. Important considerations would be whether a cooperative approach would be more or less efficient and effective than a central global approach.

Thomas Friedman (2005, 218) has proposed a global institution to regulate intellectual property laws. Now as we have just seen, the fact that different countries have different regulations in some area does not automatically mean that we need a transnational authority in that area. The major powers' implementation of intellectual property rights is geared to maximizing corporate profits rather than their true purpose of encouraging innovation.[6] Corporations assert that the best path to innovation is for them to get more profits.[7] They have successfully warped the language so that any reproduction of patented or copyrighted material is stigmatized as piracy.[8] Developing countries need access to copy-protected material at lower rates than corporations would like to charge. So there is not a commonality of interests across countries. Hence the likely impact of a global intellectual property rights czar would be to enforce the will of the major powers at the expense of developing countries. Not a good candidate for a global institution satisfying the Global Economy Difference Principle.

Another possible use for a common global tax authority would be a carbon tax administered fairly across nations. The purpose of this tax would be to lower carbon emissions to ameliorate climate change. Environmental issues, especially global warming, often need to be addressed globally. Global warming can't be handled successfully with each nation handling only the effects in its own country. So there may be a need for a global institution to handle this issue. Some of those most affected (the Inuit or Eskimos) are the least responsible. But because the environment raises ethical issues of a different kind (the environment is not and cannot be a party to a social contract), I am postponing discussion of environmental issues to Chapter 14, **IT-Enabled Globalization and the Environment.**

The next question is: Are global institutions necessary to regulate trade and commerce? We presently have a global institution regulating trade and commerce, namely the World Trade Organization. I previously concluded that the WTO probably cannot be reformed to make it ethical, and we will need a new and different transnational economic authority to implement the Global Principles of Justice. The WTO's mission of maximizing trade is not an ethical one and its governance serves the interests of the major powers. But it has the power to enforce its trade policies. Although I think it is *necessary* to create a new transnational trade authority with the mission of improving the lot of all in the global economy by making the worst off best off, I honestly can't say I know how to make this happen.

In general, where regulations by different nations conflict, we can either develop cooperative institutions and policies between the nations to resolve the conflict, or we can create a new global authority to resolve the conflict. Cooperation between nations is feasible only when there is general agreement on the nature of the regulations. When there is not general agreement, it is not clear whether anything--especially a new global authority--would be helpful. Thus the choice between cooperation within existing government institutions and a new global institution is one of the relative efficiency and effectiveness of the two kinds of institutions. These remarks would apply to a global institution to handle routine legal disputes not located in a specific national jurisdiction.

How would this apply to the Chapter 1 case of Yahoo in China? Recall that China demanded information from Yahoo which Yahoo supplied and which led to the violation of the human rights of dissidents. Yahoo claimed that it was merely following Chinese law in providing the information but subsequently lost a lawsuit to the Chinese dissidents. I concluded in Chapter 9, **IT and Globalized Ethics,** that, without some transnational legal rules or policies, Yahoo has no good ethical alternative. Without some acknowledged transnational policy, Yahoo is stuck with obeying the law of one state (China) and getting punished (successfully sued) in another (the US). The Global Greatest Equal Liberty Principle clearly requires the establishment of a transnational policy or institution. But policies arrived at through cooperation between states have much more chance of being observed than the establishment of a transnational authority attempting to impose its will on various states. The Global Network Initiative of IT communications companies, discussed in Chapter 11, **Globalized Ethics and Current Institutions,** is an agreement of this kind.

In any case, it will be interesting to watch China's future with respect to the Greatest Equal Liberty Principle. Economic power is also political power regardless of what the government wants. More individual economic power translates into more time to be concerned beyond the bare necessities of survival. The victims of Tiananmen Square may yet achieve their goal.

Whenever transnational problems are handled by cooperation between states, there is built-in oversight by states of other states. When a new transnational authority is required such as a version of the WTO with ethical rather than trade-maximization goals, it is worth considering a three-branch structure of policy-making institution, judicial institution, and enforcement institution to provide mutual oversight.

INSTITUTIONS BOTH POLITICAL AND ECONOMIC

I will consider two global functions with both political and economic aspects: Global corporate ethics; and a just global economic distribution implementing the Global Economy Difference Principle. I will also consider whether a world legislative body is necessary to make policy concerning these functions, and whether global judicial and enforcement institutions are necessary to implement policy. As before, the question concerning these functions is whether they can be handled by cooperative efforts between nations or whether global institutions are required.

As I noted in Chapter 8, **The Ethical Status of Globalized Institutions**, many of the ethical problems raised by multinational corporations are simply extensions of socially irresponsible behavior of domestic corporations. Corporations are legally individuals but they are not subject to the ethical constraints of individuals. They are often even legally mandated to fulfill the sole goal of maximizing their profits. Therefore I concluded that the solution has to be a new set of legal requirements for corporations monitored by a corporate ethics authority which will serve the function of providing the missing ethical function and also ethical accountability.

Minimal requirements were: No killing people, no deliberately not telling the truth, no thwarting the legitimate rights of your employees through union-busting, and complying with accepted accounting standards for truthfulness in financial reporting. The authority would conduct periodic ethical review on these and any other ethical requirements. The corporate ethics authority would have the power to dismantle a corporation and sell off its assets. Corporations should also be prohibited from attempting to influence public policy by advertising or campaign contributions or by financing electoral initiatives.[9] Remember that corporations are only *legal* individuals. They do not inherit rights from nor are they participants in a domestic social contract. These suggested regulations on corporations are necessary within a domestically just society in order to preserve the justice of the society. A global corporate ethics authority would therefore be necessary to prevent multinational corporations from similarly damaging or distorting global justice.

Global corporate ethics enforcement differs from global antitrust enforcement because corporate ethics are not being enforced at the local domestic level. So there is presently no corporate ethics function within various governments which could provide the basis for cooperation. Perhaps a global corporate ethics judicial agency, a global corporate ethics policy agency, and a global corporate ethics enforcement agency could be created at the same time. This would be a way of solving the oversight problem. The problem of why corporations would put themselves under such an authority does not have an easy solution. I suggested in Chapter 8, **The Ethical Status of Globalized Institutions,** that although corporations tend to treat their impact on the environment as an externality, the human agents behind corporations may come to realize that their security and survival depends on their limiting the power of corporations to damage the environment.[10] A social contract ceding some corporate power to an ethical environmental authority would gain greater security for all. I don't believe such a contract would be enforceable against the background of typical corporate non-ethical behavior of maximizing profits by lying and cheating. So this might be a way in which the global corporate ethical authority could come to be accepted. More will be said on this topic in Section 4, **Ultimate Questions.**

GLOBAL DISTRIBUTIVE JUSTICE

The two social contracts, the International Social Contract and the Global Economy Social Contract, handle global distributive justice very differently. For nations under the International Social Contract, global distributive justice is an extension of the individual principle of benevolence--to help others in need when the cost to oneself is not excessive. This would require us in the US to do more than we do now for those in poor nations--Peter Singer's discussion is persuasive. (Singer 2004, 180-185) The UN's modest Millennium Development Goal of 0.7% of gross national product for aid to the poorest is not excessive, and it is reprehensible that the US is not even close. But it is clearly excessive to say that we should give to others in other countries *just because* we have more than they do. On the other hand, global justice requires that we share our benefits when they result from someone else's burdens. And that is to be done through our second social contract, the Global Economy Social Contract and its economic principle, the Global Economy Difference Principle. Any redistribution of global economic benefits might best be accomplished through the current market economic system, modified with institutions or policies to ensure compliance with the Global Economy Difference Principle.[11]

How would this work in practice? Paul Collier, in his *The Bottom Billion* (2007) divides countries into three types: Wealthy developed countries (population 1 billion), developing countries (population 5 billion), and chronically poor countries (1 billion). The developing countries have made considerable progress in the past 20 years in improving quality of life. In the chronically poor countries, however, things are getting worse. The Global Economy Difference Principle would require us to pay the most attention to the chronically poor countries, unless there were no way their lot could be improved. It is likely that there are some ways the lot of the poorest 1 billion can be improved. At the absolute worst, if their current circumstances were in some way completely unfixable, we could migrate them a manageable number at a time until they all lived in countries with better life prospects.[12]

Here is a sketch of how the Global Economy Difference Principle might be applied using our ethical conclusions so far. The worst-off country involved in the global economy is likely to be a country in Africa providing natural resources into the global economy. If the country is not a minimalist democracy, transnational efforts should be made to move the country in that direction, perhaps through trade sanctions that impact the repressive government rather than the populace. If the country is a stable minimalist democracy, development to improve the economy overall should be considered. Infrastructure such as health, education, or access to credit should be considered, rather than the World Bank's roads to facilitate resource extraction for the benefit of developed countries.[13] Perhaps development could be managed through a social business version of the World Development Corporation, discussed below.

If the worst-off country is not involved in the global economy, we are back to the International Social Contract's principle of help when the cost is not excessive. Perhaps it would help most to get the country involved in the global economy, and a study should be done to see whether this is true.[14] If the country is not involved in the global economy, then the only principle that applies is helping others in need when the cost to ourselves is not excessive. But even there the goal should be to give aid which makes it possible not to have to give further aid. Mohammed Yunus' social businesses are definitely worth considering. Yunus points out that much outright aid goes back to the donor country in the form of salaries for administrators, and that social businesses are much more likely to be effective. (Yunus 142-144)

These considerations are schematic, but it is worth noticing that they have no place in cosmopolitan discussions of alleviating global poverty. Just shovel the money from the well-off countries to the poor countries and distributive justice will be done.

TWO PROPOSALS TO IMPROVE THE LOT OF THE GLOBALLY WORST OFF

I will consider two proposals, those of Paul Collier (2007) and Jeffrey Sachs (2005). It is worth noting right away that the Global Economy Difference Principle provides a clear basis for focusing on what Collier calls "the bottom billion." Collier's reasons for this focus depend on emotions which may not be widely shared. He says he does not want his six-year-old son to grow up in "a world with a vast running sore--a billion people stuck in desperate conditions alongside unprecedented prosperity." (2007, 175) But, like other attempts to base ethical beliefs on feeling, you can escape the ethical judgement if you don't have the feeling: Someone sipping a margarita by the side of a pool in a resort enclave in Jamaica might say, "Sounds bad, but somehow it just doesn't bother me." By contrast, the social contract basis for an obligation to help the bottom billion would be: You accept the benefits of the system of cooperation of the global economy. That system could not exist without the cooperation of--well--the entire 7 billion. Our benefits therefore require us to help make the worst off as well off as possible.

Collier notes that the 5 billion achieved their improved status by economic growth, and his aim is to determine what has prevented the bottom billion from growing in the same way. He finds four main problems: Internal conflict in the form of civil wars or coups d'etat; having abundant natural resources; being landlocked with bad neighbors; and bad governance. Having these problems seem to be symptoms rather than necessary and sufficient conditions of being in the bottom. For example, having abundant natural resources or being landlocked are obviously not always detrimental. Most of Collier's conclusions about problems and symptoms depend upon statistical econometric studies not included in the book, because "it is written to be read." This is a laudable goal, but it does mean that more of the book has to be taken on faith than I would like. The author attempts to avoid bias in constructing schemes of classification by using someone else's schemes, but this procedure merely imports someone else's bias. (2007, 26)

Unfortunately there is still plenty of bias left. Attempts to raise environmental or ethical concerns are dismissed by the phrase "politically correct." Only right-wingers accept this as a substitute for reasons for rejecting a view. For example, Collier says "the politically correct answer to the need for technical assistance is to support 'capacity building' instead." (2007, 112) In this case, Collier has a decent reason: Locals trained to international standards while conditions in the country are abysmal will simply leave. But if outside technical experts are the solution, Collier's solution implies that they can't leave or train locals until conditions in the country are good enough for trained locals not to leave. His solution to this problem is at odds with his solution to the problem of bad governance, which requires us to support the local heroes who have decided not to take their skills to more congenial countries. Is it that trained locals are less loyal or that local heroes are less attractive to foreign employers?

As in this case, Collier raises concerns worthy of attention. But I think he would have done better to take contrary positions more seriously. His types of solutions for the bottom billion are aid, military intervention, laws and charters, and trade policy. I will discuss aid last, comparing his views to those of Jeffrey Sachs. The good points in his discussion of the other solutions are accompanied by some serious flaws.

For Collier, the major consideration in military intervention is whether a cost/benefit analysis shows that regime change will be beneficial. He bemoans the fact that Iraq and Somalia have given intervention a bad name. There is no discussion about who is justified in intervening and when and why. Our extensive discussion of when it is ethical to intervene is beside the point for him.[15] He apparently sees no difference between genocidal regimes and repellent dictators, so our failure to implement regime change for cost/benefit reasons will prevent us from intervening in genocide. (2007, 184) His discussion seems to be from the point of view of an imperial power.

The fact that a country is landlocked does not have to be a bad thing. Switzerland is landlocked. But if the country's neighbors, especially those with seacoasts, are unwilling or unable to develop transportation, that effectively locks the landlocked country out of the global market. Although Collier dismisses regional organizations, if some sort of mutual advantage could be developed between a landlocked country and a coastal neighbor, that could help.[16] Some landlocked (and coastal) countries are also not viable economically on their own. Collier in effect says, that's the breaks. But when these non-viable countries are the result of arbitrary post-colonial boundaries, there must be some way to redraw them to increase their viability. Why should some arbitrary boundary decisions by the French or English in the early 20th century or before have to be permanent?[17]

Collier's discussion of laws and charters is an interesting contribution to global governance. The promulgation of international nonbinding standards (that is what a charter is) can help to bring about their adoption. Actual and possible ones include: The Extractive Industries Transparency Initiative for publication of cash flows connected with exploiting natural resources; postconflict governance in the aftermath of civil wars; campaign finance; and minimum standard for democracy, as for EU membership or other regional groups. (Collier 2007, 185-186) These can be promulgated by the UN, regional associations, or even major powers. Some of the major powers don't meet these standards--campaign finance in the US for example--so that may make it more difficult for less developed countries to adopt them.

The same is true for trade policy. His general prescription is to lower trade barriers in the worst off countries. However, he believes the bottom billion need to protect themselves against Asia, temporarily, until they are able to compete in the world economy. Otherwise, protecting bottom billion companies makes them inefficient and corrupt. Collier is mystified by NGO opposition to the MAI (Multilateral Agreement on Investment) agreement discussed in Chapter 11.[18] This agreement, written by the OECD, was to undercut monopolies in protected local markets. It removed basically all barriers to outside investment in a country as well as any labor or environmental standards. Attempts to reserve any segment of the market for local business, including state provision of low-cost health care against private transnational health providers would have become illegal. (Tabb 2004, 398-406) Collier's one-sided approach assumes the best motives for developed countries and the worst for undeveloped countries.

One more point on trade policy: Collier's discussion of the WTO can only be called bizarre. He characterizes the WTO as merely an administrator for trade agreements between different countries: "It is not a purposive organization but rather a marketplace." (2007, 170) Although it started that way, it now imposes trade standards even on the most developed countries such as no restrictions on trading with repressive regimes or no environmental restrictions. Obviously he gave no notice to the Seattle or Genoa demonstrations.

Collier's approach to aid is different from the approach of Jeffrey Sachs. (2005) Collier points out that much aid has gone to the middle five billion instead of the bottom billion. He notes that much unrestricted aid, "budget support" has been misspent, for example financing military spending. "Project support" also has the problem of incomplete and inconsistent projects funded by multiple donors. Lots of aid can also make coups more likely. The major problem is that any kind of aid to a country with bad governance is not likely to be used effectively to improve the lot of the worst off in the country.

Collier's solution is to put governance conditions on aid, and give technical assistance as well as money at the beginning of governance reform. In those circumstances, one should budget for greater administrative costs. He suggests an untried possibility: "Independent service authorities," operating independently of underdeveloped states, NGOs, churches, and private firms. These outfits would broker public services. (2007, 119) He criticizes Sachs for emphasizing aid rather than getting the poorest countries into the export market. (2007, 191)

Sachs, on the other hand, characterizes the view that market reform is the key to ending poverty as "magical thinking." (2005, 319) There is no evidence that economic freedom correlates with economic growth. (2005, 320) Further, the reason there is so much bad governance in Africa is because of poverty. Once out of poverty, governance improves. Sachs instead calls for more aid and points out that aid to Africa has in fact been extremely low, so it is not correct to say that aid has been tried and failed. He agrees with Collier that what is required is rigorous, country-specific plans developed openly with careful monitoring, backed by good governance. But instead of developing markets, he calls for aid to support infrastructure to deliver basic needs such as health care, education, and safe water. (2005, 292)

Which approach is best will be determined by the careful analysis of cases. But there no doubt that both Collier and Sachs are trying to satisfy the Global Economy Difference Principle. Both single out the worst billion as the population needing priority attention, and both claim their policies will lead to the worst off becoming better off. Sachs actually mentions that if there are poor within a country who need to be enabled to be better off, that is matter to be handled internally, thus distinguishing between domestic and global justice. But once again, I think it confuses the issue seriously to portray the remedy as just benevolence by wealthy countries. The ethical source of the obligation to help poor people is rather in the Global Economy Difference Principle, which needs to be satisfied by the participants in the global economy. Perhaps, as Sachs suggests, some part of those corporate earnings attributable to globalization should go to the UN Development Program, which will coordinate UN Country Teams administering aid on a country-by-country basis. (2007, 285) These teams would also coordinate benevolent grants by the developed countries. But it would be clear that the ultimate aim is to make the worst off, better off.

A CORPORATE SOLUTION TO GLOBAL POVERTY

George Lodge and Craig Wilson propose a new institution to deal with global poverty. Their World Development Corporation (WDC) will consist of shareholder partners from about a dozen multinational corporations, chosen by the Secretary-General of the UN. These partners will choose a board of directors. The Secretary-General will also choose a director, as well as some NGO directors. The aim of the WDC will be to facilitate viable projects which combine "maximum poverty alleviation" and sustainability. (Lodge and Wilson 2006, 157)

This project is essentially a globalized extension of corporate social responsibility and suffers the same defects. It does not differ from the World Bank and IMF in its purpose, and its structural governance differences don't guarantee any results different from those achieved by the World Bank and IMF. In fact, the underlying assumption of both institutions is that poverty will be alleviated by enough good business projects, leaving aside other social factors responsible for poverty such as health, education, access to credit, geography, or ecology.

The aims of the WDC need careful explication. If the aim of "viable projects" means "profitable," then we are back inside the circle of corporate thought, and we face the inevitable conflict between profitability and social justice. To get around this conflict, I will shortly consider reframing the WDC as the WDSC, the World Development *Social* Corporation, applying the suggestions of Mohammed Yunus. Of the other goals, I will discuss sustainability in Chapter 14, **IT-Enabled Globalization and the Environment.**

The remaining goal is maximum poverty alleviation. There are a few problems. First, it is a consequentialist/utilitarian goal which could easily ignore the worst off in favor of a greater sum of poverty alleviation. I believe it should be replaced by an application of the Global Economy Difference Principle: Projects are chosen to make the worst off in the global economy, as well off as possible. Second, projects to alleviate poverty should not be considered in isolation. It may better alleviate poverty to do a lot of projects in the worst off country, than one or two projects in twenty countries. Finally, each project should include a timeline and clear metrics for determining whether the project has actually worked to alleviate poverty. So the aim would be to choose project portfolios which most tend to improve the lot of the worst off in the global economy.

But more important than a good statement of aims is the adoption of a corporate structure that will better guarantee that the WDSC will stay focused on social aims. The WDSC's aim of alleviating world poverty is a social aim, and that makes it a candidate for being a social business by Yunus' definition. Two further changes are necessary: First, to remove the goal of maximizing profits. This can be done by making clear that a 'viable' project is not one that maximizes profits or return on investment. Rather, a viable project is one likely to achieve its goal of alleviating poverty *and* earns sufficient revenues to continue in operation. Second--and this is necessitated by the redefinition of viability--the investors and/or shareholders do not expect to make a profit. They can get their money back, but that is it. But how likely is it that corporate chieftains born and bred to maximize profits will go along with this somewhat different agenda? As we saw, even Yunus' Grameen Phone Company ran into problems when its Finnish financers reneged on an agreement to run it as a social business. But unless the WDS becomes a WDSC, it will not achieve its ethical goals.

But even if the WDC remains the WDC, it can play a useful role in the application of the Global Economy Difference Principle provided it can acknowledge that profit maximization is not its priority goal.

ECONOMIC GLOBALIZATION AND THE GLOBAL DIFFERENCE PRINCIPLE

The big question is, does economic globalization satisfy the Global Economy Difference Principle? In Chapter 11, I defined *economic globalization* as "global institutions participating in a global market economy." As we saw, a market economy goes a long way to satisfying principles of justice, whether domestic or global. But normally some constraints are required in order for a market economy to function justly. Some of these constraints have already been addressed, for example anti-competitive behavior in the global economy. Other constraints, for example environmental externalities, will be addressed in Chapter14, **IT-Enabled Globalization and the Environment.** I will now address constraints supplied directly by the Global Economy Difference Principle.

The Harvard economist Richard Freeman has noted that, although economic globalization has improved the lot of the worst off on a country-by-country basis, inequality within most countries has increased. China and India, for example, twenty years ago were worse off than Africa. And in fact economic globalization has increased the well-being of those in most countries. (Freeman 2007) But within each country, inequality has increased. In fact, in general, inequality has increased within most of those countries where globalization has increased their overall well-being. These facts raise questions about implementing the Global Economy Difference Principle. In particular, would the state of affairs that Freeman describes satisfy the Global Economy Difference Principle, namely the worst off countries doing better, but inequality in each country increasing?

First, it needs to be pointed out that increased inequality by itself does not violate either domestic difference principles or the Global Economy Difference Principle. Either difference principle is violated only if the increased inequality makes those worst off, even more worse off. I think it is probable that the increased inequality in the US does not satisfy the (domestic) difference principle. There is no evidence that huge marginal increases to top executive salaries have boosted productivity. Countries with more modest salaries have done as well or better in increasing productivity. Our executives receive such large salaries because they are the ones that set them, because they can.[19] And then at the bottom end, the US has a large number of homeless people while a 2008 presidential candidate can't remember how many houses he has. (John McCain turned out to have nine houses.) In no US state does the minimum wage come close to covering market rent on a minimal accommodation. (Claretian Publications 2007)

So let us suppose just for the sake of the current discussion, that, considering the overall well-being in each country, economic globalization has made the worst-off countries better off. Yet, within most countries, the worst off was made still worse off. (Neither is probably quite true, but it is close.[20]) Then does economic globalization satisfy the Global Economy Difference Principle or not? It clearly depends on the extent to which the domestic decrease in the welfare of the worst off is caused by economic globalization. For example, the domestic decrease in the welfare of the worst off could be caused in most countries by internal policies such as unconstrained free-market labor policies. If so, then the injustice is in the domestic labor policies rather than globalization. Economic globalization is then just because overall it makes the worst off better off. Participants in the Global Economy Social Contract could be concerned with domestic injustice and attempt to change unjust domestic labor policies, but in order to respect state sovereignty, they could not directly intervene.

If, however, the domestic injustice was due to economic globalization, then the parties to the Global Economy Social Contract would need to revise the implementation of economic globalization to reduce the resulting domestic injustice. For example, the economic development mostly responsible for the overall increase in well-being might have been financed with World Bank loans requiring the opening of capital markets without further conditions. The result of a wealthy oligarchy and a great increase in poverty could still net out to an overall increase in well-being. But the globalized development is responsible for the domestic injustice, and so the World Bank conditions need to be changed and an attempt made to reverse the consequences.

Finally, what if the situation were reversed, and the domestic economies were more-or-less economically just but economic globalization was making the worst off countries even worse off? Opponents of economic globalization believe something like this may be happening. Russia during the 90s could be an example, except globalization in the form of economic reform made things worse overall (45% drop in gross national product) *and* made things worse for individuals (poverty rate rose from 5% to 25%). (Stiglitz 2003, chapter 5). So there is no question that the economic reforms needed to be revised. South Korea in the early 90s might be a better example. For three decades, not only had overall well-being improved, but individuals were much better off. The growth rate went from about 0% to 6% per year,

Table 2. Revised possible new global institutions

	Executive	Legislative	Judicial
Mainly political	International police		International criminal court
Mainly economic	Global economic authority	Global economic authority	Global economic authority
Mainly economic	Global ethical trade authority (new)	Global ethical trade authority (new)	Global ethical trade authority (new)
Mainly economic	Global economic justice authority (new)	Global economic justice authority (new)	Global economic justice authority (new)
Both political & economic		World state (assembly)	
Both political & economic	Global corporate ethics	Global corporate ethics	Global corporate ethics

and the percentage of people in poverty went from almost 100% in 1950 to 15% in 2003. Per capita annual income grew from $87 in 1962 to $4,830 in 1989. It has had low inequality. But IMF policies of capital liberalization in Southeast Asia produced a 1997 financial crisis. South Korean gross domestic product plunged by about 7%. South Korea followed some, but by no means all, of the IMF prescriptions, especially ignoring the prescription concerning government spending, and quickly recovered. (Stiglitz 2003, chapter 4) In this case, the domestic difference principle is satisfied, but achieving global justice in this case depended upon the ability of South Korea to go against the requirements of a transnational economic organization, the IMF. A weaker country might have no option until the appearance of an ethical global trade and financial authority. Since individual countries have no direct interest in the Global Economy Difference Principle, cooperation by nations is not an option in implementing compliance with that principle. We therefore need a global economic justice authority. Such an authority needs to be structured with all three branches, legislative (for policy), judicial, and enforcement to avoid oversight problems.

CONCLUSION

Table 2 is the matrix of possible new global institutions, revised to reflect the discussion of this chapter:

We are left with two beefed-up transnational political institutions and three new institutions to handle globalized ethics: Ethical trade, economic justice, and corporate ethics. Ethical trade and economic justice could well be combined since they need to work together. And combining them would make it less likely that the trade institution would give promoting trade priority over economic justice, as the World Trade Organization currently does.

The following Chapter 13, **Ethical Implications for IT,** examines the implications for IT of the two social contracts, and the revisions to institutions and new institutions they require.

REFERENCES

Barnett, T. (2007). *Global antitrust enforcement*. Retrieved September 26, 2008 from http://www.usdoj.gov/atr/public/speeches/226334.htm

Buxbaum, H. (2004). *Jurisdictional conflict in global antitrust enforcement*. Retrieved September 28, 2008 from www.luc.edu/law/academics/special/center/antitrust/pdfs/buxbaum.pdf

Claretian Publications. (2007). *Stat house*. Retrieved September 30, 2007 from http://salt.claretianpubs. org/stats/homeless/home.html

Collier, P. (2007). *The bottom billion*. Oxford, UK: Oxford University Press.

Colliver, V. (2007, November 10). Lawsuit claims Health Net gave bonuses for policy rescissions. *SFGate*. Retrieved April 1, 2009 from http://www.sfgate.com/cgi-bin/article.cgi?f=/c/a/2007/11/10/ BUCLT9JOV.DTL

F. Hoffman-La Roche Ltd. vs. Empagran S.A., 542 U.S. 155, 165. (2004)

Freeman, R. (2007). *Inequality and global capitalism* [Jefferson Lecture at UC Berkeley]. Berkeley, CA: UCTV. Retrieved from http://www.uctv.tv/ondemand/

Friedman, T. (2005). *The world is flat*. New York: Farrar, Straus and Giroux.

Hughes, A. (2008). Corporate tax evasion and transfer pricing. *OMB Watch*. Retrieved September 29, 2009 from http://www.ombwatch.org/article/blogs/entry/5274/49

Kant, I. (1970). Perpetual peace. In H. Reiss (Ed.), *Kant's political writings*. Cambridge, UK: Cambridge University Press.

Le Bon, S. (2003 December). Interview. *Vanity Fair*.

Lodge, G., & Wilson, C. (2006). *A corporate solution to global poverty*. Princeton: Princeton University Press.

Neighbor, J. (2002 January). Transfer pricing: Keeping it at arm's length. *OECD Observer*. Retrieved September 29, 2008 from http://www.oecdobserver.org/news/fullstory.php/aid/670/Transfer_pricing:_Keeping_it_at_arms_length.html

Rawls, J. (1993). *Political liberalism*. New York: Columbia University Press.

Rawls, J. (1999a). *A theory of justice* (rev. ed.). Cambridge, MA: Harvard University Press

Rawls, J. (1999b). *The law of peoples*. Cambridge, MA: Harvard University Press.

Sachs, J. (2005). *The end of poverty*. New York: Penguin Books.

Schultz, R. (2006). *Contemporary issues in ethics and information technology*. Hershey, PA: IRM Press.

Tabb, W. (2004). *Economic governance in the age of globalization*. New York: Columbia University Press.

Tyson, J. (n.d.). How the old Napster worked. *How stuff works*. Retrieved April 1, 2009, from http:// computer.howstuffworks.com/napster3.htm

University of Maine. (2001). *The US healthcare system: Best in the world, or just the most expensive*. Retrieved April 1, 2009, from http://dll.umaine.edu/ble/U.S.HCweb.pdf

Valaskakis, K. (2000). *Westphalia II: The real millennium challenge*. Retrieved August 8, 2005 from http://ec.europa.eu/governance/areas/group11/westphalia2_en.pdf

Wikipedia. (2008). *Democratic_mundialization*. Retrieved April 11, 2008, from http://en.wikipedia.org/wiki/Democratic_mundialization

Yunus, M. (2003). *Banker to the poor.* New York: Public Affairs.

ENDNOTES

[1] Two branches would tend to fight for supremacy and four or more branches would dilute the effectiveness of the oversight.

[2] See Rawls 1996, Lecture 6, "The Idea of Public Reason."

[3] In the first decade of the 21st century, the US spends about twice as much on health care as other developed countries, for significantly worse care. About 33% of the expenditure is health insurer profit and administration. (Univ. of Maine 2001)

[4] The California health insurer HealthNet was discovered in 2007 to be giving bonuses to employees for denying customer health claims. Their response was to say they would stop doing it. (Colliver 2007)

[5] These institutions hardly work perfectly, but adding a global political *legislative* body would not fix their problems.

[6] See Schultz 2006, Chapter 9.

[7] This claim is frequently made in IT contexts. We will consider the claim in that context in Chapter 13, **Ethical Implications for IT**.

[8] See Tyson (n.d.) for a discussion of Napster which simply assumes that noncommercial copying is unethical.

[9] This prohibition on public policy influence applies to for-profit corporations. The function of non-profits is to advance social aims, so their purpose is often to influence public policy.

[10] Some corporate CEOs have come to this realization. Ray Anderson, CEO of Interface, Inc., details his epiphany in the film *The Corporation*. (Achbar, Abbott,Bakan, 2004)

[11] Aid is benevolence under the International Social Contract and so aid is not part of the Global Economy Social Contract.

[12] Obviously those in the poorest countries have already noticed this alternative and are implementing it without legal approval.

[13] Such development is a clear violation of the Global Economy Difference Principle.

[14] Involving a country in the global economy raises value issues that will be considered in Chapter 15, **The Value of IT-Enabled Globalization.**

[15] See Chapter 8, **The Ethical Status of Global Institutions,** "What is a Country?"

[16] I witnessed Turkey and Bulgaria simultaneously rebuilding a poor road linking the two countries.

[17] A sub-Saharan landlocked country like Niger has endemic problems with a Bedouin ethnic group in its north. Possibly the distinct Bedouin group should be part of a different Bedouin nation. The problems in Darfur in Sudan may be at least in part due to similar factors.

[18] See Chapter 11, **Globalized Ethics and Current Institutions,** "The United Nations, the World Court, and Other Transnational NGOs."

[19] Here is a relevant story: The rock star Simon Le Bon was once asked why rock stars always marry supermodels. He answered, "Why does a dog lick his balls? Because he can."(Le Bon 2003)

[20] Peter Singer concludes after extensive investigation that there is no definitive answer about whether economic globalization has overall made more people better off than worse off. (Singer 2004 87-90)

Chapter 13
Ethical Implications for IT

In this chapter, I will examine the ethical consequences for IT of the International Social Contract and the Global Economy Social Contract. I began considering ethical responses to global ethical problems of IT in Chapter 9, **IT and Globalized Ethics**, and continued the discussion in Chapter 11, **Globalized Ethics and Current Institutions**. Here I will examine the impact of the two social contracts on those ethical responses. The issues discussed were these:

- Internet regulation--transnational policies and equal rights
- IT and the Global Economy Social Contract
- Consequences for IT professionals
- IT and anticompetitive enforcement
- Intellectual Property
- Corporate IT ethics

TRANSNATIONAL POLICIES AND THE INTERNET

In Chapter 9, I noted that transnational legal rules or policies were needed to handle cases like Yahoo's and concluded that the Internet, as a transnational institution *par excellence,* deserves transnational regula-

DOI: 10.4018/978-1-60566-922-9.ch013

tion. The Global Greatest Equal Liberty Principle requires the establishment of some such transnational policy. I also suggested in Chapter 9 that perhaps postal or airline regulations might be a model, so that transnational regulation of the Internet could take place without having to implement some sort of new transnational authority. In Chapter 11, I pointed out that any jurisdiction (like China or the US) that found it important to restrict human rights such as freedom of speech would probably not be willing to enter into an international treaty not to restrict such rights. A transnational human rights authority may not improve matters, because an authority with enough power to override laws concerning rights within a country could easily become a "global despotism". The appropriate institution to improve the status of human rights under the Global Economy Greatest Equal Freedom Principle may be an institution like the civil society of NGOs[1] or the Global Internet Freedom Consortium. The Global Internet Freedom Consortium is a group of nonprofit and for-profit companies dedicated to developing, implementing, and disseminating technology to allow free access to the internet in spite of government restrictions. This organization thus directly implements The Global Economy Greatest Equal Freedom Principle at the transnational level. (Global Internet Freedom Consortium 2008). Another recent institution, the Global Network Initiative, also works to support global freedom. As I noted in Chapter 11, **Globalized Ethics and Current Institutions**, Yahoo, Google, and other transnational Internet companies such as Microsoft launched the Global Network Initiative in October 2008. This initiative acknowledges that global internet and communication companies are committed to respecting freedom of expression and privacy. These companies will now respect these rights even when confronted with countries which do not obey international standards. The initiative includes independent review of how well companies are implementing the principles of the initiative. (Global Network Initiative 2008) These companies acknowledge transnational freedom of expression and privacy, the part of the Greatest Equal Freedom Principle applicable to their dealings in electronic communication. The work of these two organizations is an excellent example of how to transcend unjust national laws

When Yahoo's shareholders voted against a ban on censorship on the Internet, they violated the Global Economy Greatest Equal Liberty Principle. Yahoo's shareholders have equal rights, but not the right to deny equal rights to Internet participants in the global economy. Thus they do not have the right to prevent Yahoo from enforcing equal rights (that is, banning censorship). Yahoo therefore has the right to ignore the shareholder vote. Indeed, the Global Network Initiative establishes this right for them.

A related issue is unjust restriction of NGOs or websites. The question is to what extent human rights (in the Greatest Equal Liberty Principle) should be enforced globally and through what institutions? The rights of NGOs or websites are primarily individual rights. The whistleblowing website Wikileaks (with its server in San Mateo, CA) was ordered shut down in 2008 because a Zurich bank claimed that the site had posted stolen and confidential material. Wikileaks initially argued unsuccessfully in US court that US courts did not have jurisdiction, because its spokespersons were in Paris. (Elias 2008) A US court later found that shutting down an entire website constituted illegal "prior restraint." (Kravets, 2008) In this case, the US courts came through.

A Cisco Systems executive told a Senate subcommittee in 2008 that comments in an internal document about China's goal to "combat" a religious group did not reflect the company's views on censorship. However, the Global Internet Freedom Consortium said that because Cisco offered planning, construction, technical training and other services to help China improve law enforcement and security network operations, "Cisco can no longer assure Congress that Cisco China had not been and is not now an accomplice in partnering with China's Internet repression." (Sarkar 2008)

Rep. Chris Smith, R-N.J., introduced in 2007 a House bill that would bar U.S. Internet companies from turning over personally identifiable information to governments that use it to suppress dissent. If the tech companies gave up information, they could face criminal penalties. Both Google and Yahoo want the U.S. government and other countries to make Internet freedom a top priority. "We have asked the U.S. government to use its leverage — through trade relationships, bilateral and multilateral forums, and other diplomatic means — to create a global environment where Internet freedom is a priority and where people are no longer imprisoned for expressing their views online," said Michael Samway, Yahoo's vice president and general counsel. (Sarkar 2008)

Google, Yahoo, and the other major transnational IT and communications companies indicated their seriousness about Internet freedom by creating the Global Network Initiative. Some NGOs are concerned that mandatory penalties are not included. (Sarkar 2008) But independent compliance review is included and the importance of these companies acknowledging that principles of global justice take precedence over repressive national laws cannot be overstated. (Global Network Initiative 2008)

These developments will improve the situation for transnational actors. But in some countries, there are still internal problems of justice. Problems with China are well-documented, but other countries are still far from Greatest Equal Liberty. I will cite two examples, one from Malaysia and the other from South Korea.

Malaysian blogger Raja Petra Kamaruddin was arrested in 2008. He was the founder of Malaysia Today website. A government official said the offending articles had insulted Islam and the Prophet Muhammad. He was arrested under the Internal Security Act, which human rights groups have pushed to have abolished, which allows for renewable two-year periods of detention without trial. Although normally used against suspected terrorists, it has also been used to lock up opponents of the government.

Malaysia's media is tightly controlled by the government. Malaysia's government has expressed frustration over its inability to rein in popular Internet alternative news sources. The government last month blocked access to Malaysia Today, but it quickly reappeared on alternative servers. A week before the arrest, it lifted restrictions on dozens of websites and blogs including Raja Petra's. "It is clearly hoodwinking the bloggers," an opposition spokesman said. "First you unblock the websites and people praise you, and the very next day you arrest the blogger." (Agence France Presse 2008)

South Korea's new 2008 government wants restrictions on what it calls 'infodemics,' in which, in their view, inaccurate, false information "spreads like an epidemic and prompts social unrest." (Kim 2008) President Lee Myung-bak was accused of putting the nation's health at risk by agreeing to import U.S. beef. There were daily mass protests in Seoul for weeks. Since President Lee did agree to more relaxed rules about US beef, it is not clear exactly how inaccurate the information sparking the protests was. But the government was very unhappy. In any case, the South Korean Justice Ministry is working on what it calls a Cyber Defamation Law. The Korean Communications Commission, which regulates the industry, has come up with its own rules to oblige portals to suspend sites stepping outside limits it sets and force Websites to use real names of anyone posting comments. The commission says the measures are designed to improve security and reduce the spread of false information.

Predictably, many in Korea are unhappy about government moves to restrict freedom of speech in a country with only two decades of democratic elections. "The regulations violate the autonomy of the Internet and are an effective tool for tighter media control by the government," said Lee Han-ki, senior editor at the popular citizen news Website OhMyNews. "The regulations would bring about a reverse in the advancement of the Internet media as a whole." (Kim 2008)

Before the implementation of the Global Network Initiative, large companies such as Google took the position that local laws restrictive of freedom must be obeyed. In May 2008, Google announced that it gave police information about a user of its Orkut social networking site in order to comply with Indian law. The police used the information (an IP address) to arrest a suspect for posting vulgar content about a top Indian political leader.

Although Google claimed that it supports freedom of expression and protects user privacy, it also noted it had to comply with local laws. Google's action clearly violated the Global Economy Greatest Equal Freedom Principle. In India apparently damaging the "modesty and reputation" of a person, especially a top political leader, is a criminal offense. John Ribiero, the author of a piece approving of Google's action, claims that damaging the "modesty and reputation" of a person is as bad as planning a terrorist attack. (Ribiero 2008)

There could be good reasons for complying with local law which conflicts with the Greatest Equal Freedom Principle. It may be that failing to comply with local law would produce a greater restriction of freedom. For example, if failing to comply with local law resulted in the shutdown of a valuable social networking site. But the principle that all local law goes, no matter how restrictive of freedom, is clearly wrong. At the very least, Google should have supplied the information under protest. Presumably they would have acted differently after subscribing to the principles of the Global Network Initiative.

Google's actions in Brazil were quite different. Google took action in Brazil to stop child pornography and hate crimes on a social-networking Web site used there — but Google did not offer to provide user information to officials. In August 2007, federal prosecutors said Google failed to comply with requests to provide information about users who allegedly spread child pornography and hate speech against black people, Jews and homosexuals on the popular Orkut Web site. Google eliminated the users from Orkut groups but refused to release information about them to authorities, arguing it is bound by U.S. laws guaranteeing freedom of speech. The company also installed filters to stop the spread of child pornography and increased from 30 days to six months records on users who access or spread illicit material. These actions apparently satisfied Brazilian authorities. (Associated Press 2008.) Comparing the two cases, it is interesting that Google claimed in the Indian case that it had to comply with local law, but in the Brazilian case that it had to comply with US law. Google can now claim with more consistency that it has to comply with the principles of the Global Network Initiative. But one question to be resolved is whether a government will find compliance with an intercompany agreement as compelling a reason for disobeying its laws as compliance with US law.

Yahoo's CEO Jerry Yang expressed a view similar to Google's position in India. Yang claimed he was "a big believer in American values" but added: "As we operate around the world we don't have a heavy handed American view." Some countries want major interventions in the Web and others prefer to leave the Web unfettered. So, said Yang, "We operate within these environments to the extent that the law has any clarity." (Bartz and Dobbyn 2008)

Yang's comments betray an ethical blindness which is actually contradicted by Yahoo's own actions even before the Global Network Initiative. Ethically, free speech is not just a mere matter of national preference. That would be like saying some nations prefer to oppress their citizens and others don't, and we are going to be neutral about it. The fact that Yahoo established a fund to aid victims of human rights violations shows that they really don't believe jailing people for expressing their opinions on the Internet is just a matter of national preference. I believe Yahoo's true position would have been best expressed by saying that they regrettably had to obey Chinese law to stay in business there, but that they hoped Chinese law would be changed to accord with the standards of global justice. Their endorsement of the Global Network Initiative may now make it possible for them to refuse to go along with Chinese standards.

I believe that these cases show that, with respect to Internet access, our intuitive judgements about global justice are in reflective equilibrium with the Global Economy Greatest Equal Freedom Principle.[2] These cases illustrate a consequence for IT professional: Internet companies like Google and Yahoo have a duty to uphold the Global Economy Greatest Equal Freedom Principle. Their creation and implementation of the Global Network Initiative is a major step in fulfilling this duty. Although the fact that the Initiative is a voluntary agreement without mandatory penalties raises some concern, it may be the best that can be done at the present time. As I observed earlier, there is no way that repressive regimes who currently believe they have the right to suppress speech and violate privacy will agree to international treaties banning such behavior.

IT AND THE GLOBAL ECONOMY SOCIAL CONTRACT

In Chapter 9, I noted that the Global Economy Principles of Justice must provide a place for the enabling and substantive duties of the IT professional. We now ask whether the chosen global economy principles of justice conflict with fulfilling these duties. We also need to be sure that the global principles of justice do not undermine the IT basis for the global system of cooperation they apply to. The answer in both cases is: No.

The Global Economy Principles of Justice do not conflict with the enabling and substantive duties of the IT professional. In fact, they help IT professionals fulfill their duties by mandating freedom of expression, requiring competition within the global economy, and restricting intellectual property rights within the global economy. Freedom of expression has always been essential for technological and scientific advancement, and so it is also essential in enabling IT professionals to create and maintain the best IT applications and systems. Although competition has always been a requirement for a functioning market economy, some corporate commentators feel it is unnecessary in IT. We will discuss their views shortly. Corporate commentators hold that maximizing their profits is more important than the traditional social goal for patent and intellectual property of stimulating development. This corporate view is not surprising, but it is ethically wrong. Stifling development for the sake of greater profits violates the Global Difference Principle. And clearly IT development is diminished if software copyrights are extended in perpetuity.[3]

The second question is whether the global principles of justice might undermine the IT basis for the global system of cooperation. I don't believe so. We can get an idea of why this is so by comparing the social contract global principles of justice with cosmopolitanism, a global ethical theory we rejected. Cosmopolitanism would definitely undermine the IT basis for the global system of cooperation. Cosmopolitanism requires us to transfer resources to the worst off until the greatest average level of well-being is reached worldwide.[4] We know that there are about one billion people in the developed economies, about one billion in the poorest economies, and about 5 billion in between. Cosmopolitanism leads to counterintuitive consequences concerning those at the bottom and those at the top. As I pointed out in Chapter 7, **Cosmopolitanism**, cosmopolitanism requires us to leave the worst off in their suffering if the average would be improved thereby. (In fact, this may be the actual situation right now.) But at the top, if the average would be improved by diverting the resources now used to implement high-end technology such as Internet 2, cosmopolitanism would require us to do so. So it would require us to underserve the IT necessary for global cooperation. By contrast, the Global Economy Difference Principle, like domestic Difference Principles, would require us not to worsen the lot of the worst off group in the global economy, even if the average were improved. By the same token, the Global Economy Difference Principle would not require us to divert resources from high-end technology just because the average would be improved. It is very plausible that improvements to the IT infrastructure of the global economy can contribute to making the worst off, better off, and that is all that is required by the Global Economy Difference Principle.

CONSEQUENCES FOR IT PROFESSIONALS

IT professionals must have a role in making sure that the conditions on institutions under the Global Economy Social Contract--that institutions are democratic, transparent, observant of all social contracts, authoritative-- are fulfilled.[5] But especially to guarantee democracy and transparency of institutions in the context of the IT-enabled global economy, their input is essential at all stages.

Because many if not most IT applications are implemented within corporations, the status of corporations in the Global Economy Social Contract is important. Corporations, not being ethical persons, are not parties to the global social contract and do not have rights under the Global Greatest Equal Freedom Principle. In particular, they do not have free speech rights. Actually, this is also true for the domestic greatest equal freedom principles of justice even though the courts have found otherwise.[6] An IT professional is thus faced with an organization which has a great deal of power which cannot be justified ethically. In Chapter 9, I discussed the case of an IT professional working for the World Bank, assuming that it fails to meet its own stated goals of reducing world poverty. I concluded that it was a personal decision--not even an ethical one--whether to continue facilitating an organization whose ethical flaw is not realizing its goals. There may be opportunities to provide input to improve matters, but when the scope of one's job does not include making policy, being circumspect is usually a good idea.

However, corporations can be guilty of more than just not realizing ethical goals. They can actively pursue disinformation campaigns, stonewall court decisions against them, support repressive governments in exchange for resources, and lobby for laws to decriminalize their criminal behavior--all of this both domestically and globally. What is the IT professional to do when faced with this behavior? The choice may be to comply with unethical or unjust orders or to quit. Being a whistle-blower usually costs a fair amount. Even with legal protections whistleblowers commonly lose their jobs. It is easy to say one should not obey unethical orders, but if your job depends on the judgement of possibly unethical higher-ups, the disruption to one's career and to family that may be caused by this refusal require careful consideration. It may be that refusal is more than one can be ethically required to do. It may be what is called *supererogatory*, meaning literally "above what is asked."

The relevant ethical consideration here is that, even if you feel the best thing to do is to acquiesce in the injustice, the higher level principle of justice has to be acknowledged by what you do.[7] Even if reasons of interest make it difficult or impossible for you or your company to do what you believe is ethical, it is still necessary in what you do to acknowledge the higher-level ethical principle. And this acknowledgement is ethically required. It is easy to see why. If the fact that other people are not behaving well was a sufficient reason for you not to behave well, the situation could never improve. But fortunately people are ethically optimistic and in most circumstances believe that improvement is possible. Of course, it may be foolhardy and completely unproductive to do the right thing in circumstances where ethical principles do not hold sway. It may also be supererogatory, which means that the action is not ethically required.

Exactly what form an acknowledgement of the higher-order Global Principles of Justice should take will thus depend very much on details of the circumstances. It is common that one has personal ethical family obligations which make it necessary to keep one's job. Then the extent to which a company will allow criticism of its policies and actions will determine what one can do. At a minimum, one could express regret to peers that the company could not see its way to a more ethically enlightened policy. If the company allows anonymous criticism through suggestion boxes and the like, that is another possibility.

Do such corporate environments violate the Greatest Equal Freedom Principle? I don't think that's the way to look at the situation. Corporations are not parties to the social contract and are subject only to external ethical oversight. They have their place in the global economy (and in domestic economies) because of their economic efficiency and productivity. I don't believe that the corporate goal of maximizing profits should always be *replaced* by ethical goals.[8] Rather, if restriction of speech for those working for the corporation, is necessary for the corporation to achieve its goals, that is not ethically objectionable. However, if the restriction extends to employees when not in their role as employees, that would be a violation of the Greatest Equal Freedom Principle.

IT AND ANTICOMPETITION ENFORCEMENT

In Chapter 12, **New Global Institutions,** I noted the efforts of the various nations to enforce anticompetitive policy on a global basis. Right-wing free market advocates have a different take on antitrust activity, especially in the IT area. They see it as hampering innovation by forcing successful companies to defend themselves against groundless suits. Sonia Arrison asserts that antitrust claims are made by competitors to slow successful innovators down. Consumers need no protections because IT ". . . moves fast, making true monopolies impossible to keep for long. There will always be someone in a garage with the next new thing to challenge industry leaders, all without help from the government." (Arrison 2008) According to Arrison, we can therefore assume that Microsoft is not a "true" monopoly and that it cannot stifle competition. Microsoft is not correctly characterized as a tech innovator. It has been brilliant at marketing and a fast follower. It did not develop many of its own technologies but either copied them (Windows and Internet Explorer) or acquired them. Its supposedly market-based freedom from competition has produced mediocre office applications and the underwhelming Windows Vista.[9] Of course the fact that the government convicted Microsoft of antitrust violations means nothing to right-wing free-market advocates because the government is always wrong and big business is always right. Arrison mentions with approval the contention of Brad Smith, Microsoft's general counsel, that a Microsoft acquisition of Yahoo would have *increased* market competition. Strangely enough, Smith had the contrary opinion of the Google-Yahoo advertising deal. (Peninsula 2008)

My guess would be that these free-market ideologues would not be swayed by the world financial market meltdown, happening as I write this in Fall 2008. I predict they will claim that the meltdown was not caused by lack of regulation but rather not enough application of free markets. This is an ideology impervious to facts, much like Marxist dogmatism.

Following the ideology, Arrison is alarmed by the globalization of antitrust enforcement. She claims the EU's investigation of an online advertising deal between Google and Yahoo is inappropriate because it affects only the US and Canadian markets. Google made a statement that the effects were only in the US and Canada but encouraged the EU investigation and expected it to reach the same conclusion. The EU's investigation was spurred by a US antitrust investigation. Ms. Arrison apparently doesn't see the need for such investigation. It's good that Google doesn't operate that way and encourages investigation.

So there is no reason to believe that IT needs to be exempt from antitrust legislation to function properly. And, as I noted in Chapter 12, **New Globalized Institutions**, the current shared global responsibility of different governments has been moderately effective. And when some major powers such as the US--in the 90s and especially in the first decade of the 2000s--are captured by pro-corporate free-market ideologies, other major powers--such as the EU--can take up the slack to prevent anticompetitive mergers. The case mentioned in Chapter 12 was the Honeywell/GE merger, which was approved by the US but dropped because of EU objections.

INTELLECTUAL PROPERTY

The remarks I made in Chapter 11, **Globalized Ethics and Current Institutions,** about intellectual property apply to hardware patents, software copyrights, and digital copies. Corporations are actually trying to have it both ways. As legal individuals, they hold patents and copyrights for a reasonable period of time so that they can recoup their development costs. But as corporations, they want to maximize their profits, so the idea of giving up a patent or copyright that is still making money is anathema. Also, corporations cannot entertain the idea of property as an institution which is socially useful rather than an absolute right. Their goal is not to maximize social usefulness, and they can only conceive of property as an institution to enable them to maximize profits.

Software manufacturers typically protect their software by end user license agreements rather than copyright. Copyright would make the purchaser of the software its owner and give the purchaser certain rights. The legal "first sale" doctrine gives the purchaser of a copyrighted object the right to resell it. Some legal cases conclude that copyright and end user license agreements are not different and so the right to resell remains. (Wikipedia 2008) End user license agreements frequently allow the purchaser to use the software for a limited time. Because software products change frequently and require (paid) upgrades, a constant revenue stream is available without having to extend copyright, as Disney had to do to keep Mickey Mouse profitable. Also, unlike other copyrighted or patented works, there is no effective time at which software becomes available in the public domain for others to build upon. Thus open source software may be the only alternative that preserves the original intent of intellectual property and copyright.

CORPORATE IT ETHICS

The Global Business Dialogue on Electronic Commerce is a group of CEOs of IT-related companies attempting to formulate global policy that coordinates between business and governments. Its current membership is Asian, largely Japanese with members from Taiwan and Malaysia. Its current concerns are such issues as privacy, fair business practices, a guarantee that an e-commerce concern meets certain ethical standards, eliminating trade barriers to e-commerce, and intellectual property right infringement using the Digital Millennium Copyright Act as a basis. (gbd-e.org 2008)

The aims of the GBD are clearly to promote the interests of e-commerce companies. Promoting and certifying the ethical conduct of e-business is an excellent ethical goal. But eliminating trade barriers to e-commerce could easily privilege e-commerce conducted by the most developed countries. It would probably be more in accordance with the Global Economy Difference Principle to allow some protection for developing country startups until they get off the ground.[10] And making the Digital Millennium Copyright Act a worldwide basis for handling intellectual property is unethical in two ways. First, as we already indicated, at the domestic level, the Digital Millennium Copyright Act ignores the social basis of copyright in favor of maximizing corporate profits.[11] And, at the global economic level, it again disadvantages the less developed countries in an unfair way. Charging developed country rates for materials needed to build an economy simply contributes to the continuing poverty of the worst off.

CONCLUSION

This chapter has surveyed some of the main areas in which the Global Economy Social Contract affects the practice of IT as a profession. My account differs from many others in regarding corporations as only legal and not ethical individuals. I believe that the issues discussed demonstrate the appropriateness of the Global Economy Principles of Justice for global ethical problems of IT.

REFERENCES

Agence France Presse. (2008). *Malaysian blogger arrested under tough internal security law*. Retrieved September 15, 2008 from http://news.yahoo.com

Arrison, S. (2008, September 19). The global antitrust arsenal. *TechNewsWorld*. Retrieved September 26, 2008, from http://www.technewsworld.com

Associated Press. (2008, April 9). *Google to help curb Web porn in Brazil*. Retrieved April 10, 2008 from http://news.yahoo.com

Bartz, D., & Dobbyn, T. (2008, April 3). Yahoo CEO: gray areas make foreign business hard. *Reuters*. Retrieved April 3, 2008 from http://news.yahoo.com

Center for Corporate Policy. (2008). Retrieved October 15, 2008 from http://www.corporatepolicy.org

Chang, H. (2008). *Bad Samaritans*. New York: Bloomsbury Press.

Elias, P. (2007). *Yahoo, jailed journalists, settle lawsuit*. Retrieved November 13, 2007 from http://news.yahoo.com

Gbd-e.org. (2008). *Global business dialogue on electronic commerce*. Retrieved October 14, 2008 from http://www.gbd-e.org

Global Internet Freedom Consortium. (2008). *About us*. Retrieved October 17, 2008, from http://www.internetfreedom.org/about

Global Network Initiative. (2008). *Global network initiative*. Retrieved November 11, 2008 from http://www.globalnetworkinitiative.org/

Kim, J. (2008). Bruised South Korean government takes on 'infodemics.' *Reuters.* Retrieved September 12, 2008 from http://news.yahoo.com

Kravets, D. (2008, February 29). *Judge backtracks: WikiLeaks resumes U.S. operations*. Retrieved March 11, 2008. Message posted to http://blog.wired.com

Meller, P. (2008). Europe rejects plan to criminalize file-sharing. *Yahoo! News*. Retrieved April 10, 2008, from http://news.yahoo.com

Peninsula. (2008, May 10). Google postpones Yahoo online advertising deal. *The Peninsula*. Retrieved October 10, 2008 from http://www.menafn.com/qn_news_story_s.asp?StoryId=1093214562

Ribeiro, J. (2008, May 19). Google defends helping police nab defamer. *IDG News Service*. Retrieved on May 19, 2008 from http://news.yahoo.com

Sarkar, D. (2008, May 20). Cisco Systems denies online censorship role in China. *The Associated Press*. Retrieved May 21, 2008 from http://news.yahoo.com

Schultz, R. (2006). *Contemporary issues in ethics and information technology.* Hershey, PA: IRM Press.

Wikipedia. (2008). *Doctrine of first sale*. Retrieved October 18, 2008 from http://en.wikipedia.org/wiki/Doctrine_of_first_sale

ENDNOTES

[1] See Chapter 11, **Globalized Ethics and Current Institutions,** "The United Nations, the World Court, and Other Transnational NGOs."

[2] See Chapter 4, **The Basis of Ethical Principles,** "Reflective equilibrium."

[3] See Chapter 1, **IT-Enabled Global Ethical Problems,** "Intellectual Property"

[4] This is a consequence of utilitarian cosmopolitanism. I argued in Chapter 7, **Cosmopolitanism,** that it was the most plausible of the three forms of the theory.

[5] See Chapter 10, **Elements of a Global Contract,** "General requirements of institutions implementing the principles."

[6] See Center for Corporate Policy 2008.

[7] See Chapter 4, **The Basis for Ethical Principles,** "The Rationality of Cooperative Principles." See also Schultz 2006, Chapter 3, **The Context of IT Ethical Issues,** "Partial Compliance."

[8] Although with social businesses, this is exactly what happens.

[9] See Schultz 2006, Chapter 6, **Justice in a Market Economy,** for an account of the ways in which monopolies in general and Microsoft in particular damage the justice of a market economy.

[10] See Chang's excellent discussion of why initial protection for developing countries is necessary in his *Bad Samaritans*, Chapter 2. (Chang 2008)

[11] See Chapter 1, **IT-Enabled Global Ethical Problems,** "Intellectual Property." In 2008, the EU rejected a proposal to criminalize file sharing by private individuals and also rejected a proposal to ban copyright abusers from the internet. These proposals were termed "draconian." (Meller 2008)

Section 4
Ultimate Questions

Chapter 14
IT–Enabled Globalization and the Environment

Problems of environmental ethics transcend global justice. We can behave ethically and justly toward each other across the globe, but at the same time let the environment deteriorate in catastrophic ways. I believe principles of environmental ethics have to be treated as of higher order, and therefore of greater priority than even principles of global justice.[1] The environment is not a person and therefore cannot be a participant in a social contract. So the different basis for its priority is that if the environment deteriorates, it makes all of our lives difficult or even impossible.

Challenges to the priority of the environment sometimes come from corporations when their own interests in profitability would be harmed. Very often a focus on profit maximization will make the point of view of a corporation shortsighted. Notoriously, corporate stock prices tend to value short-term financial results over longer term results. And corporate financial results do not include *externalities,* impacts on the environment that are not directly reflected in their balance sheets. Carbon emissions are an excellent example.

Developing nations sometimes object to constraints on their development for economic reasons. Their argument is that developed nations have had the benefit of unconstrained economic development, and it is unreasonable to expect them to curtail their development at its current stage. This objection was incorporated into the Kyoto Protocols of 1997 for carbon emissions: Developed countries were

DOI: 10.4018/978-1-60566-922-9.ch014

required to reduce emissions by 5 percent by 2012, but developing countries had no requirements but could be compensated for voluntary reduction. This feature of the protocols led to their rejection by the US Congress, although every other developed country adopted them. (Sachs 2008)

The value of corporations is their ability to achieve economic development. But is economic development itself always a good thing? To what extent should development be constrained by environmental concerns?

Yet even if we can answer these questions and resolve issues of the priority of economic development with the environment, there is another serious challenge to the priority of the environment from technology itself. Information technology is not directly included in this challenge, but since IT is a form of technology, there are consequences for IT. The challenge is the view that technological development should proceed unimpeded, and that any conflicts with the environment can be resolved by technology itself. The correctness of this view depends upon a view about the ultimate value of technology itself.

I will first consider principles governing our relation to the environment, then conflicts between economic development and the environment. The challenge of technology will be discussed in the next chapter, Chapter 15, **The Value of IT-Enabled Globalization.**

PRINCIPLES FOR THE ENVIRONMENT

The environmental activist Jakob von Uexkull reports an encounter with Lawrence Summers, former Secretary of the Treasury and former President of Harvard. Before a lecture, von Uexkull drew a diagram with a large rectangle labeled 'environment' and a circle inside labeled 'economy.' Summers objected and relabeled the diagram, with the economy as the outside rectangle and the environment as the small interior circle. (von Uexkull 2007) Summers' strange perspective ignored the fact that the economy is human social cooperation. It could not exist without the environment to support it, in the form of natural resources, air, water, and food.

The philosopher Thomas Pogge bases environmental ethics on the right of people to participate in decisions that affect them. Democracy, according to Pogge, is a "deeper reason" than ecology. (2002, 184) Pogge's view has the consequence that if a group chooses to live in a degraded environment, that's just fine, provided the choice was democratic. But democratic decisions may not be ethically justified. In Rwanda in 1994, the genocidal actions of the majority Hutsi (about 85%) in killing the Tutsi (about 15%) were certainly democratic, although hardly ethically justified. The same is true here: However democratically a decision is made to ravage the environment, that decision is probably not justified.

This observation makes clear the basis for extending ethics to include the environmental considerations. As I have defined ethics, it consists of principles facilitating social cooperation, either on a social contract or universal principle basis.[2] Social cooperation requires the environment, so preventing actions or policies damaging to the environment which make social cooperation difficult or impossible clearly needs to have higher priority than mere economic advantage. Clearly environmental changes which make the worst off even more disadvantaged are also unjust and therefore also are unethical.

But what if changes to preserve the environment make the worst off even more worse off? Hypothetically, if the developing countries were held to the stricter requirements of the developed countries in the Kyoto protocols and curtailed their economic development, the worst off would have been made even worse off. I think this case shows that the Global Economy Difference Principle may not have priority: Compare what happens with and without the environmental restrictions. If the environmental damage caused by making the worst off economically better off is worse than preventing the environmental damage, then preventing the environmental damage has priority over the Global Economy Difference Principle. A theoretical example would be if the only way to increase economic growth in some forested country would be to eliminate the forests and desertify the country. Then preventing environmental damage would take priority. Of course, what makes the example theoretical is the stipulation that the environmentally damaging action is the *only* way to achieve economic growth.

The Kyoto protocol case makes clear the difficulty of making these assessments. Shorter-term predictable economic benefits are balanced against the less certain longer-term harms of climate change. But a principle extending ethics to the environment is also clear: Actions and policies necessary for the long-term survival of humanity in its environment take priority over other human actions and policies.[3] My view in Chapter 2 was that higher-level principles are higher-level when those principles need to be treated that way in order to resolve conflicts between lower-level principles. Cooperative principles need to be treated as higher-level than principles of self-interest because that is the only way cooperative benefits can be achieved.[4] Similarly, environmental ethics principles take precedence over any other principle promoting human good, because without the environment there would be no opportunity for promoting human good.[5] Thus on my view, the conflict between the US and the developing nations should be resolved through an environmental ethics principle rather than through the interests of the different nations. It is worth mentioning that developed nations other than the US saw the Kyoto Protocols that way.

An environmental ethics principle still views the situation in terms of human welfare. We might call this the "Sierra Club" approach to the environment: The environment is to be preserved or protected for human use and enjoyment. In the case of the actual Sierra Club, the use is hiking and outdoor activities. By contrast, there is also the "Audubon Society" approach to the environment: The environment is to be preserved or protected for the benefit of other species, especially birds. To do this requires the protection and preservation of ecosystems. Birds can't survive without the health of the ecosystems they are part of.[6]

Over and above human interests, what kind of ethical obligation do we have to the rest of nature and what is its basis? The existence of the Endangered Species Act shows that we acknowledge such an obligation. But why should we consider the interests of other species? When we look at the environment for the basis of a higher-level principle, we see that the environment does not consist of objects provided for whatever use we want to make of them.[7] Rather, it consists of living things in complex interaction with their physical basis. We call this the *ecosystem*. And those living things become what they are through complex interaction with the rest of the ecosystem. Human beings are part of that ecosystem. Thus human survival requires the well-being of the ecosystem. The correct principle for environmental ethics is:

Ecosystem Principle: Actions and policies necessary for the long-term survival of humanity take priority over other human actions and policies. Further, the survival of the ecosystem of which human beings are a part has higher priority over actions and policies for human survival.

Thus this principle plus the various principles of justice provide a basis for the ethics of the environment. A brief statement of the priorities they encapsulate is this: Without ecosystem, no human social cooperation; without human social cooperation, no individual interests. The major levels of cooperation are global and national. I will refer to environmental principles which take priority over ethical principles as *eco-ethical principles*. We will now see how well these principles apply to recognized areas of eco-ethical concern. As always, I will be looking for reflective equilibrium with our intuitive judgements.[8]

ECONOMIC DEVELOPMENT AND THE ENVIRONMENT

Humans pursuing their interests frequently come into conflict with ecosystems. Even 60,000 years ago when humans were solely hunter-gatherers, they managed to drive the megafauna (large animals such as mammoths and saber-toothed tigers) of the Americas to extinction. Richard Leakey produces strong evidence that these megafauna extinctions in Australia and the Americas were caused in large part by human "overkill." (Leakey 1995, 194) The five previous mass extinctions were caused by environmental catastrophes, very likely asteroid collisions. Human beings are currently causing a sixth mass extinction, all on their own. As much as 50% of all species may be extinct in 100 years. (Leakey 1995, 232-245)

Things do not improve 10,000 years ago when agriculture enables human beings to build cities and develop civilization. As Jared Diamond demonstrates in his book *Collapse,* virtually all previous civilizations have outstripped their ability to produce food, ultimately impoverishing their cultivated land with the result of a collapse of population and the civilization itself.[9] (Diamond 2005) Although we tend to think of agricultural settings as paradigms of nature, they can be very much out of synch with the local ecosystem. Plowing the Great Plains of the US removed protective grass cover and produced the Dust Bowl of the 1920s and 1930s. Raising sheep in Australia causes severe damage to the protective cover vegetation and destroys the usefulness of the land. The Fertile Crescent of Iraq where agriculture originated has been desert for thousands of years, as has previously fertile North Africa.

Modern technology and the industrial revolution have accelerated the conflict with the environment and the ecosystem. Human manipulation of the environment comes to threaten the existence of the ecosystem. As human systems increase in size, their scope becomes global. The alarming feature of these systems is that there are no automatic features of the ecosystem which can bring things back into balance. As Miriam McGillis once put it, we have taken the planet off automatic pilot.[10] We are probably the first species on this planet with the capability of destroying the entire ecosystem, not just in one but a multitude of ways:

- Einstein and Teilhard de Chardin were impressed with the fact that nuclear weapons gave humankind the capability of extinguishing all life. That we haven't used these weapons in war after their first use is a sign of our intelligence. The fact that these weapons are still around and proliferating is not. (Teilhard de Chardin 1964, 145-153)
- A "safe" synthetic compound, chlorofluorocarbon, developed in the 1940s for use in air conditioners and aerosol cans turned out to be inert except in the upper atmosphere, where it destroys the ozone layer which protects us from ultraviolet radiation. There are two disturbing implications: (1) There does not seem to be any way that this result of normal chemical engineering could have been predicted. (2) All life has evolved under the protection of the ozone layer; this sudden a change has unpredictable consequences for all life forms in the ecosystem. (Asimov & Pohl 1991, 91-110) One reassuring development: All nations have recognized the threat and banned the use of chlorofluorocarbons, and the ozone layer has stabilized.
- The same unpredictable consequences are the result of the addition of gases which are the by-product of industrial technology--called the "greenhouse" gases because they increase the ability of the earth's atmosphere to retain heat, just like the panes of glass in a greenhouse. The most important gas is carbon dioxide, with much of it coming from the burning of fossil fuels in internal combustion engines. The size of temperature increase produced by the increased carbon dioxide is difficult to predict, but the size of the increase would normally happen over tens of thousands

of years. One additional current predicted consequence is storms of increasing severity. Severe strains on plants and animals are also to be expected. (McKibben 1989, "A New Atmosphere")

This issue has caused corporations whose (short-term) interests are affected to distribute false information about a lack of scientific consensus. There is consensus that there is a relatively short window to reduce carbon emissions, so the obfuscation could be very damaging. Recent credible projections of the result of lack of rapid drastic action is an average temperature increase of about 10°F by 2050. This change alone will be incredibly disruptive to all life, but will also cause great weather and climate change. There is also the possibility of what Steven Hawking describes as "runaway greenhouse," in which the earth's temperature becomes like Venus' surface temperature of 800° F. (Olesen 2006)

- Genetic engineering (genetic manipulation) also has unforeseen consequences which do not play out within individual life spans. So how can "genetic engineering" be safe? The long-range effects of such genetic manipulation as producing a more frost-resistant strawberry cannot be predicted. In nature, genetic changes are honed over time against the existing environment. By making changes out of context, we are asking for a disaster as extensive as the disappearance of the ozone layer.

Current uses of genetic engineering show that science itself is not fully conscious of its own relation to the ecosystem. We already have cases in which genetically altered individuals cannot be safely released into the environment. Salmon engineered for increased size are also sterile. Wild female salmon prefer to mate with the larger engineered salmon and thus will produce no offspring. If engineered salmon are introduced into the wild, salmon extinction would be highly probable. Genetically engineered changes are thus being judged only in the context of current benefit to current human aims.

The examples above strongly suggest that the human propensity to manipulate the environment may very well not be compatible with long-term species survival.

The economic goal is to prevent further damage to the ecosystem by making our actions, companies, and policies *sustainable,* that is, able to continue without causing any further damage to the ecosystem.[11] Given that many threats to the ecosystem have unpredictable consequences, sustainability may be the only way to satisfy the Ecosystem Principle. The eco-ethical problem is when sustainability conflicts with other goals such as short term economic benefit.[12] Here are the ways some companies have handled the conflict. (The following success stories are all from Christine Arena's *Cause for Success.*[13] (2004))

Ray Anderson, the CEO of Interface, a leading carpet manufacturer, had an epiphany about the environment.[14] He transformed his company from an environmental hazard into one that was not only environmentally sustainable to one that was, as he puts it, environmentally "restorative." (Arena 2004, 3) At the same time, Interface increased both its business volume and its profitability. As I noted in Chapter 1, there may be less incompatibility between principles and profits in the case of environmental ethics than in "regular" ethical cases. Environmentally unsound practices almost always involve waste. And eliminating waste almost always improves productivity and hence profits. This proved to be the case for Interface. Eliminating waste was a large part of their becoming a sustainable operation, and also in making sustainability profitable. It was essentially greater efficiency involving a lot of recycling which made it possible for them to have both sustainability and profitability.

Anderson's epiphany came about from reading *The Ecology Of Commerce,* a book by Paul Hawken. (1993) Hawken shares the view I stated in Chapter 8, that the predictable result of profitability as the sole goal is incompatible with human survival. My hope was that the human agents behind corporations may come to realize that their security and survival depends on their limiting the power of the corporation to damage the environment. Hawkens approach is rather to redefine the corporation so that maximizing profits is not the sole goal. Interestingly enough, it was not necessary for Interface to alter its goal of maximizing profits. Rather, a carefully-thought-out strategy yielding both sustainability and profitability was possible. My belief is that trying to add ethical motives to something that is not a human individual, will not work as a general strategy. Instead, corporations have to be left to their aim of maximizing profits but constrained from without.

From a corporate point of view, it would have made no difference whether the CEO of Interface had chosen an environmentally terrific plan or a plan producing large amounts of pollution, provided both were just as profitable. But it made a huge difference to Anderson, and he was able to get his workers and supporters to take his view--not as corporate citizens but as ethically responsible human beings.

BP (British Petroleum), the oil company, has a similar story. Its CEO Lord John Browne acknowledged in 1997 that global warming caused by carbon emissions was a serious problem. As a result, he set BP the goal of cutting carbon emissions to 10% below 1990 levels by 2010. The company achieved that goal by 2001. BP has positioned itself as industry leader for sustainability, implementing numerous social and environmental programs, which, Browne notes, "allow us to outperform our competition in the short, medium, and longer term." Each initiative pays for itself completely in line with shareholder interests. (Arena 2004, 24) BP is also investing in alternative fuels.

Stonyfield Farm, now the largest organic yogurt maker in the world, was founded with environmental goals. It invests in its farmer suppliers, requiring them to convert to organic farms. This tends to be good economically for small farmers, both allowing them to get higher prices and to survive against agribusinesses. Stonyfield actively reduces its environmental footprint by reducing carbon dioxide emissions, solid waste, and water and energy consumption. These environmental efficiencies translate directly into cost benefits. Its environmental focus has built "fierce" customer loyalty. The net result of both business success and observance of environmental principles is the same as with the previous two businesses. But the motivation is different. Gary Hirshberg, Stonyfield's CEO, from the beginning had as his goals improving public health, increasing farmer prosperity, and helping to decrease global warming. He feels "there is an absolute need for people, especially within corporate America, to change their behavior for the better." He sees his company as at the center of a "major paradigm shift." (Arena 2004, 51-52) Thus it would be fair to say that, although Stonyfield felt business success was important, its core environmental values were the priority of the business.

IT companies, when surveyed by IBM's Institute for Business Value, had views similar to Interface and BP. Two thirds demanded that Corporate Social Responsibility (CSR) activities drive revenue, and half said these activities were delivering competitive advantage. CSR activities for IT firms included green initiatives. But Rob Preston, the editor in chief of *informationweek*, notes that "it would be irresponsible for public [IT] companies to get behind economic, environmental, and social causes that don't serve shareholders interests in some way." (Preston 2008)

We saw how this potential 'irresponsibility' played out in the case of FedEx cited in Chapters 8 and 11. FedEx developed a plan for minimizing its greenhouse gas emissions, was given an EPA award for the plan and honored at several environmental conferences including one at Harvard. In other words, FedEx received and continues to receive almost the maximum possible reputational benefits for its plan. I see no discussion on the web of FedEx's decision to implement the plan in only a token way. The original plan called for replacing 3,000 dirty trucks per year with hybrids, starting in 2004. As of 2007, it had replaced just under 100, about one percent of plan. The reason, said their environmental director Mitch Jackson, "We have a fiduciary duty to our stockholders." Jackson felt there were *more responsible* uses of company capital. (Elgin 2007) 'Responsible' business management, in the absence of personal commitment by upper management or the board of directors, will not yield good environmental results.

It can be worse. Pacific Lumber, a California company that until the 1980s owned most major old-growth redwood forests, was bought out by leveraged buy-out king Charles Hurwitz with the aid of Michael Milken and Ivan Boesky, who later served jail time for related felonies. The previous managers practiced sustainable lumber harvesting. Hurwitz liquidated the old growth to pay off the debt he incurred in taking over the company, often resorting to illegal cutting when US Forestry Rangers were not on the job. (Worldwatch Institute 2008, 146) So even if a corporation is run by a management committed to sustainability, the corporation's commitments are subject to change through buyouts and acquisitions. This is another reason why external oversight is necessary.

Ben Elgin's *BusinessWeek* article "Little Green Lies" examines the case of Auden Schendler, for a time the environmental director of Aspen Skiing, a resort complex. He was unable to implement replacement of incandescent with fluorescent bulbs, saving energy as well as costs. A manager said he would rather spend the money on leather couches. Schendler later participated in buying Renewable Energy Credits to offset Aspen Skiing's use of coal-burning electricity. Wind energy developers noted that Aspen's purchase did not support building extra wind capacity; the credits were simply PR window dressing. (Elgin 2007, 51)

Corporations are in the business of selling appearance rather than reality when appearance produces more profits. One highly deceptive appearance in recent years is so-called "clean coal." Even President Barack Obama has declared that he believes in clean coal. To make clean coal possible, carbon emissions must be captured from the coal and locked away underground. So far, the technology doesn't exist to do this, and is probably decades away from commercial viability. There are also problems about injecting the amount of material required underground without causing leaks or earthquakes. The coal industry is spending $40 million on a clean coal marketing campaign, and an industry spokesman points out that if we don't continue to use coal we will say "goodbye to the American way of life we all know and love." (Elgin 2008) But increased global warming from the massive carbon emissions of coal will have even worse results. Coal produces by far the most carbon emissions of any present fuel.

Jeffrey Sachs' emphasis on reputation as a motivator for corporations to enable social justice carries over to environmental issues. But there are similar drawbacks. Some companies don't care. Exxon-Mobil, the world's largest petroleum company, may possibly be the most destructive corporation of all time. Besides stonewalling settlements to victims of the Exxon Valdez oil spill, they also got the Bush administration to fire the head of the Intergovernmental Panel on Climate Change for raising the alarm about global warming. Coal companies spend large amounts of money campaigning for nonexistent technology to make coal safe. Automobile companies fight to keep fuel economy standards from being raised and market environmental disasters such as SUVs.

A TRANSNATIONAL ENVIRONMENTAL AUTHORITY

As I noted in Chapter 11, **Globalized Ethics and Current Institutions,** some authority external to the market is required to handle environmental problems, since the environment's interests are not directly represented in the market. The environment is neither producer nor consumer. Making profits cannot be the highest and best value, because if all human beings were to vanish completely, the profits would be meaningless. Profits are therefore of use only between humans and for humans. If corporations are by their nature unable to give priority to the environment, and (as we will see shortly) multinational corporations are able to evade government edicts, we need some transnational institution to be able to formulate and enforce consensus environmental policy on both corporations and governments. The relevant group that this institution needs to be responsible to is everyone on the planet, since the actions of various economies and corporations impact everyone on the planet, from stone-age New Guineans to users of the latest technology. Indeed, their impact is not only on the *people* of the planet--it is also on all life and all processes on the planet.[15]

The motivation for ceding authority to a transnational environmental authority would be similar to individuals' motivation to enter a social contract ceding some of their authority to the state in order to gain greater security for all. Since the environment is an externality for corporations acting as corporations, the predictable result unless their power is limited is an environment unable to support human life. This result is worse than the state of nature which motivated the formation of domestic states. (Hobbes 1651)

If the human agents behind corporations come to realize that their security and survival depends on their limiting the power of the corporation, we may be able to have such limits. As we have just seen, some CEOs have seen this. But many others have not. The editor in chief of *informationweek* can say that putting environmental concerns above profitability is "irresponsible." Given that some environmental problems impact our very survival, they *must* have priority. It is all to the good that there are CEOs who see this and structure their businesses so that they are able to give priority to the environment and at the same time deliver profitability. But we simply can't expect to fundamentally alter the basic corporate goal of profitability. Corporations would lose their only reason for being, namely economic efficiency. And it is hard to see how they could even function without that goal. Consequently, their power has to be limited externally for the sake of the survival of the human beings out of which they are constructed. In the following Chapter 15, **The Value of IT-Enabled Globalization,** I believe I can also present compelling reasons restricting corporate power of communication.

GLOBALIZATION AND THE ENVIRONMENT

Just as some human institutions are now globalized, so too many environmental problems are globalized problems. Global warming is by definition global. Other environmental problems such as air pollution, the disappearance of the ozone layer, acid rain, and resource depletion are also global. In the case of these problems, the actions of any one country do not solve the problem in that country. The actions of many countries produce the problem, whose effects are distributed across countries which often had little to do with producing the problem. Some of those most affected by global warming (the Inuit) are the least responsible.

Two problems, namely depletion of the ozone layer and acid rain, are being handled by international cooperation with some degree of success. The Montreal Protocol dealing with ozone depletion took effect in 1989. It has mostly been successful in getting countries and corporations to stop using ozone-depleting chemicals such as chlorofluorocarbons, and the level of these chemicals is decreasing. If the Montreal Protocol is observed, the ozone layer is expected to recover by 2050. DuPont, cited for its pro-environment policies in *Profits with Principles* (2004), declared that the theory that its chemicals were depleting the ozone layer was "rubbish" and was still vociferously arguing as late as 1987 that the science was too uncertain to ban chlorofluorocarbons. (CIESIN n.d.) Global warming has produced very similar attempts by corporations to put corporate interests ahead of environmental reality. As we will see in Chapter 15, **The Value of IT-Enabled Globalization,** such corporate actions are a very strong reason for putting severe limits on corporate communications.

Acid rain is rain that is unusually acidic, caused by sulfur and nitrogen compound emissions. Deleterious environmental effects include death of all aquatic life in lakes, the death of forests, destruction of soil, and human pulmonary damage. As usual for an environmental problem whose solution would involve costs to corporations, electric power companies began by denying the problem and continue to drag their feet implementing a solution. Smokestack scrubbers now eliminate much sulfur emissions from coal-burning electric generating plants, and automobile tailpipe emissions controls eliminate most nitrogen oxide. The US has had success with trading excess emissions control capacity between companies. The Sulfur Emissions Reduction Protocol has been agreed to by almost all European countries and Canada but not by the United States. The agreement is part of a broader agreement on transboundary air pollution. Although there has been some progress, more needs to be done. (U.S. EPA 2008)

The remaining global environmental problems are much farther from solution, perhaps because solutions would have greater impact on corporations. To deal with global warming requires us to cut carbon emissions drastically, which means drastically reducing our use of fossil fuels or replacing them. Currently using alternatives to fossil fuels is more expensive, so it would impact profits. The most plausible assessments of what will happen if carbon emissions are not drastically reduced is that the earth's climate will become warmer permanently. The best we can do, with restricting emissions to a 30% increase by 2050, would be average temperatures increasing 5° F. If current corporate opposition continues, this much reduction will not be possible. More likely will be a 10° F average temperature increase by 2050. (Worldwatch Institute 2008, 77)

Carbon emissions trading, especially in Europe, has had some benefits. In 2006 over 1 billion tons of carbon were traded. However, this amount is only enough to begin meeting the Kyoto Protocols, which are not enough to restrict temperature increases to just 5° F. There is, however, a great deal of activity across the globe: In the US, the northeastern states have agreed to reduce emissions to 1990 levels by 2014, and then reduce them by another 10 percent by 2018. California has mandated a 25 percent reduction in emissions by 2020. Western states including California plus the Canadian provinces of British Columbia and Manitoba have set a regional emissions reduction goal of 15 percent below 2005 levels by 2020. (Worldwatch Institute 2008, 92-95) However, measures so far have not come close to making any country carbon-neutral. (Spratt 2008)

The problem of global warming is thus currently being handled by cooperation between states. Cooperative agreements between states have been very successful with ozone layer depletion, and somewhat successful with acid rain. What makes global warming more problematic to handle this way is that there is a definite deadline after which the resulting climate change will be disastrous. But although the deadline exists, no one can say with certainty when it is. The Intergovernmental Panel on Climate Change (IPCC), which won the Nobel Prize in 2007, has the job of summarizing and reporting the most recent findings on climate change. Many commentators find it extremely conservative. Its projections of effects have consistently been well below actual in its twenty years of existence. Its most recent reports neglected such topics as loss of Arctic sea ice and carbon-cycle feedbacks such as the melting of permafrost.[16] (Spratt 2008) The IPCC has been subject to political manipulation by ExxonMobil through the Bush administration. Through their efforts, the IPCC chair Robert Watson, a climate scientist, was replaced by someone more industry-friendly. (Borger 2002) The New York Times described Watson, who has distinguished credentials, as "an outspoken advocate of the idea that human actions - mainly burning coal and oil - are contributing to global warming and must be changed to avert environmental upheavals." (Wikipedia 2008a) Too radical in 2002, but now close to received wisdom. This action is part of the case for limiting corporate speech. The incalculably large danger is when corporate interests take precedence over the truth, as in this case.

Principles of rational choice strongly suggest that the dire consequences of global warming require maximin reasoning, which is to choose the course of action that gives the best results if the worst happens.[17] For this kind of reasoning, it is not relevant that the worst may not happen. We still have plan for it. Although there is some evidence that a decent number of states recognize that we need to plan for avoiding a catastrophe, there is also evidence that some do not recognize this. And corporations like Exxon-Mobil are probably incapable of maximin reasoning since it does not maximize profits.

Establishing a global climate authority may be the best idea. Such an authority could administer a common carbon tax transnationally. And a global authority may also be the appropriate mechanism to deal with some kinds of resource depletion. The collapse of fisheries is an instance of "the tragedy of the commons," where unowned or commonly owned property is overutilized until the value of the property is lost.[18] If fished at current rates, all currently harvested wild seafood will disappear by 2050. Forests are essential for biodiversity in the ecosystem and for carbon capture. Some of the ecologically important ones are being harvested or developed at unsustainable rates. The Amazon Rain Forest is disappearing at a rapid pace. Al Gore and the *New York Times* have asserted that the Amazonian rain forest belongs to all humanity. Lula da Silva, the President of Brazil, countered that "the Amazon belongs to Brazilians" and that North Americans had no ethical right to butt in. (globo.com 2008)

Considerations like these are part of the reason why cosmopolitan ethical theorists give no ethical weight to state sovereignty. But surely economic groups living in the area must have some say in their own lives. The indigenous tribes of the Amazon Rain Forest surely must have some say over their destiny. As I concluded in Chapter 8, a country has ethical legitimacy when it is just (or at least a minimal democracy) and follows just principles in dealing with other countries.[19] For smaller autonomous groups not organized into states such as indigenous rain forest tribes, the group has ethical legitimacy when it is a minimal democracy (governs with the consent of its members and does not maintain its power through repression). In either case, if the environment beyond the group would greatly suffer, then environmental concerns have to take priority. It could be helpful for a transnational authority to issue directives, rather than another state. President Lula da Silva's casting the issue as a battle between sovereign states is certainly understandable since he is the leader of a sovereign state. But to the extent that the way the Amazon Rain Forest is treated has great effects outside of Brazil, others certainly have a right to weigh in on this issue.

The Organization for Economic Cooperation and Development (OECD) is a transnational organization of states involved in environmental issues. In 2001 their Environmental Directorate issued a well-thought-out ten year environmental strategy with five general objectives and 71 concrete actions covering all of the issues just discussed. They reported after three years that very little progress had been made, citing as causes lack of agreement on the status of the problems and economic effects, including unequal burdens in remediation.[20] (OECD Environmental Directorate 2003) The OECD's plan was advisory only.

The OECD's 1995 Multilateral Agreement on Investment (MAI), scuttled after great opposition by a group of NGOs, would have eliminated any state control over environmental standards. However, control over environmental standards would not have devolved to the OECD's Environmental Directorate but rather to multinational corporations investing in various countries. Most likely this would have made things worse environmentally. As it is, the WTO sets trade rules which make it impossible to enforce transnational environmental restrictions.

Another set of transnational externalities concerns transportation. As discussed in Chapter 3, **IT's Contribution to Globalization,** the question is whether the social cost of transporting goods is greater than what companies utilizing transportation pay. Transportation for the purposes of globalization utilizes transport running on fossil fuel. The resulting air pollution and carbon emissions are externalities which do not add to the company's cost. Trucks and air transport also require massive social expenditures for such infrastructure as roads, airports, and air traffic control systems. If we took such externalities into account, would it actually be economic to import cheap plastic toys from China?

Multinational corporations can also play off states against each other to escape environmental regulations. Production can be shifted to states with looser environmental regulations. Or bribes or political contributions can be made so that environmental regulations are overlooked. Economist Joseph Stiglitz suggests enlarging the liability of corporate officers when egregious violations of environmental protection laws occur. (2007, ch. 7) But again, if this is done on a state-by-state basis, there is little chance of closing all loopholes. So it is a task for a global environmental authority.

The oversight problem discussed in Chapter 12, **New Globalized Institutions**, would apply to such a global environmental authority. So it could be better to have three branches: A global environmental policy agency, a global environmental enforcement agency, and a global environmental judicial agency. As discussed in Chapter 12, these agencies would have oversight on each other. Thus there would be no need for an authority over the global environmental authority to provide oversight.

IT AND THE ENVIRONMENT

As I noted earlier, achieving compatibility between environmental aims and business profits is perhaps easier than compatibility between profits and other ethical goals. This is because achieving environmental aims often involves eliminating waste, which improves efficiency and thus often improves profitability. This turns out to be very much the case with IT companies. The major environmental impacts of IT lie in its generation of waste (in the form of obsolete equipment, called *e-waste*) and in energy use. Reducing waste usually increases profits.

The Electronic Industry Code of Conduct was developed to provide voluntary standards for working conditions and environmental responsibility throughout the supply chain for electronic equipment. Its environmental standards call for reducing pollution and waste and complying with environmental regulations. (EICC 2007) Reducing pollution and waste is clearly the way to go. The EICC's other aim of complying with environmental regulation depends on how good government regulations are. In any case, as I pointed out in Chapter 11, **Globalized Ethics and Current Institutions,** the standard of complying with the regulations of different states is no help with transnational problems arising from conflicting national regulations.

A U.S. Environmental Protection Agency study estimates the amount of throw-away electronics at between 1.9 million and 2.2 million tons in 2005. Most of it ended up in landfill; only 345,000 to 379,000 tons—less than 20%—was recycled. Since old consumer electronics are filled with toxic substances such as mercury, cadmium, lead and brominated flame retardants in plastics, the poisons can and do contaminate the soil and underground aquifers. In the US, only CRTs not intended for reuse have special export requirements. There are currently no US restrictions on the disposal of other electronic equipment, although Canada, Australia, and other European countries have such restrictions. (EPA 2008)

There is an international standard for e-waste, the Basel Convention. The Basel Convention is an international treaty to reduce transfer of hazardous waste between nations, especially from developed to less developed countries. The Convention is also intended to promote environmentally sound management of e-wastes, both by developed and developing nations. The Convention became effective in 1992. 170 nations signed (all except a few developing nations in Southern Africa). However, as of 2008, only three have not ratified the Convention, Afghanistan, Haiti, and the United States.[21] A 1996 amendment, the Basel Convention Ban, calls for a complete ban on exporting hazardous waste of any kind to developing countries. This ban is observed by a number of countries, most notably the EU. (Wikipedia 2008b)

Exploiting transnational differences in environmental regulations is common when dealing with e-waste. Safely disassembling and recycling e-waste can be somewhat costly. So it is often cheaper--though not always legal--to ship such waste for processing to lower-wage countries where environmental regulations are laxer. Much of the exports go to China, Pakistan, India, Mexico, Brazil, Nigeria and Ghana, where toxic dumps of discarded electronics have sprung up. Children burn and pull apart the equipment to extract metals that can be sold for cash. In 1991, an internal memo of then World Bank Chief Economist Lawrence Summers was leaked to the world press. In the memo, Summers stated that "the economic logic behind dumping a load of toxic waste in the lowest wage country is impeccable and we should face up to the fact that ... under-populated countries in Africa are vastly under-polluted." (Sherman 1999)

BusinessWeek reporters Ben Elgin and Brian Grow conducted a thorough investigation into the activities of Supreme Asset Management & Recovery, one of the nation's largest recyclers of electronic waste. Their customers include such major manufacturers as Panasonic and JVC and municipalities like Baltimore County, Md., and Westchester County, N.Y. Supreme assures its customers that it lawfully disposes of e-waste after neutralizing all hazardous contaminants. Supreme's customers say they believe the company handles their e-waste properly. MIT, Baltimore County, and JVC all explain that they have visited Supreme's premises and observed nothing inappropriate. Panasonic said that it worked with Supreme on an e-waste collection drive last year. Norman Magnuson, director of operations for MIT's facilities, says that Supreme routinely provides a "certificate of proper destruction," indicating that the university's e-waste doesn't get sent overseas.

But a recent GAO probe by the U.S. Government Accountability Office found that "a large electronics recycler in New Jersey" was one of 43 U.S. companies that sought to sell e-waste for export to Asia, in apparent violation of the law. In China and elsewhere, electronic gear commonly is stripped for reusable microchips, copper, and silver; dangerous metals are dumped nearby, often close to farms or sources of drinking water. Even though the US has failed to ratify the Basel Convention, the EPA adopted rules effective January 2007 forbidding U.S. companies from exporting monitors and televisions with cathode-ray tubes unless they have approval from the EPA and the receiving country. CRTs contain lead, mercury, cadmium, and other toxins that can cause neurological damage in children and other harmful effects. The blood of children in rural Guiyu, China, a notorious e-waste scavenging site, contained lead at twice the acceptable level set by the U.S. CDC. (Elgin & Grow 2008)

Supreme doesn't dispute that it is the New Jersey recycler mentioned in the GAO report, but it denies any wrongdoing. Many of the 43 U.S. companies that expressed willingness to export items to the GAO undercover buyers "publicly tout their exemplary environmental practices," the report noted. *BusinessWeek* independently found postings on international trading Web sites in which identified sales representatives for Supreme offered to export scores of shipping containers filled with monitors requiring EPA special permission, which Supreme doesn't have. Seven former Supreme employees confirmed that they knew about the company selling large monitor shipments overseas. Despite these findings, Supreme says "We're doing everything we can to play by the law, to save the environment, and to run a successful business," says Brianne Douglas, vice-president for marketing. Many of the 43 U.S. companies that expressed willingness to export items to the GAO undercover buyers "publicly tout their exemplary environmental practices," the report noted. On its Web site, Supreme says that "100 percent of the electronic waste we receive is reused or responsibly recycled." (Elgin & Grow 2008)

Some of Supreme's rivals confirm the GAO's findings. Robert Houghton, president of Redemtech, an e-waste processor in Columbus, Ohio, stated "This industry has a tradition of no accountability." Thomas L. Varkonyi, proprietor of Metal Recycling, a scrap shop in El Paso, says that Houghton's assessment applies across the country. Varkonyi's scrap shop collects e-waste supplied by recyclers. and ships monitors and motherboards a couple of miles south to Juárez, Mexico. There, Mexican workers— "cheaper labor," he says—pry the e-waste apart, extracting valuable metals and components that can be resold. Regulation of toxins is far more lenient in Mexico. "You can pay off anyone [in Mexico]," says Varkonyi. He brings the processed scrap back to El Paso and claims he therefore doesn't need EPA or Mexican government permission. The EPA disagrees. (Elgin & Grow 2008)

The GAO stressed that the EPA's rules and enforcement efforts are inadequate because they focus only on CRTs, ignoring the export of other potentially hazardous electronic parts. The EPA has done relatively little enforcement, the GAO added. The EPA counters that it has focused on educating e-waste recyclers about its rules and now is stepping up enforcement. (Elgin & Grow 2008)

E-waste is thus very much a globalized environmental problem. An accepted transnational policy for dealing with the problem exists, the Basel Convention. The US has interesting company in not agreeing to the convention: Afghanistan, Haiti, Iraq, Myanmar, North Korea, Laos, Zimbabwe, Somalia, Angola, and a number of very small countries.[22] Enforcement of even the more limited US restrictions by the EPA is problematic. In this area, we do have the basis for transnational cooperation basically limited by lack of US support. The official reason for US non-ratification of the Basel Convention is odd. Although the Senate actually ratified the Basel Convention and all relevant US agencies and departments approved, enforcement laws were also required which have never been passed. How can there be a technical difficulty rooted in US treaty law that makes ratification that much more difficult in the US than in 170 other countries?

E-waste problems notwithstanding, reducing waste often makes business sense. This is so even if there are no government regulations to comply with. Reducing waste is very much in the spirit of the popular agile methodology. And there are lots of opportunities. *Informationweek* presented a three-part series on green IT in late 2008. Among the possibilities are consolidation of e-mail and storage, data deduplication, and increasing telecommuting. Consolidations and data deduplication not only improve service levels and reduce administrative overhead, they reduce servers and consequent energy use. Increasing telecommuting results in a reduced demand for office space, which again saves environmentally. As the author, Behrad Behtash, points out, consolidated systems have "far from a zero footprint," so it's vital to reduce the amount of data to be stored. (Behrash 2008)

Another major environmentally important use of IT applications is in cataloguing the ecosystem. It is impossible to know what needs to preserved without accurate information about the various complex ecosystems around the planet. IT has already proved indispensable in these areas.[23]

Some ecological problems stem from the nature of technology itself. IT hardware and IT applications have different ecological profiles. The rapid obsolescence of hardware has ecological consequences. There are increasing problems of pollution caused by the disposal of obsolete IT hardware. For the manager or IT professional, incorporating eco-ethical concerns often comes at little cost. The ethical manager has to insure that disposal of old equipment is done in an ecologically responsible way. Provided the cost is not too great, all that is necessary is becoming aware of this responsibility.[24] If the cost is too great, then the manager or IT professional may only be able to acknowledge his support for ecological concerns. Or, in cases like these, a legislated social policy for ecologically safe disposal may be required. A number of jurisdictions have standards for disposing of computer equipment in a non-polluting way. And there are numerous companies engaged in the business of safe disposal of old computer hardware.

There is no reason to believe the pace of obsolescence will change. There is nothing that a manager or IT professional can do about this. The forces involved are beyond human power, as we will see in the next chapter. Of course, theoretically all computer manufacturers could unanimously agree to stop improving their products. But why would they do so? From the point of view of ecology, all that matters is that negative consequences be managed.

IT application impacts on ecology are different. Attempts to streamline processes and make them more productive have the potential of benefiting the ecosystem. Reduction in the use of paper for reasons of efficiency, a common effect of the use of IT, has a positive effect in conserving forests. But there is some offset in the environmental harm caused by the disposal of obsolete hardware.

To determine fully the eco-ethical status of technology and IT requires a discussion of the nature of technology and IT and the ultimate value of both. These the topics are addressed in the next chapter, Chapter 15, **The Value of IT-Enabled Globalization.**

REFERENCES

Achbar, M., Abbott, J., & Bakan, J. (2004). *The corporation* [Motion Picture]. USA: Zeitgeist Films Ltd. (Available from http://www.zeitgeistvideo.com)

Arena, C. (2004). *Cause for success.* Novato, CA: New World Library.

Asimov, I., & Pohl, F. (1991). *Our angry Earth.* New York: Tom Dougherty Associates.

Behtash, B. (2008, October 27). The case for consolidation. *InformationWeek*, 50-52.

Borger, J. (2002, April 20). US and oil lobby oust climate change scientist. *The Guardian*. Retrieved on October 31, 2008 from http://www.guardian.co.uk/world/2002/apr/20/internationaleducationnews. climatechange

Brown, L. (2008). *Plan B 3.0.* New York: Norton.

CIESIN. (n.d.). The Montreal protocol on substances that deplete the ozone layer. *CIESIN Thematic Guides.* Retrieved April 3, 2009 from http://www.ciesin.org/TG/PI/POLICY/montpro.html

Diamond, J. (2005). *Collapse: How societies choose to fail or succeed.* New York: Viking Books.

EICC. (2007). *Electronic industry code of conduct.* Retrieved February 11, 2008, from http://www.eicc. info

Elgin, B. (2007, October 29). Little green lies. *BusinessWeek.*

Elgin, B., & Grow, B. (2008, October 15). E-Waste: The dirty secret of recycling electronics. *Business-Week.*

Environmental Directorate, O. E. C. D. (2003). *The OECD environmental strategy: Are we on track?* Retrieved October 29, 2008 from http://www.oecd.org

EPA. (2008). *Regulations and standards.* Retrieved November 10, 2008 from http://www.epa.gov/osw/conserve/materials/ecycling/rules.htm

Globo.com. (2008, May 26). Amazônia brasileira tem dono, diz Lula. *Globo.com.* Retrieved October 31, 2008 from http://g1.globo.com/Noticias/Politica/0,MUL536698-5601,00-AMAZONIA+BRASILEIRA+TEM+DONO+DIZ+LULA.html

Hall, K. (2006, August 17). *Sony fights dark side of e-waste.* Retrieved November 4, 2008 from message posted to http://blogs.businessweek.com/mt/mt-tb.cgi/7385.1284913364

Hawken, P. (1993). *The ecology of commerce.* New York: HarperCollins.

Leakey, R., & Lewin, R. (1995). *The sixth extinction.* New York: Doubleday.

McKibben, B. (1989). *The end of nature.* New York: Doubleday.

Olesen, A. (2006, June 22). Stephen Hawking warns about global warming. *USA Today.*

Pogge, T. (2002). *World poverty and human rights.* Cambridge, England: Polity Press.

Preston, R. (2008, August 11). When good corporate deeds yield good returns. *InformationWeek.*

Rowe, J. (2008). The parallel economy of the commons. In Worldwatch Institute, *2008 State of the World.* New York: Norton.

Sachs, J. (2008). *Common wealth: Economics for a crowded planet.* New York: Penguin.

Schultz, R. (2006). *Contemporary issues in ethics and information technology.* Hershey, PA: IRM Press.

Sherman, R. (1999, August 11). Toxic waste: The politics of dumping. *The Guardian.* Retrieved November 10, 2008 from http://www.cpa.org.au/garchve1/966tox.htm

Spratt, D. (2008, October 10). Global warming - no more business as usual: This is an emergency! *Links.* Retrieved October 31, 2008 from http://links.org.au/node/683

Stephens, J. (2009, January/February). Art or eco? *Sierra, 94*(1).

Teilhard de Chardin, P. (1964). *The future of man.* New York: Doubleday.

U.S. EPA. (2008). *Acid rain.* Retrieved April 3, 2009, from http://www.epa.gov/acidrain/

von Uexkull, J. (2007, February 21). *The post corporate world.* 6th annual Frank Kelly Lecture. Santa Barbara, CA: University of California.

Wikipedia. (2008a). *Robert Watson (scientist)*. Retrieved October 30, 2008 from http://en.wikipedia. org/wiki/Robert_Watson_(scientist)

Wikipedia. (2008b). *Basel convention*. Retrieved November 10, 2008 from http://en.wikipedia.org/wiki/ Basel_Convention

Worldwatch Institute. (2008). *2008 State of the world*. New York: Norton.

ENDNOTES

1   See Schultz 2006 Chapters 12 and 13.
2   See Chapter 4, **The Basis of Ethical Principles,** "Ethical principles for individuals."
3   In Schultz 2006, Chapter 12, I called this Principle the "Species Survival Principle."
4   See Chapter 4, **The Basis of Ethical Principles,** "The rationality of cooperative principles."
5   In deciding between the economy and the environment, maximin reasoning is especially appropriate. See Chapter 5, **Domestic Theories of Justice,** "Theories of Justice."
6   The actual organizations are much more alike in their activities than this schematic distinction suggests. The Sierra Club is concerned with environmental issues that go beyond human use and enjoyment.
7   This observation is the basis for a correct ethical placement of technology, discussed below in "Technology and the environment."
8   See Chapter 4, **The Basis of Ethical Principles,** "Reflective equilibrium."
9   Other factors such as drought also play an important role in collapse, but degrading the environment is always at least an important contributing factor.
10   http://www.du.edu/enviro/Events_and_Orgs.htm
11   Dow Jones publishes a *sustainability index* for different companies. Since there are differences over what sustainability is, one needs some idea of how sustainability is determined for the index. However, this information is password-protected on the website and apparently not publicly accessible. This lack of transparency renders the Sustainability Index useless for helping to preserve the environment.
12   Although support for buildings consumes 70% of US electricity and produce about half its carbon emissions, a number of superstar architects including Eisenman are not concerned with making their buildings sustainable. The motive here is not profit but rather wanting to be free of environmental constraints on their design genius. (Stephens 2009)
13   Arena's book is notable for making clear how her chosen companies reconciled economic goals with sustainability. Many other books (such as *Profits with Principles*) merely state that their companies successfully reconciled economy with sustainability without giving us a clue as to how.
14   Ray Anderson, CEO of Interface, Inc., details his epiphany in the film *The Corporation.* (Achbar, Abbott,Bakan, 2004)
15   These issues will be discussed in Chapter 15, **The Ultimate Value of IT-Enabled Globalization.**
16   The melting of permafrost releases large quantities of methane, a very potent greenhouse gas.
17   See Chapter 5, **Domestic Theories of Justice,** "Theories of Justice."

18   For a good discussion of the tragedy of commons, see Rowe 2008.

19   See Chapter 8, **The Ethical Status of Globalized Institutions,** "What is a country?"

20   A projected 2007 progress report apparently does not yet exist.

21   Are you surprised?

22   Most of these small countries would neither be suppliers or processors of e-waste: Suriname, French Guiana, Western Sahara, Sierra Leone, Cameroon, Gabon, Congo, Tajikstan.

23   See, for example //www.arkive.org/about.html .

24   The cost would be too great if doing the ecologically correct thing would interfere with your ability to fulfill your professional duties and obligations. That includes keeping up the well-being of the organization. See Chapter 4, **The Basis of Ethical Principles,** "Duties, Obligations, Rights."

Chapter 15
The Value of IT-Enabled Globalization

This chapter, like the previous one, also deals with issues that go beyond ethics as principles for social cooperation. We just saw that the environment raises issues that go beyond social cooperation. Likewise, value does not depend directly on social cooperation but rather on interest and point of view. In Chapter 4, **The Basis of Ethical Principles**, I characterized a good or valuable object as one that, to a greater degree than average, answers to the interests one has in the object from a certain point of view.[1] Thus a good disk drive is one that answers to the interests of a computer user in safely storing information. When an object is defined in terms of its function, the value of that object simply consists in its performing that function to a greater degree than average. That is, good antivirus software must prevent and destroy viruses well; good keyboard cleaner must clean keyboards well.

Often the point of view from which value is to be determined is assumed to be our own point of view, or that of our group. Most disagreements about value are in fact disagreements about the appropriate point of view to use for evaluation. But within a point of view, value is not subjective. Whether something is valuable from a point of view is a matter of fact. Thus if a bank robber and an investor disagree about whether a bank is a good one, they are not expressing merely subjective preferences. The bank that answers to the bank robber's interests is one with lax security and an easy getaway route. So the bank robber will deem such a bank, a good bank. But if this bank has squandered its capital on credit

DOI: 10.4018/978-1-60566-922-9.ch015

default swaps,[2] the investor will deem it a bad bank. The bank that answers to the investor's interests is one that is stable and provides a good return on his money. Both judgements of value are correct. The bank is both good and bad--from different points of view.

In this chapter, I consider fairly large questions of value. First, what is the value of globalization? I will consider both economic value and cultural value. Under cultural value, I will discuss the question of whether the coalescence of cultures is a good or bad thing, and in what respects. My second question is, what is value of technology and of information technology? I will consider this question from three different points of view: The point of view of humanity; the point of view of the ecosystem; and the point of view of *being*. The point of view of *being*, which is the point of view of the coming to be and passing away of all things, may be unfamiliar. I include it because it is the highest point of view and thus has priority over others. And I believe it provides the basis for a compelling argument to limit corporate power. The third question combines the answers to the first two: What is the value of IT-enabled globalization?

THE ECONOMIC VALUE OF IT-ENABLED GLOBALIZATION

IT can contribute value to globalization in two ways. First, it can enable other value produced by globalization, mainly economic value. Second, it can contribute to the value globalization produces on its own.

There is probably no question that globalization has produced economic growth. There is considerable question about whom the growth has helped. Peter Singer cites several expert opinions and concludes that data is not currently available for a clear view of the economic impact of globalization on the poor. One study found that, although income inequality between nations has increased in the last two centuries, it would have increased even more without globalization. A second study by the World Bank found that globalization benefited the majority of the population, but made things worse for the bottom 40 percent. Yet a third study found that income inequality has decreased during the era of globalization, but cautioned that this decrease might be the result of technological advance rather than globalization. (Singer 2004, 88-89)

However, it is not clear how to separate out the value of technological advance from the value of globalization. The primary way in which economic globalization increases value is through efficiencies of integration. And much global integration is completely dependent upon IT. Supply chain integration and financial integration to the degree now present in the global economy would simply not be possible without IT. There are other important enablers of the economic integration of globalization such as government policies and trade regulations. But without IT, a significant portion of globalization could not have taken place.

From the point of view of the Global Economy Difference Principle, the concern is whether or not globalization has made the worst off even more worse off. Paul Collier's discussion suggests that this is not the case. His "bottom billion" have missed the boat for the benefits of globalization, but they have not been driven further downward by globalization itself. According to Collier, the factors responsible for their not benefiting from globalization include a highly unstable political environment (and consequent unstable economic environment), the tendency of abundant natural resources to make democracy malfunction, poor governance, and unfavorable geographic location. (Collier 2007) These are internal factors making it difficult to have economic development of any kind. So, globalization has likely not made things worse.

A further question is whether economic development is always valuable. At first thought, the answer is yes. Income is an enabling good which makes it possible to pursue all one's other ends. But if economic development comes with injustice, it is less valuable. Historically the industrial revolution began with horrendous labor conditions which after much struggle and sacrifice were ameliorated. At this point in history, only a few conservative economists argue in favor of sweatshops and child labor. Certainly American and European corporations are very sensitive to claims their products are produced with labor working under inhumane conditions and make a substantial effort to eliminate such labor.

A more difficult question is how to balance the claims of the environment with economic development. I discussed this issue in Chapter 14, **IT-Enabled Globalization and the Environment.** To the extent that economic development damages the environment, it is less valuable. Some types of economic activity are valuable only if their negative environmental effects are not taken into account. The conclusion I reached in Chapter 14 took the form of the Ecosystem Principle. This principle gives priority to actions and policies necessary for the long-term survival of humanity in its environment. Such long-term survival requires giving higher priority to the survival of the ecosystem human beings belong to. The consequence is that long-term survival of humanity as part of the survival of the ecosystem has priority over economic development.

As mentioned previously, it is sometimes claimed that technology can overcome any bad effects of economic development and so the following Technology Principle supersedes the environmental principle just mentioned.

Technology Principle: Technological progress is inevitable, unstoppable, and mostly beneficial. The results of technology come about through its unimpeded progress. Hence, technological development must have priority over other considerations.

This principle licenses almost unlimited economic development. I will consider its justification and viability below.

THE VALUE OF IT-ENABLED CULTURAL GLOBALIZATION

Besides economic globalization, there is also cultural globalization. I now want to consider the value of cultural globalization. Although cultural globalization could take place in the absence of economic globalization, it is hard to see how there could be economic globalization without cultural globalization. The intensity of communication required by economic globalization makes a certain amount of cultural interchange inevitable. The question is, how much cultural globalization is a good thing, and could we stop it even if we wanted to?

The ethical cosmopolitans of Chapter 7, **Cosmopolitanism,** held that citizenship in a country or nation has no ethical significance. Cultural cosmopolitans have the same belief about cultures. For them, cultures have no value other than what is reflected in individuals. Thus for them cultural globalization has great value because it tends to eliminate the practice of people valuing their cultures.

I believe this view is counterintuitive for most people. We tend to identify ourselves primarily by what culture we belong to. When traveling to other countries, we learn to say what our names are (in Spanish "Se llama Robert," for example) and then our primary identification ("Soy norteamericano" or

"Soy ingles").[3] Cultural identification seems more important than either political or linguistic identification. We regard ourselves as participants in the artistic, economic, and athletic accomplishments of our fellow countrymen. But are we wrong?

The philosopher Anthony Appiah promotes cultural cosmopolitanism in his 2006 book *Cosmopolitanism.* Appiah asserts that value attaches only to individual attainments. So a culture consists only in individual contributions. There is no culture to be preserved over and above what individuals do. (Appiah 2006, 126) The wrongheadeness of this approach is most clear with respect to language and art objects. Language is an important part of culture, and language can hardly be decomposed into independent individual contributions.[4] The efforts of the Lithuanians to preserve their language and literature through the long Russian occupation of the 19th century were not the efforts of a number of individuals to preserve their individual contributions.

Appiah seems to think of art objects as created from scratch by individuals who have full responsibility for whatever merit or meaning they have. Art historian E. H. Gombrich decisively refuted this view in his *Art and Illusion.* (2000) Artworks belong to stylistic traditions, and it is necessary to be familiar with the tradition in order to understand, evaluate, or even create them. Some of those traditions are cultural, some transnational. When the Hungarian composer Bartók incorporates Hungarian or Bulgarian elements into his music, he did not make them up. When architects adopted the 'international style,' it was something new. If Appiah is correct, they were always working in the international style. For him there is no alternative national style.

Appiah's position inherits the fundamental problem with ethical cosmopolitanism to give absolutely no status to group membership short of the totality of human beings. I think the reason is the same for cultural cosmopolitanism. Both versions of cosmopolitanism have no appreciation of the depth of the contribution of human cooperation to human reality. Appiah quotes the 1954 Hague convention disapprovingly: "*each people* makes its contribution to the culture of the world." (2006, 126, Appiah's emphasis) Then he asks, "*which* people?" (126) The notion of collective contribution is unintelligible to him. I suppose French cuisine is only intelligible as the dishes prepared by a number of chefs.

So it seems wrong to deny any value to cultures. But Appiah's discussion does raise an important issue: What about a culture has value? And further, is all culture valuable? Should all cultures be preserved? If not, which?

WHAT IS A CULTURE?

It seems incorrect to give no value to culture. But it is also incorrect to say that all aspects of all cultures are valuable. As we saw in Chapter 6, **Political Realism and the Society of Societies**, Michael Walzer seems to hold this view. But aspects of culture which violate principles of justice have no right to preservation. Slavery, apartheid, segregation and lynchings in the US South, and pogroms in Eastern Europe and Russia are not cultural aspects that deserve preservation. To say that promoting equality of women is cultural imperialism is itself wrong. Or to hold that equal rights and democracy are "Western values" is to say that oppression is just fine if it happens to be your cultural value.

There is a problem here with what I called moral beliefs in Chapter 4, **The Basis of Ethical Principles.** Moral beliefs are religious, philosophical, political beliefs which aren't shared. If they are part of culture, perhaps they should be preserved if they are otherwise not in conflict with principles of justice. But very often holders of such beliefs (usually religious) try to force them on others or even embed them in constitutions.[5] From an ethical point of view, such attempts are unjust. By demonstrating intolerance, these religious people forfeit any claim to tolerance.[6] So from the point of view of justice, society should tolerate these beliefs only as personal rather than as a basis for law or public policy.

We now have a partial answer about what parts of culture should be valued--namely, those that don't conflict with principles of justice. To say more, we need to determine what a culture is and what its parts are. The United Nations Educational, Scientific and Cultural Organization (UNESCO) described culture as follows: "... culture should be regarded as the set of distinctive spiritual, material, intellectual and emotional features of society or a social group, . . . [encompassing] in addition to art and literature, lifestyles, ways of living together, value systems, traditions and beliefs." (2002) This gives us pieces of culture but not the unifying principle that holds them together. The unifying principle is that the social group has to regard cultural features as those passed on from previous group members (often ancestors) and passed on to newer group members (often children). Thus a belief in the divinity of Britney Spears by a group in New York would not count as part of a culture unless it were inherited from older members of the group and passed on to newer members of the group. If a Britney Spears fan club in New York all happened to believe in her divinity for a few years, that belief would not be part of a culture.

Two quite different types of culture have value in different ways. First, there are traditional ethnic cultures embedded in more-or-less self-sufficient social and economic groups. The culture usually has the name of the ethnic group. These are the cultures whose existence is threatened by globalization. Instances would be the Basque culture, the Mayan culture, the Inuit culture. Second, there are cultures which arise within the context of developed globalized civilization. They are usually better described as subcultures, and are usually attempts to achieve an identity distinct from the main culture through dress, slang, music, and such distinctive activities as skateboarding. Very often such subcultures consist exclusively of adolescents and young adults. An example would be hip-hop culture. These subcultures arise within a globalized society and are not threatened by it. They come and go, and their value (their contribution to the history of humanity) is the same as other expressions of fashion. That is to say, any value for preservation is primarily historical rather than of ongoing interest for how to live.

By contrast, ethnic cultures can embody complete world views independent of developed globalized civilization and may embody better solutions to problems of living than ours. Something is lost if all that remains of them are mere historical catalogue descriptions or even high-definition videos. They embody possible ways of living which are not found in interconnected globalized culture.[7] The possibility of such cultures remaining functionally unconnected from global culture is small. We can therefore list the possible models for such cultures to relate to global culture. They are:

- Melting Pot: All subsidiary cultures are mixed and amalgamated without state intervention.
- Monoculturalism: In a state where culture is identified with the nation, the government policy is to assimilate members of the subsidiary culture to the national culture.
- Core Culture: The subsidiary culture supports the core concepts of the culture on which the dominant society is based, although it can have an identity of its own. (Sometimes these are subcultures.)
- Multiculturalism: All preserve their cultures, interacting peacefully within one nation. (Wikipedia 2008)

The Melting Pot model is the quintessential American one. It has the advantage of minimizing internal conflicts but it also has the disadvantage of minimizing any valuable distinctive parts of other cultures.[8]

The result in America has been a shallow consumer culture promulgated and enforced by standardized corporate mass media. It is striking that the model is not enforced by the state, but is rather achieved spontaneously. This model is one of two usable for cultural globalization, and its results in America may be one reason why cultural globalization has somewhat of a bad name. The fact that it happens without explicit government policy may make matters worse, since if one dislikes the results, there is no institution to protest against. Subcultures defining themselves against the dominant culture ("countercultures") are not in a position to replace the dominant culture.

The other model possibly usable for cultural globalization is Multiculturalism. With this model, all cultures are preserved. One of the difficulties is that in the context of a state or nation, multiculturalism can be an enforced policy, but in the global context there is no single sovereign to announce and preserve multiculturalism. Of course, in the global context, there is nothing to prevent cultures from preserving themselves, and Monoculturalism or Core Culture within a state or nation may be effective in preserving that culture in a globalized context. But the institutions of globalization themselves, especially the Internet, produce strong pressure toward a globalized consumer culture promoted by the globalized corporate entertainment media. Some isolated ethnic cultures may have been economically better off outside the global culture. Some Polynesian cultures seem worse off now. But other ethnic cultures have better lives within the global economy and its culture.

GLOBALIZATION AND PRESERVING CULTURES

How should we feel about this state of affairs? Are there elements of pre-globalized cultures that deserve to be preserved? How do we go about doing this? Isolation is probably not a viable strategy. We can compare different attempts to assist indigenous peoples. On the one hand, there are projects such as the one that trained indigenous peoples of the Amazon in the use of GPS devices to help them map and register the boundaries of their lands to protect themselves against unscrupulous developers. On the other hand, there are missionaries who provide health benefits but also destroy cultural artifacts and substitute Christian elements. Perhaps the worst example occurred in 1562 when the Franciscan priest Diego Landa destroyed by fire some four thousand volumes, all but four of the extant volumes of Mayan civilization. One commentator observed, "This, not the burning of the library at Alexandria, was surely the greatest literary and cultural crime in the history of the west, and the Maya experienced it."[9] Landa thought he was destroying superstition, but we now know that he was promoting it. Proselytizing religions must believe they have the only correct set of moral beliefs--otherwise they have no reason to proselytize. But the existence of a number of mutually incompatible sets of religious beliefs leads to two conclusions: First, only one of these sets of beliefs can be correct. Second, most probably none of them are. Therefore missionaries of proselytizing religions[10] should be resisted in any attempt to convert people, either domestically or in other cultures.

We can look to anthropologists like Claude Levi-Strauss for further clues. Levi-Strauss discussed at length the anthropologist's dilemma of prizing primitive cultures and yet belonging to his own culture as a scientist. He concludes that we must take "a level-headed and unbiased view" of cultures different from our own, yet without attributing to them absolute merits. At the same time, we cannot take for granted the "naturalness" or "rightness" of our own culture. (Levi-Strauss 1961, 387) The various levels of principles of justice provide a basis for an unbiased view of our own and other cultures. But that only goes to guarantee the basic decency of a culture and provide a basis for criticism and correction. After that is done, the evaluation of what is valuable in other cultures and what needs to be preserved goes beyond ethics and justice.

Justice can tell us when to intervene and how much to intervene--generally not much unless some very bad things like genocide are going on. Landa's bad example tells us emphatically to preserve as much as we can unless there are compelling ethical--not moral--reasons not to. Since we know we cannot preserve everything, we will need to make judgements about what is more valuable to preserve. This is nothing less than judgements about what types of objects and actions in human experience are more valuable than others. For example, do we want to preserve details of how a culture made war rather than their weaving techniques? What would be the basis? From what point of view could these evaluations be made? We are asking not only from the point of view of the human species but from the point of view of *being* itself.

From the point of view of *being,* the question is: Is our goal as a species to do what the Technology Principle requires, to expand mindlessly into our environment in ways that may greatly shorten our tenure on the planet? Or are there goals beyond this that we can adopt as a species? We know as managers that a business without a strategic plan is a business likely to go out of control and therefore out of existence. Yet as human beings with the ability to affect the survival of all life on the planet one way or another by our activities, we do not have a strategic plan which includes the conditions for our own survival. The ultimate question of how we should be using our capabilities is so far unanswered.

One reason for attempting to formulate such species-level goals is the fact that our species will not always exist. Although I don't share a "manifest destiny" technologist's belief in the invincibility of the human species or its technology, I finally do hope that the human species is around for something like the normal 2-million year life span of most species. So what will happen to all the elements of all our cultures, our accumulated knowledge, our artworks, our buildings, our technology, our systems of communication, our social systems, our ethics, our spiritual connections, and so on? The only thing that prevents human knowledge from dying with its possessor is other human beings who are prepared to carry on the human enterprise. What meaning can it have for non-human species? Philosophers such as Kant and Wittgenstein have noted that our knowledge is in a very deep sense human knowledge, tied to the conditions of existence of human beings. (Kant 1787, Wittgenstein 1953) So it is very problematic to think of passing the torch to other species. They did not evolve together with us as part of the complex social web within which we can communicate with each other and share goals and values.[11]

Even so, it would be a more achievable goal to develop significant communication with other species on earth, rather than to try to locate and communicate with species on other planets who share what can only be much fewer characteristics with us. If our knowledge can continue to survive our species, it can only be through transmission to other species, and the ones here have a lot more in common with us than anything possible on another planet. There is some reason to believe this. When conditions are replicated as closely as possible, the same ecosystem does not replicate. (Leakey 1995, 167-170) Thus a whole distinct chain of DNA development on some other world will probably not bear much similarity to ours--certainly much less similarity than other intelligent species on our own world bear to us.

Even the goal of fostering communication with other species does not answer the question of a goal for the human species itself. The background goal is preserving whatever is worthwhile in what we have done as a species. But why and for whom? It would be hard for me to accept that in one or two million years (maybe a lot sooner unless we start doing more about our relation to the environment) that all that would be left of humanity would be a lot of ruins and all the waste products of technology.[12] The situation would be radically different from other extinct civilizations such as the Maya. There would be no other people, no anthropologists, to pick up the pieces and appreciate what had been going on.

So what is worthwhile in what we do as a species? And is it still worthwhile if there are no successors to appreciate it? So far as the ecosystem goes, it would be worthwhile if we did not damage it irreparably and left it capable of producing species that could recognize us as their predecessors. Perhaps (hopefully in a million years or so) we could leave a time capsule engineered to be accessible to some future successor species.

Let us return to the question of how to value cultures and parts of cultures. The same principle behind intellectual property might work: We want to preserve as much as we can that expands the range of human possibilities *and* to make it available for others to build on.[13] I think this will help with choices when we can't preserve everything. Also, it will matter whether something that expands the range of possibilities can be captured as documents or artifacts, or whether it is a way of life which needs to be preserved. We have failed to preserve the range of human possibilities if we allow Tibetan Buddhist monks to continue only as historical records, for example.

On the other hand, advocates of globalization consider it a positive value that cultures are being amalgamated. Even Noam Chomsky, a severe critic of corporate economic globalization, says that "No sane person is opposed to globalization, that is, international integration. Surely not the left and the workers movements, which were founded on the principle of international solidarity." (Chomsky 2005)

One positive value of the coalescence of cultures, or of nations or countries anyway, was noted as far back as Pascal. Pascal pointed out the irony that if one man shot and killed another on the same side of a national border, he would be a criminal. But if they were on different sides, he would be a hero. (Pascal 1670, sec. V) In general, the positive value of cultural globalization is that it tends to eliminate ethically irrelevant differences between people. Of course, cosmopolitans believe that *all* group differences are ethically irrelevant and that the only ethically relevant group is humanity as a whole. In Chapter 8, I established that membership in a country or state can be ethically relevant. Economic cooperation is organized into countries or states. Political and economic rights under principles of justice are enforced by states.

In his *The World is Flat,* Thomas Friedman argues for a different positive value of cultural globalization. In order to be able to compete in the global economy, cultures must be willing to change for economic reasons. They have to be open to adopting globalized economics. It is OK to keep cultural items that don't conflict with this aim, but other parts of a culture have to go. (Friedman 2005, 324-329) Friedman contrasts intolerant Muslim Saudi Arabia with Muslim Dubai, which he calls "one of the most tolerant, cosmopolitan places in the world," (329) according to Friedman. In 2008, "tolerant, cosmopolitan" Dubai sentenced an English Lesbian couple to jail for kissing on a beach. (Daily Mail Reporter 2008)

Friedman's attempt to lump good, socially tolerant, economically flexible and industrious cultures together and distinguish them from bad, intolerant, economically inflexible and stagnant cultures is probably doomed to failure. Ha-Joon Chang notes that in 1915 Western observers called the Japanese "lazy and indifferent to the passage of time." Koreans of that time were "dirty, degraded, sullen and lazy." In the middle of the 1800s Germans were deemed uncooperative and emotional. (Chang 2008, 182-185) In Chang's view, Friedman may be putting the economic cart before the economic horse. It is not a receptive culture that leads to development, but development that leads to a receptive culture.

Either way, there is still a tradeoff between economic and cultural globalization in valuing preglobalized cultures. The important question for value is which point of view to take? The point of view of economic globalism or the point of view of members of the culture? I think it has to be the point of view of members of the culture. Our historical tradition of treating "savages" as children has few adherents.[14] And, unless there are reasons of justice for intervening in their culture (normally genocide or something equally serious), it is their choice to remain with their culture or adopt "Western ways." Thus indigenous peoples decide themselves on the value of their culture.

There is an ethical question in the background here, namely whether participants in the global economy can, for example, ethically build a hydroelectric dam which severely disrupts indigenous lifestyles. The Global Economy Principles of Justice apply because the global economy is impacting the lives of these people. Therefore they have both Greatest Equal Freedom rights and Global Difference Principle rights in the matter of the dam.[15] In practice, this will turn out to be the legal rights of the nation they are in. But over and above these legal rights the Global Difference Principle requires that they not be made worse off by the dam project, assuming that they would be at the bottom economically if in the global economy.

I conclude that the value of cultural globalization is mixed. It is good to the extent that it promotes openness and tolerance. It is bad to the extent it causes the loss of distinctive ways of life which are otherwise ethically neutral. It is hard to regard the spread of unhealthy American fast food across the planet as a good thing, especially if it displaces healthier regional food. But again, how much do things like this really matter? If McDonalds on a global scale is the price we pay to give those at the bottom of the economy a significantly better life, then perhaps the disvalue is worth it. But yet again, will this choice really be an either-or choice? It would have the most value to have healthy regional food *and* significantly better lives. The important value insight here may be that *both* unglobalized culture *and* globalized economic benefits are worth having together even if achieving both is more difficult.

TECHNOLOGY AND THE ENVIRONMENT

I now turn to technology and its challenges for ethics, the environment, and *being*. At the beginning of this chapter, I noted another serious challenge to the priority of the environment, not from profit-maximizing corporations but from technology itself. The challenge is the view that technological development should proceed unimpeded, and that any conflicts with the environment can be resolved by technology itself. But until we gain greater insight into what we are doing as a species, human development may be from the point of view of *being* more like a disease spreading than progress. Human beings may be at this point like a disease in the ecosystem, especially if the concept of disease is correctly understood: A disease is a misunderstanding between two species. Our misunderstanding may be that we can exist completely apart from our biological basis in the ecosystem.

Technology, in many ways, reflects this separation from the ecosystem. Very often the intelligence of the human species is thought of only in terms of our ability to manipulate the environment, and the more manipulation the greater the intelligence. Indeed, many scientists and technologists hold what might be called a "manifest destiny" view of technology—that it is our goal or even duty to change the environment as much as possible, and to spread ourselves as widely as possible.[16] This is the

Technology Principle: Technological progress is inevitable, unstoppable, and mostly beneficial. The results of technology come about through its unimpeded progress. Hence, technological development must have priority over other considerations.

It is obvious that the Ecosystem Principle and the Technology Principle are not compatible. If human survival and survival of the ecosystem have priority, then technological progress does not have priority. The suggested reason for the priority of the Technology Principle is that it is not uncommon for technology developed for one use, to find another, essential, use later on. For this reason, proponents of the Technology Principle point out that you can never have too much technological development. Unimpeded growth in technological research and development is thought to be essential in correcting technology's flaws. For these reasons, it can be argued that actually the Technology Principle is the best way of serving human survival and survival of the ecosystem. We will return to this discussion after a closer look at technology itself.

THE NATURE OF TECHNOLOGY

Technology has three distinct stages:

1. The traditional technology of agriculture and cities that enabled the rise of civilization, roughly 10,000 years old.
2. Modern technology enabled by science, about 500 years old.
3. Information technology, about 50-60 years old.

The use of any technology enabling more than hunter-gatherer societies takes up a remarkably short portion of human existence on the planet. Using current estimates of the presence of human beings of our species for the last 250,000 years, civilization has been a possible human mode of existence for 10,000 years, no more than 4% of humanity's time on earth. Joseph Tainter argues in his book *The Collapse of Complex Societies* that so far, civilizations other than our current one have been unable to avoid collapsing under their own weight. He thinks our current civilization is different from previous ones in having modern technology to increase resources and thus at least postpone collapse. (Tainter 1988, 216.) Jared Diamond in his book *Collapse* is not as positive about the ability of technology to prevent collapse. (Diamond 2005)

Indeed, it is because of technology that we can even begin to have any hope of overcoming the difficulties in our current position. For it is largely science and its technological apparatus that are responsible for the knowledge of our position in the environment. If our intelligence has failed us in leading us in the direction of destroying our own ecosystem, it has not failed us in revealing this very situation to us.

Yet neither science nor technology contains within themselves directions out of the current situation. Indeed, defenders of the Technology Principle usually argue that for any problem, there is a further technological fix. There are two problems with this view: First, there is no good reason to believe it; and second, the fixes take us farther and farther away from any recognizably sustainable world. Not only do we end up existing for the sake of our technology, but the technological apparatus becomes increasingly susceptible to catastrophic failure, as Asimov pointed out in his science-fiction novel *The Caves of Steel*. [17] (Asimov 1954) Modern technology takes us in directions not previously encountered in our environment. Our changes tend to have unpredictable and dangerous side effects. Chlorofluorocarbons and their effect on the ozone layer ought to be more than sufficient to put us on notice that we really do not know what we're doing with our technological changes.[18]

Jackson and Nelson, in their *Profits with Principles,* provide a corporate misinterpretation of the correct principle that new technologies have unintended consequences which must be taken into account. Their example is Monsanto and genetically engineered food in Europe. The "unintended consequence" is failing to anticipate consumer opposition to genetic engineering in food.[19] For them, it is merely a PR problem with those superstitious Europeans that wasn't managed correctly. (Jackson and Nelson 2004, 72-73) If any technology may have unintended consequences, it is genetic engineering, because there is no way to predict how a genetic change will express itself back in the environment.

THE POINT OF VIEW OF MODERN TECHNOLOGY

It is very important to recognize how deep problems with technology are. Technologists tend to be very intelligent people. It may seem obvious to me that manipulation of genetic material is extremely dangerous given the nature of how species relate to the environment. But bioengineers are similarly baffled by objections to their seemingly totally beneficial attempts to provide more food for people who are malnourished or starving. The 20th-century philosopher Martin Heidegger saw clearly that *modern technology has its own point of view* which is completely separate from any other structure of human aims and purposes. The critical feature of modern technology is its willingness to treat anything as a resource to be reordered in the furtherance of human aims, including its own aims. Heidegger, in his essay "The Question Concerning Technology," concludes that modern technology is an independent force in human existence. It builds a new and incompatible order on top of what was there, primarily in order to extract and store energy for later uses. (Heidegger 1955, 14-17)

The point of view of modern technology regards everything as a potential resource, as "standing reserve" to be used or reused later in other processes of the same kind. A forest has status only as a timber resource. Land itself is only a resource for the building industry. Even human beings themselves, from this point of view, become "human resources." Or they become "consumers." Or ill people become a "supply of patients for a clinic." (Heidegger 1955, 17-18) Many distinctive modern technologies embody this notion of "standing reserve" in their very conception. Thus electric power, whether in the form of available current or batteries, is always entirely standing reserve, on hand for potential use.

This way of looking at things ignores the previous pattern of processes, uses, and ends. So it is inherently destructive in its effects on those processes, and hence on the ecosystem. Also, the point of view of modern technology is that technology presents itself to us as a mere means, an enabler for our other ends. But it is impossible to place technology ethically in a correct way without the realization that *modern technology has its own ends,* which are to reorder everything as standing reserve in yet-undisclosed ways.

Here is the ethical point: The general principle for the determination of the priority of ethical principles is that higher-order principles settle disputes between lower level principles that cannot be settled on their own.[20] The principle to serve technological ends cannot have priority over all other principles--the reason that technology's own ends would be furthered is not sufficient to establish this priority. The Ecosystem Principle must have priority: If technology is able to bring things into being, it is only through the agency of human beings which, at this point, require the species in order to survive. And survival of the species requires preservation of the ecosystem.

There is one other possibility to consider: Could the human species survive without the ecosystem? We probably covertly have in mind eliminating the ecosystem in favor of some substitute supplied by technology. If the Technology Principle is allowed a higher priority than the Ecosystem Principle, the aims of the ecosystem will be served only if they promote technological aims. Which principle gets higher priority depends on high-level beliefs about human technology and its relation to nature. If one believes that technology can correct its own errors in a timely manner and that a policy of unregulated technological progress is most conducive otherwise to overall human progress, then technological progress becomes the ultimate touchstone for policy. If one believes human technology has built-in unanticipated conflicts with the ecosystem, then a policy of minimum mutilation of the ecosystem is called for. An important point here is that the principles constraining the overall utilization of technology, because of the far-reaching nature of that utilization, have to be higher level than principles of justice and even those of principles of international justice and global economic justice.[21]

Might it turn out that the only way that the human species could survive is by destroying or seriously damaging the ecosystem? In this case, the kinds of changes necessary for the human species to be compatible with the ecosystem would simply not be practicable. This situation leads to two somewhat different doomsday scenarios: (1) Either human beings diminish in numbers, restrict their manipulation of the environment even when that might yield short-term benefits for the species, but allow the rest of the ecosystem to take its course; or (2) We prolong species survival as long as possible even if it would result in the extermination of all other species on the planet. These are both really scenarios for species suicide, slow or quick.[22] The first scenario acknowledges priority of the Ecosystem Principle.

The second doomsday scenario, in which we eliminate all other life on the planet in order to preserve the life of our own species, is the only one where the Ecosystem Principle does not have priority. It is almost certainly a fantasy that we can survive in the absence of any other life, and such a fantasy would again probably include the presumption that technology can replace the extensive life support we depend on. So it comes down to whether, in going extinct as a species, we take all other life with us. After all, we won't need the ecosystem as support any more. So the grounds for the priority of the Ecosystem Principle no longer apply. For this final case, we need to appeal to another point of view, that of *being* itself. With the exception of this extreme case, there seem to be good reasons for the priority of the Ecosystem Principle over the Technology Principle.

The point of view of the human species still considers us as a part of the ecosystem. Over and above that, we are part of the ebb and flow of *being* itself, of the coming to presence and passing away of all things. Heidegger does not believe that humanity can be the master of *being*, and thus the introduction by humanity of any new mode of *being* such as technology brings dangers with it. Over and above any danger to the ecosystem, there is a danger of disrupting *being* itself. For there is more to *being* than the ecosystem. The ecosystem depends on the rest of what there is for its substratum. The very air we need to breathe is the product of a dynamic relation of both living and non-living systems. Plants synthesize food from the elements and sunlight. There are levels of organization in the weather and the seasons other than those contained in animals and plants which are necessary for their existence. To say that these levels of organization are mere physical processes is exactly the point of view of modern technology.

If we can accept that there may be more to *being* than even living beings, and that as a species we have a duty to respect *being*, then we have reason to behave ethically even in the extreme case of the end of the human species just described. Thus the ultimate ethical principle may be to demonstrate the awareness of our species of our place within *being* as we leave it, and not have our final message be a path of destruction through the rest of what is. The anthropologist Claude Levi-Strauss put it this way:

. . . no species, not even our own, can take the fact of having been on earth for one or two million years-- since, in any case, man's stay here will one day come to an end--as an excuse for appropriating the world as if it were a thing and behaving on it with neither decency nor discretion. (Levi-Strauss 1968, 508)

IT AND BEING

Does the Technology Principle apply to IT? I think the answer is, only in part. Somewhat paradoxically, information technology is not entirely modern technology. Although computer hardware is part of modern technology, the application of that hardware to the world is not part of modern technology. IT applications do not look to reorder everything in the furtherance of their own aims. IT applications do not reduce everything to information; rather they provide a separate realm where certain processes representing real objects can be carried out incredibly quickly and communicated much more easily. The tendency to confuse this parallel world with the real world was common during the heyday of the dot-com bubble. People were seriously suggesting that mom-and-pop local groceries would need to convert to web businesses in order to survive, that all commerce would be web commerce. But IT web applications are a parallel world and there is no reason to expect them to replace the real world.[23]

IT application development does not have those distinctive marks of modern technology, namely its imposing itself on the world and replacing the existing order of information with its own constructs. Software development is still nowhere near regular engineering in reliability and timeliness. In 1994, W. Wayt Gibbs listed methodologies proposed over the last 30 years to regularize software development: Structured programming, CASE tools, fourth- and fifth-generation languages, object-oriented analysis and object-oriented programming. None of these were definitively shown to improve productivity. (Gibbs 1994, 96-7) Although there is no question that improvement in software productivity and reliability is possible, the attempt to transform it into a branch of engineering is probably doomed to failure.[24] For one thing, it is *provably* impossible to construct an algorithmic (i.e., calculation) procedure to find all the bugs in a computer program.[25] So software development is probably irreducibly a craft--although there is no reason why this craft can't be managed to get more reliable results, any more than saddle building or ship building.[26]

So in application development, at the heart of information technology, we find something that probably does not belong to modern technology and its drive to convert the world into resources for its own use. The mystique of computer programmers about programming is legendary, and also a source of frustration for managers trying to enforce regularity and reliability.[27] I believe the mystique has its basis in the nature of IT application development. Developing I.T. applications is more like art than engineering or science. All art uses representation and expression to interpret the real world. A painting, poem, story, or musical piece has interest for us insofar as it reveals something to us about the world we live in. But it does not *replace* anything in the real world. Artworks are thus "mostly harmless," in Douglas Adams' (1979) phrase. I.T. differs from art in that, although it does not replace the real world, it is intended to have a precisely defined impact on the real world. The information I.T. produces is used to govern real processes and to make real decisions, and thus it is not "mostly harmless."

There are ethical and value consequences. Computer hardware is part of modern technology. Modern technology, as a new way of bringing things into being, is not under human control. It would thus be pointless to try to halt the progress of technological development. However, as IT professionals and participants in the global economy, we can acknowledge that the Technology Principle can be constrained. This constraint is the Ecosystem Principle.

But, beyond this, how do we acknowledge our responsibility to *being*? Can there even be a responsibility to *being*? Since *being* cannot be under human control, all we may be able to do is to demonstrate our respect for the existence of concerns that go beyond our own self interest, our organizational or corporate interest, the interests of our society, the interests of the global economy, the interests of our species, and the interests of our ecosystem. The ground for our respect is the fact that all of these interests are ultimately grounded in *being* in ways we may never fully understand but for which we can be grateful.

The relation between the constructed parallel digital world of IT applications and the world it represents determines the impact on *being*. This *is* a relation humans have control over, in the way they implement IT application systems. The most immediate impact is for users of the system, who need to be treated with respect for their natures as human beings. And then the aims of the organization need to be served by the system. Over and above that, there are considerations of whether the system furthers the aims of a just society and just global economy as expressed in the principles of justice. And finally, does the system respect the nature of things in the real world it is involved with, or does it treat them only as resources to be on call for further use? For example, how is a timber management system (already adopting the point of view of modern technology, but let us ignore that for the moment) set up? Does the system record only facts useful for marketing the timber or will it also include facts about the age, beauty, and irreplaceability of this particular stand, so that some of the forest can be conserved? Will it be a system designed for the corporate plunderers of Pacific Lumber who liquidated the redwood forests to pay off the debt they used to acquire the firm or the older conservationist owners of the firm?[28]

More generally, which data and which processes are modeled in an IT application reflect choices. Those choices reveal specific attitudes toward the user, the organization, the society, the global economy, the ecosystem, and the *being* of the world the system models. It is the ethical responsibility of the IT application developer to represent these points of view and to show his or her respect for *being* in all his choices.

CORPORATIONS AND BEING

In previous chapters, I made the case for not treating corporations as ethical individuals. They often certainly don't behave like ethical individuals, especially with respect to telling the truth. But the difficulty goes deeper: Corporations have a different relation to *being* than we do.

The ethical basis for the wrongness of lying is that lying can't be a cooperative principle. In order for the lie to succeed, the person being lied to has to believe in the truth of what is being said. And if lying were made a universal principle, this could not happen. No one would believe what was said.[29] Even though a corporation is not an ethical individual, this universal principle consideration still applies. However, since a corporation exists to maximize profits, it often regards its profitability as taking precedence over the cooperative principle of telling the truth.

But because of the role of corporations in the global economy and the impact of corporations on the environment and on environmental policy, there is an additional consideration. Truth telling has another role besides coordinating cooperative behavior between human beings. Truth telling aligns us with the *being* of the world we live in. Corporate behavior aligns itself only with whatever will maximize profits. Perhaps that would not be so bad if profit maximization were for the very long term. But the normal timeframe for profit maximization is often the next calendar quarter or fiscal year.

Even if a corporation maximizes profits over a long time period, there is an underlying insoluble problem. Being ruled by profit maximization, a corporation is not using language to reveal the truth. Thus it can have no relationship to *being* through its use of language. Whatever happens to the world as the result of its actions cannot be something it is concerned with. The environment is an expression of *being*. Thus corporate dissembling behavior shows that it has no relation to *being* as manifested in the environment. This can only have one result if persisted in--extinction of just about everything in sight, the ecosystem, plants, animals, humans, and the corporation itself. The continuing misalignment of corporate activity and what is actually taking place can lead nowhere else.

Exxon Mobil had the head of the Intergovernmental Panel on Climate Change (IPCC) replaced, not for scientific reasons but because it would threaten their profits. If it turns out that we have missed the window for minimizing climate change because of the resistance of Exxon Mobil and its fellow corporations, I hope that will be a reason to strip corporations of influence on public policy. If the missed window will mean we can no longer prevent the runaway global warming Stephen Hawking was concerned about, no action will be necessary because no action will be possible. (Olesen 2006) We will shortly all be dead. Dupont declared that the theory that its chlorofluorocarbons were causing the disappearance of the ozone layer was "rubbish." Tobacco companies for years disputed a causal link between smoking and lung cancer. Science is one of our most powerful and reliable tools for relating to reality. There is no question which should be followed if there is a direct dispute.[30]

Thus the real danger is that corporations distort reality to serve their own ends. They are merely a human legal construct which has acquired many of the powers of action of actual human beings. Not only are they not ethical individuals with all that that implies, they are not even sentient beings--with all that that implies. They can neither suffer nor be glad; they can neither be angry nor serene; they can neither be hungry or satisfied; they can neither wonder at a marvel of nature nor be appalled at nature's destructive force. They can be productive and efficient but very dangerous in their ability to impact beings whose interests are intimately tied up with all the feelings just enumerated.

What are the ethical and value consequences? In Chapter 8, I stated that corporations should be prohibited from attempting to influence public policy by advertising or campaign contributions or by financing electoral initiatives. Given the nature of the danger, this prohibition may be a bare minimum. Corporations also fund biased pseudo-scientific studies to back their dissembling positions. So the prohibition has to be against any corporate influence on public policy in any form.

Although the environmental consequences are the most important, corporate dissembling warps human productivity in other ways. Corporations assert that the best path to innovation is for them to get more profits. They have successfully warped the language so that any reproduction of patented or copyrighted material is stigmatized as piracy. Corporations should not have any say in intellectual property laws. If corporate influence on public policy is prohibited, this will prevent influence on intellectual property laws as well.

As I suggested in Chapter 8, the disconnect of corporations with the environment may be the basis for the human beings responsible for corporate behavior to put themselves and their institutions under the various principles we have discussed: First, the Ecosystem Principle; and then the Global Economy Principles of Justice, the International Social Contract, and the relevant domestic principles of justice.

THE VALUE OF IT-ENABLED GLOBALIZATION

So far, I have provided answers to the questions, what is the value of globalization and what is the value of IT? The points of view considered have been humanity, the environment, and *being*. I now want to put these pieces together to answer the third question at the beginning of this chapter: What is the value of IT-enabled globalization?

From the point of view of humanity, cultural globalization has value insofar as it promotes openness and tolerance. IT has a central role in promoting these values, especially through the Internet. Information about virtually all parts of the world is available through the Web, as well as email contact across the whole globe. IT also has a role in promoting the possibly conflicting value of preserving local cultures. It helps in recording information about the culture and even in helping indigenous cultures to record the extent of their territory to fight encroachment by corporations. (Barclay 2008)

IT also is a major enabler of economic globalization. IT's essential feature of connectivity make it possible to manage globally distributed enterprises and supply chains, taking advantage of the best business opportunities available worldwide. IT's essential feature of speed makes it possible to make operational and marketing decisions with the most current correct information possible. Without IT, large segments of the globalized economy would simply not be possible. Connectivity and speed make possible the integration necessary for many globalized applications. IT's essential features of storage and reproduction enable the use of speed and connectivity for economic benefit. As noted, globalization increases economic value and may improve the lot of the worst off. At least it does not make them worse off.

Does IT alter the value of globalization? IT dramatically increases the value of economic globalization, but it doesn't change the nature of that value directly. Indirectly, economic globalization contributes to cultural globalization through increasing transnational contact between people. IT does change the value of cultural globalization by allowing a direct experience of global community. Regarding oneself as belonging to a global community is especially important for the correct point of view on problems of the environment and ecosystem.

IT-enabled globalization has value in this respect from the point of view of the environment and ecosystem. IT-enabled globalization also has direct value for the environment and ecosystem in allowing relevant information to be stored, processed, and available for use in sustaining and conserving the environment. Of course, IT-enabled globalization also has direct disvalue by enabling corporations to plunder the planet more efficiently and on a global scale. So overall IT-enabled globalization is neutral with respect to the environment and ecosystem.

The point of view of *being* is, as I noted, an unfamiliar one.[31] We move toward this point of view when we ask about humanity's goals as a species. What is all this for, this coming to be and passing away of humans descended from primates, coming to have the power to rearrange the entire planet to their own desires. Does all this get us anywhere in end? Can we even say where it should get us? Or where it would be good for us to get to?

Are these even meaningful questions? They are related to, but more specific than, the question "What is the meaning of life?" And, unlike that question, I believe they have answers. Not that I know what the answers are, or even how to go about finding the answers. But I know it is not acceptable to human beings to say that our existence on the planet is meaningless. We have been creating that meaning since the day we became conscious of ourselves as a species. Globalization, and especially IT-enabled globalization, is another step in that journey, and that is its value from the point of view of *being.* Becoming the nervous system of a planet is a great responsibility. The ultimate value question is, what do we use this power for?

REFERENCES

Adams, D. (1979). *The hitchhiker's guide to the galaxy.* New York: Crown Publishers.

Appiah, A. (2006). *Cosmopolitanism: Ethics in a world of strangers.* New York: W. W. Norton.

Asimov, I. (1954). *The caves of steel.* New York: HarperCollins.

Barclay, E. (2008). *Indigenous groups document environmental destruction using GPS and Google Earth.* Retrieved December 27, 2008 from http://www.treehugger.com/files/2008/01/indigenous_peru.php

Chang, H. (2008). *Bad Samaritans.* New York: Bloomsbury Press.

Chomsky, N. (2005 June). *Interview by Sniježana Matejčić.* Retrieved November 18, 2008 from http://www.galerija-rijo.hr/05/chomsky

Crick, F. (1981). *Life itself.* New York: Simon and Schuster.

Daily Mail Reporter. (2008, September 2). Lesbian couple jailed for kissing on public beach in Dubai. *Daily Mail Online.* Retrieved November 18, 2008 from http://www.dailymail.co.uk/news/article-1051753/Lesbian-couple-jailed-kissing-beach-Dubai.html

Derrickson, S. (2008). *The day the earth stood still* [Motion picture]. United States: Fox Motion Pictures.

Flaherty, R. (1999). *Nanook of the north* [Motion picture]. United States: Criterion Collection.

Friedman, T. (2005). *The world is flat.* New York: Farrar Strauss and Giroux.

Gombrich, E. H. (2000). *Art and illusion: A study in the psychology of pictorial representation, millennium ed.* Princeton, NJ: Princeton University Press.

Heidegger, M. (1927). *Being and time.* New York: Harper & Row.

Heidegger, M. (1955). The question concerning technology. In *The question concerning technology and other essays.* New York: Harper & Row

Kaiser, D. (1990). *Dolphin consciousness.* Retrieved June 7, 2004 from http://home.onemain.com/~dk1008206/html/dolph1.htm

Kant, I. (1785). *Groundwork of the metaphysics of morals.* Retrieved May 10, 2004 from http://www.swan.ac.uk/poli/texts/kant/kantcon.htm

Kant, I. (1787). *Critique of pure reason.* Riga, Latvia: Hartnoch

Leakey, R., & Lewin, R. (1995). *The sixth extinction.* New York: Doubleday.

Levi-Strauss, C. (1963). *Tristes tropiques.* New York: Atheneum. (Original work published 1955. Levi-Strauss, C. (1968). *The origin of table manners.* New York: Harper & Row.

Olesen, A. (2006, June 22). Stephen Hawking warns about global warming. *USA Today.*

Pascal, B. (2008). *Pensees.* Retrieved June 6, 2008, from http://www.gutenberg.org/etext/18269

Rawls, J. (1999a). *A theory of justice* (rev. ed.). Cambridge, MA: Harvard University Press.

Schultz, R. (2006). *Contemporary issues in ethics and information technology.* Hershey, PA: IRM Press.

Stanton, A. (2008). *Wall-E.* [Motion picture]. United States: Pixar Animation Studios.

Tainter, J. (1988). *The collapse of complex societies.* Cambridge, UK: Cambridge University Press.

Trakhtenbrot, B. A. (1963). *Algorithms and automatic computing machinery.* Lexington, MA: D. C. Heath Publishing.

Ullman, E. (1997). *Close to the machine.* San Francisco, CA: City Lights Books.

UNESCO. (2002, February 21). *Universal declaration on cultural diversity.* Retrieved June 23, 2006 from http://www.unesco.org/education/imld_2002/unversal_decla.shtml.

Wikipedia. (2008). *Culture.* Retrieved October 20, 2008 from http://en.wikipedia.org/wiki/Culture

Wittgenstein, L. (1953). *Philosophical investigations.* New York: Macmillan.

ENDNOTES

[1] Similar versions of this definition of value appear in Aristotle 350 BCE, Ziff 1960, and Rawls 1999a.

[2] Just in case credit default swaps have faded from memory when you read this, they produced liability which drove many banks out of business. They were insurance on securitized mortgages which lost their value when many mortgages went into foreclosure from 2007 on.

[3] In Spanish, a form of *ser* (to be) is used which implies these cultural identifications are more-or-less permanent. A form of e*star* would be used if these cultural identifications are temporary or changeable.

[4] The late 20th century debate about whether a private language is possible is not relevant here. Rather, it would be next to impossible for one person to develop a complete language unrelated to any other.

[5] With some regularity in the early 21st century, right-wing Christian groups have had some success embedding prohibitions against gay marriage in the constitutions of various US States. Such prohibitions are justified solely by moral religious beliefs rather than ethical principles.

[6] See Rawls 1999a, "Tolerating the Intolerant."

[7] Often distinctive features in such cultures arise because of the difficulty of obtaining food in a harsh environment. The distinctive ways of the Inuit include the possibility of starvation, as happened to Nanook, the principal subject of Robert Flaherty's astonishing 1922 documentary *Nanook of the North.*

[8] In my own family, my born-in-America parents' generation made every effort to erase the Lithuanian heritage of my grandparents. My learning the Lithuanian language was discouraged. The experience of friends with Eastern European grandparents was similar. Assimilation required losing the foreign culture pretty much completely.

9   Unfortunately google.scholar.com was able to supply the quote but unable to document the source.

10   Some religions do not claim that theirs is the only correct one, for example Buddhism, Unitarian-Universalism, and the Quakers (Society of Friends). These religions do not proselytize. Other religions such as Judaism do not proselytize, although they believe their religion is the correct one.

11   For further discussion of these issues, see Schultz 2006, Chapter 13, **The Ultimate Value of Information Technology.**

12   The film Wall-E (2008) depicts this possibility.

13   The 'making available' part is what corporations don't understand.

14   Bloggers holding such opinions can still be found in the United States. See, for example, www.boston.com/bigpicture/2008/05/indigenous_brazilians_protest.html

15   It would be sophistry to deny them rights because they are not in the global economy. For this project, they are. If, however, they otherwise choose to remain in their own culture outside of the global economy, then the Global Economy Principles of Justice would not continue to apply to them.

16   For example, Francis Crick has even suggested "seeding" terrestrial life on other planets. (Crick 1981, 117-129).

17   In Asimov's novel, set several thousand years in the future, some human beings have colonized planets in other star systems. However, further colonization from earth is prevented by the evolution of a disease-free environment on the other planets. Meanwhile, earth itself has evolved into totally enclosed mega-cities with totally engineered environments and populations of 8 billion each and climbing.

The environment on earth extrapolated in the novel is present-day New York City, and the criticism made of the environment is a cogent one, namely that the complexity required to sustain such an artificial and complex environment is fragile and that unexpected disruptions are likely to be catastrophic. The solution, however, is merely to export people to areas in which there is more space. One must wonder why a species so clearly unable to live within the parameters of its environment will do better when given more space

18   Schultz 2006, Chapter 12, contains a more extensive discussion of these issues.

19   Jackson and Nelson's position veers dangerously close to requiring advance notice of unplanned computer outages.

20   See Chapter 4, **The Basis of Ethical Principles.**

21   And therefore such principles also need to be constraints on the behavior of corporations, multinational or domestic.

22   A third doomsday scenario is suggested by the 2008 remake of *The Day the Earth Stood Still.* In that film, aliens come to earth to exterminate the human species because we are destroying the planet. This scenario requires an external agent, however. It is not conceivable that the human species should decide on its own to eliminate itself in a deliberate act of species suicide. The film unfortunately squanders what could have been an important contribution to human understanding in favor of Hollywood sentimentality.

23   The overreaction to the millennium bug of 2000 may have depended on a similar confusion of the real world with its digital representation.

24   See note 26 about agile methods.

25   For the proof about just one type of bug, namely the impossibility of detecting whether a program will go into an infinite loop, see Trakhtenbrot 1963, 86-88.

26   Currently agile methods have had promising results in improving software productivity. But agile methods are not based on technical or engineering techniques, rather on holistic insights into organizational efficiency.

27   For a recent example, see Ullman 1997.

28   The case of Pacific Lumber is discussed in more detail in Chapter 14, **IT-Enabled Globalization and the Environment,** "Economic Development and the Environment."

29   This is Kant's universal principle argument for the wrongness of lying. (Kant 1785)

30   A December 2008 statement by President Obama affirmed the precedence of science as knowledge, a hopeful break from the last eight years.

31   Here is an exercise in taking the point of view of *being*. Look into a mirror and ask yourself, why am I *here?* Not: *Here* as opposed to somewhere else but rather here as opposed to anywhere at all. If you have achieved the point of view of *being*, your response will be to feel somewhat weird. Heidegger (1927) calls this the experience of the *uncanny (Unheimlich)*. It is to see oneself as a *being-there (Dasein)*.

Chapter 16
Conclusion

My original project was to determine ethical principles for ethically globalized institutions. I also wanted to determine the role of IT in the ethics of globalization. Economic and cultural globalization are two of the most powerful forces enabled by IT. So my further question was, what is IT's ethical responsibility with respect to these forces? The two focal points in this book for considering globalization were, first, Information Technology and, second, ethical issues which emerge only at a transnational level.

I defined an *ethically globalized institution* as an institution involved in ethical problems which cannot be solved by dividing them up between existing states. Examples include governments with global reach, transnational institutions such as the United Nations, transnational economic and financial institutions such as the World Bank, other nongovernmental organizations, and multinational corporations. I also defined *globalized properties* as properties of institutions of any kind which emerge only at the transnational level and which are enabled either by advances in information technology or in transportation technology. *Globalization* is the accumulation of institutions with globalized properties. By these definitions, the globalization of the world financial markets was clearly demonstrated by the market meltdown of fall 2008. Globalized financial interconnectedness, enabled by IT, emerged in the inability of any national market to stay aloof from the changes in all the other markets.

My definitions deliberately don't prejudge the value of globalization. Globalization is a form of human social cooperation with both good and bad aspects. So globalization cannot be by its nature good or bad

DOI: 10.4018/978-1-60566-922-9.ch016

any more than human social cooperation can be by its nature good or bad. Some popular commentators on globalization such as Thomas Friedman in his *The World is Flat* (2005) define globalization so that it is necessarily positive, and any difficulties need to be ignored. Some protestors at the World Trade Organization believe that globalization is necessarily bad and must be contested at every opportunity. I take neither view in this book.

To determine ethical principles for ethically globalized institutions, I examined candidates for a globalized ethical theory. A globalized ethical theory must build on ethical theories for individuals and societies. In this book I make a sharp distinction between *ethics* as principles for social cooperation and *morality* as based on customs and religious, political, and philosophical beliefs.[1] This book is concerned with ethics and not with morality as just defined. For individual ethics, I adopt the universal principle ethics of Kant. For ethics for a society (that is, justice), I adopt Rawls' social contract two principles of justice. (1999a) Ultimately I also adopt Rawls' social contract approach for global justice. A social contract approach is attractive because it bases any enforceable ethical authority on a contract agreed to by those under that authority.

For his domestic theory of justice, Rawls describes a choice situation for the social contract which will be a model for my later global social contracts. In that situation, people are not allowed to consult their own particular interests in making a decision on the principles of justice. Also, the reasoning they use in choosing between the alternatives is *maximin* reasoning, which is to choose the alternative that leaves you best off if the worst happens. Rawls correctly points out that maximin reasoning is appropriate for life-altering decisions, which is what decision on a social contract is. The result for domestic society is two principles of justice, a political principle of greatest equal freedom and an economic principle called the Difference Principle to make the worst off as well off as possible.

The theories of global ethics I examined were political realism, two versions of social contract theories including Rawls' international social contract, and cosmopolitanism. Political realism is a theory of the relation between states, not globalized institutions. Rawls' international social contract suffers from same limitation: It is a theory that holds between the various peoples in various states. It also can't be directly extended because the guidance it provides for less-than-just states makes it too utopian to be usable. For example, it would require us to have no trade relations with China because of China's human rights deficiencies. (Rawls 1999b)

Three cosmopolitan ethical theories definitely apply globally. The three theories were a pluralist theory, a social contract theory, and a cosmopolitan theory. All three cosmopolitan theories give no ethical weight to any group short of all of humanity, and I attempted to show that this is mistaken. The pluralist cosmopolitan theory also suffers from the defect of all pluralist theories, namely that it should be chosen only if a plausible theory based on a few prioritized principles can't be found. All cosmopolitan theories give no ethical weight to the fact that societies have separate economies; I contend this is also mistaken. Consider the financial meltdown of fall 2008: Although each nation cannot think of its interests as independent of those of others, we are still organized as and make policy as national economies. The existence of separate societies and economies is disregarded by social contract cosmopolitanism. So its global difference principle requires making the worst off person as well off as possible, *regardless of which society an individual belongs to.* A massive global redistribution to eliminate inequalities is not a reasonable principle of global justice. Utilitarian cosmopolitanism shares the defect of other cosmopolitan theories of giving no ethical weight to membership in a socially cooperating group. In addition, utilitarian cosmopolitanism suffers from the same serious defects as utilitarianism as an individual ethical theory: It does not take individuals seriously. It would also allow lying about one's principles if that would produce more good.

As an alternative to these transnational ethical theories, I proposed two new social contracts, the International Social Contract and the Global Economy Social Contract. The International Social Contract is between nations. Since this is not a book about international relations, it was not appropriate to go into great detail about its derivation and application. But such a contract is necessary as part of the ethics of globalization so long as countries or nations have some ethical status. So instead of supplying my own detail, I use many aspects of Rawls' international social contract, the Law of Peoples, with some changes and additions. The major differences are these: Rawls requires parties to his contract to live in nearly just countries, requiring countries to respect human rights. My alternative, following Peter Singer, (2004) is that the people of a country acquiesce in their state and that their government respect cooperative agreements made between countries. Non-intervention in other states except for grave reasons is very similar in my contract and in Rawls'. Rawls believes that there is a duty to assist people unfavorably situated only to the extent of helping them establish just societies. I believe that this duty is rather the individual duty of benevolence extended to countries: A country has a duty to assist people in another country when the cost to itself is not excessive. Finally, as an addition to Rawls' principles, I believe it would be part of an international social contract that the nations agree to have a procedure for dealing with violations of the principles of this social contract.

The other social contract necessary for global ethics is the Global Economy Social Contract. The guiding policy for social contracts is that legitimate ethical authority must be grounded in a social contract that could be agreed to by those under that authority. Thus the Global Economy Social Contract is so-called because the parties to it are those who participate in the global economy, either because they contribute to it or benefit from it. Multinational corporations need to be under that authority. But they can't be parties to the contract because they are not ethical individuals. The major function of a social contract is to allocate socially produced goods fairly. So the parties to the contract should be representatives of stockholders, of societies involved in the global economy, and of other individuals involved in the global economy such as managers, employees, suppliers and customers. As with the domestic social contract, we want the parties deciding on principles to be able to assess their effects on different classes of individuals. They then have to decide on principles without knowing which class they will in fact belong to.

The Global Economy Principles of Justice that would be chosen are parallel to the principles of justice for a particular society, and they would be chosen for very similar reasons. The Global Economy Greatest Equal Freedom Principle states that all individuals in the global economy have an equal claim to basic liberties (but not corporations or states, since they are not individuals). The Global Economy Difference Principle states that rules for globalized institutions are arranged to make the worst off participants in the global economy, as well off as possible (but not rules diminishing productivity with the result that even the worst off is still worse off). The Principle of Respect for Other Social Contracts requires that the actions of global institutions must not impair justice in any society or international justice under that social contract.

Any institutions under the Global Economy Social Contract must be democratic, transparent, implement the Global Economy Principles of Justice, and authoritative. These conditions express the conditions of the Global Economy Social Contract.

IT has a special role in the social contract: First, the principles chosen must provide a place for the enabling and substantive duties of the IT professional. If any candidate principles actually conflicted with fulfilling these duties, they would have to be rejected. Second, the principles chosen must not undermine the basis for the global system of cooperation they apply to. IT professionals must also have a role in making sure that the conditions on institutions are fulfilled. Their role in choosing the principles themselves is no different from any other employee or manager; they must consider how the principles will affect their life prospects. But especially to guarantee democracy and transparency of institutions in the context of the IT-enabled global economy, their input is essential at all stages.

In applying these principles to new or existing institutions, it was important to keep in mind problems of authority and oversight. It is tempting to deal with a transnational ethical problem by establishing a new transnational authority to deal with that problem. But how will the authority of the new institution come to be acknowledged and who will have oversight over that authority? This potentially infinite regress can be ameliorated in several ways. One is that the social contract itself reduces the need for an overseer with oversight. A somewhat different approach is the three branch structure of the US government, legislative or policy, executive, and judicial. Each branch then has oversight over the others. Also, within the actual transnational context, two possibilities have arisen. One is transnational cooperation toward achieving shared ends. This has apparently worked well with transnational antitrust enforcement. The second is the emergence of NGO alliances such as Civil Society, which managed to prevent the adoption of a trade agreement which would have stripped developing countries of power to regulate their own economies. A third possibility dates from October 2008, when the major Internet companies promulgated the Global Network Initiative, in which these companies undertake to guarantee freedom of speech against repressive governments.

In discussing both new and existing institutions, it was important to consider whether they actually have the power to do what they are required to do. In my survey of the various institutions, I noted both limitations of power that should be removed for ethical reasons and excess power which should be limited for ethical reasons. On the one hand, the UN has not been able to be as effective as it needs to be in dealing with genocides. On the other hand, the WTO has been effective in preventing trade sanctions against repressive regimes. I concluded by making the following recommendations for institutional changes and additions: The changes were a beefed-up transnational UN police force and a broader based International Court. I suggested three new institutions to handle globalized ethics: Ethical trade, economic justice, and corporate ethics. All should have three branches, policy, executive, and judicial. Ethical trade and economic justice could well be combined since they need to work together. And combining them would make it less likely that the global trade institution would give promoting trade priority over economic justice, as the World Trade Organization currently does.

The reason for a new global corporate ethics institution is that there are currently no effective national corporate ethics bodies. My position throughout this book is that corporations are not ethical individuals, so a global corporate ethics institution is needed to provide the ethics otherwise lacking at any level. I believe it was a serious mistake to allow corporations any individual rights beyond the legal rights necessary for them to function as holders of property. Corporate behavior can be bad enough with respect to cooperative ethics within societies, but corporate actions with respect to the environment are clearly a serious threat to the survival of the human race. Of course, such a threat would also be a threat to the existence of corporations, but, given their aim of profit maximization, there is no way that they can consistently take that threat into account.

My view about corporations not being ethical individuals may seem to be contradicted by the widespread Corporate Social Responsibility movement. Remembering that the duty of corporations is to maximize profits, it is often possible for corporations to serve social purposes and make profits at the same time. But when there is a conflict, corporate managers would not (many say should not) jeopardize profits for some social aim. And, although some corporations go out of their way to resolve the conflict and further ethical aims, others don't. Within the aim of maximizing profits, the point of ethical activity is good public relations. When corporations go beyond this to be ethical, it is because of the personal beliefs of their managers. Corporations themselves have no intrinsic motivation to be ethical.

The shortfall of corporations is most striking with environmental issues. On my view, ethical principles are founded on cooperation between human beings. The environment is not a person, so our relations with it are not ethical. But environmental issues are perhaps more important than ethical issues because our survival depends on the well-being of the environment. For this reason, I call them eco-ethical issues. For corporations, the environment is often not a priority. FedEx won an environmental award to reduce dramatically the number of its polluting trucks. However, fiduciary duty to the shareholders won out and almost no non-polluting trucks were implemented.

Even worse, corporations such as Dupont and Exxon-Mobil attempted to stop action on environmental issues, putting their perception of threats to their profits over scientific evidence. When Dupont's product chlorofluorocarbon was claimed to be the cause of the depletion of the ozone layer, Dupont declared that this theory was "rubbish" and was still attempting to discredit the science when the currently effective international agreement banning chlorofluorocarbons was being adopted. Exxon-Mobil had the head of the Intergovernmental Panel on Climate Change (IPCC) replaced because they believed he would threaten their profits. The head of the IPCC was strong proponent of carbon emissions as a cause of global warming for scientific reasons.

Science is one of our most powerful and reliable tools for relating to reality. There should be no question which should be followed if there is a direct dispute between science and corporate profits. Corporations do not have a direct relation to truth, and in the case of the environment, this could be deadly. I believe the only solution is to deny corporations any influence on public policy. It is important to remember that they do not have human rights because they are not human individuals.

The depletion of the ozone layer brings up an important limitation to science and technology, especially with respect to the environment. Although science is an indispensable source of knowledge about the world, technology often has unintended consequences. The chlorofluorocarbons destroying the ozone layer were inert except high in the atmosphere, and this could not be predicted. Because modern technology attempts to impose its own order on top of what previously existed, it is likely to have destructive consequences. Hence its development has to be constrained by the priority of the ecosystem.

IT only partly belongs to modern technology because it does not aim to replace the world, only to represent parts of the world for definite purposes. IT can thus represent points of view which acknowledge individual ethics, domestic justice, global justice, the ecosystem, and *being*. IT developers have the ethical responsibility to represent these points of view whenever appropriate.

To determine the value of IT-enabled globalization, ultimately we need to take the point of view of *being*. From the point of view of humanity, IT is a major enabler of economic globalization. From the point of view of the ecosystem, environmental concerns are enabling values: They allow us to survive to do what we want. But we don't have goals as a species. Determining the ultimate value of globalization would require us to know our goals as a species. The question is, what is all that we have done as a species for? I believe this is a meaningful question even though I don't know how to go about answering it. I believe it is meaningful because it is not acceptable to human beings that our existence on the planet—for I hope the two million years ultimately given to us—has no meaning.

REFERENCES

Friedman, T. (2005). *The world is flat.* New York: Farrar, Straus and Giroux.

Rawls, J. (1999a). *A theory of justice* (rev. ed.). Cambridge, MA: Harvard University Press.

Rawls, J. (1999b). *The law of peoples.* Cambridge, MA: Harvard University Press.

Singer, P. (2004). *One world* (2nd ed.) New Haven, CT: Yale University Press.

ENDNOTE

[1]   This way of drawing the distinction is very close to John Rawls and Stuart Hampshire. See Chapter 4, **The Basis of Ethical Principles,** "Ethical Principles for Individuals."

About the Author

Robert A. Schultz received his Ph.D. in philosophy from Harvard University in 1971. His dissertation in ethics was under the direction of John Rawls. He was a member of the philosophy faculty at the University of Pittsburgh, Cornell University, and the University of Southern California, and taught courses and published articles and reviews in the fields of ethics, logic, and aesthetics. In 1980 he assumed the position of Data Processing Manager at A-Mark Precious Metals, a Forbes 500 company, then in Beverly Hills, CA. From 1989 through 2007, he was Professor and Chair of Computer Information Systems and Director of Academic Computing at Woodbury University, Burbank, CA. He regularly taught courses in database applications and design, systems development tools, and the management of information technology. He has numerous publications and presentations in the areas of database design, IT education, and the philosophy of technology. His previous book, *Contemporary Issues in Ethics and Information Technology,* was published by IRM Press (the former name of IGI-Global) in 2006. He retired and was awarded an Emeritus Professorship at Woodbury University in 2008. He continues to teach and publish in the areas of IT and ethics and taught an online course on this topic in the Applied Information Management Program at the University of Oregon in early 2009.

Index